T0367584

BUSINESS ALCHEMY:

TURNING IDEAS INTO GOLD

William R. Cobb
and M. L. Johnson, Ed.D, Ph.D.

authorHOUSE®

AuthorHouse™
1663 Liberty Drive
Bloomington, IN 47403
www.authorhouse.com
Phone: 1-800-839-8640

©2012 William R. Cobb and M. L. Johnson, Ed.D, Ph.D. All rights reserved.

No part of this book may be reproduced, stored in a retrieval system, or
transmitted by any means without the written permission of the author.

Published by AuthorHouse 6/18/2012

ISBN: 978-1-4685-8786-9 (sc)
ISBN: 978-1-4685-8785-2 (hc)
ISBN: 978-1-4685-8787-6 (e)

Library of Congress Control Number: 2012908964

Any people depicted in stock imagery provided by Thinkstock are models,
and such images are being used for illustrative purposes only.
Certain stock imagery © Thinkstock.

This book is printed on acid-free paper.

Because of the dynamic nature of the Internet, any web addresses or links contained in
this book may have changed since publication and may no longer be valid. The views
expressed in this work are solely those of the author and do not necessarily reflect the
views of the publisher, and the publisher hereby disclaims any responsibility for them.

TABLE OF CONTENTS

PREFACE

For at least 2,500 years before empiricists turned *alchemy* into the chemistry of atoms, neutrons, protons and electrons, the ancients sought to turn base metals into gold. We now realize that innovation can be turned into gold, and it is the entrepreneurial spirit within us that enables this to occur.

If "Your tomorrows will be much like today, except for the places you visit, the people you meet and the books you read," then, by simply studying this book, your future can be different from your past! As we use maps to plan routes to our destinations, this book is a traveler's map to career improvement – a guide to fulfilling your entrepreneurial dreams of business idea commercialization and for making the world a better place.

Many have traveled the route from idea to commercialization ahead of you, and they serve as guides for success. For example, having completed his physics degree and added a law degree during America's Great Depression, Chester F. Carlson was married and living hand-to-mouth in New York City. He systematically made notes about problem solutions, including how to make better copies of the patent applications he typed and re-typed at his employer's law firm. Analyzing patent applications, it occurred to him that inventing something could improve his own financial situation and perhaps do some good for the world. His patent for electrostatic photography was granted in 1942 and was commercialized two decades later – as the Xerox process.

There are multitudes of idea commercialization examples, from Carlson's billon dollar solution to the problem of reproducing dry paper copies to Muhammad Yunus' solution to the cyclical Third World poverty problem. Yunus was privileged to have earned a doctorate in economics from Vanderbilt University before returning to teach in a Bangladesh University. However, seeing the effects of his country's dire poverty, where people would quietly die of starvation on city doorsteps, he was moved to action in 1974 – creating what is now known as micro-lending. While traditional banks were not interested in loaning small amounts of money to villagers, Yunus' Grameen Bank started by providing a loan of $25.00 to 43 women to build and sell bamboo furniture – money loaned from his own pocket. The idea of micro-lending at the Grameen Bank has now grown past $7 billion to some 8 million borrowers; also earning Yunus a 2006 Nobel Peace Prize – all from the idea of loaning small amounts of money to enable people to become economically self-sufficient.

The Invention Tree has already been well picked of its low hanging fruit. However, there are plenty of inventions to be created by those who are informed and observant. For example, George H. Sweigert experience as a radio operator during WW II sparked his interest in work to improve various types of antennae, signal frequencies and different types of radios. Sweigert diligently studied the careers of Thomas Edison, Alexander Graham Bell, Samuel Morse and Albert Einstein; noting that although Bell lectured on electrically reproducing sound waves, he missed the opportunity to invent a portable radio telephone – though Sweigert initially thought a pocket telephone's use would be limited to a convenience of the elderly and handicapped. Sweigert's 1969 patent for the cordless telephone was the invention gateway for today's multibillion dollar wireless phone/ video industry.

This book will guide you through the idea to commercialization maze – identifying processes and resources for both entrepreneurial services and products. The information that you get and skills that you develop will provide the insider-level confidence needed to make informed decisions about ideas and commercialization. Along the way you will hear nay-sayers deride your idea and your abilities; against which your extensive research, meticulous planning and undaunted persistence will prevail. Remember that most nay-sayers are just acquaintances who would be embarrassed of their own laziness when you are successful. You may have heard of the "Crab Basket Phenomenon;" where one crab could easily scamper out of a wooden basket, but adding more crabs prevent any from escaping because they lock each other down with vice-grip pincers. Stay away from the crabs in your life!

The road from idea to commercialization is not without risk, and many fall by the wayside. However, preparation, for either a vacation trip or a business venture, raises the probability of success. Additionally, there are many good, honest and energetic people who want involvement in an early stage start-up – people who can help you in the venture. If you are willing to learn the entrepreneurism basics and devote time and energy to applying these basics to your business idea, you have good probability of success. "If you are willing to do what others are unwilling to do now, you will be able to do things later that they are incapable of doing." History is replete with examples of success for the inquisitive and persistent. Alexander Graham Bell was a tinkerer, a small time experimenter and elocution teacher, but he beat well funded labs in patenting the telephone in 1876 – combining the words for "distance" and "sound" for "telephone."

This book is an entrepreneur's map for idea commercialization, from the guides who has traveled the road several times. The lead author is a serial entrepreneur, an executive who has successfully moved ventures from idea to commercialization and now serves as mentor to various early stage projects. Our review of the present offerings from major bookstores revealed that no single title publication integrated the idea with concept validation, the business plan, marketing analysis, financing, management team building, business growth and exit options. The value to you, the reader, is that *Business Alchemy: Turning Ideas into Gold* is a single guide source to assist you with your new venture start up.

Best wishes for your project and let us know how you are doing.
W.R.C. and M.L.J., at: www.businessalchemy.com

CHAPTER ONE
The Entrepreneur in Hiding

"It is never too late to be what you might have been."
George Eliot

There is no evidence that they dreamed of becoming disruptive technology entrepreneurs. Mary Lerner and Len Bosack, a married couple employed in computer services at Stanford University, just thought it might be more convenient to send messages to each other through a computer network rather than using telephone calls and the paper copies prevalent in the early 1980s. William Yeager had previously written multiple-protocol router software, but discovered that its internal problems apparently hindered wider acceptance of his application. Bosack was able to modify Yeager's software, so that it could work, and together, they added Richard Troiano to help form the company that became known as CISCO SYSTEMS in 1984. Although they were not the first company to sell routers, Cisco was the first to successfully produce and market routers that supported multiple-network protocols. The company name was derived from shortening the nearby city name of "San Fran*cisco*," and a succession of CEOs scaled up the product line to make it into the international computer services firm it is today.

A company with only one product is usually at-risk as technology changes; this happened to Cisco when the introduction of Internet Protocol (IP) made Cisco's multi-protocol routing less important. However, by 1990, Cisco had successfully completed a successful IPO, and was listed on the NASDAQ Stock Exchange. This influx of new capital enabled it to expand its product offerings by means of the acquisition of companies like Stratacom and the Cerent Corporation. At the height of the dot-com boom of 2000, Cisco was ranked as the most valuable company in the world; with a market capitalization estimate of $500 billion. The company continues to develop new products and acquire promising start-ups; many of which are now $ billion in-house enterprises.

Entrepreneurs Lerner and Bosack are credited with: a) perceiving an opportunity to solve a significant real world problem, b) being capable of developing a product solution and c) carrying it through the "proof of concept stage." Wisely, they brought in professional management to help "scale-up" the flagship product and develop a larger product portfolio. By re-investing their profits back into research and development, and by making timely acquisitions, Cisco has continued to play a major role in the proliferation of the World Wide Web. Their story very well illustrates how perceptive and technically competent persons can become part of a successful start-up that benefits innovators, investors, management and society.

WHAT IS AN ENTREPRENEUR?

The term *entrepreneur* is derived from a combination of the Old French words *entree*, meaning *to enter*, and *preneur*, meaning *to take*. Thus, there has been a generous transliteration of the combined words into the business world for describing *one who moves a product or service from idea to commercialization*. Entrepreneurship is as old as the beginnings of commerce, wherein one person (a proprietor) or a group (a cartel) assumes the risk of moving a product or service to commercialization; taking something from an idea to profitability (Pirenne (1937). At some point in civilization's development, someone successfully took a useful product or service from idea to public adoption; benefiting himself/herself and the community.

Three entrepreneur roles are typically needed for a business start-up; a) the idea person(s), b) the financial backer(s) and c) the professional manager(s). Thus, if you are a competent manager and not particularly creative or wealthy, you can still be a significant player in the start-up world. Actually, you can become a player in several contexts: a completely new business, a business re-start, or a start-up within an existing business. This is often referred to as "intropreneurism" and such new entities may be later spun-off as an independent company. Social entrepreneurism, environmental entrepreneurism, or pioneering a new concept in a public agency or government, can all be examples of entrepreneurism. Someone who is starting a community foundation from scratch needs to have similar characteristics of a commercial entrepreneur and she/he will need to follow many of the processes described herein.

Imagine that you are watching the first farmer some thousands of years ago as he made a crude device to harness an ox to pull a sharpened stick; forming the first animal-powered agricultural technology. Animal power was a "low tech" innovation – "technology" simply being a tool to help accomplish a significant task – but, it was "disruptive technology" that replaced the pain of human powered farming. That plow made farming a bit less difficult and, although product launch and market penetration are now sophisticated processes, it is highly probable that there was little resistance to this new idea. Looking back with today's business sophistication, most consultants would have advised the innovator to give up the toil of farming and start incrementally improving, producing and distributing farm implements – as well as co-marketing with a breeder of bigger oxen. The new animal-powered plowing concept probably only spread field-by-field, as other farmers saw the mechanical advantage. Similarly, the diffusion of crop domestication technology, from its point of origin in Southwestern Asia, traveled at an average rate of only .07 miles per year – not sufficient market penetration by today's standards, but the adoption rate was fairly rapidly given that most ancient people lived and died within a radius of 20 miles (Diamond (2006).

Over time, the acts of improving things and disseminating such innovations, *itself, became the entrepreneurial tool for advancing civilizations*. Prototypical entrepreneurism of the ancients has been advanced and refined into high technology – an economic tool capable of dramatically transforming the wellbeing of its practitioners and improving the lives of those using the resultant products and services. The advent of money and banking facilitated and fueled entrepreneurism (See Ferguson, 2008, *The ascent of money: A financial history of the world*).

Though people had joined together for business ventures from antiquity, the concept of a "company" only emerged in the 1600 AD era; with such risky shipping trade ventures as the Dutch East India Company/West India Company, the British East India Company/Massachusetts Bay Company and the French East India Company all needing investment capital greater than could be found from just one source. Such risk-spreading companies, endorsed by monarchs and supported by a country's military, became the norm for international business ventures in the European Colonial Period.

Entrepreneuring ranges from: a) the creation and marketing of something completely different from the norm, as with Chester F. Carlson's invention of xerography ("dry copies") for making electrostatic pictures (Owen, 2004), to b) the repackaging and successful commercialization of existing business operations – as was done by Ray Kroc when he formed McDonalds. The introduction of a new idea that dramatically improves efficiency by reducing costs, or improves the human condition, or creates a competitive market advantage is called "disruptive technology." The internet's dramatic facilitation of worldwide communication is a prime example of a disruptive technology that has enabled creative commercialization across global markets and a variety of new industries.

The inventor, the project manager and the venture financer are often different persons or groups. Operating in a climate of significant risk, these entrepreneurs are major contributors to industrial dynamics and economic growth, often referred to as the engine for job creation and national economic competitiveness. Business ideas are a necessary starting point, but only about ten percent of innovations are ever successfully commercialized – largely because inexperienced people do not understand the complexity of what is required. Certainly, until well after the Depression Era of the 1930s, there were no resource guides to assist business-start-ups or to help Chester Carlson commercialize his dry copier idea. Advice from Horatio Alger's (1832 – 1879) hundred plus "rags to riches" books, idealizing hard work and moral rectitude," were of little help to Carlson and others as Alger's themes consistently connected a fortunate circumstance with aid from an outside benefactor.

The entrepreneur's objective is to realize a profit in proportion to the risk; a task achieved by creating a business process that can produce and market the new product or service. Initial entrepreneurial motivation may or may not be present prior to beginning the enterprise. For example, Michael Dell was an undergrad at The University of Texas in 1983 and he began upgrading computers for other students in the Dobie Center dorm room 2713. The fact that he had taken his first computer apart at age 15, an Apple II, to see how it worked and to make upgrades to it, had modestly prepared him for a computer career. As a university freshman, even though he had the characteristic entrepreneur's personality profile, he could not have possibly known that his idea of direct marketing from the manufacturer would result in profits measured in the billions of dollars for the Dell Corporation. He was a pre-med major not a business major.

IF YOU LOOK IN THE MIRROR DO YOU SEE AN ENTREPRENEUR?

The challenge of this next exercise is to show that you may not fully understand the typical entrepreneur's personality characteristics, and that when you look in that mirror you would only see a generally-self confident person staring back at you. A good portion of entrepreneurism does lie in self-perception; just as looking into a mirror and convincing yourself that you actually can be what you think you want to be isn't a really tough sell. The true entrepreneur is the pioneer who *ventures beyond the reality of the present into a vision of what could be,* typically creating a processes or products that solve someone else's significant problem. Actually, the problem with most new entrepreneurs is that they have no personal frame of reference with which to compare themselves. Despite the fact that no personality profile accurately describes every entrepreneur, certain characteristics are frequently associated with successful entrepreneurs. Also, as we shall see, timing and fortunate circumstances can foil the best of calculated predictions.

Characteristics of the entrepreneur/entrepreneurism – How about basic intelligence as the prime factor required for success? From the rock star adulation given to successful entrepreneurs, you might think that this is a set of exceptionally intelligent and gifted individuals – intelligence being the single trait predictor. Interestingly, Terman (Minton, 1988) certainly believed that intelligence, as measured by his test battery, was the determinant for success in a person's chosen field. His passion for the idea of identifying the super intelligent to lead society secured funding for a longitudinal study. Staff members in the longitudinal project administered Terman's version of intelligence tests to thousands of youths and selected a cohort of some 1,528 scoring between 140 and 200 to carefully study over their lifespans. Though some individuals were recognized for awards, the cohort group did not achieve anything internationally spectacular over the decades that his team tracked them. Terman's very high expectations of career achievements were not met. The fact that his cohort achieved above average socioeconomic status is as much explained by their family background as their gifted intelligence; as most of the cohort was from upper middle class West Coast families. If Terman's thesis of intelligence being the primary factor in life achievement was correct, all of his Termites should have been internationally renowned leaders in their respective fields. And, while it would seem totally unnecessary to aid the super-intelligent, Terman intervened on behalf of many of his gifted "Termites" to get them into Stanford University and to get them jobs. Yet, at least two rejects from Terman's selection program achieved remarkable success; with William Shockley (physicist and co-inventor of the transistor) and Luis Alvarez (one of the most brilliant and productive physicists in the 21st Century) earning Nobel Laureates. These Nobel Prize winners scored above average on Terman's tests, but not in the genius range. Thus, take heart, being intelligent does help, but there is far more to successful entrepreneuring than performing well on tests. One of the best analyses of success-related variables is found in Gladwell's (2008) *Outliers: The story of success*. He clearly established that multiple personal and context factors must interact to produce high level success.

Can ordinary people become successful entrepreneurs? Ray Kroc (1902-1984) is a classic example of a rather ordinary person optimizing his unique personality traits. If he was super intelligent, neither he nor his family was aware of it. Born of Czech immigrants and growing up in the Chicago area, his only advanced training was for ambulance driving. His various jobs included paper cup salesman, pianist, jazz musician and radio station employee. He was traveling from town to town selling multi-milkshake mixers to restaurants, and eventually partnered with the McDonald brothers in southern California to open and franchise restaurants. With some investors, he bought the brother's restaurants for only $2.7 million in 1961 and went national with a new kind of fast food chain; one built on Henry Ford's concept of assembly line standardization. He built McDonald's restaurant chain by standardizing production and pioneering the concept of franchising; in some 20 years Kroc went from an iterant salesman to amassing a $500 million fortune by his death in 1984. He was an ordinary man who did extraordinary things – providing hope for others who would like to develop the requisite attributes for entrepreneurial success. Kroc simply adapted the automobile assembly line concept, for product standardization and delivery speed, to the hamburger business. While McDonald's is not gourmet food, you can be confident that it is the same amount and quality in any site worldwide. Kroc also showed that age is not a limiting factor for entrepreneurs.

Characteristics – Traits are just identifiable behavior and thought patterns; the formation of which is derived from informal and formal childhood and school experiences. The term "attribute" has a similar meaning as the concept of "trait;" but it also carries the connotation of being able to "causally attribute" an outcome to a personality characteristic;

such as "running speed is a necessary 'attribute' for playing point guard in professional basketball." Fortunately, the entrepreneur's psychological profile contains many attributes that you can learn – though the acquisition process may require a great deal of effort.

While trait-based theories of both leadership and entrepreneur personality are of suspect because of low predictive validity, certain traits do seem to be associated with entrepreneurs. Age is not a factor, as high school and college students have successfully launched highly successful internet-based businesses and Ray Kroc (1998) launched McDonalds Restaurants at age 52; at an age that most people begin to anticipate retirement. Wadhwa, et al. (2009) identified family and personal motivational factors associated with successful entrepreneurs. From interviews of 549 company founders in industries from electronics to health care, they found that a) 74 percent had graduated in the top 30 percent of high school classes, b) 95 percent had earned a bachelor's degree, c) most were married with children, d) 92 percent had come from lower class or middle class families and e) 74 percent had worked approximately a decade in other companies to gain experience. Motivations for business founding included a) desire to build wealth – 74 percent, b) opportunity to capitalize on a idea – 68 percent and c) a desire not to work for someone else – 60 percent. Michael Dell has many of Wadhwa's characteristics. He is the son of an achievement oriented parents; an orthodontist and stockbroker who were financially able to purchase a new computer for him to disassemble. Though he did not work for a computer company before launching his enterprise, he had disassembled and upgraded numerous computers from age 15 to 21 years of age in the era when the computer industry was just emerging.

Problems with using a list of traits to predict entrepreneurial success include a) the fact that fortunate co-incidence of a person's ability and an opportunity can mediate success and b) skill set-specific characteristics are needed for enterprise success – those skill sets including distinctively different abilities of the inventor, the manager and the financer. A caveat of testing is that the instrument may not have yet been established for predictive validity – meaning that there is no know correlation between the test score and the degree of entrepreneurial success. Thus, you could have taken someone's "Entrepreneur Persona Test" and scored so low that you were discouraged from following your dream. Please realize that because of marketplace sector-specificity, no omnibus entrepreneur assessment device can have a high predictive value. As has been explained previously and as will be amplified later, there are three different entrepreneur's roles;

a) the inventor/innovator who comes up with the product or service idea, b) the manager who champions and guides the idea to commercialization and c) the financer who risks reputation and money to bring the idea into fruition. Some characteristics, such as enthusiasm and resilience are common to the three entrepreneurial roles, but the respective roles have several traits/specific skill sets that reduce the predictive capability of omnibus test instruments. *Skill sets* implies that the attribute can be learned, and though *personality traits* can be changed, a great deal of effort is required to change a deep-seated characteristic. Use of the word, *characteristics*, allows us to couple personal descriptors with project success, but avoids the problem of whether something is a deep personality trait or an acquired skill set.

Role-related characteristics – The following three illustrations, Figures 1.1, 1.2 and 1.3 are included to show how the three entrepreneurial roles (the idea person, the professional manager and the venture financer) inherently have differing traits/skill sets. Factors associated with the three roles are presented separately with a brief description and a Visual Analog Scale for self-assessment. Any worthwhile assessment, whether a self-assessment or a professional assessment, would have started from a) identifying a reference group of individuals deemed "highly effective," b) systematically observing these individuals in a variety of task-related contexts and c) writing test item descriptors of characteristics common to the reference group. Any identified characteristic that is found to common to individuals outside the "high effective" group would be discarded; as they would reduce the predictive capacity of the instrument.

Inventor/innovator entrepreneur role descriptors, arranged on a Visual Analog Scale, are as follows. Simply making a vertical mark on the horizontal line indicates your estimated position for each factor. Each item is understood to be preceded by, "I have the …

1. Ability to see opportunity beyond what seems obvious or common knowledge to others.

    Agree ———————————————————— Disagree

2. Ability to visualize relationships between different components or variables.

    Agree ———————————————————— Disagree

3. Ability to strongly advocate for an issue or concept in which I believe.

Agree ——————————————————————— Disagree

4. Ability to bounce back from adversity or lack of desired success of a project.

Agree ——————————————————————— Disagree

5. Ability to stay focused on a project and work at it until it is completed.

Agree ——————————————————————— Disagree

6. Ability to work with others to define and complete projects.

Agree ——————————————————————— Disagree

7. Ability to see solutions through the confusion of problems.

Agree ——————————————————————— Disagree

8. Ability to create unique solutions or products, to think divergently from accepted answers.

Agree ——————————————————————— Disagree

9. Ability to maintain a positive attitude in conflict and confusion.

Agree ——————————————————————— Disagree

10. Willingness to invest time and money into new projects in which I believe.

Agree ——————————————————————— Disagree

Figure 1.1 Factor-related self-assessment questions associated with successful inventor/ innovator role entrepreneurs.

Response to each item should be "as you typically are" and not "as you would like to become." Sort out "the real you" from "the person that you would like to become" by asking several colleagues to rank you on these factors. Photocopy Figure 1.1 to use for personal development.

Characteristics commonly associated with **inventor/innovator role entrepreneurs** include, but are not limited to, the following factors that are numbered in order as Figure 1.1. The idea persons tend to be individuals who:

1. Can **perceive** that the product is not available in the marketplace or that the new product will have a significant competitive market advantage – a vision that the product or service will solve a significant environmental, social or business problem. For example, George de Mestral returned from a Swiss Alpine hunting trip, to find small burrs stubbornly clinging to his clothing. Under a microscope the burrs appeared to have hundreds of tiny hooks, apparently ready to attach to any loop. He successfully manufactured products that simulated what he had observed in nature. This invention of Velcro revolutionized fastening.

2. Are **intuitive** in seeing relationships between seemingly different objects, processes or applications. In 1968 3M's Dr. Spencer Silver developed a "low tack" pressure sensitive adhesive that got no commercial traction in his five years of marketing attempts. It lay dormant for six years until his colleague, Art Fry, came up with the idea of applying the adhesive to bits of paper and selling them in packets. Since there had never been such a product, public acceptance lagged. To launch the product 3M issued free samples to residents of Boise, Idaho and found that 90 percent said they would purchase the product after thy had tried it. Post It products are primarily produced in the U.S. and marketed worldwide.

3. Have **enthusiasm** for a project that translates into the persuasion of others to join the venture - becomes the initial champion of the project, persisting even when others do not see the possibility of success. While a student at Yale University in the early 1960s, Frederick W. Smith wrote a paper for an economics class outlining business plan fundamentals for an overnight delivery service and reportedly received the grade of "C" because it was deemed an improbable venture. After his Vietnam War service, he purchased controlling interest in an aircraft maintenance company; a move that served as a pad from which to launch his economics class idea. In 1971 Smith invested $4 million and raised another $91 million in

venture capital to launch Federal Express (FedEx) service to 25 American cities; with worldwide express delivery service soon following.

4. Are **resilient** in the face of adversity and can bounce back from lack of success – to seek alternative ways to accomplish the task. Chester F. Carlson was rejected some 20 times over 10 years by industry and government – all who later paid a royalty for his dry copy invention. He often put the project aside in frustration, but pressed on because he could see how his Xerox Process would benefit himself and society.

5. Are **diligence** and tireless workers on projects, completing and testing numerous prototypes. WD 40 is so named because it is the 40th chemical formulation of a water dispersant development project. They remember Thomas Edison's comment that "Opportunity is often missed because it comes dressed in overalls."

6. Can **collaborate** effectively with others – even others who represent different fields or opposing views on action. Jim Collins (2001) started a project that he could not individually finish – to determine whether there are companies that turn long-term mediocrity into long-term success. And, if so, what are their common characteristics? The 20 members of the research team that produced the best selling business book, *Good to Great: Why Some Companies Make the leap and Others Don't*, are prominently listed in the front pages. Through collaboration with a team, Collins has become a very successful author and business consultant.

7. Are **solution oriented** rather than problem/blame oriented – seeing problems as merely opportunities. Great solvers do not approach problems reproductively, that is, from the same mentality as has worked in the past. Einstein did not invent energy, mass or the speed of light; he simply combined them in a novel way to express something different. His comment, that "Problems cannot be solved with the same thought processes that created the problem," is advice well taken by successful solvers.

8. Are **creative** with an inherent need to innovate – the act of creating, itself, becomes a measure of success. Pablo Picasso was a compulsive creator; once commenting that if someone gave him a gallery he would fill it. Arguably, the most financially and artistically successful multi-media artist, he produced some 20,000 works that included 1,885 paintings, 1,228 sculptures, 2,880 ceramics and 1,200 drawings – these do not include the large number of works burned for warmth in his early Parisian poverty years. In reviewing thousands of individuals, Plucker (2010) found that creativity scores were three times more powerful for predicting innovative productivity than the individual's IQ score.

9. Are **positive thinkers** who believe they can make life better for themselves and society. As a struggling patent attorney in the great Depression, Chester Carlson mused that inventing something was a good way to both improve his economic status and to benefit society. Confronted by many rejections of his patent for making cheap dry paper copies, he frequently dropped the idea; but his deep belief in its possibilities drove him to try again.

10. Make **investments** in time and effort and risk financial security for the possibility of larger rewards. After his financial success in inventing an advanced telegraph design, Thomas Edison created a high functioning innovation factory, making his 1,093 patents an unapproached record. He gave assistants ideas that they were to develop – assigning his staff the quotas of one minor invention every ten days and a major invention every six months produced the light bulb, phonograph and the motion picture camera.

Idea persons create intellectual property – IP is simply a "novel concept of value" that has legal status from patent, copyright or valid license. Even social/humanitarian organizations, such as Habitat for Humanity, need protection of the organization's mission, good will and trade name are critical to prevent dilution or theft. An innovation, "A new concept or a significant improvement on an existing product that has a potential benefit," is essentially the definition of a potential patent. Laws and court cases regarding the protection of intellectual property can be found at http://wwwuspto.gov; the home page for the U.S. Patent and Trademark Office. A patent attorney typically prepares and submits the application and a U.S. Patent and Trademark Office examiner reviews the application to determine whether it meets the standards for something that is patentable and whether the application infringes on a previously issued patent.

A note to innovators: while most start-up managers and investors are honest, there are a few sharks in the pool who will steal your IP. Just as financers conduct their own *due diligence* of inventors IP, you must do your own *due diligence* of investor or market consultants' background. One shark method is to form a company, promise millions in funding, get a majority of the stock dedicated to the new company and have the IP consigned to the new company. Then, they crash the new company, walk away with the IP and form a new company to commercialize the product or service – leaving the inventor sadder and wiser.

Professional start-up managers are entrepreneurs who tend to have unique and identifiable personality characteristics. Their start-up venture risk is to their long term reputation and, often, they leave a successful position for a lesser paying position that has potential for earning growth stock in the new company. Evidence suggests that when the innovator, who is typically best fitted to be the company Chief Technical Officer, tries to be the Chief Executive Officer in a start-up, there is only a 10 percent probability for success – as compared to a 70 percent probability of success when a professional manager launches the company.

Start-up manager entrepreneur-role descriptors, arranged on a Visual Analog Scale, are as follows. Simply making a vertical line on the horizontal line indicated your estimate on each respective factor. Each item is understood to be preceded by, "I have the …

1. Ability to manage risk – including personal risk of position, income and reputation for greater potential rewards in a business project.

    Agree ——————————————————————— Disagree

2. Ability to constantly network for potential innovations, management support and financial alternatives.

    Agree ——————————————————————— Disagree

3. Ability to look past problem impasses to generate solution alternatives.

    Agree ——————————————————————— Disagree

4. Ability to become the prime advocated for an innovation or business project.

Agree ———————————————————————— Disagree

5. Ability to envision a business project goal and its necessary action sequence.

Agree ———————————————————————— Disagree

6. Ability to assess an innovation's potential for target market penetration and share.

Agree ———————————————————————— Disagree

7. Ability to quickly put together and operate a competent management team.

Agree ———————————————————————— Disagree

8. Ability to develop and implement an effective business plan.

Agree ———————————————————————— Disagree

9. Ability to manage all facets of corporate finance.

Agree ———————————————————————— Disagree

10. Ability to effectively communicate in multiple modalities to a wide range of audiences.

Agree ———————————————————————— Disagree

Figure 1.2 Factor-related self-assessment questions associated with successful start-up manager role entrepreneurs.

Characteristics and skill sets commonly associated with successful entrepreneur-role **start-up managers** include, but are not limited to, the following factors that are listed in the same order as in Figure 1.2. Start-up managers tend to be individuals who:

1. Have the ability to analyze a business project's risks, find strategies to moderate those risks and keep risks and potential rewards in perspective. Project risks range from possible

changes in government regulations, product scale-up problems, potentially volatility of the inventor (yes, the inventor can be a major risk factor), unforeseen supply costs and military action. Experienced **risk mitigators** have learned to anticipate the unexpected and to hedge their timeline, costs, production and estimates; under promising and over delivering. The first risk to be managed is personal – the leap of judgment to "quit your day job" to manage a new project.

2. **Constantly networking** in social and business circles for innovation leads and ideas, contacts for talent and resources. Regular attendance at area venture capital events, state inventors clubs and associations, university technology transfer round tables, federal grant training workshops and start-up open house events can be informative and provide information on what is happening and who is making it happen. The start-up manager is looking for people with expertise (potential Chief Operations Officer, Chief Financial Officer, Chief Technical Officer, etc.) who may interested in making a move to a higher potential venture; a venture in which they could become a share owner. As Former President Lyndon Johnson often said; "Make friends before you need them!"

3. Are **solution oriented**; capable of generating multiple possible divergent solutions. The stereotype of managers is to use "reproductional solution thinking;" that is, relying on a past solution used in a somewhat similar situation. However, seldom are problems so identical that "cookie cutter solutions" the best answer. When W. Edwards Deming brought his ideas of manufacturing quality to American industry in post-War II, he was rejected – the very idea of a university statistics professor telling U.S. industrialist how to build better products. The 1955 Chevrolet models were far better than those of previous years, but mine frequently jumped out of gear on the highway; one time jamming the gearbox and leaving only reverse and the 2nd forward gear. Our American television sets operated satisfactorily most of the time – though at times the picture went to one inch horizontal scale that required a blow to the side of the set to restore the picture. Rejected in America, Deming took his solution for high reliability

manufacturing ideas to bombed-out Japan and taught them how to use manufacturing statistics to produce very high quality products – something now ironically called "Japanese Management." By the early 1980s Japan had risen from WW II ashes to the Number One Economy in the world – changing the "junk" phrase describing pre-War Japanese products to the "high quality" phrase describing post-War products.

4. Can be the **champion of the project.** Every project must have someone who bleeds for the idea. A venture is an event without a known end point – we frequently put the prefix *ad* to *venture* for describing an open ended trip, as opposed to family vacation in which the beginning an endings are planned. Prudent champions must be aware of the maxim, "Success has a thousand relatives but failure is an orphan." A potential venture project champion must "do diligence" in assessing the risks and potential benefits, as failure could indelibly tarnish a promising career. Although it is out of the typical corporate scene, an event occurred in the business of professional basketball that enticed a young inexperienced coach into a career venture – with many predicting the experience would end in disaster. The Los Angeles Lakers had just won a NBA championship under Coach Paul Westhead, but the team was in chaos – that talented 1980 team with Kareem Jabbar and Magic Johnson. During the post-season celebration dinner a fight broke out among the players; apparently over who contributed the most to the championship season (Feinstein, 2002). Conflict on a team with very strong player personalities led to a poor start for the 1980-81 season and Westhead was fired – with no short list of replacement applicants. Since no one else seemed to want the head coach job, Pat Riley, who had previously only been a Laker media broadcaster before filling in as Westhead's assistant coach, took the job. How he mitigated the apparent career risks has not been told, but Riley's teams won NBA championships in 1982, 1985, 1987 and 1988 - Riley also has been named "NBA Coach of the Year" three times.

5. Can **envision the action blueprint** needed to bring the enterprise concept to fruition. The controversial theoretical

physicist, Robert J. Oppenheimer, clearly had many entrepreneur characteristics. Blessed with intelligence and a good education – earned his doctorate in physics at age 23 without having taken prerequisite undergraduate physics courses – Oppenheimer was charismatic communicator, futurist and adept organizer. During WW II it was known that American enemies were frantically working to develop an atomic bomb and the country winning the nuclear race would win the war. Japan had two separate nuclear projects, Germany had a nuclear project and Russia had started an atomic project. Without an established reputation for efficiently handling large projects, Oppenheimer convinced the military supervisor, General Leslie Groves, that he could pull together the half dozen U.S. research projects and win the nuclear race – which he successful accomplished despite professional jealousy from older more established physicists and Soviet spies who infiltrated the Manhattan Project.

6. Can **perceive potential marketplace success of business ideas**. For example, a young graphic artist saw the potential for creating an *experience business* of a type and at a scale that no one had ever dreamed. He was a futurist; perceiving that he could build on his graphic art success and create a customer experience, so innovative and exciting, that visitors would flock to it from all over the world. Detesting traditional steel contraception amusement parks, thrill rides operated by people that parents would not trust alone with their children, he divined the idea of providing significant family entertainment events built around stories. He would need money for land, buildings, transportation access ways, offices, storage and parking. Hotels would be needed to house the crowds of visitors and mass transit vehicles would be needed for customer transport. He developed sketches of the facility layout from a small scale entertainment industry operation; building a comprehensive business plan and a finance plan to borrow and repay a $17 million business loan. However, banker after banker turned him down – since it had not been done before they did not see the possibility therein - so he formed a joint venture with a new television company to fund

and publicize the 160 acre project that opened in July 1955. Hundreds of millions have visited Disneyland and other resort attractions. Walt Disney pioneered a new business concept: the "Experience Industry."

7. Can quickly **build a competent management team**. From your constant networking, you will have made and vetted a list of possible candidates who can support a new project – competent persons who will help frame the project "while still at their day jobs," are good prospects. Having established good relations with corporate "head hunters" – agencies who specialize in finding and vetting potential employees – shortens time required to assemble a competent team. However, finding and training talented people is just part of the problem. The "rest of the story" is conflict management within the organization and between the staff, potential strategic partners, the supply chain, product production and product distribution.

8. Have learned how to **develop and implement an effective business plan**. The classic story of H. Ross Perot illustrates how a business plan can be launched into a successful business. After serving his military obligation in the U.S. Navy, Perot began working for IBM as a sales representative in the fledgling 1957 computer industry. By 1961 he was so successful that other sales persons complained to IBM management; resulting in strict sales quotas for sales representatives. By the end of the first two weeks in January 1962, Perot had filled his year's sales quota and spent the rest of the year as an IBM employee with nothing to do except develop a business plan for his own company. Leaving IBM he launched Electronic Data Systems (EDS) and when the company went public in 1968 its stock went from $16.00 to $160.00 per share within days. In 1984 General Motors bought the controlling interest in EDS for $2.4 billion.

9. Are skilled **financial analysts**, assessing the costs and comparative product advantage, estimating the time and money costs compared to the projected financial rewards. This is a skill set that is absolutely critical for young start-up

managers to develop. If you do not know how to dissect a business plan's financial sheet, you will have to trust someone else's word on whether or not the project is solvent. The term, "burn rate," is used to describe how fast the investor's money is being used to reach project mile-markers.

10. Are **excellent communicators**. Steve Jobs is the co-inventor of the first commercially successful lines of personal computers; the Apple II. He co-founded Apple and has led the computer industry in break-through innovations; having been the primary or the co-inventor of some 230 patents. Jobs apparently relished being on-stage presenting new products - at business conferences such as his Macworld Conference and Expo. His persuasive and charismatic personality was arguably a major factor in making his increasingly miniaturized and powerful computer products instant successes.

Management entrepreneurs move the product or service concept forward to dissemination or commercialization. There is considerable empirical research and anecdotal evidence that inventors are not the best individuals to move innovation to the commercialization phase; as companies formed by the inventor, when acting as the Chief Executive Officer (CEO), have about a ten percent probability of successfully launching and sustaining a start-up enterprise. There is a high probability that investors will bring their own professional CEO to manage the process of innovation commercialization. Expertise for inventing and expertise for managing tend to be different skill sets.

Financial entrepreneurs are called "angel investors" or "venture capitalists" and, if you want to work with them successfully, you need to know how they think and operate. Angel investment is typically from one or several "qualified investors" and venture capital is typically from a small group of investors in an innovation sector or from a venture capital fund. In either case, there is a fairly common set of thought processes and skill sets. The successful serial innovator may get start-up money before the proof of concept stage is complete; meaning that the angel or venture capital group relies as much or more on the reputation of the innovator. Prepare and rehearse your 30 second "elevator speech" pitching your innovation; as that may be only the amount time you get to pique an interest.

Investor/entrepreneur role descriptors, arranged on a Visual Analog Scale, are included as an exercise in understanding start-up capital manager's thinking and behaviors. Simply mark a vertical line on the horizontal line to indicate where you think the typical money manager would be. Each item is understood to be preceded by, "They have …

1. Deep knowledge of specific innovation technology or market sector

Agree ———————————————————————— Disagree

2. Ability to quickly analyze a financial statement

Agree ———————————————————————— Disagree

3. Ability to quickly analyze a Capitalization Table.

Agree ———————————————————————— Disagree

4. Ability to use computer-based market segmentation tools to assess potential market size.

Agree ———————————————————————— Disagree

5. Ability to network with other money sources to share the risk.

Agree ———————————————————————— Disagree

6. Ability to assess the validity of a start-up business plan

Agree ———————————————————————— Disagree

7. Intuitive analysis of project

Agree ———————————————————————— Disagree

8. Ability to quickly set up a management team from past contacts.

Agree ———————————————————————— Disagree

9. Ability to invest personal money that they do not need for living expenses.

Agree ———————————————————————— Disagree

10. Ability to achieve high return for investment ratio.

Agree ———————————————————————— Disagree

Figure 1.3 Factor-related self-assessment questions associated with successful project start-up financers.

There are two options related to your potential participation in financing project start-ups. The first possibility is for you to have sufficient disposable capital to invest personally, as an angel or venture capitalist. The second possibility is for you to develop such a track record of vetting project proposals and monitoring start-ups to success that high net worth individuals and investment groups trust you with managing their start-up money. The project start-up financers tend to be individuals who:

1. Have **deep knowledge about a specific sector**; where the field is moving and where the rapid growth opportunities are going to be. The high growth areas, such as biofuels and solar energy are so technically specific that investors tend to stay in sectors they understand. For example, with automobiles moving to electric power, improved batteries have become critical. Lithium is the lightest metal, with a mass of less than water, and performs better than traditional lead batteries. Thus, knowing where lithium deposits are found, how they are extracted and refined and how lithium batteries are optimally designed are information gateways to investing in this sector.

2. Have the **ability to analyze a financial statement** – the financial underpinnings of a business plan. Knowledge of a specific investment sector is critical to a financial analysis; for there are sector specific costs and time frames. For example, biopharmaceutical product development milestones include a) proof of concept, b) intended effect validation, c) scale-up feasibility and d) clinical trials – each with characteristic costs and time lines. However, approval for sale by the U.S. Food and Drug Administration is typically a multi-year and very expensive exercise. Investors are interested in whether it is feasible for a start-up to hit its milestone targets within budget.

3. Have the ability to **effectively analyze a proposed Capitalization Table** – a financial sheet that designates who is to get how much of the start-up company's stock equity. Though there are no standard Cap Table templates, there are key variables that financers want to see included. It is unlikely that a fledgling inventor will be able to retain a

51 percent majority of voting stock when millions of other people's money (OPM) is raised for commercialization. Big money investors will probably require majority stock position, stock compensation for the inventor and a stock incentive compensation plan for key employees.

4. Have the ability to **use computer-based market segment estimation tools**. These sophisticated data mining tools use the U.S. Census Bureau Reports to identify population age, gender, income, family size and geographic location to identify the size and demographics of a product or service market. For example, for analysis of the potential market size and location for a human reproduction management instrument, we entered the descriptors a) U.S., b) women, c) ages 17 – 26 and ages 40 – 60 and d) income above $40,000.00. Since Catholics and Moslems both use natural family planning, adding these descriptors helps to refine the search. If the resulting potential market segment size matches that of the innovator's business plan, discussion of financing the project can continue.

5. Have the ability **to network with other money sources to share the risk**. Investors talk informally at parties and formally at investment clubs and conferences. As with the European Colonial era of the British East India Company and the Dutch East India Company, investors seek to spread personal risk even if it means reducing rewards. For example, though lithium is a crucial ingredient of electric powered vehicles and very large and untapped reserves have recently been discovered in Afghanistan, finding individual investors willing to risk money in an unstable political environment will not be easy. Since many people do not have the time or expertise to individually evaluate numerous potential opportunities, they place significant funds in such organizations as the Capital Midwest Fund – see the *Dow Jones Venture Capital Alert* for periodic updates djnewsletter@dowjones.com

6. Have the ability to **assess the validity of a start-up business plan**. Though the innovator must have a firm idea of how to scale-up and commercialize the novel product or service, she/he should be assured that every part of the proposed

business plan will be dissected and assessed. Plan gaps and 'Blue sky" estimates are immediate turn-offs; not particularly invalidating the innovation, but invalidating its proposed commercialization process.

7. Have ability to **intuitively evaluate risks and potential of the whole project**. While accurate business plan numbers are critical, validity of a proposed start-up is more than an innovation and a business plan. Gladwell (2005) devoted an entire book to the subject of intuitive analysis – from the opportunity of the Getty Museum to purchase a magnificent $9 million "ancient Athenian sculpture" to military strategy decisions. A potential $ billion start-up can be abandoned by financers if the inventor appears to be paranoid about people stealing the IP. The numbers may be excellent, the cost-to-price point margin great and manufacturability feasible; but a skittish inventor can ruin the deal for everyone – including the millions worldwide who could benefit from the idea.

8. Have the ability to **quickly set up a management team from past contacts**. Both professional management entrepreneurs and investors actively look for talent – even if these persons are not immediately needed. Key personnel include the roles of Chief Executive Officer (CEO), Chief Financial Officer (CFO), Chief Technical Officer (CTO), and Chief Operations Officer (CFO). An inventor assuming the CTO role does not preclude her/him from occupying a seat on the Board of Directors.

9. Have the ability to **invest personal money that is not needed for maintenance**. There are governing rules for seeking outside money, depending upon the amount being sought. A $5 million start-up has Federal regulations governing the "offer/solicitation." While friends and family often fund "bootstrapping" to get to proof of concept outside of governmental oversight, scale-up to commercialization typically requires millions and U.S. Securities Exchange Commission Rule D 501 governs who can invest. Accordingly, an "accredited investor" must have an annual income of $200,000.00 and have a net worth of over $1 million. The

annual income and net worth values may seem elitist, but having sufficient discretionary income minimizes short term performance pressure on the start-up project.

10. Have the ability to **achieve high returns for investments**. Start-up financers are primarily interested in projects that minimally show promise of a 10:1 return - $10.00 return for every $1.00 invested – and that have a distinct investor exit strategy. High net worth investors, a synonym for *Accredited Investor*, can deposit their funds in a bank account with little risk – though the bank capitalization rate rarely exceeds five percent return. Two characteristics of venture financers is revealed herein; a) they are willing to risk some of their discretionary funds on high return ventures and b) they want a built-in exist strategy so they can move on to other ventures. Obviously, high net worth investors do not need to get more money – start-up investing simply being a high stakes game in which they can control many of the variables.

Whether the intellectual property is owned by an inventor or is a license agreement from a university from whence the invention was created, potential investors will demand evidence of IP ownership; they will subsequently conduct their own *due diligence* on the claimed ownership to a) see if claimed legal status is valid and b) to determine whether there are claimants from previous iterations of commercialization attempts. Intellectual property created at a university or research institution is frequently licensed to start-up or existing companies, called *technology transfer*, for a royalty percentage of the profits derived from commercialization. For information on issues and opportunities in the technology transfer world see Intellectual Property Marketing Advisor at http://www.ipmarketingadvisor.com or its daily electronic idea and transaction update at info@technologytransfertactics.com

Risk taking v. risk mitigating behaviors – There is a myth that participating in a start-up is risky business – and, compared to your average banking operation, it is. However, professional management and financial entrepreneurs are assiduous risk mitigators rather than high risk takers. Perhaps the best illustration of optimized risk taking behavior is from the several research studies of McClelland (1999) on *need achievement*. He studied large numbers of high achieving individuals in the private sector and the public sector; finding these high achievers more alike than different. Probing into their formative backgrounds, he found parenting styles promoting early independence and perseverance that resulted in individuals with a high level of experience-based self-confidence, persistence and moderate level of risk comfort. While some have characterized entrepreneurs as "risk takers;" the successful individuals and groups are actually "risk mitigators" because they carefully assess the probability of a project's success –minimize risks of project failure by staying within their confidence levels. One of his defining experiments came from asking people to try a simple ring toss exercise. The game rules were a) You can stand any distance from the target and try to toss rings over a vertical peg, b) The pay off is determined by the distance you stand from the target stick, c) You must get two of the five rings over the target peg in order to get the money reward and d) You must get one ring over the target peg in order to continue playing.

McClelland found that high achievement oriented people tended to start in the middle (Zone of Optimal Success) and then move back only to where they could comfortably be assured of getting at least one ring over the target peg. Two behaviors characterized high achievers; a) They are motivated to maximize their earnings and b) They see that "staying in the game" is critical to long term success. Both of these descriptors characterize entrepreneur managers and entrepreneur financers – neither are high risk takers. In reference to Figure 1.4, low risk takers tend to stay in the Safety Zone, small rewards at no risk, and high risk takers tend to start at the Gambling Zone.

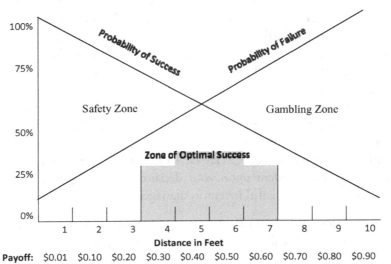

Figure 1.4 the ring toss experiment, Redrawn from McClelland (1999).

Personality profiles – While an undergraduate student at Harvard, John F Kennedy wrote his *Profiles in Courage* and a search in amazon.com shows numerous titles of profiles in business that produced some 11,818 books. Certainly these can be informative as to the processes or actions associated with an individual's success. George Sweigert certainly benefited from studying the lives of successful inventors – enabling him to envision the radio telephone – mobile telephone. However, as well described in *Outliers: The story of Success* (Gladwell, 2008), personal traits and skill sets interact with timing and circumstances to produce a particular result. To paraphrase Victor Hugo, "An idea whose time has come is the most powerful thing in the world." Thus, observe some care in transporting things from one context to another.

Prediction from a successful trait profile – As you may have noted, we asked you to position your estimates on the three Visual Analog Scales, but include neither metrics nor a sum of metrics on each of Figures 1.1, 1.2 and 1.3. This omission was by choice, as the predictive value of the respective characteristics will somewhat change with specific circumstances. And, only with an accurate statistical weighting of each characteristic factor to the success criterion, can an assessment devices be validated. Thus, simply adding a total for your marks on each of the characteristic factors would only provide the illusion of an accurate personality profile. And, citing the Johnson Paradox, "Adding more items added to an unweighted selection and prediction exercise minimizes its predictive validity."

Interpreting characteristics related profiles – Your identified position on any assessment device simply indicates where you are on a particular dimension at a particular time, not where you should be or could be. Knowing characteristics of successful people helps guide your decision for directional change. Trait labels, such as "introverted" are simply identifiers by self or others; with effort such characteristic behaviors are changeable. People, characterized as "introverted" and who observed that "extroverted" people seem to have more fun, and have taken steps to become very successful in group social situations, document the possibility thereof. However, skill sets such as for financial competency or project management, can be acquired through online or formal college classes. Thus, entry into the entrepreneurial world is largely dependent upon your decision to become prepared with characteristics of a successful inventor, manager or financier.

Case examples – Studying the components of the entrepreneur process can reveal how it typically is done. George H. Sweigert served five years as a radio operator in the South Pacific during WW II; where he learned the principles of electromagnetic wave communication. Sweigert was a student of successful inventors. Particular study of Thomas Edison's, Alexander Graham Bell's and Edwin Armstrong's careers led Sweigert to solve his own problem of getting to a telephone; as he was physically handicapped from military action.

Since case examples support concept understanding, three components of a single successful start-up are presented as follows. In this case example of creating and commercializing the dry copying process, the order of finance and management are reversed from the previous presentation because finance logically follows innovation and management is funded by venture capital.

Case example: Innovation entrepreneur – In 1930 Chester F. Carlson graduated with a physics degree from California Institute of Technology and began work as a research engineer at the Bell Telephone Laboratory in New York. Finding that work boring, he transferred to the company patent department; but was laid off in 1933 as the Great Depression worsened. With the patent experience, he found work as a clerk in a patent attorney office; an experience that motivated his study of law. Thus, as he developed his dry copying idea he was able to write his own patent applications.

Carlson had many classic characteristics of an innovator; future orientation, positive attitude, perseverance, a history experimenting and making things, technical education and perception of a future market and ability to champion his ideas. He had told a cousin at the age of 12 that he would someday make a great invention. As a high school student he bought an old printing press by working hourly to pay off the equity. Every patent application required multiple copies and those were made by placing multiple sheets of black carbon paper between white paper sheets and feeding them into a typewriter. Mistakes were a bane to correct with multiple carbon paper copies. Thus, his problem became a business opportunity. But, to devise a better method required hours of study in the New York Public Library. After bootstrapping multiple failures, he devised a electrophotography copying process and receive a patent for his idea. To commercialize the patent Carlson need a financial partner – yet more than 20 government agencies and corporations, including the Department of Navy, RCA, GE and IBM, turned him away. He had an invention that no one wanted.

Case example: Financial entrepreneur – A chance meeting with a Battelle Memorial Institute representative led to formal meetings and money to conduct necessary prototyping and production model testing. Battelle, a 501(c)(3) non-profit organization located in Columbus, Ohio, was founded by an industrialist for charitable, scientific and education purposes. Battelle saw the commercial potential for Carlson's patent and, beginning in 1944, pumped millions into product research and development. At that time they were a contract research organization and when prototype scale-up development was completed on the electrophotography project Battelle and Carlson formed a royalty agreement with a production and distribution company to take the idea public.

Case example: Management entrepreneur – In 1947 a royalty agreement was reached with the Haloid Company, a major photography paper business, to manage manufacturing and marketing of Carlson's machines. Haloid's paper business was declining and the company needed new products. The patent term, *electrophotography,* was renamed using the Greek words for dry and writing *xerograph.* The product name was shortened to Xerox. Twenty one years after the patent was issued Xerox 914 was introduced to the public and Haloid changed its name to the Xerox Corporation. The invention that no one wanted went from obscurity to being named by *Fortune* magazine as "The most successful product ever marketed in America." Carlson's multi-billion dollar dream of inventing something to perhaps improve his station in life and benefit society reached fruition; thanks to collaboration between the inventor, the financier and the manager.

Post script: Now, imagine that **you** are that person "who looks at what everyone does and sees something different" – an opportunity to benefit yourself and people around the world that you will never meet. The world is hot, flat and crowded and we need you to lead out. Your opportunity's door is now open.

CHAPTER SUMMARY

KEY POINTS

- Entrepreneurism, a tool for moving services and products from idea to commercialization, also functions to advance civilization.

- The concept of forming a company to share the financial risk of a business venture – such as The West India Company and East India Company – began in Northern Europe during the 17th Century.

- Successful innovations are typically solutions to significant problems faced by individuals or businesses.

- For various reasons few inventions ever move from idea to commercialization.

- Omnibus "Entrepreneur Assessments" cannot be valid success predictors because there are three types of entrepreneurs: a) the inventor, b) the management and c) the financier.

- The more unweighted factors/questions that are added to an assessment device the greater the prediction error.

- The respective entrepreneur's roles have separate characteristic traits and skill sets.

- It is a myth that entrepreneurs are high risk individuals; they actually are risk-mitigators and are characterized as being moderate risk-takers.

- Single trait assessments for predicting entrepreneurial success, such as intelligence, are always invalid because entrepreneurial success is dependent on multiple factors.

- Social and environmental entrepreneurism have provided powerful tools to fight global

- There are numerous formal and informal resources available to help you acquire the fundamentals of the three entrepreneurial roles.

TAKE ACTION NOW

- It is your decision as to whether you want to become a successful entrepreneur.

- Characteristic traits and skill sets if the inventor, management or financer roles help to identify the type and degree of preparation needed for entrepreneurial success.

- Since most of the low hanging fruit of invention tree has been harvested, you will need to become very well informed in a potential innovation area (such as "solar energy") in order to create a potentially viable start-up.

- Practice submitting Small Business Innovative Research grant proposals in order to augment your boot strapped innovation expenses.

- Formal classes in finance, accounting, project management and business management can help prepare you to enter the start-up management field.

- Study the lives and work of inventors, managers, and investors in your interest areas.

- Many communities regularly hold free or low cost workshops or inventors/investors round table events where you can begin networking.

- Move to a geographic area where there is action in your chosen innovation sector.

- Get on email lists for inventor, management and venture financing organizations.

- Practice *due diligence* processes as if you are an inventor assessing potential investors and an investor assessing potential IP

- Master the process of market segment analysis.

- Join a local Toastmasters International Club to sharpen your presentation skills.

- Volunteer to help someone develop their business plan, marketing plan and Cap Table.

- There are personal development resources, books, magazines, formal courses, online courses, workshops, and networking opportunities waiting for you to take action.

REFERENCES:

Collins, J. (2001). *Good to great: Why some companies make the leap and others don't*. New York: HarperCollins Publishers, Inc.

Diamond, J. (2005). *Guns, germs and steel: The fates of human societies*. New York: W. W. Norton & Co.

Feinstein, J. (2002). *The punch: One night, two lives, and the fight that changed basketball forever*. New York: Little, Brown & Co.

Ferguson, N. (2008). *The ascent of money: A financial history of the world*. New York: Penguin Group.

Gladwell, M. (2008). *Outliers: The story of success*. New York: Little, Brown & CO.

Gladwell, M. (2005). *Blink: The power of thinking without thinking*. New York: Little, Brown and Co.

Kroc, R. (1990). *Grinding it out: The making of McDonald's*. New York: St Martin's Press.

McClelland, D. (1999). *The achieving society*. New York: The Free Press.

Minton, H. L. (1988). *Lewis M. Terman: Pioneer in educational testing.* New York: New York University.

Owen, D. (2004). *Copies in second: How a lone inventor and an unknown company created the biggest communication breakthrough since Guttenberg – Chester Carlson and the birth of the Xerox.* New York: Simon & Schuster.

Pirenne, H. (1937). *Economic and social history of medieval Europe.* New York: Harcourt, Brace & World, Inc.

Plucker, P. (2010) in B. Bronson & A. Merryman, *The Creativity Crisis: For the first time, research shows that American creativity is declining. Newsweek, 7/19/2010.* 44-50.

Wadhwa, V., Aggarwal, R., Holly, K. & Salkever, A. (2009). *The anatomy of an entrepreneur: Family background and motivation.* Kansas City, MO: The Kauffman Foundation of Entrepreneurism.

SUPPLEMENTAL SOURCES:

Albion, M. (2006). *True to yourself: Leading a values-based business.* San Francisco: Berrett-Koehler Publishers, Inc.

Barbarich, S. S. (2000). *The complete manual on how to make money from your inventions and patents.* Avon, MA: Adams Media Corporation.

Barringer, B. (2008). *Preparing effective business plans An entrepreneurial approach.* Upper Saddle River, NJ: Pearson Education, Inc.

Bornstein, D. (2007). *How to change the world: Social entrepreneurs and the power of new ideas.* Oxford, EN: oxford University Press.

Craughwell, T. J. (2008). *The book of invention,* New York: Tess Press.

Deutsch, D. (2009). *The big idea: How to make your entrepreneurial dream come true, from the Aha moment to your first million.* New York: Hyperion.

Heath, D. (2007). *Made to stick: Why some ideas survive and others die.* New York: Random House.

Hess, E.D. (200?). *So, you want to start a business?: 8 steps to take before making the leap.* Upper Saddle River, Pearson Education, Inc.

Learner, J. (2009). *Boulevard of broken dreams: Why public efforts to boost entrepreneurship and venture capital have failed – and what to do about it. Princeton,* NJ: Princeton University Press.

Prahalad, C. K. (2006). *The Fortune at the bottom of the pyramid: Eradicating poverty through profits.* Upper Saddle River, NJ: Pearson Education, Inc.

Robb, A. (2008). *Capital structure decisions of new firms.* Kansas City, MO: Kauffman Foundation.

Rosen, W. (2010). *The most powerful idea in the world.* New York: Random House.

Sachs, J. D. (2008). *Common Wealth: Economics for a crowded planet.* New York: The Penguin Press.

Schroeder, A. (2008). *The snowball: Warren Buffett and the business of life.* New York: Bantam Books.

Swedberg, R. (2000). *Entrepreneurship: The social science view.* Oxford EN: Oxford University Press.

Touhill, C. J., Touhill, G. & O'Riordan, T. (2007). *Commercialization of innovation technologies: Bringing good ideas to the marketplace.* Hoboken, NJ: John Wiley & Sons.

Yanus, M. (2008). *Creating a world without poverty: Social business and the future of capitalism.* Philadelphia: Percus Books Group.

Yunus, M. (2003). *Banker to the poor: Micro-lending and the battle against poverty.* New York: Public Affairs.

CHAPTER TWO
Unleash Your Creativity

*"Discovery consists of seeing what everyone else has seen
and thinking what nobody else has thought."*

Jonathan Swift

Bob Kearns had little depth perception. In the rain he was a bad driver and in a heavy mist, he was even worse. The 1962 version of windshield wipers efficiently removed steady rain; but, wipers often screeched over dry glass in a heavy mist. While driving his Ford Galaxie through Detroit drizzle one November day in 1962, Kearns wondered, "Why can't a wiper work intermittently like an eyelid?

Though it could be argued that his was simply a, "Flash of genius that suddenly occurred to an ordinary person;" Kearns was no ordinary person. He was a brilliant mechanical engineer who was quite accustomed to putting existing components together to solve problems. Thus, began a project that would reduce accidents, earn him a fortune he never enjoyed, cost him dearly in health and family, create a legacy among inventors and the scorn of industrialists.

From his mechanical engineering training, Kearns first tried assembling mechanical parts, but soon changed to combining mechanical and electronic components. He combined an electronic and mechanical prototype with only four parts, only one of which moved. It worked effectively in his Ford Galaxie, even automatically adjusting to the amount of water on the windshield. He filed for a protective patent in 1964. Feeling confident of his protected intellectual property, he demonstrated the device to engineers at Ford Motor Company. Ford engineers had been working on a device to intermittently activate wipers, but Ford's best effort at that time consisted of the Trico System; a contraption with

29 moving parts that inefficiently operated from vacuum pressure pulled from the intake manifold.

This creativity stuff

Creativity, while often viewed as an inborn ability, is a process that can be learned. Some call it lateral thinking, some call it thinking outside of the box, some call it ingenuity. Some people can generate ideas better than others, but almost anyone can be creative. It is not so much about finding the "hand you have been dealt" as it is about improving your abilities. Creativity, for most of us, merely means getting out of the rut of our current thinking (deBono, 1970; Flatow, 1992; Michalko, 2001; Oech, 1986). While ruts are not necessarily bad, habitual behavior does not facilitate creativity. But, when current methods, systems, institutions, artifacts or behaviors are not producing competitive results or do not fit the projected time table, you need to do something different – something creative. To paraphrase Einstein, "Problems cannot be solved with the thought processes that created the problem."

Creativity starts with the conviction that you are capable of developing something unique and valuable. It is the *mental set* that starts or stops progress. Michalko (2001) cites examples of mental stop signs; erroneous statements that slow down innovation. He states:

> "In 1923 Robert Millikan, noted physicist and winner of the Nobel Prize, said that there was absolutely no likelihood that man could harness the power of the atom. Phillip Reiss, a German, invented a machine that could transmit music in 1861; but every communication expert in Germany persuaded him that there was no market for such a device, as the telegraph was good enough. Fifteen years later, Alexander Graham Bell invented the telephone and became a multimillionaire, with Germany as his first most enthusiastic customer (p. 8)."

Getting personal – This is where you start – creating something out of nothing. Actually, innovation is creating something new and valuable out of existing components, materials and prior art. Just as novelists use standard dictionary words to create literary works, innovations are made from existing components cobbled together. For example, until 1979

35

Teflon was a hard black material used for electrical insulators and heavy duty underground pipes. But, Wilbert L. Gore, Rowena Taylor and Robert Gore looked at the hard black material and saw a potential waterproof fabric. U.S. Patent 3,953,566, filed by W. L. Gore & Associates, described how Teflon could be formed into microstructure fibers characterized by nodes connected by fibrils. At that time, competitor's rainwear typically consisted of a strong polyester or nylon outer layer bonded to a polyurethane inner liner; uncomfortable waterproof material with no air transfer for breathability. Gore-Tex introduced their new all-weather wear, formed from Teflon fibers with pores (openings) too small for rain drops to enter, but large enough to allow water vapor to escape. Because it is strong, lightweight and chemically inert, Gore-Tex material is now being used in applications ranging from arterial stints, for repairing aneurysms, to automotive fuel cell technology. The foundational material for Gore-Tex products is excellent examples of a research team perceiving a potential product while looking at a seemingly un-related raw material. For details; see Flatow (1992).

To get benefit from this creativity exercise you will need to decide, at least for the near future, whether you want to create a invention or develop a lifestyle business idea and run with it or whether you want to stay in your organization and brand yourself as THE company innovator – all options can increase your own "value proposition," We do not know where your talents and interests lie; and you may not be fully aware of them either. However, we are confident that this chapter will help your identify and develop ability areas and fire a passion that can become a business idea.

Coming to terms with terms – "Creativity" gets all mixed up with problem solving, innovation, inventiveness and related terms. They are related, but not coterminous! For example, a young child's "refrigerator art" is divergently creative; but not something that solves a significant problem, nor is it an innovation of broad societal value. This is not a simple discussion; unless language precision is unimportant and you allow everyone to make up their own word meanings. Lewis Carroll (2010) addressed this "postmodern words by convenience" in *Through the Looking Glass* – Humpty Dumpty plays with words and, when confronted with obvious malapropos stated, "When I use a word, it means just what I choose it to mean."

There are many ways to cut the definitional creativity pie; your choice depending upon the context and need. For example, creativity can be divided by purpose: a) inventiveness needed to solve a problem or b) the imagination needed for inquiry into what is possible. The team that built California's Golden Gate Bridge during the Great Depression was indeed creative; ingeniously solving design problems, materials problems, local financing problems, legal problems with the railroad trying to block the project and incredible construction challenges. Stimulus for the bridge was expressed in time and dangers for ferry crossing or for roadway circumnavigating the entire San Francisco Bay.

Most creative thought is focused on solving some significant problem and such inquiry related to a presenting problem is called "applied research." However, focused thought into contemplating "what is possible" is a tough discipline; typified by independent 17th Century development of the Principles of Calculus by Isaac Newton and Gottfried Leibniz; or Charles Babbage conceiving a 15 ton computer prototype in 1822 that he called "the difference machine." By using the method of *finite differences,* Babbage avoided the need for multiplication and division. "Basic research or inquiry" is well illustrated by a recent news headline, "University scientists look for real-world applications of research." At times these two aspects of creativity overlap - basic and applied inquiry – but, both start with divergent thinking.

Reproductive v. *Productive thinking* – Creative thinking can be sectored according to activity type: *Reproductive thinking* v. *Productive thinking.* *Reproductive thinking* creates incremental improvements in existing technologies or finds niches in product or service sectors. It is sometimes called "incrementalism," "continuous improvement" or "continuous adaptation;" such as adding surround sound or larger petroleum-based automobile engines for moving people to places or divining software applications (apps) for the latest digital communications device. For example, Otterbox, Inc. designs and markets soft plastic protective solutions for personal communication devices, such as for iPhone, Blackberry, Motorola. Though many successful business models are built on incremental improvements, beware of the next generation lurking just behind a temporal success. Ridderstrale & Nordstrom (2008) present a downside of getting locked into *reproductive thinking* as follows:

> "The "surplus society" has a surplus of similar companies, employing similar people, with similar educational backgrounds, coming up with similar ideas, producing similar things, with similar prices and similar quality."

Though reproductive thinking does not produce earth shaking business ideas, there are numerous examples of businesses finding very profitable niches in product or service sectors. For example:

- John Schnatter had considerable experience in the fast food delivery business in high school and college. He perceived that people would pay for quality pizza delivered fast. His Papa John's Pizza is a great international success story.

- Heidi Ganahi saw an opportunity to provide a premium doggy day care and overnight camp service for working adults. After refining the business operation in Boulder, CO, she offered franchises through throughout the United States. After founding in 2000, the company has grown to serving some 6,500,000 happy pets annually.

- Sony engineers tried to develop a very small tape recorder and found it would only play and not record – a failure. Honorary chairman Masaru Ibuka inventively combined Sony's new ultra light head phones with the "failed" tape player and produced one of the company's all time best sellers – the Walkman.

- Candido Jacuzzi invented an at-home hydrotherapy aid for his son's arthritis treatment; using one of his company's submersible agriculture pumps and a bathtub. After limited success in marketing the invention to therapy clinics, he re-cast it as a luxury bath experience.

The other type of creativity, *productive thinking* is typified by methods for identifying possible antecedents or problem causes and then deliberately generating numerous plausible responses. This could be characterized as *C-creativity*, where the innovation is without precedent; as opposed to *c-creativity*, in which incremental improvements are made on existing technologies or niches are explored. Nobel and Pulitzer prizes are awarded for *C-creativity*; but many very successful businesses have been founded and sustained from *c-creativity* innovations. There a significant sophistication range in both *C-creativity* and *c-creativity* categories.

Breakthrough business ideas, mostly low level *C-creativity*, are generated from identifying and solving significant problems; problems that is costing time and money for many people or multiple organizations. For example, prior to the Riverbed Technologies entry into the data transmission scene, companies having numerous regional offices experienced difficulty in downloading large internet status reports; as with "Friday Reports of weekly activity to the main office." Computer connections between field and main offices are called are "Wide Area Networks" or WANs." Typically, when multiple inputs fed into the central computer the digital data reception process slowed down in proportion to the number of satellites in the company's WAN; resulting in time-related equipment and personnel costs.

Recognizing that a solution to the worldwide corporate information management problem could be a potentially profitable business start-up, Dr. Steve McCanne developed and patented infrastructure appliances to improve the performance of client-server interactions over WANs without breaking the semantics of the protocols, file systems or applications. This simply means that his novel appliances allow offices from virtually any place in the world to send and receive very large computer files with little or no speed problems. Potentially this accelerates data transfer, including copying a file from a distant file server, getting mail from a remote exchange server, backing up remote file servers to a main datacenter, or sending a very large CAD file to a colleague in another office; by optimization techniques of caching and compressing. The company's *Steelhead* appliance enables customers to improve the performance of their applications to access data across their WANs; demonstrating cost saving transmission speed increases of from 5 to 100 times and crossing any regional or national boundary.

Founded in 2002 by McCanne and two other principals, Riverbed Technologies is located San Francisco, CA. Its NASDAQ name is RVBD and it is rated as a billion dollar company. McCanne saw the potential for accelerating WANs data transfer; with that vision resulting in increased client profitability, important reduction in energy costs for data transfer and employment of thousands of people in a new product sector from *productive thinking* that created disruptive technology. See *Riverbed Technologies* at http://.www.riverbed.com

Nicholas Negroponte's often quoted criticism of *reproductive thinking,* "Incrementalism is innovation's worst enemy," cuts to the heart of merely burnishing existing art instead of considering big picture root causes of problems and then generating multiple solution scenarios. Incrementalism is the trite "Thinking Inside of the Box." Visionary breakthroughs from *productive thinking* are called "disruptive technologies;" because their very presence changes the rules for the affected sectors; if not the whole world. Some of the game changers affecting changes in lifestyle and commerce are:

1. The Shockley-Pearson invention of the transistor.

2. Jobs concept of creating small computers that the layman could operate at home - Apple.

3. Mauer, Keck, Schultz & Zimar with Corning Inc. and GE developed commercial fiber optics.

4. The Lichlider, Roberts, Bavan & Kleinrock internet development.

5. Page & Brin developed the Google search engine.

6. Bicycle repairmen Wilbur and Orville Wright invention of a heavier-than-air flying machine.

Each of these C-creativity game changers required creators to operate outside of conventional wisdom of how things should be done. For example, realizing that, in 1903, there were less than 200 miles of paved roads in America, Henry Ford's comment that, "If I had asked people what they wanted, they would have said, 'Faster horses'," places his automobile assembly line concept as "disruptive technology." Mass production of identical parts facilitated mass production of automobiles that could be sold at prices comparable to horse drawn vehicles. Ford merely adapted the decades old Chicago meat packing assembly line idea to automobile manufacture.

Flow from idea to commercialization – Figure 2.1. shows related terms in a sequence from idea-to-commercialization. Though there is a hierarchical family of related labels, some form of creativity is needed; from idea and prototyping to scale-up and commercialization.

> Level 5 Experiencing – Experiencing the results of the creative and innovative processes by living with or using benefits of services, products and processes created through entrepreneurism. This can also be applied to experiencing the results of creative ideas that have been realized and put into practice.

Level 4 Entrepreneurism – Applying service, process or product innovations to the marketplace for potentially benefit to the inventor and society. For example, Ray Kroc's synthesis process for using automobile assembly line concept for hamburger production; with subsequent divergent thinking for his franchising concept.
Level 3 Innovation – Development of service, process or product innovations. Intellectual property is simply a novel service, process or a product that has potential value – an invention. For example, Frederick W. Smith's university economics class business plan became the first nationwide overnight parcel delivery service - FedEx.
Level 2 Problem Solving – Convergent thinking focused on resolving a difficulty or predicament. For example, designing and building the Golden Gate Bridge to eliminate the ferry ride or the long road trip around the1600 square mile San Francisco Bay.
Level 1 Abstract Creativity – Divergent and convergent thinking processes or skills are foundational for developing new concepts, processes and products. For example, Pablo Picasso was one of the most successful divergently creative artists; using a variety of media and styles in his 20,000 works – sculpture, drawing and painting.

Figure 2.1 succinctly portrays the sequence of this book; namely to get you to create a business idea that can be translate through the sequence to successful commercialization – something that has potential benefits to society and subsequently benefits you.

Einstein's dictum that we should, "Strive not to be a success, but rather to be of value," ennobles the mission of your project to the level widely discussed in groups studying Warren's (2003) *The Purpose Driven Life: What on Earth are We Here For?* As is discussed in the Marketing Chapter, initially focusing on consumer or societal benefits, rather than features or potential profits, improves the inventor's focus. Similarly, Chester Carlson mused early in his law career that "Inventing was a way for individuals to both improve their economic position and to make a difference in the world" – both of which he accomplished with the Xerox innovation. Reading an account of Carlson's idea formation and refinement into a product can inform your business idea creation (Owen, 2004).

Clarifying terms – To establish a common use of the key terms introduced in Figure 2.1, consider the following operational definitions.

Creativity – Creative *divergent thinking*, imagination or ingenuity that leads to a novel concept or product. While most elementary school children produce original works of art; though valued by the young artist and the parents those arts and crafts are not typically marketable, nor did the art work solve a significant problem? No, a child's art work is simply an original expression. However, numerous artists and artisans do quite well selling their works; with Pablo Picasso arguably being one of the most divergently successful artists and clearly the most financially successful artist in history.

Problem solving – When there is a significant presenting problem, creativity is required to move from impasse to solution alternatives to project completion. Since every large bridge or building design and construction presents unique circumstances, a customized variation or a radical design solution must be created. Thus, creative *convergent thinking* is inherent in solving all real world problems; from quickly developing an H1N1 vaccine to divining multiple alternatives for resolving the rapidly growing global climate crisis.

Innovation – Creating a novel invention that has potential marketplace value is, by definition, both an innovation and a patent; patents being issued only for items that are a) original, b) have an obvious utility and c) the first to formally register an ownership claim. Patents are not issued for gadgets, other than commercially viable toys, that are simply amusing. Thus, for an invention to qualify as an "innovation" a commercial value must be demonstrated by the creator. Creativity is obviously an inherent part of the innovation process.

The word *innovation* is derived from the Latin *innovatus*; variously meaning "in + new," "into existence," "to introduce as new" or "a new idea or course of action." It involves divergent thinking, "the ability to generate new ideas" and convergent thinking, that is "the ability to synthesize different objects or processes into unique and meaningful concepts"- or to "look at the same world as everyone else and see something different." Thus, an innovation program is one that focuses on developing creativity by confronting real world problems for some utilitarian purpose – creating. It also involves convergent thinking to high potential ideas for divergent thinking into prototype stage.

Entrepreneurism – Many really good ideas that could benefit people and the planet die for lack of ingenuity in moving from *proof of concept* validation to public availability because no skilled and creative entrepreneur is available to make the transition happen. The World Economic Forum evaluates international economic competitiveness on the basis of respective countries' effectiveness in both creating commercially viable ideas and in translating those innovations into economic engines. Thus, creativity is needed for both product development and commercialization. New ideas are needed, regardless of whether the item is for commercial, social or environmental entrepreneurism.

WHY IS CREATIVITY IMPORTANT?

Human ingenuity has created a thirst for novelty; new products and services that are better and attractively packaged; typified by the contemporariness expression, "That is so yesterday!" Aside from fashion trends, spawned by creativity specific to an industry, the age of routine manufacturing job performance is waning and those who can divine better, faster, cheaper and more attractive modalities will thrive. Shape and form of every automobile starts on a paper or electronic sketch pad and, as described in Pink's (2006) *A whole new mind: Why right-brainers will rule the future*, those trained in creative skills and strategies will be advantaged:

> "The past few decades have belonged to a certain kind of person with a certain kind of mind – computer programmers who could crank code, lawyers who could craft contracts, MBAs who could crunch numbers.... The future belongs to a very different kind of person with a different kind of mind –creators and empathizers, pattern recognizers, and meaning makers. These people – artists, inventors, designers, storytellers ... big picture thinkers – will now reap society's richest rewards and share it greatest joys (p. 1)."

From decades of international research on factors related to developing economic competitiveness, the prestigious Swiss World Economic Forum concluded that developing countries should focus their educational programs on basic literacy and developed economies, such as the U.S., should focus educational programming for improving ***innovation development skills*** (www.weforum.org/). A recent IBM survey of 1,500 CEO's identified ***creativity*** as the Number One "leadership competency needed for the future" (Bronson & Merryman, 2010). Similarly, results from the 21st Century Skills survey of hundreds of business executives showed that **the development of creativity was a critically needed employee attribute** (Kay, 2004).

Individual – "If there is nothing special about your work, no matter how hard you apply yourself you won't get noticed, and that increasingly means you won't get paid much either" (Michael Goldhaber). This frustration may drive you to get creative and the employment forecast is for anything that can be done by a computer, robot or just as well by a talented foreigner will be offshored and any type of employees who only wait to be told what to do will have fewer opportunities in the New Global Economy. As Friedman explains (2009):

> "Those with the imagination to make themselves untouchables – to invent smarter ways to do old jobs, energy-saving ways to provide new services, new ways to attract old customers or new ways to combine existing technologies – will thrive …. If you think about the labor market today, the top half of the college market, those with high-end analytical and problem solving skills who can compete on the world market or game the financial system or deal with new government regulations, have done great. But the bottom half …, those engineers and programmers working on more routine tasks and not actively engage in developing new ideas or recombining existing technologies or thinking about what new customers want, have done poorly (p. 2)."

As we repeatedly emphasize, developing a product or service idea is not a business. While an invention may serve a business foundation, an invention is not a business. Once launched the business MUST add new product lines.

Corporate – New product design is a critical factor in the survival of a company; requiring a significant corporate effort to research and development (R&D). Firms with a consistent commitment to R&D consistently outperform those with little or inconsistent investment. The average U.S. corporation reinvests is about 3.5 percent of revenues in R&D; with digital techno logy companies averaging 7 percent and biotech and pharmaceuticals averaging 15 percent or more. While commitment to incrementally improving existing products is expected – making them better, faster and cheaper, focus on incrementalism can be deadly. Western Union Telegraph Corporation could have invested in R&D to develop the telephone, but they were only interested in improving a duplex system to simultaneously sent dots and dashes two ways over copper wires. And, Western Union could have invested heavily in Alexander Graham Bell's fledgling telephone company – they did not and lost out to the new voice technology. Christensen (2003) poses a paradox that can only be understood by abandoning the incremental product improvement mentality. He states:

> *"Good management* was the most powerful reason (leading firms) failed to stay atop their industries. Precisely because these firms listened to their customers, invested heavily in technologies that would provide their customers more and better products of the sort they wanted, and because they carefully studied market trends and systematically allocated investment capital to innovations that promised the best returns, they lost their positions of leadership."

Paradoxically, by pacing too much emphasis on existing products and customers, companies can fail to perceive unstated needs or future societal demands that will be created by disruptive technology. Leading edge companies, like Apple Computer, continually create customer demand by introducing innovative technology.

National – With commodity manufacturing being moved offshore, American competitiveness in the New Global Economy is at-risk and the U.S. must increasingly rely on innovations. Though the U.S. leads the world in innovation - with and average of 71 percent in the high technology fields of Telecommunications, Semiconductors, Software, Biopharmaceuticals and Clean Energy (Vella, 2008) – present success is no guarantee of the future.

The World Economic Forum identified 12 factors contributing differentially to a nation's economic progress at one of three developmental stages. These Pillars of Competitiveness are; 1) Private and public institutions, 2) Physical Infrastructure, 3) Macroeconomy of workforce and productivity, 4) Health and primary education, 5) Higher education and training, 6) Goods market efficiency, 7) Labor market efficiency, 8) Financial market sophistication, 9) Technological readiness, 10) Market size, 11) Business sophistication and 12) **Innovation**. Additionally, the WEF derived a statistical weighting index for assigning the relative contribution of each of the Competitiveness Pillar factors to any respective nation's developmental stage. Thus, the message from the World Economic Forum is clear for policy makers and policy affecters; identify the critical variables for the nation's developmental stage and address them with human and financial resources.

Although creativity is the foundation for the nation's technical and commercial innovation, **creativity is declining in America's schools** (Bronson & Merryman, 2010). Student creativity scores are inching downward – with the trend from kindergarten through sixth grade the most serious! Creativity scores were rising in children and adults for the previous decades, but they began a continuing downward trend in 1990. This does not bode well for leading the world in innovation. Florida (2005) similarly concludes that, "if we are to truly prosper, we can no longer tap and reward the creative talents of an elite minority; everyone's creative capabilities must be fully engaged. "In my opinion, the greatest challenge of our time will be to spark and stoke the creative furnace inside every human being" (p. 35).

International – Almost unimaginable creativity is needed to slow and reverse massive damage done daily to the world's environment. Creating and implementing strategies to counter increasing affects of human activity on the earth's environment is a race of ingenious countermeasures against increasing contamination. Large scale and small scale innovations to reduce population, generate renewable energy, reduce energy consumption, increase food supplies, re-vegetate barren lands, conserve water and reduce transportation costs are but a few of the critical areas needing new commercialization ideas; many of which are suggested in Hawken, Lovins & Lovins (2008) *Natural Capitalism: Creating the Next Industrial Revolution.*

After high tide there are no footprints, but as people walk on the beach each leaves a set of footprints. With the world's population growing at a faster rate than the earth can sustain, there is concern that trampling the Earth's resources can lead to disaster. Friedman's (2008) new book, *Hot, Flat and Crowded: Why We Need a Green Revolution – and How it can Renew America.* Research global environmental concepts of humanity's *Water Footprint* www.waterfootprint.org and www.gdrc.org/vem/footprinys/ water-waterfootprint.html and our *Carbon Footprint* for identifying and broadly framing problems and generating solutions that lead to innovation opportunities www.carbonfootprint.com www.nature.com .

GET CREATIVE!

I watched a two year old perform a multi-step problem solving task without cue or instruction. She had found a two cracker restaurant package, sealed with cellophane that she could not tear. Knowing that scissors were "safely stowed" in a drawer higher than she could reach, she went downstairs, found a handy stepstool, brought it up a flight of stairs, mounted it to get the scissors and then proudly cut the top off the cellophane. That was two year old creativity and you are far more creative than that! Her lesson is "No whining or pleading; take control of the situation!"

While there may be some skepticism as to the human ability to learn creativity skills, there is little controversy that creativity is effectively extinguished by rigid lecture, rote memory and drill teaching techniques; such experiences being devoid of relevance, engagement, problem solving and learning for understanding. However, it is apparently widely believed that creativity can be developed or enhanced; given the numerous trade books offered on the subject – see Michalko (2001), Tharp (2003) and Sloane & MacHale (2011) for starters.

Creativity development programs have been criticized as needing to be taken out of the "art room;" for creativity is needed in the social sciences, the sciences as well as commerce. W. Edwards Deming was a statistician who created a quality-based protocol that revolutionized manufacturing; creating a worldwide epidemic of quality. Mary Lerner and Len Bosack were university computer support staff when they created their multiple-protocol router software that became Cisco Systems. Ray Kroc was an ordinary salesman, whose visionary synthesis of two different phenomena – automobile assembly line manufacturing and hamburger production – formed the basis for McDonald's Restaurants. Thus, it is apparent that innovations are largely "skill set specific;" meaning that business sector specific information is basic to creating novelty.

Systematically developing creativity must be a foundation piece for the New Global Economy and there are numerous existing training strategies available. However, identifying where to effectively spend time and money to improve personal or corporate innovation is confusing. An internet search reveals numerous consultants pitching canned programs. Instruction in the visual arts is almost synonymous with developing creativity; yet, aside from the skills specific to that medium, "graphic art based creativity" applicable to various fields such as chemistry, agriculture and solar cell technology is suspect. Specifically, "What skills/attributes learned by artists can transfer to other contexts and tasks?" And, "How is that transfer accomplished?"

If you feel stuck, start hanging around people who are innovative. Sternberg & Williams (1996) advise that the most powerful way to develop creativity is to be a role model; people develop creativity not when you tell them to, but when you show them. Since you are the learner, apply this principle by hanging round innovative people – role models. The Homebrew Computer Club of the 1975-1986s was just an informal gathering by early hobbyists to trade parts, circuits and information. Out of that periodic gathering came several world-leading hardware and software companies. Many cities have their own Inventor's Roundtable organizations; periodic meetings of inventors, mentors, patent attorneys and prototype development service providers. See www.inventorsroundtable.com

There is considerable evidence, supporting the thesis that innovation is a skill that can be learned; after all, no one is born with this ability. As Gladwell (2008) established in *Outliers: The Story of Success*, mentoring and thousands of hours of practice create the illusion of "overnight success." For example, Paul Allen and Bill Gates both had extensive mentoring and practice during the critical developmental period of the computer industry; spending much of their high school senior year on a paid field project writing computer programs for TRW, Inc. at the Bonneville Power Station in southern Washington State. Michalko (2001) reported a similar mentor effect for Nobel Prize winners:

> "Sociologist Harriet Zuckerman published an interesting study of the Nobel Prize winners who were living in the United States in 1977. She discovered that six of Enrico Fermi's students won the prize.... This was no accident. It was obvious that these Nobel laureates were not only creative in their own right, but were also able to teach others how to think. (p. 13)."

Creative endeavors cover a very broad spectrum; from the historic human survival ingenuity and development of political systems for managing conflict to combinations of artistic and industrial arts to improve the quality of human existence. The common thread running through these diverse entities is the generation of alternative actions in response to an existing problem or opportunity. Creativity's inherent values - such as being quantitatively or qualitatively expressed as "better," "faster," "efficient," "beautiful," or "greener" – are all generated by someone's divergent thinking. For example, Advanced Energy (AE) (www.advanced-energy.com) was created from the frustration of an individual's inability to persuade an existing company to adopt a more effective manufacturing protocol. Its value proposition is that "AE creates solutions aimed at maximizing process impact, improving productivity and lowering cost of ownership for its customers, including original equipment manufacturers (OEMs) and end users around the world." AE started from someone figuring out a better way to manufacture a critical product.

Where does it start? – We know that wandering around in a desert is not inherently creative, it is just meandering. The same is true of mentally wandering "in the abstract." While meditation has numerous benefits, divining innovations is not one; else its monastic practitioners would be always at technology's cutting edge. Serious contemplation, portrayed by Auguste Rodin (circa 1880) as sculpture, "The Thinker," represents the Platonic method of trying to divine creativity by sedentary contemplation. Conversely, pragmatically tinkering and creatively dabbling in the office or garage, in search of novel solutions and designs, is the typical invention mode. An experienced teacher commented, "We learn to work creatively by confronting real problems that matter to us personally" (Gass, 2009).

You have survived and that took creativity – Let's stop looking at creativity as just something in the art room – it is practical. For example, my mother passed away at age 97 years; surviving, not because life was easy, but because she was resourceful. She solved critical problems presented by barriers to her education, extreme poverty, two world wars, a horrible economic depression that killed thousands, multiple business reversals and the death of two husbands. She had looked adversity in the eye and both survived and, starting with nothing, found means to amass a small fortune over her lifetime. She was pragmatically creative.

Primitive societies survived because they creatively used available resources; killing game animals, domesticating plants, mammals and fowls, designing effective shelter from savage elements and protecting themselves from predators and raiders. Thus, intelligence applied to the problem context is critical to survival, but what is valued as "intelligence" in one geographic or cultural context may be useless in a different context. Failure in transference of survival creativity from one geographic context to a very different geographic context was fatefully demonstrated by early European explorers of the Australian Outback; well educated people who perished in an extreme environment where Aboriginals, thought by the European settlers as having "low intelligence," had creatively thrived for eons (Hughes, 1988, *That Fatal Shore: Epic of Australia's Founding*).

The prepared person – It could be that innovation just comes to people in a sudden flash of insight; such as innovations that combine or re-combine existing components in a novel manner. However, such accidental products seldom happen and most inventions begin with a mastery of mechanics, physics, biology and/or chemistry; with artistic works requiring a similar mastery of basics. Basic knowledge prepares the inventor or artist to formulate solutions to perplexing problems and forge new frontiers. The statement attributed to Thomas Edison, "Opportunity is often missed because it comes dressed in overalls," is a way of stressing persistent work ethic. As Edison expanded his research laboratories into invention factories, the corporate quota became "to produce one minor invention every 10 days and a major invention every six months." With similar diligence, though not all of theirs were masterpieces, Mozart wrote more than 600 musical pieces in his rather short life, Picasso produced over 20,000 works, Rembrandt produced over 2650 paintings and drawings and Shakespeare's numerous plays were written along with 154 sonnets. Gladwell (2008) provides numerous examples of how unseen practice prepares people for successful launches; with each case example including basic skill development and thousands of hours of preparation. For example, by the time the Beatles hit America on the Ed Sullivan Show they had already logged more than 10,000 hours in practice and performances.

Practice framing the problem as an opportunity – In the political world, issue or candidate election campaigns are won on effectively framing the conversation – each side trying to frame the other in a manner that will be perceived as undesirable is now a high art. However, learning to frame problems is a potentially effective tool for mining business ideas. Consider Bandler & Grinder's (1981) insight on problem framing; "If you only have one choice, you're a robot. If you only have two choices, you're on the horns of a dilemma. But, if you have three or more choices then you are beginning to have the requisite variety to respond creatively." Therefore, expanding the number of potential choices by problem framing will help you creatively find, use, and even define resources in new and novel ways.

What about smarts? – High intelligence has been romanced to death! The public assumes that those who create very successful businesses are among the super intelligent. That is mostly myth! Lewis Terman (Shurkin, 1992) theorized that there as a linear relation between intelligence and career achievement. At the turn of the 20th Century Terman secured funding from

Stanford University to test thousands of children. He recruited some 1,470 students, scoring above 140 points on his Terman-Merrill Intelligence Test, as subjects in a lifetime study of intelligence and achievement. Though many of his "Termites" achieved moderate recognitions and most were successful, his prediction was that this group was destined to be the future elite of the United States did not happen. If the McDonald's Restaurants founder, Ray Kroc, was a genius, neither he nor his family was aware of the gift. While above average intelligence can facilitate achievement, other variables are more important in career success.

While less publicized, Paul Torrance (Runco et al, 2011) developed several variations of creativity testing and these have been administered to millions worldwide in 50 languages. These instruments assessed problem solving and divergent thinking using such criteria as a) the number of divergent responses to a stimulus, b) the number of different categories of responses, c) the statistical rarity of responses and d) the amount of detail in the responses. A recent analysis of Torrance data (Bronson & Merryman, 2010) revealed that the correlation to lifetime creative accomplishment was more than three time stronger for childhood creativity than childhood IQ. Thus, take heart if you are not a genius, creative ability is largely independent of traditional verbal and mathematical intelligence test scores. See Gladwell (2008) for a thorough discussion of the genius achievement myth.

Be a student of innovation – Imagine leading a second group to further explore the Northwest Passage soon after the Lewis and Clark Expedition of 1804-1806; up the Missouri River, over the Rocky Mountains and down the Columbia River to the Pacific. Considering transportation difficulty, hostiles not welcoming your presence, extreme weather variations, wild animals and undependable food supplies, at your own peril would you ignore journals and maps from the Corps of Discovery? However, published innovation journals and maps are regularly ignored by those launching business ventures. It is the good fortune of this age that successful inventors, venture capitalists and start-up managers have journaled and mapped their expeditions – available online or in your public library. Studying innovators in your own field is critical to determining the state of technical art, but studying individuals and inventions outside your area can be instructive. Some examples are listed as follows:

- George H. Sweigert (1920 – 1999) is an excellent innovation guide. Fascinated with radio as a youth, he was trained as a U.S. Army radio operator in WW II and served during intense combat in the Pacific Theater. Afterward, he experimented with various types of antennae, signal frequencies and types of radios. Sweigert studied the life stories of electronics inventors; Samuel Morse of the telegraph, Alexander Graham Bell of the telephone, Edwin Armstrong of the radio, Thomas Edison of the phonograph and motion picture machine and Philo T. Farnsworth of the color television. Their struggles to create, patent and commercialize innovations motivated him to solve his own problem – living with a severe spinal war injury that made it difficult to walk. Using a solenoid from his wife's washing machine to enable remote "lifting of the telephone receiver" when a current was sensed in the induction coil and his considerable knowledge of radio signaling, he invented U.S. Patent 3,449,750 – "Duplex Radio Communication and Signaling Apparatus." Though initially expecting that his shirt pocket telephone would be useful only for the elderly and the handicapped, he revised his prediction to forecast that in his children's lifetime half the world would own a radio telephone – his invention now having moved from cell phones to full video capacity.

- Thomas Edison (1847-1931) was a multiple inventor and entrepreneur, who invested early profits to create an invention factory – with the quota of one minor invention every ten days, one major invention every six months and a record 1,093 patents. Feeling one-upped by Bell's telephone, Edison began work to elaborate on Bell's invention; resulting in the phonograph on year later. Numerous books and media sources are available about his life.

- William B. Shockley, Jr. (1910-1989) earned a Nobel Laureate in Physics, quite an accomplishment for someone who had been excluded from Terman's longitudinal study of geniuses because he did not score high enough on the intelligence tests. While working as the Solid State Physics Group leader at Bell Laboratories, Shockley saw potential in an earlier finding that the output electrical current was greater than the input when passed through a germanium crystal. Further research led to his co-invention of the transistor; the critical device that revolutionized smaller, cheaper and better electronics. "Shockley was the man who brought silicon to Silicon Valley." See Shurkin (2006).

• Robert W. Kearns (1927-2005) invented the intermittent windshield wiper from resistor-capacitor relaxation oscillators that had been used in other applications for decades before his patent application. However, as in other inventions, no one else had even conceived of using electronics to solve the windshield wiper problem. See Seabrook (2008) and the dramatic motion picture, "Flash of Genius."

By studying innovations in your field you may find opportunities to improve on existing processes or new applications for existing technologies. For example, Edison initially perceived the phonograph to be only useful to record final statements by the elderly or for business communications – even being outraged when it began to be used to record and play popular music. Wilbert L. Gore, Rowena Taylor and Robert W. Gore did not invent Teflon; they simply developed a porous version with a microstructure characterized by nodes interconnected by fibrils. Presently, Gore-Tex has moved from creating breathable waterproof apparel to include aneurism stints in medical surgery. Gore's aneurism stints have the advantage of not being rejected by the body because Teflon is chemically inert. Unfortunately, science and technology are traditionally taught as declarative information – information about the findings of researchers without reference to the thought processes that produced an end result. However, learning the creative process, from masters of those arts and sciences, far better facilitates the creation of new products, services and processes.

Divergent thinking is necessary for progress in every field of human endeavor. Several general books are available, such as the Hawksby, Humphries & Adlington (2008) *Timetables of History*, that chronologically mate the products of divergent thought with other events in respective time periods. Almost any field has its own record of creativity that has affected conceptual transitions; including Stokstad (2007) *Art History*, Katz (2008) *History of Mathematics*, Craughwell (2008) *The Book of Inventions* and Burrow (2009) *A History of Histories*. Reading creative process examples provides a peek into the thinking and experimentation of the legends in a respective field. For example:

Physics – At the dawn of the twentieth century physical scientists had developed considerable research-based understanding of the atom; though the shape and form of such invisible particles was still largely conjecture. Ernest Rutherford postulated that atoms consisted of positive charged particles surrounded by inwardly spiraling negatively charged particles that eventually collapsed into the center. Knowing something about astronomy and planets continuing their characteristic orbital patterns, the Danish physicist, Neils Bohr (1885-1962), developed a mathematically based construct placing the proton and neutron particles in the center and negative charged electrons in fixed orbits around the core; a micro-system analogous to the solar macro-system, where the orbiting planets do not collapse into the sun. Thus, the Bohr Model of atomic structure is conceptually similar to relation of the sun to its freely orbiting planets; an easily understood model explaining the nature and structure of individually invisible atoms.

Chemistry – By definition, chemistry research requires creativity to both think of what new compounds might be formed in an experiment and to be open to opportunities presented by unexpected results. Roy J. Plunkett, of Kinetic Chemicals was attempting to make a new chlorofluorocarbon (CFC) refrigerant when a batch of tetrafluorethylene was catalyzed by its iron container and polymerized itself into a white powder. They had started with 100 pounds of gas and ended up with 100 pounds of a heat resistant and chemically inert substance that had such a low surface friction coefficient that most other substances would not stick to it – the only thing a gecko cannot mount. It was patented in 1941 and the Teflon brand was registered in 1945. The material is a hard plastic (polytetrafluoroethylene) often extruded as pipes (PTFE); because it is insoluble and inert it can carry corrosive liquids and because it has a high electronegativity it is a valuable insulator. By 1950 du Pont was producing a million pounds annually. Thus, chemical and physical property analyses of his new polymer led Plunkett to recognize that he had found a compound with greater market potential than the alternative refrigerant that he originally sought to create. As he often told audiences, his mind had been prepared by education and training to recognize novelty. See Chemical Achievers at: www.chemheritage.org/classroom/chemach/plastics/plunkett.html

Biology – Observing nature is a productive way of beginning innovation, if the observer is open to recognizing novelty. The Swiss engineer, George de Mestral had been on a hunting trip in the Alps, when he noticed burrs (small prickly seeds) sticking to his clothes and his dog's fur. Examining them under a microscope, he found each seed had hundreds of tiny hooks that caught on any soft material. He saw the possibility of creating a fastener material of hooks and loops, but no one took his idea seriously. The first prototype of cotton worked, but it wore out quickly and he turned to nylon fibers for both hooks and loops. Though the proof of concept stage was passed, it took de Mestral ten years to perfect his production methods and even then there was little public acceptance. He named the product from the French words velours, meaning "velvet," and crochet, meaning "hook." However, it was not until NASA and the ski apparel industry began using the quick attachment-and-release features, "zipperless zipper," that Velcro found its place on clothing and shoes. de Mestral was inducted into the Inventors Hall of Fame and offered advice to executives; "If any of your employees ask for a two-week holiday to go hunting, say, "Yes!'" See Freeman & Golden (1997).

Industrial arts – The utility of reducing friction in moving objects (the wheel), in reducing gravitational effects in moving objects (the inclined plane and the lever) and in developing machines as substitutes for manual labor (mechanical cotton picker) are all results of divergent thinking applied to problem situations. Imagine the difficulty of mounting a tall horse by pulling upward and jumping; a task simplified in China by creating stirrups (circa 375). This seemingly simple invention serves as an example of technology dispersal; as the stirrup quickly spread from China to Europe. Easier, faster, better and cheaper have been the technology change levers throughout history. Artisans have contributed style to objects of utility.

Three craftsmen – a paper maker, a jeweler and a scribe - created a business from combining commonly available elements. Though ink and moveable printing had been developed much earlier in China, the smaller European alphabet facilitated typesetting print; as compared to the thousands of characters in the Chinese language. Thus, when Gutenberg printed his Bible around 1455, he simply had the good sense to combine six technologies in a novel way and his innovation spread quickly across Europe. Diamond (2005) succinctly describes the Gutenberg's technology recombination as follows:

> "Of those advances – in paper, moveable type, metallurgy, presses, inks, and scripts – paper and the idea of moveable type reached Europe from China. Gutenberg's development of typecasting from metal dies, to overcome the fatal problem of non-uniform type size, depended on many metallurgical

developments: steel for letter punches, brass and bronze alloys ...for dies, lead for molds and tin-zinc-lead alloy for type. Gutenberg's press was derived from screw presses in use for making wine and olive oil, while his ink was an oil-based improvement on existing inks (p. 259)."

Gutenberg's clever re-fitting an agricultural wine press for printing is arguably the single most important factor in accelerating civilization from the Dark Ages to the Industrial Age; for the recording and transmission of knowledge is critical to technological progress.

Because of its strategic location rail and geographic location, Chicago had become the Nation's meatpacking center of by the mid-1800s. Chicago processors adoption of Alexander Twining's 1849, 1850, 1853, and 1872 refrigeration patents enabled year round meat packing even during hot summers. In 1882 Augustus Swift installed the new refrigeration machines to railcars; enabling centralized processing and shipping to distant markets. Legendary meatpackers, Swift, Wilson and Armor, simply adapted developing technology into their business plans to very significantly change; low level business creativity that had a powerful effect on both an industry and the American society. Finding unique combinations for existing components has always been a major innovation source.

Visual art – Industrial arts are not divorced from creative graphic arts; as, when machines become standardized with the same features, appearance becomes the commercial attractor. Pink (2006) describes how art is increasingly integral to design for commercial advantage in the marketplace. For example, a toaster is used for only a fraction of the day and, as it sits on the kitchen, countertop it becomes an "art object." Attractive art objects sell better than plain or ugly objects of the same utility.

Beginning with cave drawings of the ancients and architecture in cities of lost civilizations, creative visual expressions virtually define humanity. Young children produce remarkably creative artwork, a characteristic skill too often lost by adulthood. While fine art has transitioned from representational portrait and landscape painting through impressionism to abstract themes, art has invaded the corporate world in product design and marketing. Additionally, there are business ideas in the art world that include a) operating your own or a collective art studio and gallery, b) contract work for video game developers and c) becoming an art dealer. Your business idea information may come from published materials or visits to such market centers as New York City or Santa Fe, NM.

How can creativity be improved? – Numerous creativity training books, seminars and workshops are readily available; with an internet search of "Creativity Training" finding some 7,210,000 items in .21 seconds and Amazon lists 218 titles. Though many very clever activities are available from texts, consultants and internet services, there is little formal documentation connecting such training with breakthrough innovations – be somewhat skeptical. However, since a first step in developing an innovation is "Seeing what everyone else has seen and thinking what nobody else has thought," an experience designed to move outside your paradigm comfort zone could help. And, it is axiomatic that geographic innovation zones – Silicon Valley and research universities – foster invention. Experiences shared and gained from networking interactions can stimulate possibility thinking. The Goodman and Goodman (2010) virtual book, *Creating the New American Dream: The Spiral Renaissance Theory*, is an excellent example of an experience designed to stimulate possibility thinking. Some textbook creativity training examples are as follows:

- The triangles problem – Take three toothpicks and form a triangle that touches only at the ends. Next, using three more toothpicks, form as many triangles as you can with the six toothpicks – touching only at the ends and without bending any of them. You should be able to make four triangles.

- The box problem – Draw the figure of a box of any size as long as it is reasonable square. Without lifting your pen, link all nine dots below using four straight lines, without crossing the same line more than once.

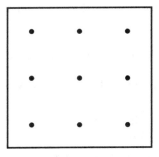

- The brick problem – List uses for a common brick in a two minute time period. Evaluate your results using the Torrance Test criteria described earlier in the chapter.

- The cardboard problem – With eight inches of mechanic's wire and a five cent 12 inch square of thin cardboard, design a product that typically sells for 50 cents in a hobby shop. This is a commonly used product.

It is also important to note that creativity is rarely due to "one great person." Much more often important creative discoveries have been made, and especially implemented, cooperatively. It has even been suggested that large groups of people can, rather than digressing to the lowest common denominator, generate solutions that are better than those suggested by the most expert individuals in the group (Surowiecki, 2004). The two most important factors in successfully solving problems in groups are a) the context, b) method used and c) the people who are included in the process. The "right people need to be on the bus and sitting in the right seats" (Collins, 2001). This usually means finding the people who are most impacted by the problem, the people whose authority is needed to solve the problem and the people who will be instrumental in implementing the solution. Consider Takahashi's (Michalko, 2001) NHK protocol to avoid "Jumping to a Solution" that is paraphrased as follows:

1. In response to a problem statement, participants write down five ideas on separate cards.

2. Each person explains her/his five ideas and others write down other ideas that are generated.

3. Cards are collected and sorted by themes.

4. New teams are formed, card ideas are discussed and any new ideas are written down.

5. Cards are organized by theme and recorded on a flip chart.

6. Groups of ten are formed and the ideas are vetted.

Careful record keeping during product development is absolutely critical; recording what was done, under what conditions, for what outcomes. The value of diaries, *Inventor's Notebooks* or research reports include a) a record of conditions that caused success or failure, b) remembrance of what not to repeat under those same conditions, c) record to establish ownership of a new idea and d) the basis of directing promising research. Leonardo da Vinci was a meticulous record keeper; as were Charles Darwin and Robert Hutchins Goddard. Thomas Edison described and illustrated every step and misstep of the way to discoveries. The technical procedures for his 1,093 patents are described in his 3,500 record books. Imagine Roy J. Plunkett in 1938 at work meticulously recording the weight, chemical description, pressure applied and temperature reduction needed to test a promising refrigerant; only to find that a hard waxy solid had been somehow produced. Because of careful recording Plunkett was able to reproduce the experiment, scale-up a production process and give du Pont one of its most profitable products – Teflon.

PARADIGMS

"If you do not like change, you will like irrelevance even less" (General Eric Shinseki). History's roadway is lined with carcasses of once-successful businesses – businesses that had dominated their respective sectors. Many died from self-inflicted wounds, such as a) the Blockbuster, Inc. Board of Directors infighting that absorbed corporate energy from innovation and b) an insularly attitude typified by the statement, "We are successful and we do not need to change!" The latter statement portends almost certain death – a disease called "paradigm paralysis," in which past success virtually paralyzes innovation - blocking perception of changing environments. History is replete with examples of new ideas being ignored because the new concept does not fit with "the way we do business." For example, the quiet quartz watch, a thousand times more accurate and durable than ticking watches, was ignored by its developers, the Swiss watch making industry, because it did not have gears and a mainspring. The Swiss watch makers so ignored their invention that they did not patent the idea; leaving the door open for opportunistic Seiko and Texas Instruments to commercialize the billion dollar concept that has almost destroyed the Swiss watch making empire that once cornered well over 50 percent of the market. As has been previously explained, the Swiss watch makers were blinded by paradigm paralysis, a condition in which there is an assumption that "the present technology **is** the technology of the future."

Blockbuster, Inc. was once a multibillion dollar corporation, renting videos and charging high late fees to consumers – high flying and a bit arrogant. However, because Blockbuster basically stayed with its business model, while only reducing late fees and allowing customers to use their own bankcards in an attempt to stay relevant, it had to file for Chapter 11 bankruptcy protection on September 23, 2010 – citing competition from Redbox, Netflix and on-demand video streaming. Strangely, Blockbuster did not see potential in on-line video deliver, as it scrapped its own concept of Total Access online video service in 2004. "Your successful past will block your visions of the future," (Joel Barker).

While we all use paradigms – from the Greek preposition *para* and the noun *deigma* that together mean "to go along with the pattern or routine" – to simplify our lives, historic success has blinded many people and organizations to new opportunities presented outside the edges of the prevailing system. IBM saw no potential in the xerography process and Xerox saw no opportunity to expand its product line into personal computers. Consider the paradox offered by Di Lampedusa (2007) from *The Leopard*, "If we want things to stay the same, things will have to change."

Your strategy for using effective paradigms and creatively resisting paradigm paralysis should include mastery of the fundamental arts and concepts of the field - critical to creating alternatives and search for opportunities at the edge of the business paradigm. For example, writing a quality piano concerto would be improbable without first having mastered the instrument and creating a breakthrough internet advancement that increased capacity, speed and reduced energy consumption would be impossible without mastery of requisite fundamentals. However, there is an inherent problem with mastery of an art or science; in that being married to the past can blind experts from perceiving breakthrough alternatives that could lead to future success. Paradigms, that tendency to follow a tradition or existing pattern, may blind us to opportunities that lie outside of the present successful methods. Thus, "the key to dancing with paradigms is to master the existing concepts and skill sets without allowing the paradigms to master you." For more information see Joel Barker's website at www.starthrower.com

INTELLECTUAL PROPERTY RIGHTS (IPR)

If the business idea is based on a product, you need to consider how to protect what you have created and if it is a unique service you could consider establishing trademark protection. Intellectual property rights legislation and agreements are made to ensure the ownership rights for creators, as the individual or corporation avails public viewing or use of the object or service. Some have argued that IPR deprives the public from invention benefits that could improve and advance the social order. In the case of Ford, et al v. Selden (1911) Henry Ford broke the monopoly enjoyed by the Association of Licensed Automobile Manufactures (ALAM) on a technicality. After winning the Selden patent case on appeal, Henry Ford just ignored the U.S. Patent and Trademark Office, preferring instead to "take" inventors' ideas and order his own engineers to develop their own versions of the products. Seabrook (1993) described Ford's distain for intellectual property protections as follows:

> "This gave the young automobile industry the unique advantage of having free access to technology as soon as it was invented.... This was not necessarily the best thing for those who invented the technology – the designers of carburetors, sparkplugs, radiators, rubber tires, power steering, overdrive, the convertible top, rack-and-pinion steering, rear-window defroster, cruise control, air bags, and intermittent windshield wipers. However, Ford, in defense of his position on patents, often pointed out that his invention – a light, cheap, durable car that could be mass-produced... would not have been possible if he had been forced to pay for inventions of other men (p. 10)."

However, though free access to IP is an interesting theory, if there is no incentive to invent there is no long term benefit to society. While he claimed the high ground of "benefiting society," it was Henry Ford who amassed a family fortune on the backs of other men who had labored to benefit themselves and their own families. Ford's engineers simply employed "reverse engineering;" whereby an expert takes a device apart and maps the necessary steps that the originator would have used to create the product.

Protection of IP is a major problem. *MindMatters* (2010) reports that "U.S. based companies lose an estimated $45 billion annually in intellectual property (IP), yet 62 percent have no procedures for reporting information loss and 40 percent have no formal IP protection program. This is frightening when you consider that IP can represent up to 70 percent of company's valuation."

Categories of intellectual property (IP) protection – There is a constant tension between those who innovate and those who seek to profit from the work of others; with legitimate business cooperating with the inventor to develop and promote the product or service and others with a mission to steal the intellectual property. The innovation is safe as long as it remains in the inventor's brain, but that benefits neither the inventor nor society. Thomas Jefferson (Kanwar, 2009) anticipated the IP disclosure problem; the problem of displaying a new product concept:

> "If nature has made any one thing less susceptible than all others of exclusive property, it is the action of the thinking power called an "idea," which an individual may exclusively possess as long as he keeps it to himself; but the moment it is divulged, it forces itself into the possession of every one and the receiver cannot dispossess himself of it."

Thus, if an innovator is to benefit from the fruits of her/his labor, intellectual property rights (IPR) must be assured. The first, and most basic, precaution is to make sure that no one sees the invention without adequate confidentiality. Casually showing the object to "friends" or having a prototype visible in a workshop for invited or uninvited visitors to see places the IPR at-risk. Also, lest someone may perceive the innovation process and work to be the "first to file," adequate non-disclosure precautions must be exercised for invited viewers.

Non-disclosure agreement – A non-disclosure agreement is typically a one page document wherein individuals formally affirm that they will not use the IP that they are about to see and that they will not disclose anything about the matter to others. This is an instrument used in early stage product development when the innovator needs to get technical advice from others or when presenting to possible project funders. If anyone refuses to sign the non-disclosure agreement, that should be the end of the conversation.

Types of formal protections – As your idea progresses you will need to consult a patent attorney to secure you intellectual property. You could also consider patent insurance; a policy that assists you in court if there is infringement.

Provisional patent – As the project develops, the innovator may choose to file a provisional patent, particularly if there is an apparent race to be the first to file. The up-side of a provisional patent is that it established a date for filing. But, the down-side is that a formal patent must be filed within one year or the concept may revert to the public domain.

Utility patent – Utility patents, or industrial patents, are for IPR protection of manufactured objects. The utility requirement ensures that the device will have some beneficial use. A Rube Goldberg device, wherein an initial momentum precipitates a subsequent series of events to reach the final action, would not be patentable unless its utility was defined a being a "toy." Thus, the utility of the several objects designed, manufactured and distributed by Sprigtoys (R) is that they are children's toys (www.sprigtoys.com).

Design patent – Design patents are issued for the protection of artistic or visual features of a product, such as the shape of stapler or athletic brace. Design does not necessarily relate to function, as function would be covered in a utility patent.

Copyright – Copyrights are issued for the protection of original expressions of art, music, drama or literature. Typically the third page of any book contains the copyright reservations. To reduce the risk of ownership questions, do not reproduce any literary piece without the author's name and date, as argument can be effectively made that unmarked copies belong to the public domain. For beginning authors, one economical method of establishing ownership is to place a complete copy in an envelope and mail it to your self; as an unopened postmark dated envelope can be handed to the judge as authorship evidence.

Trademark – Trademarks are issued for the protection of brand identification. In the U.S, the Lanham Act is the federal trademark statute; giving the manufacturer or seller the exclusive right to the brand identity and preventing competitors from infringement; providing that a) it had a "symbol" or "device,' b) it had developed a secondary meaning in the marketplace and c) if the trademark is granted, will competition be stifled? The Supreme Court, in Qualitex Co. v. Jacobson Products Co. Inc. 514 U.S. 159 (1995), used the Lanham Act criteria in determining that that a particular color could be registered as a trademark.

Trade secret – Trade secrets are those items that are essential to production of identifiable product qualities, such as the qualitative difference in the taste of Coke Cola and Pepsi Cola. Both are produced from closely held chemical formulas, trade secrets that have persisted for decades. Patent applications require disclosure of process; thus divulging trade secrets. Obviously, any employee working in critical IP areas is required to sign binding non-disclosure agreements as a requirement for such employment.

Innovations with significant potential monetary value should be protected with appropriate legal action through the U.S. Patent and Trademark Office. However, as Bob Kearns unfortunately discovered, in trying to protect his intermittent windshield wiper invention, even official government ownership certification is insufficient to prevent infringement. A patent is only as good as it can be enforced with expensive legal action While Ford, Chrysler, General Motors, Mercedes and most other automobile manufacturers clearly profited handsomely from Kearns' invention, collections are only enforced by plaintiff court action and not by the government.

Patent office principles – The U.S. Patent and Trademark Office (USPTO) is a self-funded government agency that issues patents to individuals and businesses. Its patent reviewers tend to be scientists and engineers, those knowledgeable of industrial processes, and the trademark application reviewers tend to be licensed attorneys. Approximately 150,000 patents are issued annually to applicants worldwide and over 7,950,000 patents have been issued. Some of the criteria used to evaluate application validity include the following:

Relationship to prior art – The innovator and the patent attorney must show diligence in building the case for the application from the series of work that others have done. However, clearly demonstrating that the new device is different from all prior art.

Principle of non-obvious conclusion – Establishment that the new device is not just a minor modification of prior art is now mandatory. In the case of Bob Kearns' intermittent windshield wiper, Ford Motor Company claimed that the Kearns device was just an obvious next step in their engineering research and that his components had been known for years. However, the state of the art prototype then being engineered by Ford was a complex mechanical device of some 29 parts; whereas Kearns' device was electronic with few moving parts.

Principle of public disclosure – As has been previously stated, patent applications are at risk of being declared in the public domain if there has been public showing. Engineers for Seiko and Texas Instruments quickly created patent applications based upon their viewing of the Swiss quarts watch that was demonstrated at the watch exhibition.

First to file – Generally, the first application for a particular device is awarded the patent, though there are extenuating circumstances when virtually simultaneous filing occur.

PROJECT NARRATIVE

At some point you will need to tell your business story; to investors and to start-up colleagues. Steve Jobs is a master of corporate message; stories designed for employees and stories designed for eager consumers (Gallo, 2009). Consider the abbreviated from his 1984 address to staff members (Gallo, 2010); where he positioned Apple's Macintosh against IBM's potential domination of the computer industry. He started with a historical review as follows:

> "It is 1958. IBM passes up the chance to buy a young, fledgling company that has invented a new technology called xerography.... The early eighties, 1981...IBM enters the personal computer market in November 1981 with the IBM PC. Will Big Blue dominate the entire computer industry? (shouts of, "NO" from his audience) (pp. 64-65)."

Message principles – Why search for a message template when an effective one is already available? Again, borrowing from Steve Jobs' playbook (Gallo, 2009), consider the following:

- Sell dreams, not products – Those who buy Apple products are not consumers. They are people with hopes, dreams and ambitions. Apple products are designed to help bring these to fruition.

- Create insanely great experiences – Apple Stores have become the gold standard for service. The products are innovations that individuals and businesses can easily adopt.

- Master the message – Love of the innovation process and products must come through in the business story. You can have the most innovative idea in the world, but if you cannot get people excited about it, your innovation does not matter.

Power of the story – In his book, *A whole new mind: Why right-brainers will rule the world*, Pink (2006) makes the case for expressing complexity in simple story form. Businesses that cannot tell their story, in terms of what they do and how that affects people, are at risk; as are inventors who cannot succinctly tell their stories to potential investors. Pink states, "Our tendency to see and explain the world in common narratives is so deeply ingrained that we often don't notice it – even when we've written the words ourselves. In the Conceptual Age, however, we must awaken to the power of narrative" (p. 106).

Converting innovation problems to story form would be like changing numerical expressions into mathematical story problems. Many innovations are grounded in the classic hero's story, described by Pink (2006) as follows:

> "And the one overarching story, the blueprint for all tales since humankind's earliest days, is the "hero's journey." The hero's journey has three main parts: Departure, Initiation, and Return. The hero hears a call, refuses it at first, and then crosses the threshold into a new world... then he returns, becoming the master of two worlds, committed to improving each (pp. 104 – 105)."

Steve Jobs is arguably the world's preeminent corporate story teller and his message has only grown since his being fired from leading his own company, departure to a very successful side career in Pixar and, subsequent return to lead a floundering Apple Corporation. Though your corporate story may not be as dramatic, it must have compelling elements that get investors, employees and customers excited. The following is a story example from the Sprig Toy website.

CREATING SPRIG TOYS

Consider that four unemployed toy designers planned to challenge the big guns with an untried technology. Toy manufacturing and distribution is a multibillion dollar business sector; with annual retail sales of over $45 billion. The International Council of Toy Industries (ICTI) was formed as a center for a) discussion and information exchange on trends and issues important to the industry, b) to promote product safety standards, c) to reduce or eliminate trade barriers, and

d) to advance social responsibility in environmental and workplace safety. (See http://www.toy-icti.com) Products are designed for both children and adults; with adult hobbyists collecting such toys as miniature electric trains. The International Toy Fair is held annually in Nurnberg, Germany to display product lines to wholesale buyers. (See http://www.spielwaremesse.de) Most toys are now manufactured in China for cheap labor and reduced surveillance of fair employment practices, though during the 1950s the Louis Marx & CO. (U.S.A.) was the largest toy manufacturer in the world. (See http://www. marxtoymuseum.com)

Sprig Toys, Inc. tells its own story on their website as follows: "Once upon a time there were four talented toy designers who were taking the industry by storm. Their award-winning toys were selling like hotcakes. They were happy and successful. Then one day the designers visited the factories that turned their computer renderings into real toys. They eagerly watched the assembly line with anticipation, and quickly realized the harmful impact their toy production had on the nearby air, soil, water, plants and people. They went back to the drawing board, only to face another disturbing trend that threatened to control their designs. Passive "watch-me" electronic toys were gaining popularity, encouraging otherwise healthy kids to become more inactive. The designers refused to be part of the problem, so they joined forces to become the solution. Our brave young designers made a pact. They vowed then and there to make the best toys the right way. They were on a mission to keep the kids active and the planet healthy, and the quest became personal when they started having children of their own. In 2007, they formed Sprig Toys, Inc., turning their vision into reality. The designers packed their families and moved from opposite coasts to reunite the foursome in the heart of the Rocky Mountain west. It was in Fort Collins, Colorado where Team Sprig created their top-secret high-tech toy laboratory – and where they designed an exciting line of battery-free, eco-friendly, paint-free, kid-powered toys sure to dazzle the most discriminating preschooler."

Consider the design and prototype construction process that would have enabled the following user comment from http://www.amazon.com/review/product "My son is a little young (two years), but the Discovery Rig is one of his favorite toys. It can easily go over rocks and stairs, but there's not a scratch on my hardwood floors. He loves the music and will often stop pushing to do a little dance and then he's back on his adventure. I love that I don't have to worry about how it's made. It may be part plastic, but it smells like wood which gets a great reaction from all of my adult friends."

The prototype would have been designed, molded, electronics created, and tested numerous times in the laboratory, before having focus groups of parents and children examine and play with the toys. A multi-million dollar A Round of venture capital financing was raised to initially manufacture and distribute the product line. With only one round of financing the principals have kept more of the company equity. Sprig Toys, Inc. has been offered an exclusive distribution option by a major international distributor, but they have opted to sell by internet and multiple walk-in stores.

The Sprig Adventure Series harnesses the natural kinetic energy of push-and-pump action play to generate lights and sounds – all without batteries. Interchangeable characters plug into rugged yet appealing vehicles, engaging children in audio tales of exploration. Designed for the active preschooler, the vehicles and characters are molded from Springwood – a durable child-safe bio-composite material made from recycled wood and reclaimed plastic. The materials are dyed in-process, so no external paint is needed. The product line and it has merged with Wham-O Toys for manufacturing and distribution. See http://www.sprigtoys.com and http://www.sprigwood.com)

CHAPTER SUMMARY

KEY POINTS

- Creativity has multiple definitions, each beginning with divergent thinking.

- Problems cannot be solved with the thought process that created the problems.

- Concept and skill mastery is a prerequisite for being able to identify critical problem areas or areas of opportunity.

- Think of creativity as a "craft" that almost anyone can learn.

- You, the Nation and the World need more creativity and more creativity brought into action.

- Technically, innovation and intellectual property are synonymous.

- Without patent and copyright protection there is no motivation to invent.

- Innovation is the technology driver for economic development.

- Paradigm paralysis blinds experts and traditionalists to new innovation opportunities.

- A country's political policies can stimulate or stifle innovation.

- Lessons learned from studying other successful inventors can serve as your guide.

- Adding value to an existing technology is a form of innovation.

- Unfortunately, only ten percent of inventions are ever successfully marketed.

- Creativity can be learned (taught) in any school subject or activity. Creativity development programs and activities may be effective; with numerous training resources available in books and from training consultants.

TAKE ACTION NOW

- Repeat after me, "I can be creative ... I will be creative ... I am creative!" Do this daily in front of a mirror while looking directly into your own eyes.

- In your business, business and social networks and significant conversations, pose the question "What is it that is keeping you or your business from becoming great?" They may identify critical areas for innovation.

- Become a student of innovation in your technical area as well as creativity in other areas that has led to significant innovation – master the process.

- Practice backwards-engineering innovations out of your field and in your field.

- Re-write the history of something like "Building the Golden Gate Bridge" from the project manager's perspective; using personal pronouns – "I ...." This could be a publishable venture!

- Learn to re-frame "problem statements" into "opportunity statements."

- Read futuring books – a list is included in the Supplementary Resources section.

- Become an active member of your local Inventor's Roundtable group.

- Sign-up for the Dow Jones "Venture Capital Alert"- djnewsletters@dowjones.com

- If you have an innovation, practice writing "Your story." Use Steve Jobs as a guide to effective corporate storytelling.

- Study the process of protecting intellectual property and identify patent attorneys that you feel comfortable with.

- Though film script writers sometimes take liberty with reality, study inventor's stories such as Thomas Edison and Robert Kearns.

REFERENCES

Bandler & Grinder, (1981). *Trance-Formations: Neuro-linguistic programming and structure of hypnosis.* Boulder, CO: Real People Press.

Bronson, B. & Merryman, A. (2010). The creativity crisis: For the first time, research shows that American creativity is declining. What went wrong – and how we can fix it, *Newsweek,* 44-50.

Burrow, J. (2009). *History of histories: Epics, chronicles and inquiries.* New York: Vintage Books

Carroll, L. (2010). *Through the looking glass.* Tribeca Books.

Christensen, C. (2003). *The innovator's dilemma: The revolutionary book that will change the way you do business.* New York: HarperCollins Publishers, Inc.

Collins, J. (2001). *From good to great: Why some companies make the leap and others don't.* New York: HarperCollins Publishers, Inc.

Craughwell, T. J. (2008). *The book of invention.* London: Black Dog & Leventhal.

De Bono, E. (1970). *Lateral thinking: Creativity step by step.* New York: Harper & Row.

Burrow, J. (2009). *A history of histories: Epics, Chronicles, and inquiries from*

Herodotus and Thucydides to the Twentieth Century. New York: First Vintage Books.

Diamond, J. (2005). *Guns, germs and steel: The fates of human societies.* New York: W. W. Norton & Co.

Di Lampedusa, G. T. (2007). *The leopard.* New York: Pantheon Books.

Flatow, I. (1992). *They all laughed... from light bulbs to lasers: The fascinating stories behind the great inventions that have changed our lives.* New York: HarperCollins.

Florida, R. (2004). *Rise of the creative class: And how its transforming work, leisure, community and everyday life.* New York: Basic Books.

Freeman, A. & Golden, B. (1997). Why didn't I think of that: Bizarre origins of ingenious inventions we couldn't live without. New York: John Wiley & Sons.

Friedman, T. L. (2009). The new untouchables. *The New York Times,* www.nytimes.com/2009/10/21/opinion/21friedman.html?_r1&sq=thomas

Friedman, T. (2008). *Hot, flat and crowded: Why we need a green revolution – and how it can renew America.* New York: Farrar, Straus & Giroux.

Gladwell, M. (2008). *Outliers: The story of success.* New York: Little, Brown and Company.

Gallo, C. (2010). *The innovation secrets of Steve Jobs: Insanely different principles for breakthrough success.* New York: McGraw Hill.

Gallo, C. (2009). *The presentation secrets of Steve Jobs: How to be insanely great in front of any audience.* New York: McGraw Hill.

Gass, L. (2009). Teaching creativity in science. *Creativity at Work: Articles and Tips,* http://www.creativityatwork.com/

Goodman, D. & Goodman, E. (2010). *Creating the new American dream: The spiral renaissance theory.* Dana Point, CA: Goodman Experiences, LLC.

Hawken, P., Lovins, A. & Lovins, H. (2008). *Natural capitalism: Creating the next industrial revolution.* Boston: Little, Brown & Co.

Hawksby, L., Humphries, C. & Adlington, F. (2008). *Timetables of history.* New York: Random House Reference.

Hughes, R. (1988). *That fateful shore: Epic of Australia's founding.* New York: Random House.

Kanwar, M. (2009). *Intellectual property – Its meaning and development in India* http://www.linlroll.com/Intellectual-Property-Legal-4973-Intelelctual-Property

Katz, V. J. (2008). *History of mathematics* (3rd Ed.). Reading, MA: Addison Wesley.

Kay, K. (2007). *A framework for 21st Century learning.* Tucson, AZ: partnership for 21st century Skills.

Kidder, T. (1987). *The soul of the new machine.* (2nd Ed.), New York: Penguin Books.

Michalko, M. (2001). *Cracking creativity.* Berkeley: Ten Speed Press.

MindMatters (2010). *Do you know how to protect your "Know How"?* MindMatters, http://www.us-mindmatters.com 12/22/2010.

Oech, R. V. (1986). *A kick in the seat of the pants: Using your explorer, artist, judge, & warrior to be more creative.* New York: Harper & Row.

Owen, D. (2004). *Copies in seconds: How a lone inventor and an unknown company created the biggest communications breakthrough since Guttenberg – Chester Carlson and the birth of Xerox.* New York: Simon and Schuster.

Pink, D. (2006). *A whole new mind.* Berkley Publishing Co.: New York.

Ridderstrale, J. & Nordstrom, K. (2008). *Funky business forever: How to enjoy capitalism.* www.funkybusiness.com

Runco, M. A., Millar, G., Acar, S. & Cramond, B. (2011). Torrance tests of creative thinking as predictors of personal and public achievement: A fifty year follow-up, *Creativity Research Journal,* 22(4).

Seabrook. J. (2008). *Flash of genius and other true stories of invention.* New York: St. Martin's Griffin.

Shurkin, J. (1992). *Terman's kids: The groundbreaking study of how the gifted grow up.* Boston: Little, Brown & Co.

Shurkin, J. N. (2006). *Broken genius: The rise and fall of William Shockley, Creator of the electronics age.* New York: Palgrave Macmillan.

Slade, P. & MacHale, D. (2011). *Lateral thinking puzzles: Killer brainteasers that will slay you.* New York: Puzzlewright/Sterling Publishing.

Stokstad, M. (2007). *Art history, combined* (3rd Ed.). Upper Saddle River, NJ: Prentice Hall.

Surowiecki, J. (2004). *The wisdom of crowds: Why the many are smarter than the few and how collective wisdom shapes business, economies, societies, and nations.* New York: Doubleday.

Tharp, T. (2003). *The creative habit. Learn it and use it for life.* New York: Simon & Schuster Paperbacks.

Vella, M. (2008). Global innovation leaders, *BusinessWeek,* 44) http:// images.BusinessWeek.com

Warren, R. (2003). *The purpose driven life: What on earth are you here for?* Philadelphia: Running Press.

SUPPLEMENTARY RESOURCES

Aguayo, R. (1991). *Dr. Deming: The American who taught the Japanese about quality control.* New York: Fireside.

Benyus, J. M. (2002). *Biomimicry: Innovation inspired by nature.* New York: William. Morrow Co.

Brown, K. (2004). *Penicillin man: Alexander Fleming and the antibiotic revolution.* Stroud: Sutton.

Businessweek (2009). *20 most important inventions of the next 10 years.* February 25, 2009.

Borden, L. & Blegvad, E. (1995). *Sea clocks: The story of longitude.* New York: Margaret K. McElderry Books.

Bordessa, K. (2005). *Team challenges: 170 + group activities to build cooperation, communication, and creativity*. Chicago: Zephyr Press.

Caney, S. (1985). *Steve Caney's invention book*. New York: Workman Publishing.

Clements, G. (1994). *The picture history of great inventors*. New York: Alfred A. Knopf

Clegg, B., & Birch, P. (2007). *Instant creativity: Simple techniques to ignore innovation & problem solving*. Philadelphia: Kogan Page Limited.

Correll, L. C. (2004). *Brainstorming reinvented: A corporate communications guide to ideation*. Thousand Oaks, California: Response Books.

Csikszentmihalyi, M. (1996). *Creativity: Flow and the psychology of discovery and invention*. New York: HarperCollins Publishers.

De Bono, E. (2008). *Creativity workout: 62 exercises to unlock your most creative ideas*. Berkeley, CA: Ulysses Press.

Deming, W.E. (2000). *The new economics for industry, government and education*. New York: Fireside.

Deming, W. E. (2000). *Out of the crisis*. Cambridge, MA: MIT Press.

Florida, R. (2008). *Who's your city: How the creative economy is making where you live the most important decision of your life*. New York: Basic Books.

Florida, R. (2005). *The flight of the creative class: The global competition for talent*. New York: HarperCollins Publishers.

Friedman, T. L. (2005). *The world is flat: A brief history of the Twenty-first Century*. New York: Farrar, Straus and Giroux.

Harvard Business Essentials (2003). *Managing creativity and innovation*. Boston, MA: Harvard Business School Publishing Corporation.

Hyman, C. (1982). *Charles Babbage, Pioneer of the computer*. Princeton, NJ: Princeton University Press.

Jacuzzi, K. & Holloway, D. (2005). *Jacuzzi: A father's invention to ease a son's pain*. Lincoln, NB: iUniverse.

Jacuzzi, R. (2007). *Spirit, wind & water: The untold story of Jacuzzi family.* New York: Welcome Rain Publishers.

Kauffman (2009). *Kauffman thought book.* Kansas City, MO: The Ewing Marion Kauffman Foundation.

Kordis, P. L., & Kordis, S. J. (1998). *Name your passion: A user's guide to finding your personal purpose.* Fort Collins, CO: Delphinus Press.

Krupp, F. & Horn, M. (2008). *Earth: The sequel.* New York: W. W. Norton & Company.

Laurin, C. (2009). *The Rudolph factor: Finding the bright lights that drive innovation in your business.* Hoboken, NJ: John Wiley & Sons, Inc.

Lynch, D. & Kordis, P. L. (1988). *Strategy of the dolphin: Scoring a win in a chaotic world.* New York: William Morrow and Company, Inc.

CHAPTER THREE
Testing Your Business Idea

*"In today's turbulent markets, you must make connections
to create value that competitors can't see."*

Marcus Powe

Of course your idea is brilliant ... or maybe it could just possibly need a little more work. Here's how to find out whether or not you're ready to move forward. Somewhere between scribbling an idea on a cocktail napkin and actually starting a new business, there's a process that needs to be carried out that can actually improve your chances for success. Oftentimes, would-be entrepreneurs get so excited about their innovation that they forget to find out whether or not it can translate into a viable business.

In Chapter Two we focused on creating a product or service that could potentially be commercialized. Theoretically there is a clean differentiation between creating the product or service and developing a successful business. However, in reality, the lines are blurred. For example, Chester Carlson's xerography patents defined the machines that would eventually make cheap dry copies; but he needed funding and technical assistance from the Battelle Foundation and the Haloid Corporation to commercialize the product. Xerography became the dominant business product so Haloid was renamed the "Xerox Corporation." Conversely, John Schnatter's idea for rapid delivery of high quality fast food was simultaneously a product and business idea that resulted in Papa John's Pizza – more on the business idea than the product. The history of invention documents describe how even master inventors fail to perceive commercialization potential. For example,

Thomas Edison invented the phonograph as a spin off from Bell's telephone; but Edison thought it to only be useful for recording final wishes of the dying and for business dictation. He had no plans for commercialization. In fact, Edison was incensed that his phonograph had become a tool for recording popular music. Recognizing these blurred lines of invention and commercialization, we assume you have a product or service formulated and we now try to focus on business development – the business side of innovation.

WILL YOUR BUSINESS IDEA SUCCEED?

A business feasibility review is a deliberate process for identifying problems and opportunities, determining reasonable objectives, describing situations, defining successful outcomes and assessing the range of costs and benefits associated with several alternatives to solving a problem (Drucker, 1985). It is an analytical tool used to assist stakeholders and decision makers in determining if a business concept is worth pursuing. Therefore, a business concept feasibility test is an effective way to safeguard against wasteful investment of time and resources. There is no one best analytical tool for all market sectors, so several analysis strategies are presented herein.

A well done feasibility analysis not only looks at the technical feasibility of creating the product or service; but also tests the potential of the market and industry, the ability of the entrepreneur to create an organization that can run the business, and the financial prospects of the planned venture. While many entrepreneurs address these issues when writing their business plan, that's not the same as examining the venture's feasibility. Bruce Barringer (2009), co-author of: *Entrepreneurship: Successfully Launching New Businesses* says this of first time entrepreneurs: "They get an idea and immediately proceed to the stage of writing a business plan. At that point, they're in the mode of looking for facts that support their idea, rather than testing it." Though, writing a business plan is a good idea, it should be preceded by business concept feasibility testing." Save yourself the time and effort of meticulously writing a detailed business plan by first determining whether or not your business concept will fly.

Business concept feasibility analysis also considers where the entire market sector is trending and where the market sector is in its life cycle. The bottled drink industry is a relatively mature market sector that seems to maintain its discretionary product market share; with Coca Cola and Pepsi having successfully stayed at the peak of the business idea life cycle. Sport drinks and bottled water are two of the few products that have successfully been able to enter that market sector. On the other hand, digital technology innovation is continuing to evolve at unbelievable acceleration. Specific digital technology software and hardware have a very brief commercial life span – as Marshall McLuhan prophetically stated decades ago, "If it works, it's obsolete." Study your market sector and be ready to abandon a great business idea in a dying market sector.

John Mullins (2003), *The New Business Road Test*, hypothesizes that successful entrepreneurship consists of three crucial elements: a) market and industry differentiation b) both macro and micro analysis of your market secretor and c) the entrepreneurial team's critical skill sets. It isn't enough to be able to build a better mouse trap; you have to know where that mouse trap fits within the economy, the industries that are affected by it, and the market segments that will hopefully purchase it. Does working through this micro-market analysis actually pay off? The *Nike* Corporation is a good example of this approach, and a brief analysis is included at the end of this chapter.

Getting the business idea and imagining its vast possibilities is the easy part. But it is the research that doesn't come so naturally. "It's a big red flag when someone outlines the size of the market, (multibillion dollars), but doesn't clearly articulate a plan for how their idea will meet an unmet need in the marketplace" (Keller 2006). Moving from divergent creativity, which birthed the business idea, to convergent thinking yielding a commercialization plan that meticulously answers launch and operation questions requires an accountant's realism.

The type of information you will need to gather to answer these questions will depend upon the type of product or service you want to sell. If you are planning a retail business - selling to the general public - you will seek different sources of information than someone who is planning to sell only to other businesses (B2B) for consumption or for resale. Regardless of the kind of enterprise you are considering, there are several basic analysis steps you should explore to help you scope out the size and conditions of your market opportunity.

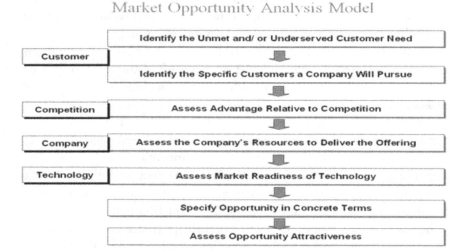

Figure 3.1 Opportunity Assessment Process Model re-drawn from The Gatton College of Business and Economics, University of Kentucky

The first step in the process is to identify the value proposition that your new business will bring to the marketplace. Recognize that everyone has been doing just fine up until now without you, and that there will need to be a reason to pay attention to your firm once you get started. The best way to get the attention of the marketplace is by offering a product or service that solves a problem or meets an underserved need. Here are some questions to ask to help discover unmet or underserved customer needs:

- What is the ideal customer buying experience for what you plan to offer?

- Is there a gap between the customers' current actual and an ideal buying experience?

- What are the customer beliefs and associations about the buying process?

- What existing barriers block some or all customers from acquiring what they need?

- What are the opportunities for your company to enhance the customers' current experience?

The purpose of asking these questions is to test if what you are going to provide is new or different enough to be recognized as different within the existing market. Many new companies are often met with a "so what" reception from the marketplace because they haven't taken the time to understand their customer's perspective. Make sure to understand the problem you intend to solve or the need you intend to address so that you can present the benefits of what you intend to offer to your prospective customer in an understandable way.

The second step in the process is to make sure that you know who your "ideal" or targeted customer is. Once you know what they look like, you then need to take the steps necessary to determine where they are and how many of them there are. This process is called market segmentation, and it is accomplished by breaking down a group of the population or industry into addressable purchasing units. The resulting targeted market(s) should be the one(s) that can be easily identifiable, can be readily reached, and described in terms of its growth, size, profile and attractiveness.

Conducting a meaningful market segmentation exercise is a worthwhile undertaking, but it does require some discipline. What you are trying to discover is the size and scope of the market opportunity you are pursuing, the actual number of potential customers that are available to buy your new product or service. Here are some useful guidelines that can help you to recognize customers within a market segment:

- Customers within a segment behave similarly, while customers across segments behave in different ways.

- Customers within a segment have similar purchasing motivations, and common purchasing criteria.

- Customers within a segment face the same set of barriers when they buy or use a product or service.

- Customers within a segment can identify with how others within the segment currently (or could) buy or use the product or service you plan to offer.

- Customers within a segment correlate to differences in profitability or cost to serve. They have similar purchasing characteristics.

- Customer within a segment have differences large enough to warrant a different set of actions by a company that serves them.

The results from this exercise should be a quantification of the size and scope of the marketplace your new company is going to compete in. You should also come away with a better understanding of the kind of customers you intend to sell to, their buying characteristics, and some insight into their buying motivations. This is critical information for assessing the viability of your business opportunity, as the better you understand your "ideal" or targeted customer, the greater your chances for success.

The third step in the process is to assess the competitive environment within your chosen market space and determine how your new venture is going to compete. Recognize that you will encounter three distinctively different kinds of competition: Direct competitors, those who sell similar products or services to the same targeted customers; indirect competitors, those who though they reside in different industries, offer products and services that perform the same function as what you will be proposing; and adjacent competitors, firms that have the potential to provide products or services like yours that are substitutes.

The best approach to examining this environment is to undertake a process called competitor mapping. What you are hoping to discover from this exercise is to identify underserved market needs, which provide the greatest opportunity, and areas that are the most competitive, which are niches to avoid. You want to identify who the current competitors are and what are their attributes and strengths. You may also want to identify industry collaborators as part of this process, the "other firms" that could benefit from your arrival in the marketplace. Finally, you need to assess any competitive hurdles; barriers to market entry that you feel could be challenging to overcome.

In figure 3.2, we have identified some very basic requirements that today's consumer finds desirable in their relationship with product and service providers. Note that we are not analyzing product differences, but rather looking for ways to make our new venture different from existing providers that already exist in the marketplace. What will our new company do differently that could make it more attractive than all of the others?

Buyer's Requirement	Competitor A (Direct)	Competitor B (Indirect)	Competitor C (Adjacent)	Our Plans
Product Availability	Large Inventory	Limited Inventory	Catalogue Order Only	Inventory & Catalogue
Purchase On-line	Order and Pay Online	Online Sales are Final	Order and Pay Online	Order and Pay Online
Volume Pricing	Volume Discounting	No Discounting	Volume Pricing	Volume Discounts
Able to Return	Only direct to Manufacturer	No Exchanges or refunds	Only direct to Manufacturer	Exchange or Refund
Knowledgeable Representatives	Not Available	Not Available	Not Available	Knowledgeable Representatives
Product Warranties	Manufacturer Only	Manufacturers Only	Manufacturer Only	Warranty plus Services

Figure 3.2 Simple Competitive Assessment Matrix

This example may be somewhat simplified, but it will hopefully help to make the point. By constructing this kind of a matrix, you can readily see which of your customers' needs are being met by the existing competitors and which ones are being neglected. Obviously, where the existing providers are lacking is where you want to take advantage. In our simple example, you could distinguish a new retail outlet by simply providing knowledgeable sales representatives, and a reasonable return and exchange policy. If you were to add to that profile an easily understood warranty and service policy, you just might possibly position yourself to begin attracting customers away from some of the already established competitors. Find your niche!

The fourth step in the evaluation process is to assess your resource needs; those things that you will need to acquire in order to establish your company. You will most likely require three different kinds of resources to launch your enterprise: Customer facing resources, a sales force or distribution channels that communicate directly with your potential customers; internal resources, technology, management information systems, financial controls, and a support staff; and up stream resources, like suppliers, and depending upon your product or service offering, perhaps even manufacturing or assembly needs as well.

You do not need to generate a great deal of information on these subjects at this stage of the evaluation process because you will do that as part of your business planning. But you do need to test the feasibility of your assumptions and determine if the things you will need to operate are available for you. Speak with potential supply sources, identify the kinds of business systems you would need to utilize, and start looking for key individuals who possess the skill sets you need to execute your plans. Become comfortable that you can identify and have access to the operating resources you will need to actually make your new venture happen. We will address finding the financial resources for the business in a later chapter.

The fifth step in the process is to test the market's receptivity to the product or service you intend to offer. For example, if the product is a tangible item, let a focus group from the target market see and touch a prototype. For intangible products, show prospective customers an illustration or a draft, and use your website to convey clear communications. Continually tweak your plans!

Consider building a product demonstration capability into your business planning. Develop a prototype, a model and a description of operation mechanics. Few ideas for new products or services work the first time – the concept validation problem. Make sure yours works; as failure can set back even the best innovation. Consider nitrous oxide's set-back that stalled modern dentistry for twenty years. Joseph Priestley synthesized N^2O in 1772 and Humphrey Davy validated its potential for surgical anesthetics in 1800. However, Horace Wells' 1844 tooth extraction demonstration to the Boston Medical Society went terribly awry because too little N^2O was administered – the patient shrieked in pain, the spectators jeered and it was not until 1863 that the anesthetic gained popular acceptance for use in dentistry.

Calculate your price point – Determine the price that you can sell the product for in the current marketplace. Get accurate prices and delivery dates from suppliers, especially if you're purchasing the product for resale. Ask your friends and family if they would buy this product at the price you will have to charge. Production costs versus sales margins are different for each market sector. For example, manufactured goods, to be physically displayed and retailed, may need a 1:5 production cost to sale price point ratio for profitability – the big box stores often take up to half of the retail sale margin to cover their own overheads. But, software sold over the internet for example, particularly where there is an annual upgrade, produces a very attractive profit to cost ratios because these products are delivered electronically.

Field testing – Initially your start-up may only have one product or service. Go to your potential customers with a sample or prototype and ask if he or she would buy it for the benefits the product provides. Arrange a demonstration if you are sure the prototype works. If selling business to business, be sure to call on the individual who makes the buying decisions. Then ask how much the product's benefits would be worth. If people criticize your new product idea, ask them why. Ask how the product could be modified to make it more attractive.

Product comparisons – Though start-ups are disadvantaged in entering an existing market sector, they have the advantage of comparing competitor's features, benefits and price points. Thus, compare your product with the value and price for other products on the market. Continually ask yourself, "Why would someone switch from their current provider and buy from me?" Solicit the negative opinions of others as well; as falling in love with your own business idea can prove costly. Simultaneously, be an optimist and a realist by selling the benefits of what you will provide and also looking for the flaws in both the business idea and your marketing assumptions.

Attend trade shows and exhibitions – These are terrific places to get immediate feedback. You can get into a trade show by signing up as either a product exhibiter or just a participant. Once you're in, find out what else is available that's similar to or performs the same function that your product will. Other companies marketing similar products will have their products on display; take a good, hard look at what they have to offer. Then talk to product buyers, as sophisticated buyers at the trade show can provide information about market sector needs – needed features, benefits and price points.

Get people talking by asking questions – There are several ways to gathering feedback. Write a one-page concept sheet describing your business, then show it to several people whose opinions are relevant and respectable, including potential customers, investors, partners and employees. Unfortunately, "People will spend years developing a product without ever talking to anybody who might buy it. If you get 15 (potential) consumers in the room, you'll end up with 20 different opinions" Wise (2008). Virtual or actual focus group volunteers in defined categories can be recruited via www.Craigslist.com – "personal."

Test marketing – The ultimate feasibility test for a new product or service is a market test; where you actually take your new product or service to a customer who can buy it to see if they like it. As soon as you know your cost and price, make a sales call on a potential buyer. Listen carefully to the comments and objections of the buyer--their feedback is priceless. Savvy companies like Microsoft, for example, regularly solicit beta testers to assess new products during their development (support.microsoft.com/ kb/833520); as does digital product maker IC Tomorrow (www.register. ictommorow.co.uk/).

It should not take more than a few weeks to gather product feasibility feedback. However, analyzing the feedback can be confusing. But, for initial feasibility purposes, feedback can be very easy to understand; especially if it's extremely negative or positive. If you get a lot of negative feedback or product concept rejections, it is time for some soul searching. Do the reviewers just not get it or is yours just a bad idea. Analyze the product, its value proposition and the way in which you have presented it. However, remember that Chester Carlson's xerography business idea was rejected by many of America's leading companies and U.S. government agencies - none of them "got it!" And, J. K. Rowling was repeatedly advised by international publishers that her books were too long and complicated for children – all prior to her spectacular success with the Harry Potter series. There is typically an acceptance lag time for disruptive technology.

Clarifying the opportunities to introduce a new product or service in the marketplace is an important step, as it helps to "shape" the potential and structure of your business idea. But, you are creating a new business, not just introducing a new product, so it is important that you look a little deeper into your value proposition and test more than just the attractiveness of the product or service you intend to offer. You may need to consider offering more than one product or service to be of value to the marketplace. Listen to the feedback.

The sixth step in the process is to summarize everything that you have learned into an "opportunity story." When you put it all down on paper, (or key it all into your electronic files) the summary of your findings, it should portray a "picture" of your new venture. "Story Boarding" is a technique that movie makers use to organize the scenes and sequences of the motion pictures they produce. You are going to "Story Board" the value and benefits of the enterprise you are going to create, and this will prove to be very useful to you when it comes time to develop your formal business plans.

A "Story Board" is not necessarily a narrative, but more of a "power point" summary of what you have been able to learn in the first five steps of this process. The following is a suggested list of the items that should be part of this exercise. Here are some critical points that will help you decide whether or not your business idea is a go.

- Describe the target segment(s) within the selected market. Who are the targeted customers you intend to serve? What do they look like? How many are there? How can you reach them? How do they buy?

- Articulate you high-level value proposition. What will your new venture provide that does not already exist within the marketplace. Why do you feel that this is important?

- Spell out the expected elements of the customer's benefits. Why should your targeted customers buy from you? What underserved need will you address? What benefit does your customer derive as a result of purchasing from you?

- Identify the critical capabilities and resources needed to deliver the customer benefits. List the critical functions that you will need to perform and the kinds of skill sets necessary to perform them. Identify the materials you will need to create, support, or assemble for the product or service you intend to offer. Summarize why you feel that you can acquire these resources and the sources where you will find them.

- Lay out the critical "reasons to believe" that the identified capabilities and resources will be a source of relative advantage over the competition. Once you are up and running, the capabilities that your new venture provides will be more highly valued because they are different then existing alternatives in some definable way. What are they?

- Categorize these critical capabilities (and supporting resources) as in-house, build, buy, or collaborate. This is your first draft of your future operating model. What functions will you employ, which can you contract or "out source?" What materials will you need to make, buy or obtain from other industry participants on a collaborative basis?

- Describe how the company will capture some portion of the value that it creates for its customers. This is all about your pricing models, what you will be able to realize from the sale of your products or services. The greater the value you offer your customers, the higher the price you can charge for it. You need to quantify these assumptions.

- Provide an initial sense of the magnitude of the financial opportunity for the company. This is the segment where you connect the dots, so to speak, of what you have learned about your market. If there are "n" number of targeted customers identified, who spend "x" dollars on the kinds of products and services you intend to offer, then the market opportunity for you is "n" times "x." If the demand for the types of products or services you are going to provide is growing at "y" percent per year, then there is "new market" being created each year in the amount of "n" times "y" percent times "x" dollars. If you believe that you can capture some percentage of the new market being created, and some portion of the existing market, than that is your opportunity.

The final step in the process is to assess the overall attractiveness of the business venture you are going to pursue. There are five criteria that have been identified by the investment community as important to making this kind of an assessment. They are:

- The level of underserved need or the magnitude of unconstrained opportunity, your market opportunity. (An example of a company that had unrestrained opportunity would be E-bay, they can auction off anything)

- The level of interaction that exists between major customer segments, the consumers or industries that you will server. (Zoomerang.com, the electronic survey company, is an example of a business that bridges multiple customer segments and serves multiple industries)

- The likely rate of continued market growth (the higher the percentage of expected market growth, the greater your opportunity to enter and grow with the market.)

- The overall size and volume of the market (the more customers there are to pursue, the greater the opportunity for success)

- The levels of profitability that can be achieved (profitability is always a critical success factor)

Although it is always worthwhile to understand how the investment community sees opportunity, it is not necessarily the only criteria to evaluate the desirability to start a business. Every entrepreneur has their own set of expectations for their business, and it is for this very reason that we wanted to introduce other evaluation models for consideration as part of this feasibility chapter. For example, the Arkansas Small Business Development Center has come up with a more personal model for examining the feasibility of a new business.

As the result of a partnership between the Small Business Administration and the University of Arkansas, Little Rock, College of Business, a "workbook" was developed that explored the question of business feasibility from three three very distinctive perspectives: 1) An examination of the entrepreneur's personal skills, objectives and resources; 2) A review of their business idea and its requirements; 3) an evaluation matrix to help the entrepreneur with the decision making process. While completing these steps does not guarantee success in business, paying attention to them will improve your chances of success. They will certainly help you to evaluate your business idea before you or other people make a financial commitment.

Personal Evaluation

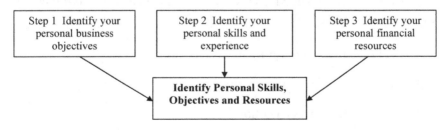

Figure 3.3 Phase 1 from the UALR Feasibility Model

Step 1. When evaluating your business idea, one of the elements to consider is its ability to satisfy your wants and needs. Stating the risks you are willing to take for the potential rewards will help you decide whether the business is right for you. The UALR process provides a questionnaire designed to help you to identify the financial and personal needs objectives that are important to you. Objectives are very personal; each person's will be different. The importance of developing these lists is to make you think about the real reasons you are considering starting your own business.

The list that is offered includes everything from the importance of taking vacations to your desire to become well-known in your community. Other inquiries explore your willingness to concentrate on the business to the exclusion of family and friends, the number of hours you are willing to work, and amount of income you will need to cover your living expenses. It also asks you to evaluate your comfort with uncertainty, the amount of money you are prepared to risk.

Step 2 Your chances for success are usually much better if you have direct work experience in the type of business you plan to start. Past experience provides key contacts in the industry or community that can help as you establish your own operation. Past experience provides firsthand knowledge that cannot be learned from a book. It gives you credibility.

The Management Skills Checklist that comes next in the process identifies some of the skills that business owners need in order to insure that they can adequately control their businesses. The management skills checklist offers help to the entrepreneur to evaluate how well prepared they are to manage their new business. The matrix provided requires the entrepreneur to identify those skills which they possess, those that they would need additional training for, and those that they would rely on someone else, (partner, employee, or contracted), to provide.

The list of skills provided from UALR is quite inclusive, and it includes skill requirements such as:

- Establish & maintain financial records

- Compile financial statements

- Project & control cash flow

- Purchase & manage inventory and/or supplies

- Determine credit worthiness of customers

- Promote my product/service/business

- Negotiate agreements/contracts with suppliers,

- Schedule production work, including labor, machinery, & material needs

- Install quality control methods & conduct follow-up measurement

- Meet basic legal requirements, including those related to employment, zoning, safety/health, waste disposal, etc.

- Identify & make changes necessary to maintain the business's success

They also suggest that the entrepreneur identify the names of people or places that will satisfy the "I Need Training" requirements, as well as the names of people or places that will satisfy "Someone Else Will Do" requirements.

Step 3 A critical element in the analysis of your business idea's feasibility is evaluating how much of the business's financial needs you can meet from your personal resources. It is unrealistic to assume that you will be able to borrow all of the money you need to start your venture. Virtually every lender — aside from family and friends — will require you to put in some money of your own, either in the form of cash or assets. In order to determine whether you have an adequate amount of money to put into the business, you need to summarize your personal financial resources.

Essentially you need to complete an updated balance sheet, recognizing your assets and liabilities. In addition, you should record any "off-balance sheet" liabilities, such as leases, and any other sources of income, such as interest, dividends, rental property, etc. The objective of this step in the process is to try and quantify how mush capital you have a available to invest in your new business venture. This is an important step, because what you plan to invest is going to be what you are putting at risk.

William R. Cobb and M. L. Johnson, Ed.D, Ph.D.

Business Concept Evaluation

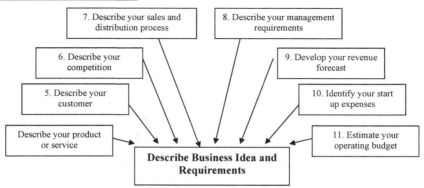

Figure 3.4 Phase 2 from the UALR Feasibility Model

The next set of steps in the process concern themselves with gaining an understanding of the business you are about to undertake and recognizing those elements that can effect your plans. It is important that you know, in your own mind, precisely what business you are going to engage in. While there are hundreds of types of businesses, most can be classified into one of four main categories: service, retail, wholesale, or manufacturing.

Service businesses are currently the most frequently established operations. They are similar to retail businesses, though location is often less important and advertising is often more important than in retail. Service operations usually sell a specialty or skill, so credibility is very important. Start-up costs are often low, and many service businesses can be operated from the owner's home.

Retail stores are a common type of business start-up. Their main advantage is that they can be owned and operated by one person with minimal assistance. Compared to manufacturing operations, they are relatively easy to start, both financially and operationally. However, they have a high failure rate due to undercapitalization, poor site location, and poor market analysis.

Wholesale operations serve as the link between the manufacturer of goods and the retail merchant, industrial customer or end user. They take title to the products they sell and, thus, often have a larger dollar investment in inventory. Location is important even though they often serve a large geographic market.

Manufacturing start-up costs are higher and the setup times are longer than with the other three business types. Cash may become a problem as the time span between purchase of raw materials and payment for finished goods can be weeks and often months during which many fixed expenses must still be paid. Also, manufacturing operations require more people, both for production and management, than all the others but it is the largest of the other three types.

Step 4 -This next step in the evaluation process requires you to describe your product or service. This may seem like a relatively basic question to answer, but it is an important one to get right. ULAR offers a questionnaire to help you gain an understanding of what you will need to support your products success. It starts with identifying the type of business you are planning to start, (*service, retail, wholesale, or manufacturing*) and its business classification code. [The North American Industry Classification System (NAICS), approved in April, 1997, has replaced the former Standard Industrial Classification (SIC) and enables the U S Department of Commerce to better compare economic and financial statistics necessary to keep pace with the changing global economy.] The UALR questionnaire provided asks the entrepreneur to provide answers for the following kinds of questions:

- What will my business' image be?

- What specific products/services will I offer?

- Are these products/services already available in the marketplace?

- If so, how and where? If not, why not?

- Will my products/services be different from what is already available?

- In what way? (*e.g., convenience, quality, service, price?*)

- How will I deliver my product or service to the marketplace?

- What kinds of equipment or raw materials will I need to run my business or produce my product? How available are these?

- Can my equipment be used to manufacture other products or produce other services?

- Are there other services or products I could offer to increase my lines of business?

Although the list provided has to be generic to meet the general requirements of "all businesses," it does encourage the entrepreneur to think carefully about the value proposition of the product or service he or she is planning to bring to market.

Step 5- Without customers, you will not have a business. Yet it is amazing how many companies know next to nothing about the people or businesses that purchase their products or services. You have to know who your potential customers are before you can determine how to sell to them. When it comes to your potential customers, you need to know two things: what they are like and how many of them exist in your target market segment.

For consumers, common traits include things like age, occupation, marital status, income, number of children, etc. For business customers, some characteristics to consider are dollar sales volume, type of business, markets served, authority to make the buying decision, and location. Business trade journals for specific industries often provide subscriber characteristics in their "media kits."

To help the entrepreneur understand how to identify their potential customers, the UALA provides a list of questions to ask that includes the following kinds of inquiries:

- Describe your "ideal" customers in detail. What will be their age? Sex? Income level? Education? Occupation? Marital status? Location? etc.

- If customers will be other businesses, what types? Sizes? Location? etc.

- Why will customers buy your products/services? (Possibilities include need, luxury, impulse, replacement, improvement, status, pleasure, quality, price, guarantee, and durability.)

- When will these customers buy your products/services? (Particular times of the year, month, week, day.)

- How often will customers buy your products/services? In what quantity?

- Where are your potential customers located?

- How many potential customers are in my market area?

- If customers have to come to your store location, how far will they be willing to travel to get to your business?

- Is the population growing or declining in my market area?

- What percent of your customers will use the Internet to purchase your product/service?

There are some excellent publications available that explain how to do your own market research. *Do-It-Yourself Marketing Research* (1991) takes the mystery out of gathering market data and using it to make sound decisions. *The Insider's Guide to Demographic Know-How* (1993) tells you how to find, analyze, and use information about your customers.

Step 6- This next step in the process is to identify and analyze your competition. Starting a

Business successfully can depend to a great degree upon how well you understand your competition, their products, their marketing methods, and their competitive advantages and disadvantages. Once again, UALR provides a set of questions for the entrepreneur to answer to provide insight into the analysis of potential competition. The list includes topics such as:

- Who will my major competitors be and where are they located?

- What are the major strengths and weaknesses of each competitor?

- Do any of my major competitors plan to expand? If so, at what location?

- Have any competitors gone out of business in the past two years?

- If yes, why did they go out of business?

- Will growing market demand permit a new business to enter the market or will I be attempting to take business away from my competitors?

- What is the impact, if any, of the Internet on my industry?

Do not overlook the possibility of interviewing other people and potential customers to learn about the competition. Talk to the people or businesses that fit your profile. Ask about their current sources for the goods and services you plan to offer. Ask them to identify what they like and dislike about their current sources of supply.

Step 7- This step in the process addresses the need to examining how you are going to sell and distribute your products. For many new businesses, it is the element known as distribution that causes product sales problems. An understanding of the advantages, disadvantages, and costs of different channels of distribution will help you avoid making mistakes that could cost you your business. For the purposes of this section, UALR has divided the information into *sales processes* for those starting a service or retail business and *distribution* for those going into manufacturing. This is because retailers are a part of the distribution channel, always dealing directly with the end user. Manufacturers, on the other hand, rarely sell to end users, but instead sell to a variety of intermediaries, of which retail stores are one.

Since most retail operations sell directly to the end user, marketing for a retail operation is 90% location. Though advertising can increase traffic to your store considerably, your facility must be accessible in terms of finding it and getting to it. So the kinds of questions you may need to answer would be:

- Can I initially operate the business out of my home?

- What time of day will customers shop my business?

- What sales-per-square-foot ratio is typical for my type of business?

- How can I best communicate with my customers?

- What types of promotional and marketing techniques are available to reach them?

- To what extent might an Internet web site influence local business?

- How much retail space will my business need?

- If I lease, will I have the option to renew my lease?

For manufacturers, there are many channels of distribution for you to consider. While they will vary from industry to industry, the following are the main ones with which you should be familiar so that you can select the one that is best for your business:

- Direct to the end user (via the internet)

- Sales representative either employed or contracted

- Retail and specialty stores

- Catalogue, direct mail, or mail order

- Distributors and wholesalers

The UALR suggests that you ask yourself these kinds of questions if you are going to be a manufacture and distribute a tangible product:

- Do I have the skills to manage operations and the sales process?

- Could my product be sold by an independent sales representative?

- To what extent will a presence on the Internet influence my distribution process?

- Does selling the product /process require technical education or support?

- Can my product/process be sold with a picture?

There are many other factors to consider in the actual development of a sales and distribution strategy, but it is important that you explore the feasibility of what you perceive you will need.

In today's complex business environment, it isn't enough to build a better mousetrap. You have to find a way to get your message in front of your targeted customer, and that is what sales and distribution discussion is all about.

Step 8- One of the most critical, yet most intangible, requirements for a successful business is management skill. In Step 2 you identified your personal skills and experience, what you "have." The next question is to find out what you "need." This is not an easy question, but it is one that you must answer. Your business will fail if you are not able to control and direct the business once it is operating.

UALR suggests that you should talk with at least five people running similar businesses to get a range of opinions and experiences. You need to understand the day-to-day life of the business operator, the hours involved, the skills and experience required, the conflicts, the travel required, the customer skills and experience needed, and as many other elements of the business as you can. With an increased understanding of the day-to-day and overall skill requirements of the business, you are now in a better position to evaluate your own skills and experiences and identify areas in which you might need additional training or support.

Other possible sources of information are national or regional trade associations for your type of business and your local chamber of commerce. The *Encyclopedia of Associations* identifies trade associations which you can contact for useful industry information. It is good to contact your local chamber to help develop local connections and support for your business. They may also have profiles of people in your line of business.

Step 9- This next step in the process is gaining an understanding of what the value of the opportunity is for your new business. In evaluating how much of the market you can get, concentrate on why customers will buy from you and not your competition. Data on selected industry sales is included in Sales and Marketing Management's *Survey of Buying Power*. Information is given by state, county, and metropolitan areas, and is updated annually. Consult the *Census of Retail Trade, Census of Wholesale Trade, Census of Manufacturing,* and *Census of Service Industries* for industry data on sales receipts and value of shipments. This data is also presented on a statewide, county, and city-wide basis and available at www.uscensus.gov.

If you are planning a retail operation, an excellent predictor of sales volume for a storefront operation can be obtained from *Dollars and Cents of Shopping Centers*. This reference provides data on median sales per square foot and median size of location. Multiply the sales figure by your potential location's square footage to arrive at an estimated annual sales volume. You should also compare your potential location's size to the median to determine if your site's size is in line with the industry.

UALR also suggests that you consider other business owners and owners of similar businesses that may have failed. Don't expect competitors to share this data with you. Owners of similar businesses outside your market area may, however, since you will not be in competition with them. You may be able to obtain valuable information and advice, based on their experiences.

Step 10- This segment of the process concerns itself with identifying the actual costs associated with getting your business started. These start-up costs must be identified as you analyze your business idea's feasibility. Only by knowing the total costs to get your business to an operating stage can you decide whether you have enough personal financial capacity to approach others about financing for the remainder of the money that you need.

Identify the specific expenses that must be paid, and also your needs for operating cash to support the business until it begins to generate enough cash to meet continuing costs. The amount of operating cash you need depends on the amount of your recurring monthly expenses and the number of months it takes for the business to generate a positive cash flow. It is wise to be conservative when projecting the operating cash you will need during the start-up phase of your business enterprise.

UALR suggests that you develop a worksheet that identifies common start-up costs. Use this form to develop an estimate of the amount of money you will need to get started. Omit or add items to suit your business. Check with trade associations and franchisors for industry data on start-up costs for your potential business. You may also want to ask other business owners outside your market area for guidance.

Step 11- In this segment of their process, UALR suggests that you develop a twelve month "pro-forma" or estimated operating budget. The operating budgets for your business are summaries of the business' projected sales and expenses, cash flow, and balance sheet. They are the road maps by which you can project and chart the business' future.

Developing a detailed operating budget, cash flow projections and such are usually reserved for the business planning stage of launching a new company, as some types of businesses may not achieve profitability in the first year. If this is the case for your business, you would need to extend your profit or loss projection up to the point where your projected figures show an annual profit.

UALR provides some templates with their workbook for the entrepreneur to use to help organize and categorize this kind of information. For evaluation purposes, you are initially looking for "road blocks," things that would cause you to believe that your business idea is financially unviable. The projected profit or loss statement should include all the known costs associated with the day-to-day operation of your business. Some of these expenses are often fixed; that is, they continue whether or not the business has sales. Others are variable, they are controllable and, sometimes, these costs are directly tied to your business' sales volume. Be sure to consider miscellaneous expenses, all the things you have not thought of or anticipated.

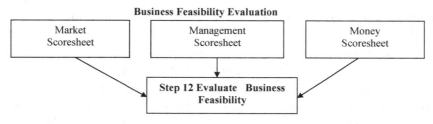

Figure 3.5 Phase 3 from the UALR Feasibility Model

Step 12- This final step in the UALR process is where you pull together everything that you have discovered and actually evaluate the feasibility of your new venture. At the very minimum, the right question should be "Will this business work for me?" not the more general "Will the business work?" You are the critical and personal element of your business success. Ultimately, only you can answer that question. However, UALR does provide three sets of scoresheets for the entrepreneur to populate, to help assess the answer to this critical question. Here they are:

MARKET SCORESHEET-

Rate your level of agreement with the following statements concerning the sales and marketing issues of your business. Check the appropriate column and total the number of choices at the bottom of each column.

Question	Strongly Agree	Agree	Neutral	Disagree	Strongly Disagree
I have demonstrated that my product/service is needed in the proposed market area.					
The proposed product/service is different from anything already available from competitors.					
Based on research and conversations, I have identified why customers will buy my product/service.					
I have described ten key characteristics of my customer(s) in detail.					
I have described five geographical sites where my customers are located.					
I have estimated the number of potential customers in the proposed market area.					
I have identified and described the strengths and weaknesses of at least 50% of my potential competitors.					

As a manufacturer or distributor, I have researched at least three ways to get my product to my customers.					
I have identified and spoken at length with at least five suppliers of my raw materials.					
I have researched, priced, and spoken with key people concerning the advertising and sales techniques that I will use to reach my customer.					
Total Number of Choices in Each Category					

MANAGEMENT SCORESHEET-

Rate your level of agreement with the following statements concerning the management issues of your business. Check the appropriate column and total the number of choices at the bottom of each column.

Question	Strongly Agree	Agree	Neutral	Disagree	Strongly Disagree
I have a strong need to achieve.					
I possess a large amount of energy which I am willing to put into my business.					

I am persistent — I keep trying until I get it right.					
I am comfortable taking risks.					
I have good reading, writing, and arithmetic skills.					
I know the most common skills needed to operate this business and possess them myself or will get training.					
I have owned or managed a business before and it was successful.					
I have work experience in the type of business I want to start.					
I am comfortable with hiring, firing, training, and managing employees.					
I have researched, priced, and spoken with key					

I have considered the consequences if the business fails and I know how I will handle them					
Total Number of Choices in Each Category					

Money Scoresheet –

Rate your level of agreement with the following statements concerning the financial issues of your business. Check the appropriate column and total the number of choices at the bottom of each column.

Question	Strongly Agree	Agree	Neutral	Disagree	Strongly Disagree
Based on research about similar businesses, my business' projected sales per square foot is typical for the industry.					
The business will show a profit at the end of the first year, based on the expected sales volume minus all anticipated expenses.					
The estimated sales are built on researched assumptions about how much product can be sold at the projected selling price.					

Start-up costs and business expense estimates for the last year are based on actual dollar costs where quotes or documented estimates could be obtained.				
Trade associations and/or financial publications have proven to be good sources of useful information about the typical financial performance of businesses similar to mine.				
My business' projected sales and expenses are comparable to the industry information I have obtained for similar businesses.				
I have personal assets, such as land, stocks, etc., that I can and will use as collateral to get a loan to start this business.				
I have cash savings that I will use to start the business				
The business will be able to pay me a salary on which I can live.				

I need to borrow no more than 70% of the money required to start the business.					
I know what lenders will expect of me if I seek a loan to start the business.					
Total Number of Choices in Each Category					

ANALYZING THE SCORESHEETS-

You can now analyze the results from the Market, Management, and Money Scoresheets. Please fill out the following form below, as described:

	Multiply by:	Market		Management		Money	
		# of Choices	Total Points	# of Choices	Total Points	# of Choices	Total Points
Strongly Disagree	-10						
Disagree	-5						
Neutral	0						
Agree	5						
Strongly Agree	10						
Total Points for ea. Scoresheet							

If your score for a particular scoresheet is above 50, it indicates that, based on your opinions and analysis, you have a relatively positive business proposal with respect to the particular topic. A score between +50 and -50 for a particular scoresheet indicates that, based on your opinions and analysis, it is hard to predict whether or not this is a solid proposal. You can proceed to steps beyond this study of business feasibility, but be aware that some areas may require further work. A score below -50 for a particular scoresheet indicates that, based on your opinions and analysis, you have a relatively poor business proposal in respect to this topic at this point, and you should not proceed further until you have sorted out some of the issues raised.

Still another approach to determining feasibility is to test your business concept is with a "S.W.O.T." analysis; meaning: an analysis of the strengths (S) of your industry, any weaknesses (W) of your product (such as design flaws) or service (such as high prices), your market opportunities (O) and for your product or service potential threats (T) such as competitors and market sector trends

The S.W.O.T. analysis model came from research conducted at Stanford Research Institute from 1960-1970. The background to S.W.O.T. stemmed from the need to find out why corporate planning failed. The research was funded by the fortune 500 companies to find out what could be done about this failure.

It all began with the corporate planning trend, which seemed to appear first at Du Pont in 1949. By 1960 every Fortune 500 company had a 'corporate planning manager' (or equivalent) and 'associations of long range corporate planners' had sprung up in both the USA and the UK. However a unanimous opinion developed in all of these companies; that corporate planning in the shape of long range planning was not working, did not pay off, and was an expensive investment in futility.

It was widely held that managing change and setting realistic objectives which carry the conviction of those responsible was difficult and often resulted in questionable compromises. The fact remained, despite the corporate and long range planners, that the one and only missing link was how to get the management team agreed and committed to a comprehensive set of action programs.

To create this link, starting in 1960, Robert F Stewart at SRI in Menlo Park California lead a research team to discover what was going wrong with corporate planning. He was asked to find some sort of solution, or to create a system, for enabling management teams to agree and commit to development work, which today we call 'managing change'.

The research carried on from 1960 through 1969. 1100 companies and organizations were interviewed and a 250-item questionnaire was designed and completed by over 5,000 executives. Several key findings lead to the conclusion that in corporations, the chief executive should be the chief planner and that his immediate functional directors should be the planning team. Dr Otis Benepe defined the 'Chain of Logic' which became the core of system designed to fix the link for obtaining agreement and commitment.

Can such a sophisticated approach be applied to the evaluation of a new business concept? Of course, as the model is relevant to any new business undertaking, its just that the data points for a new enterprise will be much different than those of an established organization. Using the basic elements of the model, test you plans for your new business in each of the four categories. As you ask yourself each of the critical questions suggested, you will begin to identify what will probably work for your new company, and what it is you will have to improve in order to launch your business successfully.

This SWOT example is for a new business opportunity. Many criteria can apply to more than one quadrant. Identify the criteria appropriate to your own SWOT situation.

Strength criteria examples
Advantages of proposition?
Capabilities?
Competitive advantages?
USP's (unique selling points)?
Resources, Assets, People?
Experience, knowledge, data?
Financial reserves, likely returns?
Marketing - reach, distribution, awareness?
Innovative aspects?
Location and geographical?
Price, value, quality?
Accreditations, qualifications, certifications?
Processes, systems, IT, communications?
Cultural, attitudinal, behavioral?
Management cover, succession?
Philosophy and values?

WEAKNESS CRITERIA EXAMPLES

Disadvantages of proposition?
Gaps in capabilities?
Lack of competitive strength?
Reputation, presence and reach?
Financials?
Own known vulnerabilities?
Timescales, deadlines and pressures?
Cashflow, start-up cash-drain?
Continuity, supply chain robustness?
Effects on core activities, distraction?
Reliability of data, plan predictability?
Morale, commitment, leadership?
Accreditations, etc?
Processes and systems, etc?
Management cover, succession?

OPPORTUNITY CRITERIA EXAMPLES

Market developments?
Competitors' vulnerabilities?
Industry or lifestyle trends?
Technology development and innovation?
Global influences?
New markets, vertical, horizontal?
Niche target markets?
Geographical, export, import?
New USP's?
Tactics: eg, surprise, major contracts?
Business and product development?
Information and research?
Partnerships, agencies, distribution?
Volumes, production, economies?
Seasonal, weather, fashion influences?

THREAT CRITERIA EXAMPLES

Political effects?
Legislative effects?
Environmental effects?
IT developments?
Competitor intentions - various?
Market demand?
New technologies, services, ideas?
Vital contracts and partners?
Sustaining internal capabilities?
Obstacles faced?
Insurmountable weaknesses?
Loss of key staff?
Sustainable financial backing?
Economy - home, abroad?
Seasonality, weather effects?

Figure 3.6 The S.W.O.T. Analysis Matrix (Alan Chapman 2005-2009)

Business idea feasibility testing is designed to reduce uncertainty, but it won't eliminate it. Mathematical analyses are not always valid; as reduction to numbers may misidentify some winners as losers. Market size can be mathematically estimated; as can elegance of the invention or business idea. However, it is difficult to correctly estimate the potential of new teams. For example, Paul Allen and Bill Gates, of Microsoft Corporation, were newcomers to business and Gates was a university dropout. Steve Wozniak and Steve Jobs, of Apple Corporation, had never managed a business and Jobs was a college dropout. A mathematical model would not have predicted either management team to dramatically succeed. However, the model would have been more favorable to *Nike's* co-founder, Phillip

Knight; as he was a business major at Oregon and was a certified public accountant before leading the Corporation for decades.

There is no single approach that can be taken to insure success, or predict failure, of any new business venture. There are, however, fundamental characteristics that consistently appear in all of the models we examined: market opportunity, a viable product or service concept, and talented entrepreneurs. *Inc.com* (2010) suggests that your consider these *"10 Things to Do Before You Start Your Start-up:"*

1. Scope out your industry - Find the best industry to fit your style and talents.

2. Size up the competition - Study your competition by visiting stores or locations where their products are offered, and search the Internet.

3. Second guess yourself - Make sure you have an adequate amount of capital set aside to enable a successful launch.

4. Think about funding - Money is a big topic for entrepreneurs and you'll want to identify your financial options early on.

5. Refine your business concept - When you position your company, think in terms of what makes you different from your competition.

6. Seek advice from friends and mentors - A mentor can be a boon to an entrepreneur in a broad range of scenarios, whether he or she provides pointers on business strategy, helps you bolster your networking efforts, or act as confidante when your work-life balance gets out of whack.

7. Pick a name - You want to choose a name that will last and, if possible, will embody both your values and your company's distinguishing characteristics.

8. Get a grasp on your marketing strategies - Be clear on who your customers are, because you don't have any time to waste on marketing to those who aren't.

9. Do a little test run - Solicit feedback on the cheap by using online

survey tools available through such services as Zoomerang.com, Surveymonkey.com and Constantcontact.com.

10. Start searching for future talent - This might sound premature, but don't forget that your business is supposed to grow someday. Identify people who might fit into your organization.

Entrepreneurship can be challenging, and the resolve necessary to undertake the effort does not get much more challenging than during the start-up process. It is critical that founders share the same passion for the business and remain mutually supportive of one another. For example, *Nike's* co-founders had a passion for track competition; each contributing their first $1000.00 to incorporate. But, Coach Bowerman mainly wanted cheap high quality shoes for his runners and Phillip Knight wanted to start a business. Their collaboration and conflicts are legendary; with Bowerman frequently wanting to leave and Knight refusing it. In a way both won – Bowerman stayed and cashed out $9 million at the IPO.

NIKE CORPORATION: THE BUSINESS IDEA

Nike Corporation's story is now a familiar one. Phil Knight, a distance runner, and his Oregon University track coach Bill Bowerman incorporated as Blue Ribbon Sports in 1964. Initially they served as distributors for the Japanese shoe manufacturer ASICS; selling shoes at track meets out of Bowerman's car. Profits from selling the ASICS Tiger enabled the company to launch its own line of shoes and the corporate name was changed in 1974 to Nike, Inc. – as derived from the Greek goddess of victory.

In 1974 the University of Oregon resurfaced its track and Bowerman wanted to find some type of outer sole that would grip the track's urethane surface more efficiently. He poured liquid urethane into the family waffle iron and refined the new material into the now iconic Waffle Trainer. The new design was embraced by distance runners because it gripped artificial track surfaces better, it was lighter (Benefit: faster race times), had better cushioning (Benefit: fewer shin splints and stress fractures from miles and miles of training), and had superior lateral stability (Benefit: reduced chance of ankle sprains caused by running on uneven terrain). Note: The product customer benefits are highlighted rather than any shoe technical features.

Distance runners particularly liked Nike shoes and advertising was largely word-of-mouth through the 1970s. However, by expanding product lines to include specialty shoes for other sports, Nike was able to capture some 50 percent of the U.S. athletic shoe market by 1980. The "Swoosh" design, the ad line "Just do it!" and high profile athlete marketing has propelled Nike into manufacture and sales of anything athletic that can be worn or used. Success in the distance running segment led to later successes in tennis, basketball and other sports.

The founder's were initially focused on selling track shoes; serving as distributors for shoes designed and produced in Japan. At the macro-level, the U.S. market for athletic footwear was stagnant in the 1960s. Athletic shoe designs were rather utilitarian. Most people had only one or two pairs of sneakers and saw no need for another. Smartly, Nike's president, Phillip Knight, chose a high value and high price position in the athletic shoe marketplace.

At the micro-level, Knight and Bowerman saw initially was a chance to offer a demonstrably superior product that customers, distance runners, would prefer and pay for; one that could then lead to similar success in other sharply targeted footwear niches. Their sport-by-sport advance across the formerly stagnant athletic footwear market was propelled by astute marketing that made high-priced athletic shoes a fashion item, leading the market's stunning growth – (How many pairs of different athletic shoes are in your closet today?) - and to Nike's leading position in the marketplace.

Nike's marketing strategy has left few stones unturned. For cash and equipment contributions to athletic departments, high schools and universities showcase the Nike logo on athlete's uniforms during practices and games; getting advertising exposure to spectators and television audiences. For example, in 2010 the Nike Pro Combat jersey collection was worn by football teams from the universities of Alabama, Boise State, Florida, Miami, Ohio State, Oregon State, Pittsburgh, Texas Christian, Virginia Tech and West Virginia.

Thus, a business idea moved from just selling track shoes to designing and manufacturing, marketing and distributing multiple types of sport shoes; later expanding to virtually all things related to sports. Most notable is the corporate decision to market quality and self image – Nike product wearers become one with celebrity athletes who endorse the products.

Chapter Summary

KEY POINTS

- An innovation is not a business; though it could serve as the basis of a business idea.

- There are numerous formats for business idea feasibility testing.

- Test your own willingness to participate in what may be required to establish your new enterprise

- Business idea feasibility testing should preceded writing a business plan.

- Different market sectors have unique product/business life cycles.

- The digital technology product sector lifecycle is very short; meaning that the business idea must include not only an aggressive research and development concept, but an aggressive marketing plan.

- Your business idea is most valuable when it can solve a problem or satisfy an unmet marketplace need.

- Think of your business idea in terms of its product/service benefits to the customer.

- Analyze your potential customer base in terms of purchasers, influencers and end users.

- Document your business idea feasibility analysis with sufficient detail to allow investors to track your thought processes.

- A S.W.O.T. analysis can both reveal problem areas in the business idea and validate your assumptions for presentation to investors.

- Business idea feasibility analysis includes realistic comparisons of competitors in your market sector.

- Documentation of price point estimates, with costs from production to distribution points, can validate business idea assumptions.

- Asking your potential customers what they think of your new product or service and would they be willing to purchase them at your desired price point is among the best ways to gain a realistic assessment of its future market success.

TAKE ACTION NOW

- A feasibility test is an analytical tool used to assist stakeholders and decision makers in determining if a business concept is worth pursuing.

- The idea stage of your business concept can be examined in terms of the kind of company you envision, the kinds of customers you will serve, the companies you will compete against, and stakeholders you could impact.

- The Developing a prototype, model, or detailed description of your offerings will help you to communicate your thoughts more effectively to potential customers.

- Ask your potential customers if they would purchase your products and ask at what price points they would make that purchasing decision.

- Check out your competition and understand what they offer, at what price points, and why customers currently purchase their products.

- Understand the complexity of what you will provide and how it would need to operate with other elements that exist within your targeted customer's environment.

- Conduct a S.W.O.T. analysis to better understand the strengths and weaknesses of your business proposition and the opportunity you are about to pursue.

- Recognize your resource requirements in terms of both capability and financial support to successfully launch your venture.

- Understand the dynamics of the industry you will be part of and the economic model by which you will operate going forward.

- Review the "10 Things to Do" to make sure you are ready to move forward.

- Business ideas are not static, as they can grow and change in the sector environment.

REFERENCES

Barringer, Bruce (2009). *Entrepreneurship: Successfully launching new businesses.* Upper Saddle River, NJ: Pearson Education, Publishers

Breen, George & Blankenship, A.B. (1991) *Do It Yourself Market Research,* New York, McGraw- Hill Inc., Publisher

Crispell, Diane (1993), *The Insiders Guide to Demographic Know-How,* Ithaco, American Demographic Press, Publisher

Drucker, Peter (2006). *Innovation and Entrepreneurship. New York: Harper*

No author credited, (2004) *Business Blueprints: Is your Business Idea Feasible?* Arkansas Small Business Development Center, Publisher

No author credited, *Market Opportunity Analysis; Will Your Business Compete,* Gatton College of Business and Economics, University of Kentucky, Publisher

Inc.com Staff (2010) "10 Things to do Before You Start Your Start Up," www.inc.com , 8/17/2010.

Keller, Aaron (2006). *Design matters: Packaging.* Beverley, MA: Rockport Publishers

Mullins, John (2006). *The new business road test: What entrepreneurs should know before writing the business plan.* (2nd Ed.). Upper Saddle River, NJ: Prentice Hall Publisher

Ortutay, B. (2011). *Investments put Facebook value at $50B.* Coloradoan, 1/4/2011, B1.

Silver, David (2007). *Smart Startups.* Hoboken, NJ: John Wiley & Sons, Publisher.

Survey of Buying Power, provided annually by *Sales and Marketing Management Magazine*

SUPPLEMENTAL RESOURCES

Barringer, B. (2006). *Business feasibility analysis.* Upper Saddle River, NJ: Prentice Hall.

Hass, K. B. (2008). *The business analyst as strategist: Translating business strategies into valuable solutions.* Vienna, VA: Management Concepts, Inc.

Kurowski, L. & Sussman, D. (2011). *Investment project design: A guide to financial and economic analysis with constraints.* Hoboken, NJ: Wiley.

McManus, G. & Powe, M. (2009). *The creation of sustainable value.* Edithvale, Vic, Australia.: Marcus Powe.

Wyckham, R. G. & Wedley, W. C. (2005). Factors related to venture feasibility analysis and business plan preparation. *Journal of Small Business Management.* 28(4), 48-60.

Zimmer, T.W., Scarborough, N. M. & Wilson, D. (2007). *Essentials of entrepreneurship and small business value package.* Upper Saddle River, NJ: Prentice Hall.

William R. Cobb and M. L. Johnson, Ed.D, Ph.D.

Excerpts from an *Entrepreneur.com* article entitled: *"How to Research your Business Idea"* by Karen E. Speader, a freelance business writer in Southern California.

Henricks, Mark (Dec. 1, 2007) excerpts from *Test Run,* Entrepreneur. com

The Public Forum Institute, (2009) *Entrepreneurship Success Stories*

Alan Chapman 2005-09. This free PDF version of this tool and information about SWOT analysis methods are available at www.businessballs. com/swotanalysisfreetemplate.htm. This is a free resource from www. businessballs.com, which contains lots more useful tools, diagrams and materials.

CHAPTER FOUR
Business Planning for Success

"Goals are dreams we convert to plans and take action to fulfill."
-Zig Ziglar

You are about to embark upon a journey into the local, regional, national, or global economy to establish a new enterprise and to make your mark in this world. And, as with any other journey, you are well advised to have a destination in mind and a road map to help you get there. The business planning process is all about building a roadmap. It's about having a logical path that will enable you to accomplish the goals and objectives you have set for the venture. As children are reminded each day on television by "Dora the Explorer," to find your way use "The Map, the Map, it's the Map," Creating your business plan is not just about "marking the box on the checklist," as a prerequisite for attracting investment capital; although good plans do improve the probability of successful financing. Factors such as a) the situation, b) the innovation and c) the market, all determine the degree of sophistication needed in a business plan. Entering a market sector early makes product positioning easier and cheaper.

Decades ago, the concept of spicy bread-based finger food was a novelty in America. John Schnatter got into this market sector before the field became crowded. From working in fast food sales and delivery businesses in high school and college, he realized there was potential in expanding an existing market by delivering a quality product to the customer's door. In 1983 he knocked out a broom closet in his father's tavern, sold his car to buy $1,600.00 of used restaurant equipment and began selling pizzas to the bar customers; also delivering to homes from out of the back door of the lounge. Astute business management, and a global franchising model, has spread the business idea to over 3,000 locations worldwide; making

Papa John's Pizza the third largest take-out and delivery pizza operation in the world.

Among the many challenges you will face in formalizing your business plans will be the need to identify the role your business will play, and the value that your new business will bring to your specific industry. Every industry has its own "consumption cycle" that has evolved over time as the result of various participants playing various roles in the production and delivery of these goods and services. Understanding the role that you are about to play is critical for you so that you can develop your marketing plan; operating plans and financial models.

Within the United States economy, goods and services are delivered as the result of different industries providing different support capabilities. In simplified terms, raw materials are extracted; they are then manufactured into both consumer and industrial goods, often distributed through "middle men," and eventually purchased by consumers, businesses, or government. Thus, the first task is to determine where your industry, and your business, fit into this cycle of raw materials extraction, manufacturing, distribution and sales. For professional services organizations, such as marketing, advertising, computing or accounting, it is important to identify the unique capabilities you plan to introduce into these already established industry sectors. John Schnatter entered his market sector early by applying the commercialization process shown in Figure 4.1, and as a result, he had the time to informally develop his own recipes, learn how to manufacture his own product, and retail it directly to the consumer; providing both a "quality product" and "delivery convenience to the ultimate buyer."

Figure 4.1 Generic Innovation Consumption Model.

The second step is to construct a specific consumption model for your specific industry. For example, if you are planning to design, produce, and sell a product into the consumer marketplace, than you would need to account for the various "touch points" that will occur to complete the consumer consumption cycle, as shown in Figure 4.2. Identify which of these touch points you intend to perform and which ones are you going out source or rely on others to perform is critically important to this process. Each out-sourced touch point reduces the profit available to your enterprise or it raises the product price point; both of which will affect your market position.. It is imperative that you understand the economic impact of these touch point influences in your customer's consumption cycle in order to construct a meaningful business model for your venture.

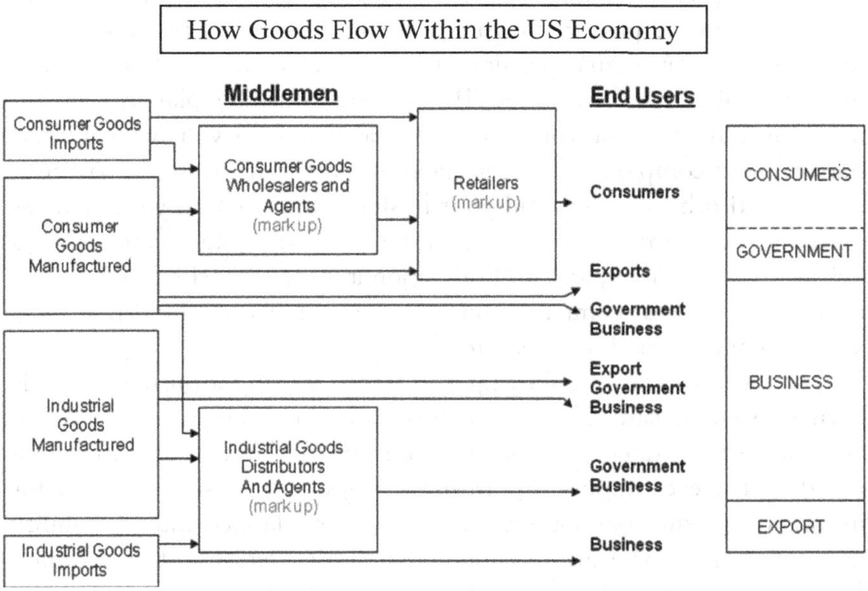

Figure 4.2 Touch points affecting the price point of a product. The innovator's mandate to "develop a product that can be manufactured for at least one fifth of its retail price point," realistically considers all of these respective touch points. Redrawn from Bonoma & Garda (1983), as originally proposed by Alexander, Cross & Hill (1973).

WHAT IS A BUSINESS PLAN ANYWAY?

It is a formal statement of goals; including the reasons why they are believed attainable and the plan for reaching those goals. It may also contain background information about the organization or team attempting to reach those goals. Both non-profit and for-profit organizations must have solid business plans. For-profit business plans typically focus on financial goals, such as profit dollars or the creation of wealth. Non-profit, as well as government agency business plans, tend to focus on the "organization's mission." Though, for-profit investors want to see how and when the venture will be profitable, non-profit contributors want to see the type and degree of affect efficiently made by their money. When starting a new venture, a three to five year business plan is essential.

Because he entered a developing market, John Schnatter's initial business plan, to open a take out and delivery pizza business, was little more than a mental image. Since he bootstrapped his venture, there was no need for a solid plan to convince a financier to invest in his idea; but he astutely developed an expansion plan that included a standard business model for all of his franchisees. Thus, a good business plan is a living, breathing blueprint for your business that can help you navigate and manage your company while also helping potential investors, partners, lenders, and others understand your business strategy and your chances at success. A business plan is never quite finished because you're always revising it, reviewing it, and building upon it. Once launched, you should no more shelve your company's business map than you would fold away your map once started on a long road trip.

For those of you just starting a business, writing a business plan is a crucial step. It can help you describe your product or service, detail your marketing strategy, and lay out your sales and operational forecasts; including the ever important cash-flow projections to stay on track for meeting the product development, manufacturing, launch and profitability milestones expected by any investors. With the proliferation of the internet, there are now scores of websites that offer to sell cheap business plans; a computer file designed to let you enter your company name and specifics and generate a plan. Unless you do a lot of editing, these are of little value since each business is unique. A business owner should also be fully invested and fully aware of every aspect of their plan. Take your time, understand what you want to do, and recognize what it takes to make it happen.

A business plan usually starts out with the current status of an organization and sets out an overall business strategy for the next three to five years with a more detailed operational and financial plan for the years immediately ahead. Although plans vary from organization to organization, they generally focus in on: a) management, b) product, c) marketing and d) sales. Yes, the financial projections are important as well, but they are meaningless unless you can demonstrate how they are going to be achieved. The entrepreneur should be fully invested and fully aware of every aspect of their plan because any competent investor will thoroughly dissect their business plan – deep preparation will assure any investor that you know of what you speak.

Robert Reiss, (2009) has been involved in 16 start-ups, is a three time INC 500 Winner, a graduate of Columbia University and the Harvard Business School. He suggests that you consider that: "The smartest entrepreneurs plan on growing and are prepared for change." His advice, for first-time entrepreneurs and for seasoned business owners looking to hit a new stage of growth, is "Write your business plan in pencil." This may be strange advice; but, the metaphor illustrates two important principles.

Change is inevitable – There is little doubt that you will shortly have to change, amend, modify, or possibly scrap your original business plan. Virtually every construction project will have multiple "Change Orders" to be approved by the owner, because of things that the architects did not or could not anticipate. One of the attributes of successful entrepreneurs is flexibility. "Writing your business plan in pencil," forces you to look at "change as the only constant." Make change your friend, embrace it and work it to your benefit. The reasons why your original plan will need modification after your company is operational are myriad. It's likely your projections under or over-estimated your competition, the profit margins, company cash needs, personnel competencies and suppliers ability to meet quality and delivery schedules. Or, you misjudged market need and size. If open to change, you will discover new opportunities that did not appear until the business was actually up and running.

Avoid business plan worship – When we produce documents that are neatly typed and bound we are reluctant to change them. This phenomenon is especially true for those who may have attended business schools where the plan took on a larger than life importance. Those whose business plans were lavishly praised, received high marks or, even worse, won a business plan contest, tend to feel their plan is infallible/bullet proof. Premature true believers feel that if they rigorously adhere to the well-vetted plan it will yield the riches of their dreams. However, Reiss' mental image of a penciled document reminds us that change is good and it can help reach your goals.

COMPONENTS OF A TYPICAL BUSINESS PLAN:

With an understanding of your limited ability to peer into the future to both a) know what the important variables are and b) control these variables, here are some general guidelines and components that most business plans need to follow. Jot these headings on a sheet of paper and start making notes relating your business idea to the descriptive narrative.

Company Description – Describing your business in the plan may sound deceptively simple. In reality, a nuance company explanation is needed, and it will serve as a strong foundation for your entire plan document. To write a complete description of your proposed business, follow these few simple suggestions:

Identify Your Type of Business – From the business categories listed below, find the one that most closely matches your business. Use one of the descriptions that follow as a reference when you describe your own business. Figure 4.3 shows a variety of general business sectors that could be entered; with almost unlimited specific substrates of these major areas.

- *Retail* - Retail describes a commercial transaction in which the buyer intends to consume the product or service being purchased for personal or household use. These businesses buy merchandise from a variety of manufacturers and wholesalers and sell it directly to the end user or consumer.

- *Wholesale* - Persons or firms that buy large quantity of goods from various producers or vendors, warehouse them, and resells to retailers. Wholesalers who carry only non-competing goods or lines are often called distributors, and they buy merchandise from manufacturers or brokers and resell the goods to retailers and other consumer outlets.

- *Service* - A valuable action, deed or effort performed to satisfy an identified need or to fulfill a demand. People with a particular skill or capability sell it to consumers or to other businesses.

- *Manufacturing* – Is the process of converting raw materials, components, or parts into finished goods that meet a customer's expectations or specifications. Manufacturing commonly employs a man-machine setup with a division of labor in a large scale production. Manufacturers convert raw materials into products for consumers or other businesses.

- *Project (product) development* – Is a planned set of interrelated tasks to be executed over a fixed period and within certain cost and other limitations. Project companies create a salable commodity by assembling teams for a one-time project.

Select one of these general business sectors and drill down in a major area to identify potential competitors and market entry space.

Write a value proposition – All successful businesses share a common attribute: They do something that is valued by their customers. One way to determine what is valued by your customers is to identify and describe the problem that your business will address – market the consumer benefits not the product features! For example, a car wash solves two customers' problems: wanting a clean automobile; not having enough time or the physical ability to clean the automobile themselves. If you can accurately understand your customers' problems or needs, your answering these types of questions will be crucial to the writing your business plan and to the success of your venture.

If you are the inventor of a new product, there will be a tendency to "romance the innovation" – to focus on the product features that you identified in your initial "product description." Your invention may be fantastic, but your business plan is not about the invention; it is about marketing it! Therefore, do your own market analysis first.

Develop a series of related questions when you are developing your business description. Consider asking the following kinds of questions to challenge your beliefs about the value of what it is you are about to provide and your ability to provide it:

- What is the problem I plan to solve, or unfulfilled need I plan to address for my customers?

- How large is the market I plan to serve?

- What are the characteristics of the market I plan to serve; is it growing? How fast?

- What does my "ideal" customer look like? How many are there and where are they?

- How will I reach my target customers and get my market message to them?

- Will the products and/or services I am planning to provide solve their problem or fulfill their needs? Are there any additional products or services my customers may expect me to provide that I don't currently plan on providing?

- Where should I locate my business?

- Have I identified my supply chain needs and have I determined where I will buy the products I need to operate?

- Have I identified the key human resources I will need and do I know where I can find these individuals and how I need to compensate them?

- How am I planning to introduce my business to the marketplace, and what mediums will I use?

- Who are my competitors going to be and what are their strengths and weaknesses?

- How will my business be different from these competitors and why should my target customers select my products and services instead of my competitions?

Be Sure to Describe Your Business Operations – Many new entrepreneurs neglect to think through how they are going to operate their new enterprise. Take your time, as it is very likely that the first time you attempt this task, you will discover new questions that you didn't consider previously. The important thing is not to overlook the operational elements of what it actually takes to provide the goods and services you are planning.

To sum up, writing a precise description of your business is an essential part of the business planning process. Make sure you've considered as many details of your operations as possible, well before you open your doors. Remember: A business plan is the process of determining a commercial enterprise's objectives, strategies and projected actions in order to promote its survival and development within a given time frame. Business planning typically has two key aspects, one focused on making profits and the other focused on dealing with risks that might negatively impact the business. Here are some additional thoughts regarding the plan's components:

Market Analysis – It's a big world out there, so how can you precisely identify your potential market sector and size? Learn to apply the simple principles of segmenting your market and drilling down to a more precise view of your target customer base. After you have quantified the data and analyzed the market, you will need a succinct and clear approach to best communicate this information as part of your plan. To be successful, you have to know who your potential customers are, where they are, and how you are going to reach them.

Competitive Analysis – You can gather endless information regarding potential competition by immersing yourself into the Internet. However, for start-ups the best strategy may be to stay local and get a firsthand look at competitors. Make meticulous notes and source references for competitor product/service a) features, b) price, c) customer support if needed, d) geographic location and e) warranty.

- *Mine the free database research online* - Start with Google. com., although you should consider using other search engines to find the one that gives the best results for your industry. On Google and AltaVista, type in "link: www. whatevercompanyyouwant.com" and you will get link listing to a specific company's Web site. This identifies companies that have an interest in your market sector or are doing business with the company you are researching. InvisibleWeb. com is a directory of more than 10,000 databases, archives, and search engines. Use it to research companies, industries, and business publications.

Northern Light conducts searches of industry-focused Web pages, market research, economic analysis, and company reports. It also sells research by the page, so you can buy only the pages you need, instead of having to buy the entire report. Before you pay for information, check whether you can get the same information for free from another site like PR Newswire. Marketresearch.com is another source with a collection of more than 40,000 publications from more than 350 leading research firms.

Enlist the help of your team members, your potential customers, vendors, and others. Though you can do a lot of research on the Internet, talking to key people remains an excellent way to gather market intelligence. Ask your friends to be your eyes and ears in the marketplace, in your industry and even in your current company's reception area.

Capitalizing on internal resources is one of the best ways to acquire competitive intelligence. Leverage the relationships your employees have with other people in your industry, especially their colleagues from previous jobs. For example, recently an aspiring screen writer serving as the key liaison to security consultants for his "day job" employer mentioned his frustration in breaking into the film industry. A week later, thanks to a volunteered contact by the security consultant with a very successful screen writer, the aspiring screen writer received a phone call offering assistance.

- *Establish communications with experts* - Identify individuals within your industry or market and develop a relationship with them. The Web can help you identify experts, but a "blog" is no substitute for a personal relationship. Gaining access to experts helps you keep ahead of published reports. Be sure that you remember to reciprocate with these individuals by sending them interesting information you discover.

Financial Security Analysts are especially helpful for researching public companies. However, they may follow private companies if the companies have potential to become big players in their industries. Use *Nelson's Directory of Investment Research*, available at business libraries, to find names of analysts.

- *Trade or Industry Associations* - They can be very valuable, especially if you want to learn about an industry, and some association membership lists can help you to identify suppliers. Some associations will send you their membership directory, even if you're not a member. Find the names of associations in the *Encyclopedia of Associations*, usually available at public libraries. (Consult the <u>*American Society of Association Executives*</u> for information on associations in a variety of industries.)

- *Journalists* - Go to Bizjournals.com to find local business journals. To find other print publications, consult *The Standard Periodical Directory*, available at public libraries. Call the local paper and ask the business editor who covers the company you are interested in. If there are photos with a story, talk to the photographer, especially if photos were taken inside a manufacturing facility.

Bigger is not necessarily better when it comes to doing market research on your competition. Corporations may have entire departments dedicated to market analysis, but smaller companies may have the speed, drive, and dedication to get it done better and faster. It is doubtful that John Schnatter formally knew that by 1973 American spending for "food prepared away from home" was reaching parity with "food prepared at home." His was an intuitive analysis of a market demand trend that he personally observed while delivering food as a high school and college student. His Papa John's Pizza entered the up-swinging "food prepared away from home" market sector. Thus, look to market trends as a way to get ahead of the competition; to know where the market is going before it gets there. Document your findings by citing experts -- a market expert, market research firm, trade association, or credible journalist.

Business operations – It's not just *what* you're doing in your market sector, but *who* will be doing the business management. In the management section of your business plan, describe your organizational structure and put your team in the best possible light – briefly describing team member attributes and successes. A business plan needs to not only explain what you intend to do; it also needs to explain how you expect to do it, including any technology that is critical to your competitive advantage.

- *Display the organizational structure* - The management structure of a company is what you frequently see as an organizational chart. Use an organizational chart (from a drawing program, or one of the specialized organizational charting software packages available) to present a professional layout. Or, use text layout design to describe the organizational structure in words, without a chart.

Explain how job descriptions work and how the main company functions are divided up. Are your organizational lines drawn clearly? Is the authority properly distributed? Do you have jobs that include responsibility without authority? Do your resources seem proportional with your organizational needs? In other words, does your proposed structure support the accomplishment of the tasks necessary to get the job done?

- *List team members and their backgrounds* - List the most important members of the management team – typically the Chief Executive Officer (CEO), the Chief Operations Officer (COO), the Chief Financial Officer (CFO) and, for innovation-based start-ups, the Chief Technical Officer (CTO). Include summaries of their backgrounds and experience, using them like succinct résumés. Describe their functions within the company. Résumés should be attached to the back of a plan.

- *Discuss your management gaps* - You may have obvious gaps in management, especially in start-up companies, but often even in more established companies. For example, a manufacturing company without a production manager has some explaining to do, and a computer company without service is a "Red Flag." It is far better to define and identify a weakness than to pretend it doesn't exist. Specify where the team is weak because of gaps in coverage of key management functions – as the COO role could be described but a person not employed until needed. How will these weaknesses be corrected? How will the more important gaps be filled?

- *Other Management Team Considerations* - Applicability of management roles depend on your company. However, some questions that should be answered include: a) Do any managers or employees have "non-compete" agreements; b) Who is on your board of directors, and what do these members contribute to the business; c) Who are your major stockholders and what is their role in management of the business; and d) Do you have an advisory board and what is its role?

Technology needs – Every business needs technology – technology simply being "a mechanism employed to achieve a task." Even if your company makes old-fashioned chocolate chip cookies, you'll rely on multiple technologies to handle routine business operations; from maintaining financial records, to processing orders, to staying in contact with suppliers and customers. Also, since technology is central to running a competitive business, you need to specify the a) type, b) function – office or manufacturing, c) initial cost, d) maintenance expense, e) life span and e) critical training associated with technology.

Decisions made about digital technology, such as the choice of your database program, may be costly or cumbersome to change later. When outlining your technology plan, keep in mind how your company might grow or change; trying to choose technology that is flexible enough to grow and change with you. Choose technology that meets your requirements and is simple, rather than overly complex. All those extra "features" may just make your technology (whether it be a software program or a telephone) harder to use.

- *Specialized or "Off the Shelf"* - Some industries have vendors who produce software or hardware tailored to meet industry-specific demands. Your trade association can help you identify vendors of such industry-specific technology, and you can typically find many sources exhibiting at industry trade shows. Although these products may be more expensive than general off-the-shelf software, these tailored products may better suit your company's specific needs, and they're less expensive than having software created specifically for you by a consultant.

Financials – Many people find finances intimidating or tedious; but they are critical. The financial section of a business plan is not the time to add creative flourishes; instead, stick to a conventional approach that bankers and investors can easily follow. The first order is to describe the process to be used in accounting for income and expenses. The second is to tie investor financing to expenses incurred for product development, scale up and production milestones. Third is prognostication. Predicting the future is hard; but making financial projections of company quarterly, annual and multi-year progress is necessary.

Here is how you can avoid some common mistakes – It doesn't matter whether you're applying for your first bank loan or your tenth, or whether you are seeking venture capital or debt financing. Sooner or later, you must prepare a set of financial projections that are credible. Lenders will look for a strong likelihood of repayment; investors will calculate what they think is the value of your company and what it will become. Here are some dos and don'ts for financial modeling:

- Don't provide only an income statement; include a balance sheet and a cash-flow statement. It is understandable that you are focused on sales and net income, but your banker or investors will also want to know how much money you intend to leave in the business as retained earnings and how much additional debt or equity financing you will need to grow the company.

- Do provide a minimum of monthly data for the current year and quarterly or annual data for succeeding years - Many entrepreneurs prepare projections using only monthly or only annual data for the entire three- or five-year period. The financial results of your first year will probably end up being different from your projections, so there's no point in thinking that you can accurately forecast monthly results for the future years. But some business planning may require that you itemize future capital costs and operating expenses on a month by month basis. Only in cases where you may be looking for long-term financing for equipment or real estate is it likely that your stakeholders will want these longer-term projections.

- Don't provide more than three years' worth of projections unless your lender or investor has asked for more. This is an extension of the less-is-more concept – under promise and over deliver. Realistically, it is a stretch to accurately forecast your company's sales or net income for even three years.

- Don't provide more than two scenarios in your projections - Loan officers and investors are already drowning in paperwork and multiple projections can easily confuse them. We have seen projections with the following three scenarios: a) base (or likely) case, b) worst case and c) best case. Our advice is that you prepare just the base case and the break-even case. The base case should show what you realistically expect the business to do; the break-even case should show how low sales could go before the business begins runs into difficulty.

- Do ensure that the numbers reconcile - Everybody knows that assets must equal liabilities plus equity, and that the debits and credits all need to add up. But, too often entrepreneurs will simply plug a figure into a slot to make things settle up. If the numbers do not add up from one period to the next, you will need to explain. Even though everyone makes mistakes, this is one you want to avoid because it makes you look like you did not take this aspect of your planning process seriously. Also, if after the mistake is corrected, your company has a smaller potential than you had originally presented, your banker or investor may think you were being intentionally misleading them.

- Do not be too optimistic about sales growth or operating profits - All bankers and investors want to do business with ambitious entrepreneurs, but there's a big difference between a realistic business plan and one that is unlikely to be realized. While it is true that companies that have low revenues can grow their sales quickly in percentage terms, it may not be realistic to assume that your business can double in size every year. Also, entrepreneurs often try to convince investors and stakeholders that as the company grows it will achieve economies of scale and operating margins will improve. If you insist that the economies can be achieved, you should be able to explain your assumptions.

- Do account for interest expense on the income statement if you have debt on your balance sheet If you expect to have an average loan balance outstanding at the end of the year, and you forecasted an average interest rate of six percent, then you need to budget that cost item as annual interest expense. Do not budget less than a realistic amount; this is one line item where you're always better off coming in under budget.

- Don't include every individual line item for each expense, asset, and liability figure - Although your banker or investor will probably be interested in knowing details about sales from major product or service lines, as well as the direct cost of sales associated with them, keep to the basics in other categories. For operating expenses, those would be salaries and payroll taxes, lease and rental expenses, depreciation, amortization, and any other kind of expense that consumes a measurable percent of revenues. Also, do not forget to distinguish the owners' compensation from that of non-owners, particularly if you and your co-owners are drawing above-market salaries as a means of reducing business income taxes. For assets, focus on cash and investments, accounts receivable, inventory, the major categories of fixed assets (including capital-lease assets), and any amounts that may be due from shareholders or affiliated companies. Also, be sure to include any of your intangible assets that you consider material, such as patents or licenses.

• Identifying liabilities is straightforward. You should have *one* line item for all accrued expenses and a line item for each of the following: accounts payable, a revolving line of credit, term loans, capital leases, amounts due to related parties, dividends payable, and income taxes payable. Finally, if your business has deferred revenue (meaning that you collected a cash deposit from your customers before having actually provided the goods or services), add a line for it in liabilities.

• With your projections, do include any assumptions that you used, and be able to explain them - In addition to the income statement, balance sheet, and cash-flow statement, you should provide a one-page summary that explains your assumptions about revenue growth; cost of goods sold; operating expenses; interest expenses; turnover of accounts receivable, inventory, and accounts payable; capital expenditures; dividend policy; and income-tax rates. Also include any ancillary information that has an impact on the financial success of your business. Examples of that might be your projected growth in employee head count and a need for future office or warehouse space requirements.

There are many guidelines available from many different sources for you to use in creating your plan, so we felt that we should include at least one as part of this Chapter. Maricopa Community College in Phoenix Arizona has published the following guideline to assist new entrepreneurs in creating their first business plan:

BUSINESS PLAN GUIDELINES

Your business plan is very important to your success. It represents your "roadmap" toward a successful venture. This set of guidelines does not address every aspect of every possible business plan. You should consider more questions than those that are posed in each section – be sure to ask them – your success often depends on the completeness of your planning process.

Each numbered section below (I, II, III, etc.) should be a page heading, while other underlined items will probably be one to three paragraphs long.

I TITLE PAGE

The Title Page should contain the following items, doubled spaced, horizontal centered, and positioned just above the center of the page:

- Business Name
- Business Address
- Business Telephone
- Owner's Name(s)

II TABLE OF CONTENTS

The Table of Contents should list the title of each section of the document and indicate the page number where each is located. It should also list specific support items (appendices) by name. This page will be done last, since it requires the entire document as input. It allows the reader to quickly locate specific sections.

III BUSINESS CONCEPT OR EXECUTIVE SUMMARY

The Business Concept, or Executive Summary, should be a one-page explanation of what your business is, and its competitive advantage. Provide a clear description of the industry in which you are competing, and a precise explanation of you business's unique qualities that set your venture apart form others who are competing for the same customers.

Your explanation should answer these questions:

- In what general market does your business compete?
- What does your business do?

- What quality image will it have?

- In what price range will it compete?

- What volume of sales is expected?

- What customer needs are met?

- What makes it unique form the competition?

IV Marketing Plan

This section should contain a narrative description of the following five factors:

A. Industry Description and Outlook

1) Describe your primary industry.

2) Describe the size of the industry; historically and currently.

What is the total expected market volume?

What is the growth potential in five years? In ten years?

3) Describe your industry characteristics and trends; historically and currently

What benefits are sought by the market that your product/service will satisfy?

Where in you industry is its life cycle?

Future potential?

4) Describe your customer base.

Consumers – It is important for you to develop a clear, mental picture of your ideal customer. Describe your potential customers using the following factors:

Age, Sex, Income Level, Education Level, Geographic Location, Occupational Area, Leisure Interests, Buying Habits, Goals and Aspirations

Business – If you intend to provide a product or service to another business, your description would include:

Type of business (service, retail, manufacturing, etc.), Size of business, priority placed on purchasing your product, projected image of the business markets that the business services, trade publications read by the business, trade organizations memberships of the business

B. Competition:

A description of your competition should answer the following questions:

Who are you major competitors?

Why are they successful?

What substitutes are there for your product?

What impact do these substitutes have on your sales?

What distinctive difference separated you from your competitors ?

Why should customers leave your competitors to choose your product?

What market share do you expect to get? Why?

C. Location Analysis:

Describe your business location and how it will enhance the sale of your product or service. Your description should answer the following questions:

What strategic advantages do you have at this location?

Is there opportunity for expansion?

What are the neighboring businesses?

Do they complement/detract form yours?

Are building renovations needed? Cost?

Is there a limiting zoning classification?

Is the neighborhood stable, changing, improving, deteriorating?

William R. Cobb and M. L. Johnson, Ed.D, Ph.D.

How is customer access, parking, etc.?

NOTE: Include in the appendix a photograph of the building, a drawing of the immediate area showing road access and identity of adjoining businesses, and a drawing of the floor plan of your business.

D. Price Determination

A description of the price structure for your product or service will answer the following questions:

What price will you set for your products or services?

How does your price compare with the competition's?

Why should customers pay your price?

What image (perception) will be projected by this price points?

What advantages do your customers get that are included in the price?

Will you offer credit terms?

E. Marketing Approach

A description of your marketing effort should answer the following questions:

Were the preliminary or test market results favorable?

How does your product or service satisfy your customers' needs and wants?

How will your image be clearly and consistently conveyed to potential buyers?

Which media are most suitable? Why?

How will you evaluate the effectiveness of each advertising and promotional effort?

How will a sales staff be used? Evaluated? Incentives?

V. MANAGEMENT OR OPERATIONAL PLAN

This section contains a description of who will run the business and how they will do it, including the following:

A. Management Team

Your description of how the business will be managed will answer the following questions:

> What management background do you have?
>
> What is your business track record?
>
> How is the education and/or experience of key people related to this type of business?
>
> What legal form (corporation, partnership, proprietorship, etc.)?
>
> Who does what? Who reports to whom?
>
> What other resources (accountant, lawyer, etc.) will be used?
>
> (NOTE: Include in the appendix the resumes for key personnel.)

B. Employee Relations

Your description of your methods for hiring, training, compensating and communicating with your staff will answer these questions:

> What are your personnel needs now? In the future?
>
> What skills will be required?
>
> How will you go about hiring and training?
>
> What salary and benefits will be provided?
>
> How will you determine and communicate wage increases to employees?
>
> How will personnel policies be provided to your employees?

C. Operational Controls

Your description of the kinds of management systems and how they will be used will answer these questions:

What is your production capacity?

What operating advantages do you have? How will you capitalize on them?

What elements are critical to your success? How will you make sure they

are available?

What will be key indicators of success?

How will you monitor these factors?

What hazards do you anticipate for your business? What protection

And / or alternate plans do you have?

What policies will you establish for the operation of your business?

VI. FINANCIAL PLAN

A description of how your business will be financed and how you will maintain a sound financial condition will answer the following questions:

A. Current Funding Requirements

How much money will be needed for start-up?

What will be the sources of start-up capital (debt, equity, etc.)?

What business and personal assets will be pledged as collateral?

B. Use of Funds

How will the money be spent (working capital, debt retirement, capital expenditures, acquisitions, etc.)?

How will borrowed funds make your business more profitable?

C. Long-Range Financial Strategies

How will you liquidate your investors' position?

What terms of repayment are feasible?

What back-up plan will be used if repayment cannot be accomplished as planned?

D. Financial Statements

To support this section, several types of financial statements may be required, such as the following:

Personal Financial Statement of Owner

Business Start-Up Costs

Pro Forma Cash Flow Analysis (expected)

Balance Sheet (actual or proposed)

Income Statement (actual or proposed)

Capital Equipment List

(NOTE: Work sheets can be provided for each of these statements.)

VII. STRATEGIC PLAN

It is very important to include a description of where you want your venture to be in the next few years and how you intend to move toward those goals. This strategic plan should focus on Years 2 through 5 and include descriptions of the following items:

Strengths within your organization

Weaknesses within your organization

Opportunities available to you (and your competitors)

Threats impeding you (and your competitors)

Using the preceding four factors, you should describe strategies that use your strengths to take advantage of opportunities and overcome threats; and strategies to reduce weaknesses and avoid threats to your business. The strategies should identify intermediate goals (yearly) and the marketing, management, and financial resources that will be used to accomplish these goals.

Even with all of this careful planning, it is possible that you could find yourself falling into the same traps of those who have gone before you and struggled with the task of communicating business plans convincingly. Here are the top 10 mistakes that entrepreneurs make when crafting their business plans, offered by Hirai (2010), a business consultant who advises start-up companies on the elements of business-plan writing; including competitive analysis and financial forecasting.

 # 1 Being All Things to All People – You cannot expect a business plan to appeal to every possible audience. With this in mind, try to pick one business model, and to focus on one industry or one problem. Otherwise, you risk spreading yourself too thin, and potentially creating a sprawling plan that makes a bad first impression.

 # 2 Being Boring – If a potential client gets two pages into your plan and is bored, that's a terrible sign. It is important to have the reader interested right from the executive summary on the very first page. And don't neglect your cover page: a well-designed logo never hurts.

 # 3 Measuring the Size of the Market Too Optimistically – Although it may seem impressive if you project vast markets and the potential for huge sums of revenue, outsize financial estimates often appear gimmicky to investors. Big numbers can often make you sound as if you don't know what you're doing or recognize how hard it will be to penetrate your target market. Don't make big promises unless you're absolutely sure you can keep them.

 # 4 Lacking the Confidence to Sell Your Product – In an effort to portray confidence, too many business plans ignore the competition that a new business will face. Few ideas, if any, face zero competition. Even if your concept is completely original, you should take into account forces that compete with your product or service, including different solutions to a problem, different ways that customers might choose to spend their money, and inertia in the marketplace.

 # 5 Repeating Yourself Too Much – Avoid repeating a few catchphrases and a few simple ideas in ten different formulations. Nobody wants to hear the same thing over and over again. Be sure to keep your plan's fundamental message consistent throughout, but employ creative language and appealing imagery to flesh out your ideas.

 # 6 Using Too Much Jargon – Remember that not everyone in business is familiar with cross-industry lingo. If you have a background in a specific industry, this is especially true in science and engineering, try to use simple, specific, and concrete phrases to describe your business. Rely on general terms that most everybody will understand.

 # 7 Not Being Consistent – Eliminate contradictions. Make sure that the information in your plan is consistent. For example, a financial chart deep within the plan does not undermine a fact used in an earlier section. Make absolutely certain that every fact about your industry, the market, and key competitors is accurate and readily verifiable.

 # 8 Failing to Incorporate Feedback – Presenting a business plan about which you have not received feedback is an easy amateur mistake to make. Remember: Presenting to a top investor a draft business plan that contains silly errors or gaps in logic is worse than presenting no plan at all. Try reaching out to a few friendly contacts who have vetted business plans in the past before you begin to share it with qualified potential investors.

 # 9 Taking Too Many Perspectives Into Account – Do not go so overboard in anticipating lines of questioning or identifying possible flaws in your thinking that a reader will have a hard time following the narrative thread. Make sure you address some likely investor objections, but balance the desire to be clear-eyed with the overall objective, which is to make a persuasive pitch.

 # 10 Failing to Acknowledge the Competition – Successful plans come in all shapes and sizes and formats, so don't worry about crafting one that looks and reads exactly like every other plan that's out there. Your goal isn't to fit in; you want your business plan to stand out. Remember: If you create a proposal that expresses your idea and your personality, you will be more comfortable and confident when you are called on to present it.

PRESENTING YOUR BUSINESS PLAN –

Every entrepreneur has to present a business plan to outsiders if he or she is seeking a loan or investment. Obtaining venture capital funding, angel investment or even bank loans for a business is increasingly difficult in a tough economy. Do not let a poor pitch impede your ability to score financing for your business. In fact, it's imperative to have a pitch and presentation that showcases your idea, your potential, your market and your ability to provide investors with a return on their investment.

The business pitch is different than the business plan. But you need to have your plan drafted before you can fine-tune your pitch. According to Berry (1999), president and founder of Palo Alto Software, "People misunderstand that the pitch is a different medium than the plan. They misunderstand that somehow their plan is going to sell the business. The plan is the screenplay for the business. You have to have it before you can put together your pitch. The pitch is a high communication summary of the plan."

Prepare Your Pitch and Presentation – A business pitch is an effort to convince others that you have a great idea for a business. The pitch involves a) summing up your business plan, b) going over your product/service offerings, c) your market, d) product/service benefits to customers, e) your leadership, and f) why you will succeed. Informally, you may have done this a thousand times already. "It can be as simple as your reality check in a one-person business, or agreeing with a spouse or significant other, your team members or your boss" (Berry 1999).

The more formal process of pitching and presenting your plan is usually reserved for an audience of venture capitalists, angel investors, or bank loan officers in an effort to secure a loan or investment for your company. Most of the time, the entrepreneur will make a formal presentation, often with a power point display. The formal presentation is typically followed by a question and answer session. Investors will often mull over the details and, if they decide to consider investing, will perform due diligence on the plan and its financials before turning over any funds.

Know Your Business Plan – The first rule of thumb is to write a business plan and to know that plan inside and out before pitching and presenting to outside investors. The written business plan is often the way to get in the door with investors. If they like your plan, they may invite you to pitch and present. You may get only one chance to present to an investor group. Do not waste it by seeming ill-informed or being unable to answer questions.

Venture capitalists, for example, may have 100 or more business plans piled on the desk at any given time. They only listen to formal pitches and presentations from a handful. Your business plan needs to include the necessary critical components, the business concept, market, management team, financial projections, marketing plan, etc. You should have a hand in drafting the plan if you are the presenter so that you are intimately familiar with all the details. The goal of the business plan is to convince investors that you are worth the risk of investment.

Your pitch and presentation need to build on that theme - "It really has to excite them," says Linda Pinson (2009) *Automate Your Business Plan for Windows® and (2008) Anatomy of a Business Plan* and author of the U.S. Small Business Administration's business plan publication. It must say to that investor: "what's in this for me?' It has to have an overview of what you're asking for and what you're trading for it. Is this a business that looks like it will have fast and sustainable growth and get the returns to the investor that he or she is looking for?"

Determine How Much Funding to Request – The reason an entrepreneur makes a pitch is most often to request funding. But just how much to ask for is often key. "Match your financing goals to reality," Berry (1999) says. "Don't think you're going to get millions in venture capital unless you have a good track record with previous startups, a very strong potential business, and a realistic exit strategy. If you're looking for a few hundred thousand dollars, look into angel investors, seed money investors and/or seed money funds. Understand which investors want high-growth and high-risk strategies, and which will accept lower growth and lower risk."

Many of the decisions by investors are based upon more than just financials. There are intangibles of personal confidence you have convinced them to have in you and the business idea. Your financials are simply validations of what they have come to believe. The present recession is a very difficult time to raise investment capital. One way to prove to investors that you are investment worthy is to show them that you too are investing in the business, by putting in your own capital and being willing to trade equity for proportional financing. Funding requests should always be tied to defensible expense categories, industry standard amounts and progress milestones.

Prepare Your Message – A pitch needs to be prepared in a variety of formats to take advantage of not only the formal pitch and presentation meeting but the informal chance meeting on an airplane or in an elevator. Here are a few types of pitch situations you will need to prepare for:

- *E-mail message and elevator pitch -* Every entrepreneur should have a short, concise speech ready whether they step onto an elevator or prepare to travel on an airplane. You never know who is going to be sharing the ride with you. The key words to keep in mind while crafting this message are: quick, powerful, and condensed. You won't have the investor's attention for long so condense this message. A one-page e-mail and/or a 60-second elevator speech should be sufficient.

- *Summary memo* - This is a lengthier treatment of your elevator pitch. It consists of a 2-5 page memo summarizing the need or want you fill as a business offering, your target market, differentiation, growth prospects, management team, and your financing plan. It's important to emphasize how much money you need from investors, how much of your company ownership you're prepared to give in exchange, and how you're going to turn that back into money for them, including when and how much.

- *Pitch presentation* -This is your more formal pitch presentation that you make to investors. Cover the same elements included in your summary memo and in the executive summary of your business plan. Plan on 20 minutes maximum with no more than 10 to 12 slides, and use pictures and diagrams, not bullet points, to illustrate the points you are making.

Investor Pitch and Presentation Tips – It's important to be versatile and to be able to deliver your pitch in a variety of different media. There are a growing number of businesses using YouTube, Go-to-Meeting or Skype, to deliver their business pitch. Some angel investors review YouTube pitches before scheduling a face-to-face meeting with an entrepreneur. "It's a new world that lets me see the people as they talk about their business and how they manage communication. It gives investors more access to more information faster" (Berry, 1999). Here are five steps to consider when delivering the perfect pitch:

- Be specific and concise. Know what you want to say. Know your business plan. Pick out what matters most.

- Sell yourself. This is the "why me" section. Talk about your skills, background, vision and why you can make it work.

- Sell your offering. What need does your business fill? Why is anyone going to buy your product or service?

- Close the deal. This is where you put your salesman's cap on. Make sure to make a strong finish.

- Nail your delivery. Practice makes perfect. So practice your pitch and presentation in front of family, friends, business associates, etc. and get feedback on how to improve it.

Avoid deadly pitfalls – College students and serial workshop attendees have reached their saturation point with long and boring lectures and computer generated video projections that are read verbatim. They call them "Verbal regurgitation" and "Death by Power Point!"

- Do not memorize your presentation - Know it like the business plan is and old friend and be able to give it fluidly, using different words each time.

- Avoid PowerPoint faux pas - The formal pitch is usually accompanied by a presentation, most often a slideshow, which you should also hand out to attendees at the pitch presentation. Do not load frames with lots of detail; that you will dutifully read! Three lines per frame is standard formatting for non-technical copy.

- Keep in mind "What's in it for the investors" – Emphasize the benefits you offer to specific investors and how that will make your investors money.

Stay Flexible – The text book standard process is that you a) make an elevator speech that produces a request to see your business plan, b) followed by an opportunity to pitch, which ends with c) investors offering you funding. However, the real world is not nearly as orderly as these books suggest. Try to establish a follow up date with the investor; but remember that the relationship is only going to work if it is mutually advantageous. If no chemistry is generated from a presentation, ask for suggestions for business plan improvement. If you have gotten to the business plan presentation phase with investors, they will have done enough homework to render valuable suggestions – suggestions that you need to gratefully receive without defensiveness! It's all part of the learning process.

We wanted to remind entrepreneurs that the real value of the business planning process is that it requires the founder, owner, and stakeholders of the new venture to recognize the critical paths necessary to achieve success and the cost associated with executing each phase of these requirements. Everyone is familiar with Gordon Moore's, (one of the founders of Intel) famous law regarding the incredible rate of development for processing technology: "it advances exponentially every 12 to 18 months." But most of us are not as familiar with his second famous law regarding business development: "Everything takes longer and costs more than you think; but money always runs out on time!" Preparing a credible business plan with a representative financial model will help you to mitigate many of the risks associated with starting you new venture.

Even with careful planning, a good plan can go astray, as occurred with our example for Infinitec Communications. The principles of this company thought that they had covered all the bases, but the environment surrounding their opportunity was changing quickly and dramatically. A great deal can be learned from the thoroughness of their planning discipline, but the need to pay attention to those "substitute products" that can come into your industry niche from new sources is equally important. Infinitec did not anticipate the pending changes within the regulations governing the communications industry. The Federal Communications Commission (FCC) released radio spectrum (bandwidth) to the private sector for commercial use. This resulted in the proliferation of the new wireless technologies that we currently enjoy as it has offered a more mobile and less expensive way to enable access to the public switched telephone network and the Internet.

INFINITEC COMMUNICATIONS BUSINESS PLAN

Business Origin: Infinitec Communications was founded by Dan Carter and Perry Brown, two electronics engineers living in Tulsa, Oklahoma. Their idea was to use new developments in technology to improve digital communications in low traffic environments. They used their personal savings along with some seed capital from local angel investors to launch the venture.

Business Description: Infinitec Communications was created to design, produce and market communications equipment that serves rural regions of the public switched telecommunications network.

Management: In order to build a electronics company capable of producing commercial products, Infinitec needed to raise additional funds. Venture capital partners joining Infinitec felt that they needed to compliment the capabilities of the founders with additional industry talent. The management team that was ultimately selected to bring Infinitec to life included: a CEO with 20 years of telecom industry experience; a Marketing / Sales Vice President with 15 years of distribution experience; a CFO with 10 years of financial reporting experience; an Operations Vice President with 15 years of production and logistical experience. The two founders assumed the roles of CTO, (Chief Technical Officer) and Vice President of product development.

Market Opportunity: During the 1990's, the pace of technology advancement was accelerating rapidly within the telecommunications industry. The policy makers saw that the deployment of digital communications, (the Internet) could have a profound impact on economic development and crafted new regulations that nurtured the introduction of new entrants into the marketplace. This market had previously been occupied by only highly regulated large scale telephone companies, and opening the market to this expansion led to the creation of the "DOT.Com Boom.: The Telecommunications Act of 1996 enabled the formation of new companies and the introduction of newer technologies to accommodate the onslaught of enhanced digital services.

The AT&T Spin offs, (The Regional Bell Operating Companies)

along with the Inter-exchange carriers, (AT&T, MCI, Sprint, etc.) were concentrating their digital network expansion in the top 100 Metropolitan Statistical Areas (MSAs). These highly populated areas accounted for 243.4 million of the U.S. population. Next, these big corporations planned to move into the second 100 MSAs; which represented an additional 39.2 million potential users. Infinitec Communications elected not to focus on these larger carriers, but rather on the smaller carriers in the tier two and tier three cities. These MSAs represented 55.3 million of the population living in more than 700 small cities and towns.

These smaller communities were principally served by local, independently owned telephone operators, rather than the large conglomerates. Infinitec intended to provide these independent operators with the electronic products they needed to help them narrow the "digital divide" that existed between major metropolitan areas that had access to the Internet and the neglected rural communities. The larger equipment providers, Lucent Technologies, Northern Telecom, Cisco and others were all chasing the large telecommunication carriers and were pre-occupied with meeting that demand. Infinitec's strategy was to focus on the independent telephone companies who were being ignored by the larger equipment providers and had special needs for smaller "line size" electronics.

Initial Product Description: Infinitec Communications entered the market by offering a product known to the industry as a "digital loop carrier system." This piece of electronic equipment is found at the very end of the wire-line communications network and is the device that connects the wires to home or business. Infinitec's product was unique because 1) it was offered in smaller line sizes, 24 lines and 48 lines, 2) It contained a software algorithm that allowed compression of a traditional voice call from 64 kilobits to 16 kilobits without noticeable quality derogation, 3) It was able to detect the difference between a "voice" call and an "internet" connection and would only compress the voice call so that the internet call could "pass through" at the higher bandwidth rate. This technology was patented, and considered the company's most valued intellectual property.

Market Plan: Infinitec Communication's analysis of the independent service provider's business practices revealed that these independent telephone operators had an opportunity to access incremental revenue from their existing customers by deploying Infinitec's equipment. For the same capital cost, they could now offer both internet services and traditional telephone voice services. Not only could they provide both, but the cost of the Infinitec product was actually less expensive than their existing equipment choices, (because of the smaller line size options) and the technology was more efficient because of the compression benefit. The added internet connection feature had also improved because the technology within the Infinitec product allowed for "clear channels" of data transmission.

Infinitec did not have an existing relationship with these independent rural telephone operators and needed a channel partner to introduce the products line. They chose Power & Tel, an established distribution firm that was already supplying these telephone companies with wire, cables and connecters. Power & Tel was not providing any of the electronic components necessary to run a network, so there was an opportunity for them to expand their business interest with the Infinitec product. Infinitec and Power & Tel solidified a mutually beneficial distribution arrangement.

Since Power & Tel was not familiar with sophisticated electronic equipment, Infinitec needed to hire sales engineers to compliment Power & Tel's sales efforts. Regional sales engineers were deployed that worked with each of the offices of Power & Tel to address any customer technical questions or concerns. The arrangement worked well for all parties and Infinitec enjoyed rapid product and service acceptance.

Operations: *Infinitec* Communications understood that in order to sustain its revenues and maintain a position within the market that it needed to continue to develop new products and features benefiting its customers. It also knew the value of minimizing as many fixed operating costs as possible to control expenses. The company's operational plans reflected this and included the following major categories:

- Research & Development - dedicated to new product

development and responsible for patenting and licensing technology for the firm

- Contract Manufacturing- arrangements for the supply of components and the production and assembly of circuit boards and finished products

- Warehousing and Fulfillment- logistical support to enable timely shipments of customer orders to various regions around the country

- "Tier Two" Technical Support- a help desk that operators could call into for support of installations and trouble shooting of Infinitec equipment

- General & Administrative Needs- facilities, computer systems, and outsourcing arrangements for administrative services such as payroll processing and employee benefits administration

Financial Model: Infinitec Communications began its life as a development company, and all of its initial employees were engineers and technicians. The cost of this activity was recognized as "cash" expenses, and the first two and one half years of operations consumed cash and produced no revenues. Once the prototypes were validated, and production models were finalized, the company was able to manufacture and sell products to generate cash flow. The ultimate goal of Infinitec was to reach sufficient sales volumes to become attractive to the public equity markets via an Initial Public Offering (IPO).

INFINITEC COMMUNICATIONS PLAN SUMMARY					
Operating Statement	Yr. 1	Yr. 2	Yr.3	Yr.4	Yr.5
Revenues	$ -	$ -	$12,500,000	$36,000,000	$ 72,000,000
Cost of Goods Sold	$ -	$ 350,000	$ 7,250,000	$18,000,000	$ 36,000,000
Gross Margin	$ -	$ (350,000)	$ 5,250,000	$18,000,000	$ 36,000,000

Research & Development	$ 2,250,000	$ 3,500,000	$ 3,750,000	$ 4,000,000	$ 4,350,000
Marketing & Sales	$ -	$ 250,000	$ 2,250,000	$ 6,300,000	$ 12,600,000
Operations	$ -	$ 150,000	$ 1,000,000	$ 1,800,000	$ 3,600,000
General & Administrative	$ 250,000	$ 350,000	$ 550,000	$ 525,000	$ 555,000
Total Operating Expenses	$ 2,500,000	$ 4,250,000	$ 7,550,000	$ 12,625,000	$ 21,105,000
E.B.I.T.D.A.	$(2,500,000)	$(4,600,000)	$(2,300,000)	$ 5,375,000	$ 14,895,000

Footnote- *During this time period more than 200 telecommunication ventures were started and less than ten exist today. The Federal Communications Commission approved the sale of spectrum (radio / wireless communications) for commercial use thereby changing the economics and technical requirements for serving rural environments. Sadly, Infinitec Communications became one of the victims of the "DOT.Com Bust."*

CHAPTER SUMMARY

KEY POINTS

- An industry consumption model is a representation of how value is created and distributed within a given industry structure.

- A business model is a representation of the specific role that your enterprise will play in participating within its industry's consumption model.

- A business plan is a formal statement of a set of business goals, the reasons why they are believed attainable, and the plan for reaching those goals.

- Change is inevitable. There is little doubt that you will shortly have to change, amend, modify, or possibly scrap or abandon your original business plan thoughts altogether. One of the attributes of successful entrepreneurs is flexibility.

- A business plan must contain a minimum of vital components: a business description, executive summary, market analysis, competitive analysis, management and operations, technology plan (if required) and financial projections.

- Ten mistakes to avoid in constructing your plan: a) being all things to all people; b) being dull or boring; c) overestimating your opportunity; d) lack of confidence in your product; e) being repetitious; f) using too much jargon; g) being inconsistent; h) failing to incorporate feedback; i) considering too many perspectives and j) failing to recognize the competition.

- A business presentation or "pitch" consists of an effort to convince others that your idea for a business is a good one.

- Know your business plan and how to say it concisely.

TAKE ACTION NOW

- Study several books on writing business plans and identify the elements that relate to your business sector. Your local public library is a good starting point.

- Perform a market position analysis for your service or product; identifying competitors and your value in the market sector.

- Write a business plan simulation for a company that has recently been successfully launched – identifying product or service, value proposition, competitive positioning, probable financing for A, B and C Rounds, Capitalization Table, Management and launch. For example, there is a great deal of information about Fred Smith's FedEx.

- Start mapping a business plan table of contents for your company – considering the main headings and their contents.

- Write your own business plan and get at least three informed persons to critique it. Do not be defensive if something is not understood; as a reviewer's comments will be far less caustic than those of a potential venture funding source reading an ill prepared document.

- Since you will probably be asking strangers for money, demonstrate that you have accurately researched costs, timelines and projected income.

- Potential investors will ask, "How much skin do you have in the game?" Thus, prepare a list of items and costs that you have invested in the project. Your "sweat equity counts" so put numbers to your hours of work on the project and a reasonable hourly valuation.

- Prepare a 30 second "Elevator Speech!" Your pitch and

presentation need to build on that theme, and needs to be prepared in a variety of formats to take advantage of not only the formal pitch and presentation meeting but the informal chance meeting on an airplane or in an elevator.

REFERENCES:

Alexander, R., Cross, J. S. & Hill, R. M. (1973) *Industrial marketing.* (4ᵗʰEd). Homewood, IL: Richard D. Irwin, Inc.

Berry, T. (1999). How to write a marketing analysis that will really sizzle, *Inc. Magazine*, www.inc.com

Bonoma, T. V. & Garda, R. A. (1983). *Marketing manager's handbook.* Chicago: Dartnell Press.

Hirai, A. (2010). The top 10 mistakes entrepreneurs make when writing a business plan. www.inc.com

Reiss, Robert (2009). Write your own business plan in pencil, *Inc. Magazine*, www.inc.com

Reiss, Robert, Howard Stevenson, Jeffrey Cruikshank (2000), *Low Risk, High Reward,* New York, NY, The Free Press, Publishers

Maricopa Community College, SBDC (2002), 2400 N. Central Ave., Suite 104i Phoenix, AZ

Pinson, Linda. (2008). *Anatomy of a business plan.* Tustin, CA: Out of your Mind …and into the Marketplace, Linda Pinson, Publisher

Pinson, L. (1997). *Automate your business plan: Quick start manual.* Tustin, CA: Out of your Mind…and into the Marketplace.

SUPPLEMENTAL SOURCES

Abrams, R. (2000). *The successful business plan: Secrets and strategies.* Palo Alto, CA: Running "R" Media.

Bronti, P. A. (2000). *Persuasive Projections.* Rockville, MD: Mercury Partners.

Berry, T. (2009). *Hurdle: The book on business planning.* Palo Alto, CA: Palo Alto Software.

Gardner, J. (2001). Competitive intelligence on a shoestring. *Inc. Magazine.* www.inc.com

Gumpert, D. E. (2003). *How to really create a successful business plan.* (4th Ed), Needham, MA: Lauson Publishing Co.

Mansueto Ventures (2010). A presentation at World Trade Center. *Inc. Magazine,* www.inc.com

Reiss, R. (2009). *Bootstrapping 101: How to build your business with limited cash and free outside help.* Boca Raton, FL: R&R.

Reiss, R. (2000). *Low risk, high reward.* New York: Simon & Schuster.

Rule, R. (2004). *Rule's book of business plans for startups* (2nd ED.). Madison, WI: Entrepreneur Press.

Wassermann, E. (2010). How to write a great business plan, *Inc. Magazine,* www.inc.com

CHAPTER FIVE
Find the Money to Finance Your Project

"Money never starts an idea: it is the idea that starts the money"
William J. Cameron

The metaphor used to describe the critical elements of a business start-up is a "three legged stool;" without any one of the legs the stool falls - the business fails. The legs are a) Intellectual property (IP) or the Business concept, b) Financial backing and c) the Management team. The world of business ideas is replete with stories of frustrated inventors who think they can do the engineering, manufacturing, marketing, distribution and financial controlling; "if only I could get the right investors." They either "Don't get it" or "Don't want to hear it;" but, investment money follows the business model and not just the invention. Enterprises, with the inventor as the manager, have a success rate of approximately 10 percent; as opposed to the 70 percent success probability when professional managers run the operation. Money is almost always available for good business ideas; but *big money* is also *smart money,* and it invests in the logic of the business plan and not just in a unique product idea or invention.

Raising adequate financial support is essential for an early stage enterprise (start-up) and there are several sources of funding; each with advantages and disadvantages to the enterprise. The advantage/ disadvantage considerations are typically in terms of getting enough financing to move from the conceptual idea, to the prototype stage, to scale, and to successful commercialization. Accomplishing this while trying to minimize giving up too much operational control and ownership of the company is a formidable challenge. Choosing the wrong financial instruments, such as commercial loans that only move the business idea past the "proof of concept stage," may leave the inventor at risk of bankruptcy and without a clear avenue to commercialization. This is a condition called "the valley of death;" a situation where the start-up dies for lack of funding to move it along. As you continue through this chapter, remember the second generalization by Intel's cofounder, Gordon Moore; "Everything takes longer and costs more than you think; but the money always runs out on time."

All new ventures go though a predictable development cycle, regardless of their size or potential. They all start with an idea or a business concept, they all need some amount of capital to get started, they all require some early stage financing to initiate operations and they require additional financing to grow. Understanding the amount of capital required for each stage is the first step in developing your financial plan. Figure 5.1 shows how increasing amounts of capital is needed as a project progresses through the developmental stages.

Startup Financing Cycle

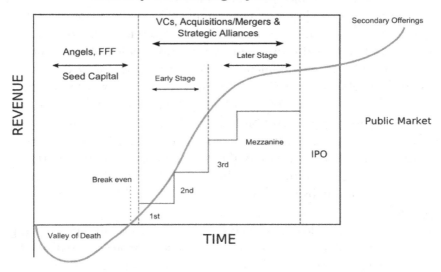

Figure 5.1 Capital needed and its uses during the new venture project stage progression. Image representation from The TAPMI BLOG, T. A. Pai Management Institute

The Kauffman Foundation (Robb, 2008) conducted the largest longitudinal study of new businesses in the world, a cohort of nearly 5000 firms; asking questions on a range of topics including a) the founder's back ground, b) sources of financing, c) type of innovation, d) business strategy and e) profitability and survival outcome. Regarding financing, contrary to widely held beliefs that start-ups rely heavily on family and friends, the research revealed that 75 percent of start-up funding was from equal parts of owner equity and bank loans; underscoring the importance of liquid credit markets to the formation and success of new firms. Kauffman is continuing monitoring these cohort firms and findings will be periodically reported (See www.kauffman.org).

Boot Strapping

Imagine trying to raise both of your feet simultaneously while standing on the floor and pulling up on your boot straps. Impossible, but the task is a metaphor for starting up an enterprise with your own financial resources - "Boot strapping." Lean and hungry inventors are not famous for initially having adequate financial resources. Service start-ups may require little cash and the entrepreneur may be able to "Keep her/his day job" while scaling-up the new project; but business recessions have often hastened these entrepreneurial decisions. For example, Wilson (2009) described how skills and contacts can be leveraged for a quick service industry start.

When Ashish Gadnis was laid off from his position of president of a Minnesota software development company (2004), he managed to launch his new life before even leaving the parking lot. On the way to his car, he ran into the vice president of operations who had also been let go, and the two decided to start their own business. Right after receiving the bad news of his unemployment, Gadnis soon found a business partner, thought up a business name, Forward Hindsight Inc., and registered his new strategy and risk management consulting business before the day was over. In 2008, the Minneapolis-based company made about $3 million in sales.... (pp. 74-75).

For product development projects, you will need to fund prototyping, manufacturing, marketing, distribution and sales. Money is needed to file patents, rent laboratory space for testing, and often for third party validation of your invention or business idea. You need to fund primary market research to determine the product's price points and competitive attributes. Introducing a new product into an economy requires considerable effort and a rational amount of investment is necessary to bring your concept to life.

If you plan to start a consulting business or a service enterprise, you may be able to "bootstrap" it from your home office and realize some short term positive cash flow. But, even these undertakings need cash to get started. The U.S. Small Business Administration reports that it takes an average of $175,000.00 to launch a small business in the United States.

However, if you plan to develop and introduce a new product, you will need a much larger capital investment; with the critical two questions being a) "How much money will be needed?" and b) "From what source(s) will it be obtained?" Your business planning from Chapter Three and Four will help you to answer the first question, and now we need to discuss possible funding sources to answer the second question.

Entrepreneur resources – Money for early stage product development typically comes from the inventor…for she/he is the one who can visualize the product concept and its applications. Inventors can uniquely "see" the form and utility of the product long before there is a prototype to show someone else. Early prototype money typically comes from savings or household discretionary cash flow, and family members may not rejoice at fund diversion for tinkering with new gadgets. But, in the end, it is the entrepreneur, the extended family and friends who will be most willing to support your excitement about the project – long before there is a prototype or business plan to support it.

The budding entrepreneur typically has few desirable personal funding choices; including a) pay-as-you-go from the monthly budget, b) sell something valuable, c) pledge real property or securities, d) take out a second mortgage, e) take a second job, f) float a personal loan or g) pledge a share of the business if it becomes profitable. Charging project items on a credit card is an invitation to disaster; as interest rates will be in double figures and a record of repayment delinquency will jeopardize future rounds of financing. However, each of these options has advantages and disadvantages. For instance, taking a second job could provide needed cash, but it would consume valuable project time and energy. John Schnatter sold his prized Chevy Camero to fund the Papa John's Pizza start-up. Steve Jobs sold his Volkswagen micro-bus and Steve Wozniak sold his Hewlett-Packard scientific calculator to raise $1,300 for Apple Corporation's start-up funds.

Friends and family – Friends and family are frequently the early stage funding sources, as this group is willing to invest in you. For the most part, they will find your ideas interesting; but their faith will be in you as an individual. Your character alone will persuade them to invest in your venture. When considering funding from these sources, it is best to construct your arrangement in the form of a loan. Promissory notes can easily be generated to include interest rates and due dates. Promissory notes eliminate later discussions with friends and family concerning ownership and it limits the amount of their influence over company management. This approach allows you to reserve 100 percent of the ownership for future financing rounds and major funding negotiations.

Regardless of the amount or the source, there needs to be written documentation of the following: a) the amount, b) the proposed use of the money, and c) and the repayment conditions. The typical promissory note structure specifies interest accrual over the life of the note and the final settlement amount at maturity. Occasionally there are provisions for converting to common stock at maturity; but this must be clearly defined in advance of note signing. Friends and family money must present the same formal obligations as financing from professionals at banks, angel investors or venture capitalists.

PUBLIC MONEY SOURCES

There are several sources of public money; some available as grants, as contracts or as cooperative agreements. Almost every public agency has problems to solve that are unique to the respective agency. For example, with the imminent worldwide need for energy there are at least two hot research and development areas of interest to both federal and state governments: a) find ways to make traditional fuels cleaner and more efficient and b) find renewable sources that are economically competitive and efficient. Look for problems to solve that are within your ability level and interest areas.

Some have the idea that business and government should never mix; preferring to have a totally unregulated free market and no government assistance. However, when pirates attacked U.S. merchant ships off the Somalia coast, it was the U.S. Navy that ousted the pirates and saved the private enterprise. Government has a historic role in ensuring fledgling ideas get vetted and supported to create start-up business jobs. For example, in 1958, Russia's launch of Sputnik spurred the U.S. to create the Advanced Research Projects Agency (ARPA); to gain a technological advantage in information networking. Various programs by military branches and the federal National Science Foundation from 1958 to 1988 when the U.S Networking Council approved connecting the National Science Foundation Net (NSFNET) with commercial electronic mail services; and the modern internet was born. During the 1990s the internet grew by 100 percent per year; born from federal research and development and commercialized by private industry.

Federal government – The U.S government has a vested interest in promoting research and development that facilitates economic development, national security, improves infrastructure and supports the nation's human capital. While there are several sources of information, many departments use http://www.grants.gov/ as the grant announcement mode; any business can sign up for these daily alerts. The *Federal Register* is the official news source for federal funding sources; however, it is a cumbersome source to search. Each department has its own website and searching such topics as "Grant Forecast" and "Grant Reports" will give clues as to the types of projects of current interest. The federal government typically makes grants only to businesses – not to individuals; thus, a quick incorporation with your own Secretary of State may be necessary.

Departmental focus areas – Every federal department has research and development areas in which they are interested, along with discretionary money to fund projects that fit their missions. While not particularly brave and frustratingly nearsighted, proof of concept start-up funds, disguised as research and development, are commonly available. To his frustration Chester Carlson was rejected by the Department of Navy before the Battelle Institute and the Haloid Company commercialized his xerography device. However, after commercialization, the Defense Department provided numerous refinement grants in the 1950s, in recognition of the need for a dry copy device that would work in a nuclear environment.

When working with the federal government there may be an intellectual property issue to be considered; as the agency providing the financing may want exclusive use rights for what it is that is being developed. For example, if there is a strategic national security implication for the research, the military, not wanting a device to fall into the hands of an unfriendly nation or international terrorists, may become your only customer. But, if the profit margin is sufficiently high, or every soldier needs one of your products, that single customer may secure your company's future. The father of modern guided rocketry, Robert Hutchins Goddard, was cursorily dismissed by the American military, though he openly launched 34 one and two stage rockets from 1926 to 1941; also patenting 214 devices and improvements; some of which were created under government contract. A successful patent suit against the U.S. Government for patent infringement brought about the largest settlement amount paid up to that time. In the later stages of WW II, the U.S. military awoke to Germany's intercontinental ballistic missiles, only later to find that Dr. Werner von Braun had simply gotten copies of Goddard's patents to create Hitler's rocket program.

Small Business Innovative Research (SBIR) – The SBIR program was established by Congress in 1982 to increase opportunities for small businesses – "Small business" is defined as "Having under 5000 employees" - to a) help meet federal research and development needs, b) increase employment from business start-ups, c) foster innovation research participation by the socially and economically disadvantaged and d) increase private-sector commercialization of priority federal research and development areas. SBIR grants are competitive, meaning not earmarks or subject to one's lobbying efforts; as historically only 15 percent of Phase I proposals are funded and only 30 percent of Phase II proposals are funded. Each department must allocate 2.5 percent of its extramural research and development budget to its SBIR program. The SBIR actually has two forms; the traditional slow SBIR application process and a fast track program for promising technology transfer; meaning a "Faster route to commercialization." The Small Business Technology Transfer (STTR) program is the fast track research to commercialization vehicle.

THE TRADITIONAL **SBIR** FORMAT HAS THREE PHASES:

- Phase I – This is basically the "proof of concept stage" – where you clearly establish that your idea works and validate the feasibility of developing a valuable product. Funding varies with departments – in the $50,000.00 to $100,000.00 range. Typically, Phase I projects are for only six months duration, so once notice is received the project must become a time and effort priority. The completed report must be ready at the end of six months; ready to immediately apply for a Phase II project continuation.

- Phase II – This is the "concept scale up stage" – where you develop the proposed product through sufficient prototyping and testing to validate both product function and potential for commercialization. A preliminary business plan will be required in the proposal. Funding varies by department, but typically ranges from $200,000.00 to $750,000.00 for the two year project time period.

- Phase III – This is the "roll out stage" – where the company is expected to either bootstrap the start-up or seek capitalization financing for commercialization. No federal funds are available for Phase III. However, having the product vetted through two and one half years of development ought to have resulted in a viable product that would be attractive to venture capitalists.

Each department has its own solicitation schedule, submission deadlines, submission format and published guidelines. If in doubt about how to interpret a submission requirement, seek a clarification from the Program Contact identified in the solicitation announcement; as even a slight infraction, such as having one extra line in the proposal "Abstract," will allow the reviewer to disbar the proposal that you spent 100 hours preparing. One important feature of the SBIR program is that any intellectual property created in the research and development project belongs to the business proposing the project. SBIR proposers find the guidelines to be difficult to initially understand, the required proposal format somewhat archaic and the reviewer response time abysmally slow. However, the prospect of having the both a) proof of concept stage and b) product scale up stage funded, with no loss of project equity, may make the risk of time and effort worthwhile.

State government – Many states now realize that both economic development and population stability are dependent upon home-grown innovation. Thus, there may be seed funding for select initiatives such as solar power conversion or promising energy storage (battery) innovations. New energy is a hot topic. Check with the various departments in your state for seed funding opportunities.

Local institutions – Regions and municipalities are becoming aware of the need to support local innovation – in hopes of well paying jobs being generated to sustain the community. Contact the Office of Economic Development in targeted cities. These officers have a vested interest in finding start-up capital for promising innovations.

City/Local – Municipal or local area research and development to support economic development – job creation, can result in a public/private initiative that provides leadership, technical support, financial networking and office space for promising start-ups. For example, the City of Fort Collins, CO initiated a project to connect entrepreneurs, advisors and investors; the Rocky Mountain Innovation Initiative (RMI^2); providing a part time coordinator and office space for prospective start-ups. RMI^2 provides high-potential innovation-based start-ups with facilities access to networking opportunities with seasoned advisors and business planning and management education programs. As a relatively new initiative, RMI^2 has spun-off several successful companies and will shortly build its own state-of-the-art LEED Gold building, complete with office space, bioscience laboratories, conference facilities and other amenities. Contact them at http://www.rmi2.org

U. S. Small Business Administration (SBA) – When planning to start a business or expand an existing business, SBA provides a number of low-interest loan programs designed for small business owners who may have trouble qualifying for traditional bank loans. SBA sources are listed here because, though the loans are somewhat secured by federal resources, individual loans are administered through local institutions. To start the process, visit a local lending institution that participates in SBA programs. Local institution applications are structured to meet SBA requirements, in order to get a Federal guarantee. This guarantee represents the loan portion the SBA will repay to the lender if you default on the loan.

The SBA does not offer grants to start or expand small businesses. Their grant programs generally support non-profit organizations, intermediary lending institutions, and state and local governments in an effort to expand and enhance small business technical and financial assistance. Since its inception in 1953, the SBA, has helped thousands form businesses; with offices in every state, the District of Columbia, the Virgin Islands and Puerto Rico. The SBA can also assist with business planning, financing and other forms of financial and management training. Search http://www. business.gov/ for information, the application forms and the official SBA Loan Application Checklist.

DEBT FINANCING/COMMERCIAL MONEY

Banks are under fiduciary obligations to their depositors and investors to prudently manage funds and they are also regulated by the Federal Reserve Banking System. Because the success rate of innovation-based business start-ups is only 10 percent, this makes unsecured loans from banks improbable. Banks will require some real property collateral as surety of loan repayment, meaning that the borrower must pledge real assets equal to the request in order to secure a loan. Thus, while commercial loans are appropriate for later stage operations, they are not very practical for early stage ventures without pledged surety. Loans, whether from friends and family or commercial institutions, must be paid back with interest; but the advantage of loan arrangements is that they do not require dilution of ownership (equity).

Collateral needed to support leveraged financing is usually something that can be sold easily for the approximate declared value. Collateral pledged to secure business loans must be relatively liquid; with your own venture's start-up corporate stock, valuable baseball cards or antique cars holding little financial leverage as collateral. However, real property, blue chip stocks and certificates of deposit (CD) held at the respective bank are good leverage for a line of credit. For example, Resnik (2009) reported that, "Back when I was building my internet marketing company in 1997, we found ourselves in a cash-flow bind, and I called my banker for help. Thankfully, I owned a $1 million Brooklyn brownstone that I was willing to pledge as collateral. I also had several hundred thousand dollars in an S&P 500 index mutual fund. Otherwise, I doubt Citibank would have given us that $100,000.00 credit line on the strength of our accounts receivable alone – much less the $1 million credit line we were able to get later on" (p. 34).

While collateral is critical to securing commercial loans, both relationships and character are also very important. Choose a local bank and establish a relationship with its loan officers; informing them about your business ideas well before a loan is needed. Heed President Lyndon Johnson's motto, "Make friends before you need them." Lending institutions largely define character in terms of your loan repayment history – your FICO Score. See www.myfico.com/

Commercial financial institutions – Savings and Loan Corporations, regional commercial banks and local banks are potential funding sources. However, their typical strategy is to make as much money as possible with as little risk as necessary. The advantage of commercial money is that loss of corporate equity is minimized and the interest rate on the principal borrowed is somewhat tied to the Prime Rate set by the Federal Open Market Committee (FOMC); with local institutions varying their offered rates in regard to the borrower's credit history and estimates of timely repayment probability. Prime Rate is based upon the discount rate, the interest rate by which banks can borrow money from the Federal Government; rates varying from 1.75 percent in December 1947 to 21.50 percent in December 1980. Building a long term positive relationship with your local banking institution is extremely important; as trust in the borrower is a critical variable. If it is a rental property real estate deal, showing realistic cash flow in the business plan will be critical.

Microlending – The natural progression from corporate story analyses is for individuals and groups to form their own micro-corporations (mini-corps). Perhaps a preface to actually starting the respective mini-corps, would be to study the processes used by the 2006 Nobel Peace Prize winning economist and banker, Dr. Muhammad Yunus - http:// muhammadyunus.org - of Bangladesh. Dr. Yunus completed his doctorate on a Fulbright Scholarship at Vanderbilt University and returned to the Bangladesh Chittagong University to teach economics. During the 1974 famine he got involved in fighting poverty and discovered that even very small loans could make a disproportionate difference to a poor person. For the first loan, and from his own money, he lent to women in the nearby village of Jobra so that they could make bamboo furniture. Beforehand, to buy the raw materials, the women usually took out usurious loans from money lenders and sold the finished items back to the lenders for only a two cent profit; from which they were unable to support their families. Traditional banks were not interested in lending small amounts to poor people, who were considered to be high repayment risks. Yunus established the now very successful Grameen Bank to make micro loans to the working poor, who were without credit, without collateral and without legal contracts. He found that trust is a value that is nourished by the financial transaction. Millions of people are now working their way out of poverty with such mini-loans and Yunus and the Grameen Bank shared the considerable funds of the Nobel Prize. Preview the 2008 film "Slumdog Millionaire" for context reference of the Grameen Bank, as the extreme poverty found in India is comparable to that of Bangladesh.

Analysis of debt financing – Our purpose is to inform you of funding options. Inasmuch as there is great variation in innovator and innovation funding needs, the following analysis of borrowed money is offered.

Advantages of Debt Financing – You keep all of the company equity and:

- Debt financing allows you to have control of your own destiny regarding your business. You do not have investors or partners to answer to and you can make all the decisions. You own all the profit you make.

- If you finance your business using debt, the interest you repay on your loan is tax-deductible. This means that it shields part of your business income from taxes and lowers your tax liability every year. Your interest is usually based on the prime interest rate.

- The lender(s) from whom you borrow money does not share in your profits. All you have to do is make your loan payments in a timely manner.

- You can apply for a Small Business Administration loan that has more favorable terms for small businesses than traditional commercial bank loans.

Disadvantages of Debt Financing – You keep all of the company equity, but:

- The disadvantages of borrowing money for a small business may be great. You may have large loan payments at precisely the time you need funds for start-up costs. If you don't make loan payments on time to credit cards or commercial banks, you can ruin your credit rating and make borrowing in the future difficult or impossible. If you don't make your loan payments on time to family and friends, you can also strain those relationships.

- For a new business, commercial banks may require you to pledge your personal assets before they will give you a loan. If your business goes under, you will lose your personal assets.

- Any time you use debt financing, you are running the risk of bankruptcy. The more debt financing you use, the higher the risk of potential re-payments issues. Calculate the debt-to-equity ratio to determine how much debt your firm can sustain, compared to its equity.

- Some will tell you that if you incorporate your business, your personal assets are safe. Don't be so sure of this. Even if you incorporate, most financial institutions will still require a new business to pledge business or personal assets as collateral for your business loans. You can still lose your personal assets.

PRIVATE MONEY

If the business appears to have potential to either a) create a new market category, b) deliver higher quality in an existing market category or c) reduce the cost of manufacturing or production, the entrepreneur may attract corporate sponsorship for prototype refinement, manufacturing and distribution, in exchange for a portion of the new company's stock. Most start-ups require several financing round, as the invention moves from idea to successful prototype to scale-up manufacturing; termed sequentially as A Round, B Round and C Round financing. Angel investors are usually in A Round funding proof of concept and elementary scale-up. The critical phase between *proof of concept*, and commercialization, where product development, market analysis and manufacturing scale-up financing is needed, is often called "the valley of death;" as many projects die here without the next round of B financing. For example, Chester F. Carlson was granted a patent for his process to print dry paper copies in 1942, but struggled for decades to attract investor interest in refining his prototypes and scale-up manufacturing. The idea nearly died – several times. He was turned down for financing by more than twenty companies and the U.S. Department of Navy; even being dismissed by the National Inventor's Council. Fortunately, in 1944, the Battelle Memorial Institute sponsored Carlson's product refinement through a third party manufacturer and distributor, the Haloid Company that was later re-named the Xerox Corporation. With billions of dry paper copies being made daily worldwide, Carlson's long derided idea has turned into one of the most profitable inventions in history.

Corporation internal funding – The business world is moving too fast for any company to successfully rely on the type and quality of existing services and products. Seventy percent of executives surveyed said that innovation is a top priority and corporations should focus their efforts on innovation around what they do best (Meyers, 2009). Maintaining focus on product innovation is critical, especially in the high tech market sector.

For example, Palm helped originate the hand held computer market in the 1990s, but was shuffled around with purchase by U.S. Robotics, 3Com Corporation before it was spun off as an independent in 2000. During these transitions product development suffered and Apple Inc.'s iPhone took most of the market. Jon Rubinstein, (Metz, 2010) head of the smart phone maker, Palm, described the scenario as follows:

> "… the company's attempt to turnaround – which ended earlier this year when it was bought by Hewlett-Packard for $1.8 billion in cash – was thwarted by competitors that simply moved too quickly."

Palm Inc., a pioneer in the smart-phone market fell behind in recent years, had many of the necessary elements for success when it launched its fresh operating software, webOS, and accompanying Pre and Pixi smart-phones in 2009. Still, the world moved faster than they expected and they ran out of time (B2).

The intrapreneur – In addition to standard R&D department activities some companies establish a corporate culture of encouraging employees to take direct responsibility for creating an idea and moving it through concept validation by assertive risk-taking and innovation. For example, Google Inc. encourages its engineers to spend one day per week (20 percent of their time) on projects that interest them and have no connection to regular assignments; resulting in Gmail, Google News, Orkut and AdSense. Google estimates that half of its new product launches come directly from Innovation Time Off. The advantage of inside entrepreneurism is that the company financially supports the employee's product idea. However, carefully asses your corporate culture; for many profitable employee business ideas have been commandeered by corporations.

Spin-out initiatives – A spin-out is a legal action where the company split off sections of itself as separate businesses. A new firm is formed when an employee or team leaves to develop an independent start-up - when the new business idea is outside of the perceived corporate mission or when the parent company sees potential profitability in the separation. The spin-out innovator benefits because product development costs, legal services and office space are covered prior to the legal split. For example, Agilent Technologies was spun-out of Hewlett-Packard in 1999 and HP stockholders were given shares of the new company.

Angel investors – Angel investors provide early-stage financing to get IP through the concept validation and business start-up phases. The advantage of working with angel investors is that financing is available when the risk of project failure is the highest. Angels are willing to share the risk, but, require both a substantial part of company equity (shares) and an understood exit strategy; usually within 3 – 5 years. They will normally be seeking an exit event that will reward them with 15 – 100 times their initial investment.

If an inventor has established a track record of start-up success, angel investors may finance the project based only upon a product idea; before proof of concept is clearly established. These angel individuals typically have a net worth exceeding $5 million and will often use limited liability companies to make their investments. Angel individuals, angel groups or angel networks, specifically focus on market areas – like "renewable energy" - to reduce risks by establishing product sector expertise. Angel investors are often entrepreneurs who have done exceptionally well with their own business start-up and are willing to help someone else get started.

An internet search of "angel investors" produced some 669,000 citations; varying from angel investor groups and matchmaker services to a region by region directory of angel networks. An internet search for "seed stage venture funds" yielded some 124,000 items. Corporate descriptors of seed stage funders included "We're looking to invest in extraordinary entrepreneurs who have the ability to build great teams and great companies." Note: This descriptor emphasized entrepreneurial team building and company building skills rather than simply identifying high potential intellectual property. Three seed stage venture/angel groups cited in the search that request project submissions include:

- Garage Technology Ventures – http://www.garage.com

- First Round Capital – http://www.firstround.com/

- Joystick Labs – http://games.venturebeat.com/

Angel investors also tend to seek smaller deals, prefer to invest in risky, early-stage enterprises and invest in practically all industry sectors. Additionally, many desire a small amount of control in their invested firms and tend to avoid follow-on investments. Some angel investors are truly enthusiastic about investing to promote local economic development; while others are only concerned about monetary gain. It is critical that you are aware of these different motivations in order to make an informed decision. See Benjamin and Margulis (2000) for more leads.

Analysis of angel investor funding – Bringing investor funding into your project is much like getting married; as there must be a good relationship between all parties at the start. Additionally, consider the legal agreements defining the relationship as a prenuptial agreement.

Advantages of angel investment – You give up some of the corporate equity to get operating capital and:

- It can provide the needed capital for a startup. According to the Center for Venture Research at the University of New Hampshire, nearly 2/3 of funding for new enterprises is obtained from angel investors. Therefore, angel investor capital can provide a great source of funding for new businesses that have a high potential for growth

- Ability to raise capital in small amounts. Most early-stage ventures require small amounts of money, typically less than $500,000. Angel investors can provide this needed amount, using their own personal funds for the investment.

- Flexible business agreements - Angel investors have a more informal investment criteria compared to the traditional financial lenders, including banks and venture capitalists because they are investing their own money.

- Can often bring forth vast knowledge and experience to a new company - Many angel investors were once entrepreneurs themselves and have founded several successful companies under their leadership; therefore, they will not only provide the needed capital that entrepreneurs need but they can also offer desired support, expertise, and contacts in making a business grow.

- Involved in high risk investments - An angel investor's capital in a new business is considered to be a high-risk investment since the new company has not yet established a solid track record of success. Despite the fact that most new businesses fail in their initial years, angel investors tend to be quite optimistic about their investment choices and often request a large amount of returns to counterbalance the risk.

- Does not require high monthly fees - Another benefit from raising angel capital is that there are no outstanding payment rates such as the ones that bank loans and credit cards require.

- Community involvement- Many angel investors choose to invest locally. Many angel investors take pride in using their expertise and in giving back to their community. These are the angel investors who look beyond monetary return.

- Angels are located everywhere, in practically all industries - Today, angel investors can be found everywhere, not just in traditional financial centers and districts. They also invest in nearly all markets worldwide. The majority of them are involved in industry-specific investments, according to the level of their expertise.

The disadvantages of angel investing – You give up a portion of company equity and get operating capital, but:

- Angels rarely make follow-on investments - The reason why most angel investors are less likely to make second round follow-on investments is because of the risk associated with losing even more money when reinvesting in an unsuccessful company

- They can actually be deceptive - While the majority of angel investors truly look beyond the promise of monetary return, there are a few angel investors who are greedy and motivated by money rather than in promoting the good of the firm. These angel investors tend to be less patient with new entrepreneurs and do not provide any mentoring or guidance during a company's early stage of development.

- Can be costly - In exchange for providing the needed startup capital for a new company, many angel investors often require a certain percentage of stake in a company, starting at 10% to 20% or more, and they expect a large ROI from their exit.

- Active company involvement can lead to problems - Each level of company involvement varies from investor to investor; however, it is not uncommon for an angel investor to have a certain amount of control in running a company. Another problem that may arise is the angel investor's lack of industry experience. This limited knowledge adds very little value to a company's success. That is why entrepreneurs should only seek angel investors with proven experience in their industry.

- Do not have national recognition - While there are well-documented directories of venture capital firms available, there is no national register for angel investors. They remain hidden and mysterious; choosing to do so in order to have a degree of separation from entrepreneurs, who may pester them with their business plans and telephone calls.

There are pros and cons in angel investing, yet despite these differences, the advantages seem to considerably outweigh the disadvantages. Some benefits lie in the unique characteristics of angel investors and their added value to a company. They are also geographically dispersed and can provide the amount of needed funding that most startups may require.

Venture Capital *(VC)* – Venture capital has enabled the U.S. to support its entrepreneurial talent by turning ideas and basic science into products and services that are the envy of the world. Venture capital funds the building of companies from the simplest form – perhaps just the entrepreneur's business idea – to established mature corporations. Venture capital firms are managed by institutional professionals who use risk capital to support innovative and promising companies. Venture capital funds new ideas that, because of failure risk, could not be financed with traditional bank loans – projects that typically require five to eight years for successful launch.

Venture capital is unique as an institutional investor class. When an investment is made in a business venture, it is an equity investment in a company whose stock is essentially illiquid and worthless until successful launch as long as five to eight years later. Venture capital firms can arrange for follow-on investment to provide additional funding as the company grows – as shown in Figure 5.1 These rounds typically occur at scheduled intervals as development milestones are reached; with the allocation of shares to investors and the management team being based on a stipulated valuation. But, until a venture is acquired, goes public or produces revenue dividends, the company stock is not easily sold or liquidated. .

Typically, for every 100 business plans submitted to a venture capital firm, only 10 get a serious look and only one gets funded. The investment firm looks at the management team, the concept and the marketplace; looking for a fit with the fund's objectives, the value added potential for the firm and the total amount of capital needed to build a successful business. In the present environment, the business concept must address global markets, have superb scalability, be successful in a reasonable time frame and be truly innovative. A concept that only promises to a 10 to 20 percent improvement over existing competitors will hardly get a serious consideration.

Many currently funded technologies have potential to be truly disruptive and do not lend themselves to being embraced by established companies whose products would be threatened. Also, with the increased pressure on publicly traded companies to show positive quarterly results, larger corporations tend to reduce R&D spending and innovation funding. Many highly talented teams now seek institutional venture capital when their ideas are rejected by their companies.

Until the second half of the 20th Century, private equity investing was the exclusive domain of wealthy individuals or families. Until after WW II aspiring investors had few vehicles to pool their money for moderate risks that potentially could return far more than the typical single digit interest from bank deposits. George Doriot, former dean of Harvard University Business School, and others, founded American Research and Development Corporation (ARDC) and pooled small investor money of $70,000.00 to invest in the start-up Digital Equipment Corporation (DEC) in 1957. DEC's initial public offering (IPO) to other investors through the New York Stock Exchange in 1958 yielded a return of over 500 percent of initial investment and an annual rate of return of 101 percent.

Presently, venture capital funds invest $ billions annually in projects that have passed the proof of concept and elementary scale-up validation phases. These start-ups are ready to begin serious manufacturing, marketing, distribution and sales. For major financial support of a start-up, VCs will typically want a large portion of company equity, a position on the Board of Directors and selection rights of the Chief Executive Officer (CEO). If the start-up is being spearheaded by an inventor with high technical skill and little management experience, the VC Group will probably insist on forming its own management team.

In general, business resources that are provided by venture capital firms who have taken an equity position in a start up company can be invaluable to the success of the company. Many start-up firms that are able to secure venture capital are able to thrive and become giants in their industries. The following table represents a few of the better known larger success stories that attribute their beginnings to venture capital funding.

VENTURE CAPITAL BACKED COMPANIES
KNOWN FOR INNOVATIVE BUSINESS MODELS
EMPLOYMENT AT IPO AND NOW

Company	As of IPO	Current	# Change
The Home Depot	650	331,000	330,350
Starbucks Corporation	2,521	176,000	173,479
Staples	1,693	75,588	73,895
Whole Foods Market, Inc.	2,350	52,900	50,550
eBay	138	15,500	15,362

VENTURE CAPITAL BACKED COMPANIES
KNOWN FOR INNOVATIVE TECHNOLOGY AND PRODUCTS
EMPLOYMENT AT IPO AND NOW

Company	As of IPO	Current	# Change
Microsoft	1,153	91,000	89,847
Intel Corporation	460	86,300	85,840
Medtronic, Inc.	1,287	40,000	38,713
Apple Inc.	1,015	35,100	34,085
Google	3,021	16,805	13,784
JetBlue	4,011	11,632	7,621

Source: IHS Global Insight. Data is FY 2007 Year End Data. Reported by the National Venture Capital Association

An internet search of "venture capital" yielded some 17,000,000 entries; ranging from the National Venture Capital Association, a Directory of Venture Capital Firms to a listing of the Top 100 Venture Capital Firms. Information sources about venture financing and venture capital firms include:

- National Venture Capital Association (www.nvca.org) is comprised of more than 400 member firms, and is the premier trade association representing the U.S venture capital industry. NVCA's mission is to foster greater understanding of the importance of venture capital to the U.S economy, to support innovation and entrepreneurial activity. The NVCA represents the public policy interests of the venture capital community, strives to maintain high professional standards, provides reliable industry data, sponsors professional development and facilitates member interaction.

- Venture Wire Alert (djnewsletters@dowjones.com) is an update service provided by Dow Jones Company; the same group that calculates the daily Dow Jones Average. Their daily updates, *Dow Jones Venture Capital Alert* delivered electronically as "Dow Jones Venture Wire," mainly cover industry trends, regulatory actions and financial deals made by corporations and venture capital groups. These email updates include a summary of significant financial events, planned IPOs and "Corporate Personnel Changes." The service is free by request, though the offer is for several weeks of free trial and the following subscription offer is for several hundred dollars. However, at the end of the trial period they keep sending the daily summaries.

- Price Waterhouse Coopers *MoneyTree Report* (www.pwcmoneytree.com) is a quarterly study of venture capital activity in the U.S. Price Waterhouse Coopers collaborates with the NVCA to analyze data from Thomson Reuters to produce industry endorsed reports. The *MoneyTree Report* is the definitive information source for both funding amounts and funding sources. *MoneyTree* is a staple for the financial community, entrepreneurs, government policy makers and the worldwide business press.

- Stanford Center for Entrepreneurial Studies (http://www.gsb. stanford.edu) is an initiative of the Graduate School of Business. While most of the information is for high level venture capital and management, there are numerous links to real world problems, like a) "What should an executive summary include?" "What topics should be included in the business plan?" and "What are common reasons startup plans are rejected?" Some videos are available online from seminars held by the Center.

- Rockies Venture Club (www.rockiesventureclub.org) is a regional venture capital clearing house that tries to stimulate economic development by connecting innovators with startup capital.

VENTURE CAPITAL GROUP EXAMPLE

Rockies Venture Club – communications@rockiesventureclub.org/ For over 25 years the Rockies Venture Club (RVC) has helped create Colorado success stories. For example, TerraLUX is a Colorado-based company that specializes in accelerating the adoption of LED-based solid state lighting. They apply their patented technologies in thermals, optics and controls to a variety of applications by way of standard and portable devices, light engines and embedded light modules. The key to its 1.8 inch TLM-R16 LED module's abilities is an integrated micro-processor-based drive technology that allows smooth dimming operation with existing low voltage magnetic or electric halogen transformers.

For the first time, lighting fixture manufacturers have a complete, high performance, cost effective LED module option that performs as required by lighting designers; and is simple and cost-effective to use. By constantly monitoring and managing LED temperatures, LEDSenseTM ensures that the module will deliver long-term lumen maintenance; keeping LED and other component temperatures within the manufacturers prescribed operating range without having to build in thermal headroom. Regardless of fixture position, type of fixture or environmental temperature, designers and users can be assured that the maximum amount to light is being delivered while preserving long-term performance.

Founded in 2003 by Dr. Tony Catalano, TerraLUX initially targeted the portable device market – flashlights – and grew from that foundation into the general lighting market. Initially bootstrapped, early seed capital came from the Denver, CO and Austin, TX Access Venture

---

Partners (www.accessvp.com), an early stage venture capital fund investing in clean technology, data integrity and new media companies that have exceptional management teams capable of success in world markets. Recent $5.6 million A Round venture capital financing was led by the Zurich, Switzerland Emerald Technology Ventures (www.emerald-ventures.com), a global leader in clean tech venture capital; advanced technology for water, energy and materials. Emerald manages five venture capital portfolio funds valued at $440 million.

In general, formal documents are intended to reflect current practices and customs, and venture funds do have some differences between the West Coast and East Coast firms in a number of their practices. However, one of our goals is to introduce industry "best practices," and inform you of both the pros and the cons of your different financing options. It is important that you carefully review all agreements you enter into with these investment groups and have them reviewed by an attorney as well. Typically, venture capital financing documents will include the following:

- Term Sheet – summarizes the terms and conditions under which the venture capital firm is willing to make an investment, including "pre-money" evaluation

- Stock Purchase Agreement - sets forth the basic terms of the purchase and sale of the preferred stock to the investors (such as the purchase price, closing date, conditions to closing) and identifies the other financing documents.

- Certificate Of Incorporation - The Certificate of Incorporation is a key document produced in connection with a venture capital portfolio investment. Among other things, the Corporation's Certificate of Incorporation establishes the rights, preferences, privileges and restrictions of each class and series of the Corporation's stock. If you already have a similar document, it is not uncommon for the venture capital investor to want to amend it to suite their investment requirements.

- Investor Rights Agreement - An Investors' Rights Agreement can cover many different subjects. The most frequent are: information rights, registration rights, contractual "rights of first offer" or" preemptive" rights (i.e., the right to purchase securities in subsequent equity financings conducted by the Company), and various post-closing covenants of the Company.

- Voting Agreement – A voting agreement is evidence of an understanding between the original owners of the company and the new venture capital investors as to who can represent what stockholder voting rights and for what purpose. Typically the new investors will want representation on the governing board of the company and be able to influence decision concerning the future management of their investment.

- Right of First Refusal and Co-Sale Agreement – This document is provided to insure that in the event of a transfer of ownership, all of the existing "key holders" of the company's stock would have the right to participate first ins such transactions, and any sale or transfer of company stock to others without their knowledge and consent would be prohibited.

- Management Rights Letter – this is an agreement between the management of the company and the venture capital investors they provides the investors with the right to consult with and advise management on issues effecting the performance of the company. It provides the right to examine the books and records of the firm and any other highly confidential information they may need to.

- Indemnification Agreement - Some companies choose to provide mandatory indemnification for directors (i.e., the company is required to indemnify a director if the applicable conditions are met) and discretionary indemnification for officers (i.e., indemnification is at the discretion of the company even if the applicable conditions are met). Such an agreement is normally accompanied with an indemnification insurance policy referred to as "D & O Insurance," which defends Directors and Officers from frivolous law suits.

- Legal Opinions – These accompany opinions reflect the due diligence performed by the respective attorneys confirming the existence of the company, its ownership, and any public filings or patents that are relevant to the valuation of the transaction.

Analysis of venture capital funding – To reiterate the relationship caveat described earlier, you may not want the money offered if the conditions are not suitable for you. The following analyses provide bases for negotiations and decisions. See Martel (2010) for details on pros and cons.

Advantages of venture capital funding = There are some benefits to venture capital funding. In many cases, the company that is able to secure venture capital funds can receive services that may include:

- Business Consultations - Many venture capital firms have consultants on their staffs that are well versed in specific markets. This can help a start up firm avoid many of the pitfalls that are often associated with start-up business ventures.

- Management Consultations - Unfortunately, not all entrepreneurs are good business managers. Since venture capital firms almost always require a percentage of equity in the start-up firm, they likely will have a say in how the firm is managed. For the non-management expert, this can be a significant benefit.

- Human Resources - In terms of finding the best talent for start up firms, venture capital firms often provide consultants who are specialists in hiring. This can help a start up firm avoid the pitfalls of hiring the wrong people for their company.

- Additional Resources - Starting a new business is fraught with concerns about legal matters, payroll matters, and tax issues. It is not unusual for a venture capital firm to take an interest in providing these resources since they have a vested interest in the success of the company.

The disadvantages to venture capital financing – The following are only a few of the possible problems that an entrepreneur could face when they secure venture capital funding. Securing venture capital typically means that you have to give up something in exchange. In fact, there are some things that venture capital firms may ask for that may surprise you. These include:

- Management Position - In many cases, a venture capital firm will want to add a member of their team to the start up company's management team. This is generally to ensure that the company can be successful, though this can also create internal problems.

- Equity Position - Most venture capital firms require that the company give up an equity position to them in return for their funding. This amount is not small, in many cases it can be as much as 60 percent, or more, of the equity in the company. In effect, this means that the entrepreneur is no longer controlling their business; it is now being controlled by the venture capital firm.

- Decision Making - One of the biggest problems that many entrepreneurs face when they agree to accept venture capital is that they often are giving up many key decisions in how their company will operate. Venture capital firms that have taken an equity position want a "seat at the table" when any major decision is made that affects their investment and they often have the power to override management decisions.

- Business Plans - When a business plan is written and submitted for financing considerations, most finance companies will agree to sign a non-disclosure agreement. This is not the case in most venture capital firms. Venture capital firms will nearly always refuse to sign a non-disclosure agreement due to the legal ramifications of doing so. This can put ideas from an entrepreneur at risk.

- Funding Plan - If an entrepreneur writes their business plan and determines that they need $500,000 to get the business launched, they may be lulled into thinking that these funds will come up front. This is simply not the case. Venture capital firms almost always set goals and milestones for releasing funds. Funding from venture capital firms is typically done in stages with an eye on the expansion of the business.

Strategic investors – Seventy percent of executives surveyed said that innovation is a top priority and corporations should focus their efforts on innovation around what they do best (Meyers, 2009). Maintaining focus on product innovation is critical, especially in the high tech market sector. For example, as we explained earlier in this chapter, Palm helped originate the hand held computer market in the 1990s, but was shuffled around with purchase by U.S. Robotics, 3Com Corporation and Apple Inc.'s iPhone took most of the market.

If your business appears to have the potential to a) create a new market category, b) deliver a higher quality product within an existing market category or c) reduce the cost of production, you may be able to attract corporate sponsorship in exchange for a portion of the your company's stock. Such investments are the lifeblood of the venture capital industry and an increasingly popular tool for large companies. Some of these larger corporations even have their own venture capital entities, known as corporate venture capital, or CVC, arms. Perhaps the most famous is Intel Capital, which has invested $7.5 billion in about 1,000 companies since 1991, according to the company. While strategic investments come in many forms, there are some generalities. For example, a strategic investment is often a minority stake and part of a syndicate of other investors (usually venture capitalists).

A strategic investment can also validate a new technology. One example is INSIDE Secure, which was attempting to build microprocessors for the emerging industry of near-field communication. As a result, the company snagged strategic investments from Samsung Ventures America, Nokia Growth Partners, and Motorola Ventures. A strategic investment may also provide access to substantial infrastructure. For instance, Intel Capital encourages networking among its portfolio companies and holds events and workshops across the world. Another benefit is getting access to technology and product road maps.

A strategic investor might ask for a so-called "right of first refusal" (ROFR) for an acquisition. Simply put, the fear is that another competitor will make an offer for your company. If you agree to this, it means it will be difficult to sell the company to anyone other than the strategic investor. In other words, this could ultimately reduce the valuation of a potential sale. So, if you want to get the best return for your company's shareholders, it's desirable that you get rid of the ROFR clause. A strategic investment can be enormously beneficial, especially if you need to conquer a new market. It requires lots of communication and planning and time, but it can definitely be worth it for the long-term value of your company.

Private placement financing – If your company is seeking investment capital from $50,000 to $10,000,000 from individual investors, then you will definitely benefit from the structure of a Securities and Exchange Commission Regulation D private equity offering. From simple deals like seed capital for opening a coffee shop to million dollar raises for high growth companies, these programs will give you a legal, practical method of raising capital from private investors.

A private placement memorandum (PPM) is the document that discloses everything the investor needs to know to make an informed investment decision about your company. This includes: the offering structure, the share structure of the company, SEC disclosures about the shares being purchased, company information, information on company operations, risks involved with the investment, management information, use of proceeds, information on certain transactions that could affect the investor, and investor suitability data. The PPM also includes the subscription agreement which is the actual "sales contract" for the shares of stock. This is the document that the investor will sign and send in with their investment funds.

The PPM is very important because it provides the investor with all of the prescribed data they will need to make an investment decision and includes the actual documentation to effect the investment transaction. PPM's are designed as a stand-alone document - meaning that there need not be other information presented to the investor for them to make an accurate investment decision. Many companies will, however, attach their business plans to the PPM as supporting documentation. This is an acceptable practice so long as the information in the business plan properly corresponds with the information in the PPM and that the investor is made aware that the business plan alone does not constitute an offer to sell securities - only the PPM can make that offer.

A private placement arrangement may also enable you to hand-pick investors with compatible goals and interests. Since the investors are likely to be sophisticated business people, it may be possible for the company to structure more complex and confidential transactions. If the investors are themselves entrepreneurs, they may be able to offer valuable assistance to the company's management.

There are also a few disadvantages associated with private placements of securities. Suitable investors may be difficult to locate, and the ones you do locate may have limited funds to invest. In addition, privately placed securities are often sold at a deep discount below their market value. Companies that undertake a private placement may also have to relinquish more equity because investors will want compensation for taking a greater risk and assuming an illiquid position during the start up phase. Finally, it can be difficult to arrange private placement offerings in multiple states.

The SEC has formerly placed many restrictions on private placement transactions. For example, such offerings can only be made to a limited number of investors, and the offeror is required to establish strict criteria for each investor to meet. Furthermore, the SEC requires private placement of securities to be made only to "sophisticated investors"— those capable of evaluating the merits and understanding the risks associated with the investment. Finally, stock sold through private offerings could not be advertised to the public and can only be resold under certain circumstances.

In 1992, the SEC eliminated many of the more onerous restrictions in order to make it easier for small companies to raise capital through private placements of securities. The rules now allow companies to promote their private placement offerings more broadly and to sell the stock to a greater number of buyers. It is also easier for investors now to resell such securities. Although the SEC restrictions on private placements were relaxed, it is nonetheless important for small business owners to understand the various federal and state laws affecting such transactions and to take the appropriate procedural steps. It may be helpful to assemble a team of qualified legal and accounting professionals before attempting to undertake a private placement.

Regulation D, adopted in 1982 and has been revised several times since, consists of a set of rules numbered 501 through 508. Rules 504, 505, and 506 describe three different types of exempt offerings and set forth guidelines covering the amount of stock that can be sold and the number and type of investors that are allowed under each one. Rule 504 covers the Small Corporate Offering Registration, or SCOR. SCOR gives an exemption to private companies that raise no more than $1 million in any 12-month period through the sale of stock. There are no restrictions on the number or types of investors and the stock may be freely traded. The SCOR process is easy enough for a small business owner to complete with the assistance of a knowledgeable accountant and attorney. It is available in all states except Delaware, Florida, Hawaii, and Nebraska.

Rule 505 enables a small business to sell up to $5 million in stock during a 12-month period to an unlimited number of investors, provided that no more than 35 investors are non-accredited. To be accredited, an investor must have sufficient assets or income to make such an investment. According to the SEC rules, individual investors must have either $1 million in assets (other than their home and car) or $200,000 in net annual personal income, while prospective investing institutions must hold $5 million in assets. Finally, Rule 506 allows a company to sell unlimited securities to an unlimited number of investors, provided that no more than 35 of them are non-accredited. Under Rule 506, investors must be sophisticated. In both of these options, the securities cannot be freely traded.

Regulation D Offerings can be an effective method for private companies to raise investor capital. As regulated by the SEC, the money is then available to the company for osperations. A Regulation D Offering also provides the framework that allows individual investors to invest in your company easily and efficiently. A Regulation D offering can be a valuable addition to your business planning if you are seeking to raise private investor capital.

Wealth Management Firms – These firms are actually in an investment advisory category that incorporates financial planning, investment portfolio management and a number of aggregated financial services. High Net Worth Individuals (HNWIs), (business owners, professional athletes and wealthy families) who desire the assistance of a credentialed financial advisory specialist call upon wealth managers to coordinate estate planning, legal resources, tax professionals and investment management. Wealth managers can be independent Certified Financial Planners™ (CFAs or MBAs), Charter holders or any credentialed professional money manager who works to enhance the income, growth and tax favored treatment of long-term investors. Professional management of pooled finances accounts for some $61 trillion worldwide; with approximately $30 trillion in the U.S. alone.

We introduced these investment management groups as a potential source of "accredited investors" to purchase interests in your company. Depending upon the make up of their clientele, many of these financial consultants will often advise their clients to consider investing a portion of their portfolio into higher risk, higher reward opportunities. If your new company meets their criteria, then you may be able to "locate" your accredited investors by working with a wealth management firm to introduce your private placement. Although you will eventually be transacting with the individual investor, the financial advisor can serve as a catalyst to bring you both together, and provide a basic level of due diligence for the investor.

Raising external money to advance the enterprise is largely predicated on creating something that helps investors understand your value proposition. Thus, the independent innovator will need to pony-up some early stage cash to develop something that creates excitement – a business idea supported by targeted market research. The following quote from the film "Kate and Leopold" (Rogers & Mangold, 2001) is descriptive of the inventor's dilemma in conveying a project's value proposition, "I'm the dog who **saw** a rainbow, only none of the other dogs believe me."

Financial Terminology – It is critical that you become totally conversant with the "investor language," otherwise you may be dismissed as naive or be taken advantage of by investors. Level the negotiation table by learning the language. Selected concepts are listed as follows, and we have provided a glossary of financial terms as an appendix to this book. Use the internet as a handy research tool; starting with *Wikipedia* and then entering your term to get a quick overview of its usage and background.

Accredited investor – An accredited investor is legally defined and regulated by the U.S. Securities and Exchange Commission (SEC), Rule 501 of Regulation D; as a natural person with assets exceeding $1 million and having an annual income of at least $200,000.00. Trusts, banks and other organizations have higher limits. The purpose of the high asset limit is to protect start-ups from having to liquidate prematurely because someone needs living expenses.

Capitalization Table (Cap Table) – A cap table details who owns what in a business start-up; listing the company's stockholders and their shares. Standard spreadsheets specify equity reserved for the founder, equity available to investors, equity available for the option pool and statement about dilution for subsequent financing rounds. Numerous cap table templates are available on the internet; such as at http://venturehacks. com/articles/cap-table

Equity – Legal interest in or ownership of an asset after liabilities have been paid. Inventors typically have 100 percent of the IP's equity; but that is diminished as stock is traded for operating cash. Obviously, there is a tension point between the inventor and potential investors as to the "correct" valuation of the start-up and its IP; with both trying to negotiate favorable proportions of the company's stock. See http://www.ustyleit. com/LOI.htm for template.

Natural person – This is a restrictive legal term meant to differentiate a person from a corporation. Corporations are not natural persons.

Private Placement Memorandum - (PPM) – A document explaining a new offering of securities for private placement. Private placement involves selling securities without registering with the SEC. A private placement memorandum must then explain exactly why the offering complies with SEC Regulation D exempting certain companies from registration; this is done to protect both the issuer and the investors. According to Regulation D, a PPM must contain a complete description of the security and the terms of the sales. It must also include applicable information about the issuer's financial situation and applicable risk factors

Term Sheet – Term sheets or letters of intent (LOI) are non-binding bullet formatted documents detailing the terms and conditions under which an investment will be made.

Valuation – The process of examining various economic factors of a business using predetermined formulas to assess the value of the business or an owner's interest in a company. Business valuation may be conducted to provide an accurate snapshot of the company's financial standing to present to current or potential investors.

FELD, BRAD* (2009). "VC OR ANGEL MONEY,"
ENTREPRENEUR. FEBRUARY, P.50. (USED BY PERMISSION)

As a venture capitalist, I get approached several times a day by entrepreneurs looking to raise money. One of my typical responses is, "You shouldn't be talking to me; you should be targeting angel investors." The source of this confusion varies; sometimes it's a misunderstanding of the different roles and expectations of a venture capitalist vs. an angel investor. Other times it's a lack of clarity on the part of the entrepreneur regarding what he or she wants to accomplish with both the business and the financing. Regardless of the source of the confusion, here are a few guidelines for determining whether you should be approaching angels or venture capitalists for your financing.

The amount of money you're raising is in this round: If you're raising less than $1 million, you're likely wasting your time targeting venture capitalists, with two exceptions: 1) you specifically target funds that do seed rounds, or 2) you have a preexisting relationship with a VC firm and want to put together a seed round to get going quickly.

The total amount of money you're looking to raise over the life of you're company: If you think you can get you're company to a point where it is cash flow positive on less than $3 million, stick with angels.

The type of company you're building: Venture capitalists love to fund businesses with the potential to be enormous. Angels love this too, but they're much more willing to fund smaller companies that will presumably require less capital. In addition, most venture capitalists want to fund businesses that have clearly defined economies of scale (such as software companies) vs. ones that scale linearly with some factor (such as service companies).

Your experience: Successful serial entrepreneurs always find it easier to raise money from venture capitalists. If you're a first time entrepreneur, that doesn't mean you can't raise VC money, but you will find it more difficult than an experienced entrepreneur will.

Your network: If you have never met a venture capitalist before and none of your colleagues have built companies with VC money, you're at a disadvantage having to start from scratch. In contract, if your best friend's father is the CEO of a Fortune 500 company, you have a good shot at quickly getting plugged into a powerful set of angels.

As with all guidelines, there are plenty of exceptions. One generalization seems to hold in most angel financings: the rule of thirds. A third of your financing will come from one investor, the second will come from a set of people following that investor and the last third will be random. So make sure you go hunting for your lead investor.

* Brad Feld has been an early-stage investor and entrepreneur for more than 20 years. He is co-founder of

Foundry Group (www.foundrygroup.com/), an early stage VC firm. He blogs at feld.com and asktheevc.com.

CHAPTER SUMMARY

KEY POINTS

- The three critical elements of a successful start-up are a) intellectual property, b) financial support and c) a professional management team

- Institutional money is also smart money that invests in the logic of your business concept and not just your invention.

- There are often investor and management tensions until the contract is made and then everyone has a vested interest in cooperating to make the start-up successful.

- Most start-ups are funded by a combination of inventor contributions and bank loans.

- Commercial money (banks) is available to individuals with collateral.

- Angel investors provide early stage funding with the expectation of a high rate of return for undertaking the risk.

- Venture capital typically come into start-up projects that have moved passed proof of concept and need funds to expand and grow.

- Private placement offerings are federally regulated and require legal services for preparation and execution. You do not want a federal investigation for securities fraud.

- Federal government agencies have grants and contracts to perform research and development in their respective areas of interest – biopharma and alternative energy are currently hot topics.

- Local and state governments support innovation as part of their economic development.

- Inventors skill sets typically do not include the mastery of business language; such as cap table, term sheet and equity dilution. Learn the language or lose positioning in negotiations.

TAKE ACTION NOW

- Assess the funding needs for your business idea; recognizing that the further you can develop your product concept the more equity, (ownership,) you will be able to keep.

- Be sure that you develop several scenarios for your business valuation; be able to state your assumptions and explain your market analysis processes.

- Master the "language of investment funding" before you approach investors.

- Develop a relationship with your local Small Business Administration Office – before you need the money.

- Start networking in local investor-inventor groups – check with the local Chamber of Commerce for events.

- Find local, regional and state Offices of Economic Development – discuss your project with the appropriate officer.

- Study funding strategies of successful start-ups in your technical area.

- Online term sheets, cap tables and PPMs are available for modest fees – practice completing these for your business.

- Conduct online searches of U.S. Government departments to identify contract and grant topics that fit your technical areas.

- Practice in submitting Small Business Innovative Research grant proposals. Get registered with www.grants.gov to get daily updates on Federal grant project descriptions. Businesses specialize in SBIR grant writing for an upfront fee, but with some study you can write your own.

- Research venture capital fund application requirements – complete the checklists.

REFERENCES:

Benjamin, Gerald A., Margulis, Joel, (2000), *Angel Financing; How to Find and Invest in Private Equity,* John Wiley & Sons, Publisher.

Feld, B. (2009). VC money? *Entrepreneur,* February, p. 30.

Kawasaki, G. (2009). Top 10 lies of venture capitalists. *Entrepreneur,* February, p. 36.

Martel, Doreen, (2010) Pros and Cons of Using Venture Investments, www.BrightHub.com

Metz, R. (2010). Palm CEO says swifter peers stalled company's turnaround, *Coloradoan,* 12/8, B2.

Meyers, T. (2009). Special report: Innovate in a recession, *Entrepreneur,* February, 107-110.

National Venture Capital Association , (2006) *Venture Impact- The Importance of Venture Backed Companies to the US Economy*

Peters, B. (2009). *Exit strategies for entrepreneurs and angel investors: But maybe not for venture capitalists.* Lake Oswego, OR: First Choice Books.

Resnik, R. (2009). Liquid assets keep the credit flowing. *Entrepreneur,* February, p. 34.

Robb, A. (2008). *Kauffman Foundation to extend groundbreaking study of new businesses,* Ewing Marion Kauffman Foundation. http://www. kauffman.org/Details.aspx?id=5845

Rogers, S & Mangold, J. (2001). *"Kate and Leopold."* MiraMax Films.

Wilson, S. (2009). Laid off in 2008?: Start a business in 2009, *Entrepreneur,* February, pp. 73-77.

Supplemental Sources :

Excerpts taken from: *Pros and Cons of Angel Financing*, (no date or author) Go4Funding.com, 545 East John Carpenter Freeway, Irving Texas, Publisher

Deutsch, D. (2008). *The big idea: How to make your entrepreneurial dream come true, from the Aha moment to your first million.* ??

Hess, E.D. (2008). *So, you want to start a business?: 8 steps to take before making the leap.* Upper Saddle River, Pearson Education, Inc.

Kroc, R. (1990). *Grinding it out: The making of McDonald's.* New York: St Martin's Press.

Owen, D. (2004). *Copies in second: How a lone inventor and an unknown company created the biggest communication breakthrough since Guttenberg – Chester Carlson and the birth of the Xerox.* New York: Simon & Schuster

Learner, J. (2009). *Boulevard of broken dreams: Why public efforts to boost entrepreneurship and venture capital have failed – and what to do about it.* Princeton, NJ: Princeton University Press.

Schroeder, A. (2008). *The snowball: Warren Buffett and the business of life.* New York: Bantam

Touhill, C. J., Touhill, G. & O'Riordan, T. (2007). *Commercialization of innovation technologies: Bringing good ideas to the marketplace.* Hoboken, NJ: John Wiley & Sons.

Yanus, M. (2008). *Creating a world without poverty: Social business and the future of capitalism.* Philadelphia: Percus Books Group.

Yunus, M. (2003). *Banker to the poor: Micro-lending and the battle against poverty.* New York: Public Affairs.

Supplemental Reference
Security & Exchange Commission Regulation D Offerings

Under the Securities Act of 1933, any offer to sell securities must either be registered with the SEC or meet an exemption. Regulation D (or

Reg D) contains three rules providing exemptions from the registration requirements, allowing some companies to offer and sell their securities without having to register the securities with the SEC. For more information about these exemptions, read our publications on Rules 504, 505, and 506 of Regulation D.

While companies using a Reg D (17 CFR § 230.501 et seq.) exemption do not have to register their securities and usually do not have to file reports with the SEC, they must file what's known as a "Form D" after they first sell their securities. Form D is a brief notice that includes the names and addresses of the company's executive officers and stock promoters, but contains little other information about the company.

In February 2008, the SEC adopted amendments to Form D, requiring that electronic filing of Form D be phased in during the period September 15, 2008 to March 16, 2009. Although as amended, the electronic Form D requires much of the same information as the paper Form D, the amended Form D requires disclosure of the date of first sale in the offering. Previously, disclosure of the first date of sale was not required. The Office of Small Business Policy has posted information on its web page about the filing requirements for the new Form D.

If you are thinking about investing in a Reg D company, you should access the EDGAR database to determine whether the company has filed Form D. If you need a copy of a Form D filed as a paper filing (which will include any Form D filed before September 15, 2008) that has not been scanned into IDEA, you can request a copy using our online form. If the company has not filed a Form D, this should alert you that the company might not be in compliance with the federal securities laws

You should always check with your state securities regulator to see if they have more information about the company and the people behind it. Be sure to ask whether your state regulator has cleared the offering for sale in your state. You can get the address and telephone number for your state securities regulator by calling the North American Securities Administrators Association at (202) 737-0900 or by visiting its website. You'll also find this information in the state government section of your local phone book.

For more information about the SEC's registration requirements and common exemptions, read their brochure, Q&A: Small Business & the SEC. http://www.sec.gov/answers/regd.htm.

CHAPTER SIX
Selecting and Retaining Your Team

*"The primary skill of a manager consists of knowing how to make
assignments and picking the right people to carry out those assignments"*

Lee Iacocca

Depending on the type and the potential size of the business you are
planning to start, you may have already been challenged on this topic by
your potential investors and stakeholders. Very few of us, (actually none of
us,) know everything there is to know about everything we need to know,
and therefore, we have to admit that we need help. Coming to terms with
this reality is the important first step in putting together a successful team
to move your business forward. Even if you could do everything that is
required to operate your business, you will not have the time to get it all
done.

ORGANIZATION MODELS

Different business models will have different staffing requirements
that reflect the unique skill sets necessary to carry out their plans.
Although certain functional skills are needed in virtually all enterprises,
such as accounting and legal services, different skills may be needed to
perform other critical functions within your business, such as design and
engineering. Since the first step in the process of building your team is
recognizing that you can't do it all yourself, then the second step is to
define what it is that needs to be done.

Too often an entrepreneur will start this process by designing an
organizational chart of functional areas that are perceived to be important
and assume that highly paid individuals are required to manage all of these

activities in order for the business to develop. In some cases this could be true, but we would like to suggest that you come to that conclusion from a different perspective. Instead of identifying the positions to manage the work, why not start with identifying the work that needs to be managed. If there is enough work to be done, appointing someone to oversee it will become obvious.

One way of approaching this topic is to view the three major components of what makes up an organization: 1) the tasks to be performed; 2) the individuals involved; 3) the formal organizational arrangements. An organization can therefore be thought of as a set of components. The question is not what are the components, but what is the nature of their interaction and do the relationships among the components produce the desired output.

Tasks – Look at the inherent work to be done by the organization and its units, or the activity in which the organization is engaged, particularly in light of what your business strategy is. The emphasis here is on the specific work activities. Task analysis would include a description of the basic work and the work flows, as well as an assessment of the characteristics of the work. For example: gaining an understanding of the required knowledge or skills that are necessary to perform the work.

Individuals – Who has the knowledge and skills? Other considerations can be individual preferences, their perceptions and expectations, and other demographic considerations such as age or sex that can influence individual behavior. Early stage companies have a need for high energy, highly committed individuals who are willing to work in an environment where there is a significant degree of ambiguity, and a constant need for improvisation. It's not for everyone.

Organization – This is the structure, processes, methods and procedures that are explicitly developed to get individuals to perform tasks. The goal here is to develop a structure that will, over time, lead to congruence, or good fit, among the different elements of business strategy, tasks, individuals, and organizational arrangements. Recognize as you begin this process that your organization will continue to evolve, particularly if you are able to grow, or required to make a change in your business strategy.

Component	Task	Individual	Formal Structure
Definition	The basic and inherent work to be done by the organization and its parts	The characteristics of the individuals in the organization	The various structures, processes, and methods that are created to perform tasks
Critical Features of Each Component	Degree of uncertainty associated with the work, including factors like interdependencies and routines , types of skills and knowledge demands, types of rewards the work inherently can provide, constraints on performance demands inherent in the work	Knowledge and skills individuals have, Individual needs and preferences, perceptions and expectancies, background, demography	Grouping of functions, structure of units, coordination and control mechanisms, job design, work environment, human resource management systems, reward systems, physical locale

Figure 6.1 Three Major Organization Components (From Nadler & Tushman, 1988).

DEFINING YOUR ORGANIZATIONAL STRUCTURE-

Managers must make choices about how to group people together to perform their work. In the recent Detroit automobile crisis, where Ford, GM and Chrysler nearly crashed from legacy costs and import quality competition, Bill Ford hired Alan Mulally from Boeing to run the company. The astute Mulally quickly realized that Ford had become a dysfunctional international organization; one in which the respective virtually autonomous international satellites created their own designs and mechanics. He directed that there would be "ONE" Ford, efficiently centralizing design, component use and manufacturing process for use in every geographic region. Mulally's reorganization was central to Ford's return to profitability (Vlasic, 2011).

We have identified five common approaches for you to consider, (functional, divisional, matrix, team, and networking) to help you determine departmental groupings (grouping of positions into departments). The five structures are basic organizational structures, which are then adapted to fit your organization's needs. All five approaches combine varying elements of mechanistic and organic structures. For example, the organizational design trend today incorporates a minimum amount of bureaucratic features and displays more of an organic design; with a decentralized authority structure, fewer rules and procedures.

A functional structure – Position groups into work units based on similar activities, skills, expertise, and resources. Production, marketing, finance, and human resources are common groupings within a functional structure. As the simplest approach, a functional structure features well-defined channels of communication and authority/responsibility relationships. Not only can this structure improve productivity by minimizing duplication of personnel and equipment, but it also makes employees comfortable and simplifies training as well.

A divisional structure – Semi-autonomous divisions are normally found in larger companies because managers in large companies may have difficulty keeping track of all their company's products and activities, and specialized departments may develop. These departments are divided according to their organizational outputs. Examples include departments created to distinguish among production, customer service, and geographical categories. This grouping of departments is called a divisional structure. These departments allow managers to better focus their resources and results. A Divisional structure also makes performance easier to monitor.

A matrix structure – combines functional specialization with the focus of a divisional structure. This structure uses permanent cross-functional teams to integrate functional expertise with a divisional focus. Employees in a matrix structure belong to at least two formal groups at the same time; a functional group and a product program, or project team. They also report to two bosses, one within the functional group and the other within the team.

A team structure – This system organizes separate functions into a group based on one overall objective, accomplishing a particular task of completing a project. These cross-functional teams are composed of members from different departments who work together as needed to solve problems and explore opportunities. The intent is to break down functional barriers among departments and create a more effective relationship for solving ongoing problems. Volvo traditionally has cross-functional teams build motors, rather than have individuals adding parts on an assembly line.

A network – Networks rely on other organizations - outsourced companies - to perform critical functions on a contractual basis. In other words, managers can contract out specific work to specialists. This approach provides flexibility and reduces overhead because the size of staff and operations can be reduced. On the other hand, the network structure may result in unpredictability of supply and lack of control because managers are relying on contractual workers to perform important work.

One thing for certain is that the structure you start with will continue to evolve to meet the changing needs and requirements of your business. It is quite possible that you may choose to start with a network structure, and then evolve into something more formal once your business processes become better defined, and your customer's needs better understood. Figure 6.2 provides a framework for you to use as you consider your present and future needs, and will also serve to remind you that nothing is as constant as change.

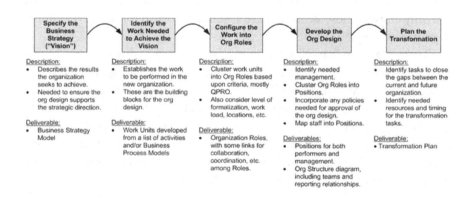

Figure 6.2 Organizational Design (From Clowse, 2006).

DEFINING YOUR TEAM

The next step in developing your organization is to examine each of the critical skills you have identified to determine which skills you need to employ, and which of these skills you may choose to contract. The advantages to considering this "out sourcing" approach is obvious; you only pay for the skill when you have a need for the skill. For example, you will need the help and counsel of an attorney as you design your by-laws, construct your contracting documents, and gain a deeper understanding of the laws and regulations that are applicable to your business. However, you probably do not need to employ an attorney full-time in order to acquire this expertise; you can purchase their services *ala carte*.

The same can be said for your accounting and tax preparation services. In the developing stage of your business, you may only need to employ someone to keep your accounting entries up to date, and then let an outside C.P.A. firm use this information to construct your financial reports. There are any number of excellent firms that work with developing companies in this fashion, and once again, your are only purchasing the required amount of their services when you need to.

Many other services can be viewed in this same fashion during the formulation stages of your business. Some companies utilize professional engineering firms to test and critique their designs, others utilize contract manufacturing for production, and still others develop marketing relationships with third parties to keep the cost of customer acquisition as variable as possible. The concept is simple; in the early stages of your company's evolution, you want to keep your fixed costs as low as possible and only employ those skills that are absolutely critical for the development of your company.

The remaining "tasks" are going to be unique to your business model and your business strategy. You have identified the things that you can trust to others, and now you have to look for that "someone" with the knowledge, skill, understanding and experience with a particular set of tasks that you need to employ. As a matter of fact, there is probably more than one of these identified positions that you need to fill in order to get your business off the ground. This is going to cause you to invest the time and energy in a meaningful recruiting effort.

RECRUITING YOUR TEAM

There are a number of factors that can impact the success of your recruiting efforts, many of which are outside of your control because they are influenced by external factors. In recruiting new employees, management must consider the nature of the labor market; what sorts of potential employees are available, and how do they look for work. These are questions that economists have studied for years, and their findings are relevant to the recruiting process.

Labor market boundaries – A labor market consists of a geographical area where the forces of supply, (people looking for work) and demand (employers looking for people) interact and thus affect the price of labor (wages and salaries). The actual boundaries depend upon the type and number of job candidates being sought. The labor market for certain skills may be half the United States, whereas the best labor market for software engineers may be Silicon Valley, Austin, Texas, or Boston, Massachusetts.

Available skills – Very few companies hire "labor"; rather, they hire specific kinds of workers. Companies that need to hire numbers of highly skilled tool and die makers must locate in areas where these tradesmen have established homes. When fully trained workers are required, a new company may have no choice but to locate near the facilities of a competitor. Companies that require a large number of a certain type of worker will have more difficulty recruiting than organizations that are seeking to fill a smaller number of diversified skills.

Economic conditions – Economic conditions in the labor market itself effect recruitment. A new plant located in an area where there is a depressed labor market may be overwhelmed by unemployed workers, whereas trying to establish the same operation in an area where few qualified workers are out of work creates a very different recruiting problem.

Attractiveness of your company – Potential employees will find some organizations far more attractive than others. If your plans are to build an expanding company, engaged in an expanding industry, that enables the payment of high wages and attractive benefits, it will be viewed as a desirable place to work. However, if your plans are to compete within a commodity industry where low wages and employment uncertainty are the norm, it may be viewed as a less desirable place to work. High skill individuals consider both the company, geographic location and area demographics in their selection process - considering quality of life and public school quality.

PERSONNEL SOURCES

The next step in your process is to determine where these potential employees are available for your consideration and how do they seek employment? There are essentially four answers to this question, as everyone eventually experiences one or more of these phases as they progress through their careers.

New employees taking their first job – An inexperienced employee who has only a sketchy idea about job possibilities. They are likely to take several jobs within the first five or six years of their employment life, and eventually settle down after recognizing a more realistic expectation of job satisfaction.

Currently employed, but dissatisfied – This is another source that firms recruit from as many existing employees are convinced that their talents are going underutilized and at some point feel a need to rebel against authority. The fact is that there is only a small percentage of this "dissatisfied group" that is actually seeking other jobs. There are exceptions to this generalization though. During periods of high employment when companies actively compete for labor, and jobs are easy to get, employees do begin to consider alternatives.

Unemployed workers – This is a current and continuing source to consider, and it is important not to view the unemployed as "unemployable." Economic uncertainty, business relocations, organizational re-structuring, etc., have displaced many a qualified worker. Many firms tend to be suspicious of those who have been discharged from a previous assignment, but there are circumstances where these events are not the fault of the employee. Take the time to know the facts before you judge. Many highly productive individuals have found themselves unemployed simply because of off-shoring of their former manufacturing or technical jobs. Enrollment in re-training programs is an indication of motivation

METHODS OF RECRUITMENT

The mere availability of the new jobs you're creating will not bring applicants to your office door. You are starting a new company, no one knows you exist, what you plan to do, or the depth of the resources you have to do it with. Even companies that have established operations, good reputations within their communities, and have a history of providing "good jobs," still need to recruit on occasion. Here are some approaches that you may want to consider:

Word of mouth – Informal personal communication is a great tool to utilize to begin your recruiting efforts. Recommendations from friends, professional co-workers, and other stakeholders provide you with a more "personalized endorsement" of the kind of organization you are striving to create. Equally important, the recommendations they provide can be more readily scrutinized because of the trusted sources they have been provided from. When you are first getting started, it is important to have a few key people in your organization that you know and you trust.

Employment agencies and recruiters – Commercial agencies (Head hunters) are a useful source to consider because of the recent trend of employees to acquire specialized occupational skills. Agencies now focus on providing technical talent, clerical talent, or other specific skills and employers select these sources based upon their reputations to provide them. Executive recruitment falls into this category as well, as founders and investors will often scour the country looking for an individual with specific industry experience and prescribed personality traits.

Advertising – Traditional newspaper and magazine adds "help wanted' have now has transformed into electronic formats. There are a number of "job boards" out on the internet that compile résumé's and make them available to prospective employers for reasonable fees. Among the largest are CareerBuilder.com, Monster.com and HotJobs.Yahoo.com.

Raiding – The practice of hiring employees from other companies introduces the controversial practice of raiding. Some companies scrupulously refrain from recruiting employees from other companies within the same industry. Others will employ the services of a third party recruiting firm to make these contacts for them. However, significant legal liabilities can be incurred when a company lures a key employee from a competitor in order to learn a trade secret or a specific technical "know-how." Be very careful here!

Professional contacts – Networks are becoming more and more of a source for finding and recruiting talent. Social networks have expanding the reach to just about of all of us, and specific professional networks, such as linkedin, are invaluable for finding new sources. Other professional associations, such as the Institute of Electrical and Electronic Engineers, (IEEE), provide career guidance and job sourcing for their members. These kinds of industry associations are good venues to find qualified professionals.

Selection alternatives

Attracting qualified job applicants is only the first step in the process of acquiring your new employees. You must also have techniques for selecting, among those applicants, the ones that are suitable for employment in your new company. Hiring and training costs can be substantial, so trying to avoid hiring someone who will quit or turn out to be unqualified has to be the objective for this initial screening process. While selection methods tend to differ significantly from company to company, there are some common practices that can help with this process. Here are some thoughts:

Screening out applicants that don't fit – Screening is the first step in the process. Since the primary objective of any selection procedure is to find applicants who fits the company's image of "good," "reliable," or "fit with our values," then eliminating those who obviously don't match this initial criteria is a good first step. Definition of the "right type" varies, and some companies define this in terms of physical appearance, background, age, degree of ambition, or similar characteristics. There are also other, more definable, selection criteria that can be appropriately used as screening variables. This could include technical abilities, or some minimal educational requirement.

Fitting people to jobs – Job match is the more typical selection approach. This selection philosophy assumes that the requirements of a given job, and the characteristics of a given applicant, are sufficiently unique and explicit to make possible an intelligent match between them. Essentially, the selection process is one of prediction; making an informed estimate as to which of the various applicants is most suited for the job being filled. But, in order to make these decisions, one needs reliable information about the tasks and the applicants themselves.

Fitting jobs to people – Circumstances may dictate an alternative approach that requires adjusting the job requirements to the people that are available to fill them. For example, during World War II, many traditional "male" jobs were adjusted to enable them to be performed by women. In recent times, flexible work shifts have been introduced, and many skilled jobs have been broken down into components that can be performed by lesser skilled employees. Psychologists have now introduced the concept of "human engineering" that seeks to make equipment design and work processes better adapted to "typical" human characteristics so that a larger universe of individuals can perform the work.

SELECTION TOOLS

There are a number of selection instruments available, four of which will be introduced here for your consideration. They are: applications, (biographical inventories), interviews, (human interaction), physical examinations, (when appropriate), and formal tests. Each of these can be used with some degree of certainty for the purpose for which they were designed. However, individual behavior can be different in the interview process then it can be in the workplace, and there will always be some degree of uncertainty in any selection process.

Application forms – Standardized forms are the traditional device used to record biographical information, such as education, training, and work experience. Standard forms for all applicants provide some insight into the nature of previous work assignments, the duties performed, length of time in each assignment, and the salary or compensation earned. Although many applicants will often exaggerate their previous experience, there are ways of verifying the information provided and it gives the hiring manger a good summary of the qualifications of the applicant.

Interviews – Personal conversation is almost universally used as a selection device. The interview enables the person responsible for hiring to view the "total individual" and to appraise his or her behavior directly. An effective interview involves two-way communication, and allows both the candidate and the hiring manager an opportunity to get to know one another. Even at its best, the interview is still not a precise technique, and skillful interviewing *is* difficult to conduct. Candidates react very differently depending upon who is interviewing them and how the interview is handled, and the interviewer can bias the outcome by incorporating their own stereotypes. Consider letting more than one member of your group speak with a new applicant before making a decision.

Physical examinations – Relevant physical evidence of capability may be required for certain kinds of jobs. For example, a pilot would need to be physically able to fly a plane, so a physical examine would be an appropriate requirement for someone seeking that position. In recent times, many employers have been requiring "drug tests" of new employees as part of their screening process. The practice has become so prevalent that most applicants anticipate it as part of the process, and very few consider this request as unreasonable. If you encounter an applicant who refuses to participate, this may be an indication of a larger issue that you should avoid.

Testing – Formal assessment of applicants was at one time almost synonymous with the selection process, but today, some companies don't utilize testing at all. Employment tests were originally designed to find a more objective method of measuring the qualifications of a job applicant, as well as to evaluate their qualifications for promotion. There have been a number of different tests designed for different purposes, but for employment and selection here are some of the more common ones:

A performance test is perhaps the most obvious and simplest form of testing, and it is the "work sample" test in which the candidate demonstrates their ability to do a specific job. For example, a machinist may be asked to interpret a drawing.

Aptitude tests have been designed to measure an applicant's likelihood to learn a specific skill required for a job. Individuals differ, for example, in their ability to learn work involving precise eye-muscle coordination, such as the work done by a skilled shop craftsman or a mechanic. Aptitude tests do not test motivation and, on the job, motivation may be more important than aptitude. For this reason, many companies have substituted aptitude tests with personality tests.

Interest tests have been introduced to measure the applicant's interest in certain kinds of work or work environments. For example, do they prefer to work indoors or outdoors? While these tests have been utilized for vocational testing in the educational arena, they are used by companies to determine an applicants suitability for certain jobs. Similarly, these tests help predict whether employees will be happy in their occupations.

Personality tests are much like interest tests, as neither has a set of "right answers." These tests are designed to determine how individuals will relate to interpersonal and situational stress. Personality tests seek to assess an individual's motivation, their adjustment to the stresses of everyday life, their capacity for interpersonal relationships and self image. These are expressed in terms of the relative significance of such traits within the person as self-confidence, ambition, decisiveness, optimism, patience, fear, and distrust.

Very few of us are experts at assessing others, but there is a great deal of help available from a number of "free sites" out on the internet. Consider going to the Department of Labor website, (www. Dol.gov) or to (www. HR-Guide.com) for some additional guidance. They can provide you with insight into labor laws, compensation issues, testing tools, and evaluation techniques to help you with this process. Finding the right candidates to help launch your new enterprise is a critical step in your success.

SELECTING EXECUTIVES

Executive selection involves some special challenges, in part because of the greater vagueness as to what it requires to be an executive, and therefore, there is even less agreement as to how to pick one. Some companies rely entirely on interviews, others on personality tests, and still others rely upon "assessment centers" to do the screening for them. Although personality tests can be used to identify leaders and innovators, they are used most commonly to weed out "misfits."

According to the Ninth House, Inc. (2011), a leadership development company headquartered in San Francisco, California, dramatic changes in the U.S. economy has resulted in unparalleled changes in the skill sets companies will require of middle and top-level executives. Ninth House has partnered with 12 world-renown business experts in creating a library of interactive training courses that address the most critical organizational issues. Mastering and integrating the following five management skills may mark the difference between the leaders and the losers:

1. Creating a Compelling Organizational Vision: "The organizational leaders of today will be those individuals who are able to create a compelling vision that tells everyone who you are (purpose), where you are going (picture of the future) and what will drive your behavior (values). If your people don't know what you stand for, they will fall for anything. Once your vision is set, then the goals or strategies you establish will have a bigger picture context" (Blanchard, 2005).

2. Understanding and Coping with a Constantly Changing Economic Environment: "The pace of change is greater than ever, and there are signs that our individual ability to assimilate it is reaching the limit. Today's leaders are faced with the daunting task of sustaining productivity under conditions that will certainly undermine it. Without them, productivity will suffer, and our hair-trigger economy won't stand that" (Bridges, 2009).

3. Developing and Mentoring Employees: "Over 100 years ago, Henry Ford said: "Why when I only want to hire a pair of hands, do I get a whole person?" In today's complex world that is moving more and more into a knowledge economy, the challenge for leadership is to "use the whole person." Leaders can no longer have the answers. Instead, their task is to release and focus the potential of everybody within their organization. Only when that is done will excellence be achieved" (Bradford, 1997).

4. Building a Workplace Community: "The growth and uncertainty experienced in recent times caused some leaders to return to basics-building workplace communities of respect, affirmation and inclusion. It worked. Employees and the marketplace responded positively. If this trend becomes a strategic priority for leaders, we predict the workplace of the future to be one of risk-taking, shared knowledge, increased productivity and a reduction in the impact of change" (Taulbert, 1999).

5. Negotiating and Managing Critical Relationships: "The ability to negotiate and manage relationships with strategic partners is essential. Productivity within companies who partner could be three times higher than the normal productivity per employee. Look for growth in partnering, which spreads capital risk and shortens time-to-market." (Segil, 2004).

If you are considering bringing in professional management to help lead, develop and mature your company, this list can certainly be of value to you in conducting your interviews. Ideally, you want to find these key individuals who are compatible with your values, knowledgeable of your industry, and capable of conveying your vision of the future to your organization and its stakeholders. Take your time with these kinds of selections, as the individuals you choose will have a significant impact on the future of your business for many years to come.

COMPENSATING YOUR TEAM

Compensation, simply stated, is pay provided by an employer to an employee for services rendered. Employees expect an acceptable monetary reward in return for the time, effort and skill they invest in a job. Compensation lies at the center of the implied, and sometimes formal, employer/employee contract. Getting pay right is critical to keeping your work force motivated and attracting top talent to your organization.

Compensation can be categorized into two basic elements: fixed and variable pay. Fixed pay is a constant, it does not regularly vary according to performance or results achieved. Variable or incentive pay is earnings given in addition to base salary that is contingent on discretion, performance or results achieved. Fixed pay is a guaranteed amount while variable pay is not. The objective of any compensation plan or program, regardless of how formal or informal it may be, is to be internally equitable, externally competitive, affordable, and appropriate.

New companies face many of the same human resources challenges that larger, more mature companies face. In terms of employer staffing costs, it is more expensive to replace employees than it is to retain them since turnover costs can range from 50 percent to several times an incumbent's salary. It makes sense to start with a pay program that fairly and equitably compensates all employees. In order to remain competitive, your organizations must:

- Attract qualified personnel

- Pay employees for excellent performance

- Maintain fair and competitive market pay for employees

- Encourage employees to improve skills and assist them in that effort

- Retain a skilled and effective workforce

In order to compete effectively for valuable talent, you need to assess what the competition is doing. Collecting salary data from organizations that are similar to yours allows you to compare your salaries to what your competitors pay for the same positions. When you analyze pay competitiveness by collecting market-based pay rates for jobs, you can recruit more effectively for positions in your organization and be certain that you are not overpaying for that job.

When it comes to researching salary information, both job seekers and employers are often lost. From too much information to no information, almost anything could sideline your research. The key is to review a number of reliable sources and surveys, avoiding dependency on any one resource alone. Here a few sources that could help you research salary information:

PRINT RESOURCES

For researching average salary data, your local librarian is probably your best resort when it comes to print resources. Most public libraries subscribe to a wide range of salary surveys. In addition, print resources could include general periodicals, newspapers, trade magazines, professional literature, industry associations and organizations, Occupational Outlook, etc.

ON-LINE RESOURCES

For researching average salary and general information you can go to:

Career Journal's Salary Data and Hiring Trends – A neat resource for researching average salary based on occupation and location.

Salary.com – You can research salary information using their salary wizard. Basic information is free; there is a fee, however, if you would like to purchase a personalized salary report.

SalaryExpert.com – Features a salary calculator; basic information is free but you may have to pay for a personal salary report.

JobStar's Salary Surveys – JobStar has prepared an excellent page with links to profession-specific salary surveys.

Riley Guide – Features an excellent section entitled "Salary Guides & Guidance."

GOVERNMENT RESOURCES:

America's Career InfoNet – A great resource for salary and occupational trends. Also look at the Occupation Profile section.

Occupational Outlook – Excellent resource; you can search your occupation to review earnings trends.

Bureau of Labor Statistics: – wages by area and occupation; current employment hours and earnings, both nationally and by state.

National Compensation Survey – Provided by the Bureau of Labor Statistics; provides comprehensive measures of occupational earnings, compensation cost trends, etc.

According to a recently published article by Erisa Ojimba, (2012, Salary.Com) a company's pay structure is the company's method for administering its pay philosophy. The two leading types of pay structures are the internal equity method, which uses a constructed grid to ensure that each job is compensated according to the jobs above and below it, and market pricing, where each job in an organization is tied to the prevailing market rate.

A company needs some sort of job descriptions for all of its positions so that people know where they fit within the organization. A formalized pay structure helps to answer questions about who's who and why people are compensated differently. It also helps the human resources personnel to fairly administer any given pay philosophy. Opportunities for incentives are also dealt with in the pay structure. For example, people with strategic roles will likely have opportunities for higher incentives.

Your reward structure should also be based upon results and not simply the activity level of the employee. Just because they try doesn't mean they have earned a bonus that should be available for those who actually produce results for the company.

EMPLOYEE BENEFIT PROGRAMS

According to the Bureau of Labor Statistics National Compensation Survey (2009) about 64 percent of both full-time and part-time civilian employees in the United States have access to both an employer-sponsored medical care plan and an employer-sponsored retirement plan. Another 15 percent of civilian employees have access to either a medical care plan or a retirement plan but not both. The remaining 20 percent of civilian employees do not have access to either a medical care plan or a retirement plan. Health insurance (which includes medical care) and retirement plans are among the larger benefit costs for employers. Health insurance costs represent about 8.1 percent of total compensation (wages and benefits) and retirement about 4.5 percent of total compensation. Combined, these two benefits represent 12.5 percent of total compensation and 41.3 percent of the average total cost of employee benefits.

Access to both medical care and retirement benefits varies for employees in different occupations and industries but is more available for workers with high pay. About one in three civilian workers in the lowest 25th percentile of earnings have access to both medical care benefits and a retirement plan, while access to both benefits ranges from 67 percent to 86 percent for workers in the highest three quartiles. Workers in the lowest 25th percentile of earnings are more likely to have access to neither type of plan than to have access to both types of plans. However, those in the highest three quartiles are more likely to have access to both types of plans than access to neither (Grensing-Pophal, 2005).

Compensation component	Cost per hour worked	Percent of total compensation	Percent of benefits
Total compensation	$29.39	100.0	–
Wages and salaries	20.49	69.7	–
Benefits	8.90	30.3	100.0
Paid leave	2.08	7.1	23.4
Supplemental pay	0.71	2.4	8.0
Insurances	2.52	8.6	28.3
Health insurance	2.37	8.1	26.6
Retirement and savings	1.31	4.5	14.7
Defined benefit plans	0.80	2.7	9.0
Defined contribution plans	0.51	1.7	5.7
Legally required benefits	2.28	7.8	25.6

Figure 6.4 Employer costs for employee compensation, (From Bureau of Labor Statistics, US Dept. of Labor, National Compensation Survey, 2009A).

Total employee compensation then becomes the cost of wages and salaries plus the employers' cost of employee benefits (Bureau of labor Statistics (2009B). If you are competing for talent within an industry that provides these kinds of benefits, you will also have to provide them in order to attract a comparable level of talent. If you are competing for individuals who do not necessarily expect these benefits, then you may be able to postpone providing them until you are more able to absorb the cost.

Providing a minimum of health insurance and a 401k plan are becoming the norm as more and more workers expect to find this as part of their employment arrangements.

Employee ownership programs

Louis O. Kelso (1913-1991), a lawyer, an investor and economic scholar, sought to find a way to preserve capitalism from the rhetoric of communism; searching for an philosophical commerce alternative within the context of the early Cold War. He is credited with the creation of the first Employee Stock Ownership Plan (ESOP). His non-conformist "capitalism" might be compared to the peoples' capitalism ideas of G. K. Chesterton, in which ownership is distributed to as many people as possible within the economy. Kelso developed the idea of Binary Economics to explain the need for expanded capital ownership in light of industrial production and the dominance of capital instead of labor.

In 1956 Louis Kelso invented the Employee Stock Ownership Plan (ESOP) to put his ideas into practice. The first ESOP which was used by the employees of Peninsula Newspapers Inc., based in Palo Alto, California, to acquire the newspaper chain. Since that time, ESOPs have been used by hundreds of companies, including Avis, Exxon Mobil, Standard Oil of California and Atlantic Richfield. In 1958, Kelso collaborated with the philosopher Mortimer Adler (1958) to write *The Capitalist Manifesto* that is considered the primary source of his economic theories. They (Kelso & Adler, 1961) followed with *The New Capitalists*. Both books are readable online from the Kelso Institute (www.kelsoinstitute.org.)

In today's world, stock options are still important, but other equity compensation plans are rapidly assuming greater importance. Companies such as Amazon.com and Microsoft are moving from stock options to restricted stock, and still other companies both large and small are doing more with *phantom stock, stock appreciation rights*, or *direct stock purchases*.

Traditionally, stock option plans have been used as a way for companies to reward top management and "key" employees and link their interests with those of the company and other shareholders. More and more companies, however, now consider all of their employees as "key." Since the late 1980s, the number of people holding stock options has increased about nine-fold. Broad-based options remain the norm in high-technology companies and have become more widely used in other industries as well. Larger, publicly traded companies such as Pepsico, Starbucks, Southwest Airlines, and Cisco now give stock options to most or all of their employees. Many non-high tech, closely held companies are joining the ranks as well.

A stock option gives an employee the right to buy a certain number of shares in the company at a fixed price for a certain number of years. The price at which the option is provided is called the "grant" price and is usually the market price at the time the options are granted. Employees who have been granted stock options hope that the share price will go up and that they will be able to "cash in" by exercising (purchasing) the stock at the lower grant price and then selling the stock at the higher market price. There are two principal kinds of stock option programs, each with unique rules and tax consequences: non-qualified stock options and incentive stock options (ISOs).

Limited liability companies (LLCs) are a relatively recent form of business organization, but one that has become increasingly popular. LLCs are similar in many ways to S corporations, but ownership is evidenced by membership interests rather than stock. As a result, LLCs cannot have employee stock ownership plans (ESOPs), give out stock options, or provide restricted stock, or otherwise give employees actual shares or rights to shares. But many LLCs want to reward employees with an equity stake in the company, and they search for innovative ways to do so.

The most commonly recommended approach to sharing equity in an LLC is to share "profits interests." A profits interest is analogous to a stock appreciation right. It is not literally a profit share, but rather a share of the increase in the value of the LLC over a stated period of time. Vesting requirements can be attached to this interest. In the typical arrangement, an employee would receive an award and would be treated as if an 83(b) election had been made. An 83(b) election fixes the ordinary income tax obligation at the time of grant. The employee would pay taxes on the value of any difference between the grant price and any consideration paid at ordinary income tax rates, and then pay no further taxes until paying capital gains tax on subsequent appreciation *at sale*. If there is no value *at grant*, then, the tax is zero, and taxes would only be paid when the interest is sold, at which time capital gains tax rates would apply.

Restricted stock refers to shares whose sale or acquisition is subject to restrictions. In employee ownership plans, this typically would mean that an employee would be given shares or the right to buy shares (perhaps at a discount), but could not take possession of them until some time later when certain requirements have been met (or, to put it differently, restrictions have been lifted), such as working for a certain number of years or until specified corporate or individual performance goals have been met. If the employee does not meet the requirements for restrictions to lapse, the shares are forfeited.

One of the great advantages of these plans is their flexibility. But that flexibility is also their greatest challenge. Because they can be designed in so many ways, many decisions need to be made about such issues as who gets how much, vesting rules, liquidity concerns, restrictions on selling shares, eligibility, rights to interim distributions of earnings, and rights to participate in corporate governance (if any).

Direct Stock Purchase Plans are plans can also be considered in which employees can purchase shares with their own funds, either at market price or a discount. In some cases, employers will provide below-market or non-recourse loans to help employees purchase these shares. Employees then hold the shares as individuals with the same rights as other holders of the same class of securities.

If your principal objective is to motivate the participants in the program to grow the value of your business, a Stock Appreciation Right (SAR) grant is typically more appropriate. The holder of a SAR award receives no benefit in the form of a cash bonus. Rather, a bonus based upon an increase in value of his or her "equivalent" shares is provided at a future date.

Other equity or allocation formulas could be used as well. The taxation of the bonus would be much like any other cash bonus; it is taxed as ordinary income at the time it is received. Phantom stock plans are not tax-qualified, so they are not subject to the same rules as ESOPs and 401(k) plans, provided they do not cover a broad group of employees. If they do, they could be subject unless the underlying stock value appreciates. As a result, the holder has an incentive to improve financial performance with the expectation of growing the stock value. SAR grants are frequently made subject to a vesting schedule to encourage retention, as well as to provide an incentive to grow value. However, the vesting element of a SAR grant is successful as a retention tool only to the extent that the value of the underlying stock continues to appreciate.

If the underlying stock declines in value from the date of grant so that the SARs have no value, the employee might be more willing to entertain an offer to go elsewhere because he or she forfeits no value upon departure. For example, assume an employer makes annual SAR grants with a graded five-year vesting schedule for each grant. Assume further that the underlying stock value appreciates each year during the first four years from $10 to $15, $20, $25, and then $30. If, at the end of five years, the underlying stock is valued at $40 per share, the employee would have a significant unvested build-up of the early awards. In this case, the annual SAR grants, with their five-year graded vesting schedules, become a valuable retention device. If, however, the underlying stock is more volatile and the value at the end of five years drops to $20, then the retention value is more limited.

Phantom stock is another form of a compensation, simply a promise to pay a bonus in the form of the equivalent of either the value of company shares or the increase in that value over a period of time. The employee does not own "real equity" in the company, but rather "equivalent" equity. For instance, a company could promise Tom, its new employee, that it would pay him a bonus every three years equal to the increase in the equity value of the firm times some percentage of total payroll at that point. Or it could promise to pay him an amount equal to the value of a fixed number of shares set at the time the promise is made. In either case, Tom is paid to ERISA rules. Unlike SARs, phantom stock may reflect dividends and stock splits. Phantom stock payments are usually made at a fixed, predetermined date.

If you consider offering such a plan, then the first issue to address is how much phantom stock to give out. Care must be taken to avoid giving out too much to early participants and not leaving enough for later employees. Second, the equity of the company must be valued in a defensible, careful way. Third, tax and regulatory problems may make phantom stock more dangerous than it seems. Cash accumulated to pay for the benefit may be subject to an excess accumulated earnings tax (a tax on putting too much money in reserve and not using it for business). If funds are set aside, they may need to be segregated into a "rabbi trust" or "secular trust" to help avoid causing employees to pay tax on the benefit when it is promised rather than paid (Adams, et al, 2010).

STOCK OWNERSHIP PLAN ADMINISTRATION

It's easier then you may think to get lots of technical information about stock options, restricted stock, stock appreciation rights, phantom stock, performance shares, and other equity sharing tools. It's also easy to find guidelines for executive ownership of equity in public companies. It's a different matter, however, to learn how to tailor an equity-sharing program in a closely held startup or established entrepreneurial company that is just getting started. Here are some tips from the National Center for Employee Ownership to consider.

Decide How Much to Share – The typical approach is to say "we'll give out x% of the stock." Often, that's 10%. Ten percent of a company with an established product and a history of profits is a very different matter than 10% of a company with no product, no profits, and a lot of debt. But owners often think "there is some percentage of ownership we are willing to give away, so let's settle on that." This could creates a number of potential problems. What if you give away most of the 10%, but then need more to give to new hires when you grow? What if 10% of the equity turns out to be not worth much and thus is not much of an incentive? What if it is worth more than you really need to give out to attract and retain talented people?

We suggest that you take the approach recommended by the National Center for Employee Ownership (2010). Give out ownership based on meeting company targets, with more given out if a stretch goal is met, and none given out if the base goal is not met. This can be done on a regular basis, with amounts set so that they are sufficient to get people's interest, but not so high as to make majority owners feel like they are giving too much away.

Decide Who Gets Ownership – Most people start off with the assumption that they just want to reward "key performers." It's easy to agree with this premise but there is cause for disagreement with the usual definition of "key." No matter how good your product or service is, if the receptionist is rude, the customer service agent uninformed, the warehouse clerk too slow, or the programmer distracted, then not much good is going to happen. Everyone in your company has the potential to make a contribution, often well beyond what their narrow job descriptions entail.

Decide How Much Each Person Gets – Many new companies look to comparison data to ask how much people at various levels get in terms of a percentage of total equity. That does not seem very constructive to us, for the same reasons setting a percentage to give away overall doesn't make much sense. Instead, the key should be to provide a reward that is financially meaningful to employees; one big enough to attract, retain, and motivate them, but not so large as to waste corporate assets. Once a range of value has been set, then decide whether to base the award on merit, salary, or some other formula. Merit-based approaches are very popular, but just be sure that the process of determining merit is considered fair.

Think About Frequency – Many companies load up equity grants in the first year, reserving much less for later. But this practice can create a lottery effect for employees. If you join when the stock is at a favorable price you do much better than someone who comes in later at a less favorable one. Smaller, but more frequent, grants smooth out this effect and allow for ongoing incentives for future employees.

Pick a Kind of Equity – Stock options come in two flavors, nonqualified and incentive. The increase in value of nonqualified options is taxable as income on exercise to employees and deductible to the employer at that time; incentive options can qualify for capital gains treatment and not be taxed until sale if certain rules are met. But the employer gets no deduction and the employee may have to pay alternative minimum tax (AMT).

Restricted stock gives or sells employees actual shares but requires some condition, such as years of service, to be met before they can actually take possession of them. Tax treatment varies and your accountant can help you work through this issues. Stock appreciation rights give employees a cash or stock award for the increase in the value of shares over a period of time; phantom stock gives employees the actual cash value of the stock, instead of the stock itself. Both are taxable in the same way as a cash bonus.

Choosing a professional advisor with extensive experience is essential in this process. Make sure they can provide all the alternatives, instead of just trying to sell you on their favorite approach. The National Center for Employee Ownership provides consulting services to help you review your alternatives. The NCEO does not actually set up plans, so they can approach this in a more objective way than consultants who hope you will go on to hire them. Generally, a one- or two-hour phone consultation is sufficient to help new company leaders make some essential choices.

Starting a new enterprise involves facing many new challenges, and building your team is certainly an important part of your effort. Recognizing what skills you need to help you, finding the individuals who possess those skills, and then convincing them to join your efforts is a critical step toward your success. If you take the time to research what is fair, structure your plans so that they provide the appropriate incentives for accomplishment, and enable your team to participate in your success, you just may be creating a successful company and a great place to work.

The SAIC Solution:

In 1969, Dr. J. Robert Beyster founded Science Applications International Corporation (SAIC) with a unique vision of creating an employee-owned organization. The following summary is taken from Dr. Beyster's remarks on the topic of employee ownership.

"Company owners and managers often wonder why their employees don't feel the same dedication to the job that they do. Who hasn't witnessed the 4:59 pm rush to the parking lot, or the employees who provide the minimum levels of customer service necessary? While there are many possible explanations, in my mind, there is one key reason why employees don't feel or act like owners: it is because they *aren't* owners.

Soon after I founded Science Applications International Corporation (SAIC), I realized that in order to attract and retain talented employees I would need to offer them real ownership in the business, backed with deeds and not just words. So, while I owned 100 per cent of SAIC's stock on Day One, within a year after I founded the company, my ownership stake was reduced to 10 per cent, with the balance set aside for employees. By the time I retired in 2004, I owned less than two per cent of the company's stock."

SAIC was built on the belief that a company in which employees thinks and acts like an owner creates the potential for numerous synergies to enhance corporate performance. The employees benefit by working in an environment that challenges them, values their opinions and ideas, and then rewards them with an ownership stake.

The shareholders, including employees, benefit by enjoying the increased returns that this innovative, efficient organization creates. Ultimately, SAIC believes its their customers who are the real winners, benefiting from the good work of motivated and highly skilled employee owners who help solve critical problems.

A growing body of evidence supports this direct link between employee ownership and performance. For instance, in a review of employee ownership studies for the National Bureau for Economic Research (NBER), Joseph Blasi and Douglas Kruse of Rutgers University reported that on average companies with significant employee ownership had better economic performance although there are some variations between companies.

A series of studies by NBER's Shared Capitalism project by Blasi and Kruse and Richard Freeman of Harvard University help explain these variations. They reported that employee empowerment, good employment relations, and various other work practices help determine whether employee ownership will succeed or not. Employees with the right corporate culture and different types of equity and profit sharing will more responsibly monitor fellow employees. The U.S. General Accounting Office conducted a study of 110 American firms and found that participatively managed, employee-owned companies, increased their productivity growth rate by an average of 52 per cent per year.

Finally, a study of 45 employee stock ownership plans (ESOP) and 225 non-ESOP companies conducted by the National Center for Employee Ownership (NCEO) revealed that companies that combine employee ownership with a culture of participative management grow 8 per cent to 11 per cent faster than those without such plans in place. So what exactly is it that causes employee ownership to work its magic on the organizations that choose to adopt it?

The following attributes of an employee-ownership culture seem to be at the heart of this phenomenon:

Employee ownership allows a focus on long-term goals. Employee ownership helped to insulate SAIC from outside shareholders who had no direct ties to the company. Free of the need to meet short-term performance goals dictated by pressures from outside shareholders, the company could establish growth and profitability goals that best suited its own short- and long-term objectives and the interests of patient stockholders.

Employee ownership helps attract and retain a superior workforce for decentralized growth. SAIC enjoyed greater freedom to use stock ownership to maintain a highly decentralized and entrepreneurial corporate culture and to preserve a focus on individual effort and initiative. Being employee-owned also gave the company greater latitude in designing stock incentive programs geared to a decentralized company. SAIC's equity compensation plans were very diversified and could reach a greater proportion of its employees than virtually any of its competitors.

Employee ownership facilitates the alignment of key corporate constituencies. At SAIC, the roles and interests of owners, employees, and managers were potentially more mutually supportive and overlapping than in traditional corporations that often experience the divide between executive management and the majority workforce with no ownership stake. As an employee-owned company, management perceived an obligation to be more responsive to employees' needs and concerns.

SAIC's interdependent and self-regulating work environment placed a priority on open communications, employee participation in decision-making and greater mutual accountability. This helped the company in numerous ways, from controlling salary levels, and costs in general, to getting employee feedback on important corporate issues, to implementing quality improvement efforts that enhanced not only results to the customer and the corporate bottom line but also the return to employee-shareholders.

Employee ownership at SAIC promoted adaptability to maintain customer focus. As a high-tech company in an extremely dynamic and competitive business environment, SAIC had to regularly restructure its operations to respond to changing market needs and opportunities. The company's performance-based ownership incentives encouraged SAIC's employee-owners to maintain a customer-driven focus. SAIC's employee-owners treated the business as if it was their own, and they made a point of constantly gauging customer satisfaction. Dissatisfied customers can easily result in lost business, which can result in decreased stock value.

In short, ownership put employees' fingers right on the organization's financial pulse, encouraging them to do the right thing for customers, their colleagues, and the company. The result? An $8 billion business success story one that is poised to continue its growth and success far into the foreseeable future.

Chapter Summary

KEY POINTS

- Organizational requirements are discovered by examining three key components: the tasks that need to be performed, the individual skill sets required to perform the tasks, and the relationships between the two that enable work processes to produce a desired outcome.

- There are five basic organizational designs: functional, divisional, matrix, team, and networking

- A functional organization groups positions into work units based on similar activities, skills, expertise, and resources.

- A divisional structure is normally found in larger organizations that have a need to track a variety of organizational outputs.

- A matrix structure combines a functional structure with the focus of a divisional structure. This is often refereed to as the creation of cross functional teams.

- A team structure organizes separate functions into a group for one overall object, to accomplish a specific goal ro the completing of a project.

- A network structure relies upon other organizations to perform critical functions, (usually contracted,) to perform specific work functions.

- Personnel recruiting efforts are often impacted by external factors, such as: labor market boundaries; available skills; economic conditions; attractiveness of your industry or market.

- Sources for human resources can be found from: new employees seeking their first job; individuals who are currently employed, but dissatisfied; "raiding" from existing firms; and unemployed workers seeking opportunity.

- Recruitment can be accomplished from: word of mouth efforts; advertising; professional contacts; employment agencies and recruiters.

- Selection methods for new candidates can consist of: screening out obvious "misfits;" fitting people to jobs; fitting jobs to people.

- Selection tools can consist of: applications forms; interviews; physical examinations; and testing.

- Common personnel tests consist of: performance testing; aptitude testing; interest tests; and personality tests.

- Selecting executives is more comprehensive and can include: interviews, personality tests, and the help of professional "assessment centers" to screen candidates.

- Compensation consists of fixed pay, variable pay, benefits provided, and any additional form of either ownership or bonus tied to company value creation

- Sources of compensation information can be found at: web-based providers, (such as Salary.com, www.salary.com), published surveys, (the National Compensation Survey, www.bls.gov); customized third party surveys, (www.HRGuide.com), self-conducted surveys and other free sources, such as job advertisements.

- Employee benefits are part of the compensation equation and, according to the department of labor, comprise almost 30% of total compensation. Healthcare and 401k plans are the most predominant.

- Employee ownership plans are provided as a source of incentive compensation and as incentive for employees to remain with the company.

- Employee ownership programs can be in the form of E.S.O.P.'s (Employee Stock Ownership Plan); restricted stock plans; direct stock purchase plans; stock appreciation rights; and phantom stock

- Administration includes: how much total ownership to provide; determination as to who receives an allocation; and the amount of the individual grants.

TAKE ACTION NOW

- Recognize your strengths and your short comings and select the role that you will play in the development of your enterprise.

- List the tasks that you will need to have accomplished and the skill sets that will be required to accomplish these tasks

- Select an organizational model that will enable you to perform the work and provides the flexibility to realign reporting structures as the business matures

- Identify the functions that you will "out source" to others and the work activities that you will need employees to accomplish.

- Develop job descriptions for the positions you need to hire and determine what competitive compensation rates are for these kinds of positions.

- Begin recruiting efforts to identify potential sources for the skills you require and labor pools from which they can be obtained.

- Utilize a combination of selection tools to sort out the best available candidates for the job categories you need to fill.

- Develop you compensation structure to include employment benefits if appropriate, fixed pay rates and incentive plans.

- If you are considering employee ownership, select a model that fits your business requirements and obtain "expert" help in designing your plans.

- Determine who will qualify for your ownership plans, how much of an interest they will be able to earn, and the format in which it will be distributed, (e.g. vested over time).

REFERENCES

Adams, J.; Baksa, B., Coleman, D. D., Janich, D., Johanson, D. R., Jones, B., Kemp, K., Rodrick, S., Rosen, C., Staubus, M., and Struve, R., (2010) *Beyond Stock Options*. Oakland, CA: The National Center for Employee Ownership, Publisher.

Beyster, J. R. Economy, P. (2007). *The SAIC Solution- How We Built an $8 Billion Employee-Owned Technology Company*. New York: John Wiley & Sons, Publisher.

Blanchard, K. (2005). *Self-leadership and the one minute manager: Increasing efficiency through self-leadership*. New York: HarperCollins.

Bradford, D. & Cohen, A. R. (1997). *Managing for excellence: The guide to high performance in contemporary organizations - influence without authority*. San Francisco: John Wiley.

Bridges, W. (2009). *Managing Transitions: Making the most of change*. Philadelphia: Da Capo Press.

Bureau of Labor Statistics (2009A). *National Compensation Survey: Employee Benefits in the United States*, Washington, DC.

Bureau of Labor Statistics, (2009B) *National Compensation Survey: Occupational Earnings in the United States:* Washington, DC.

Clowse, Steve (2006) *Organizational Design Methodology*, Advanced Strategies, Inc. Publishers 16 (1)

Grensing-Pophal, Lin, (2005), *Employee Management for Small Business*, Bellingham, WA: International Self-Counsel Press, Ltd. Publisher

Kelso, L. O. & Adler, M. (1958). *The capitalist manifesto*. New York: Random House.

Klieman, Mel; Klieman, Brent (April, 2002), *Recruit Smarter Not Harder*, New York: HTG Press, Publisher.

Economy, P. & Beyster, J. R. (2007), *How we built an $8 Billion Employee-Owned Technology Company,* John Wiley & Sons, Hoboken, N.J.

Nadler, David A. , Tushman, Michael I., (1988) *Strategic Organization Design,* New York: HarperCollins, Publishers

National Center for Employee Ownership, (2010) *Sharing Equity in a Startup or Established Entrepreneurial Venture,* NCEO, Oakland California, Publisher. Ninth House, Inc. (2011). San Francisco.

Rosen, C.; Case, J.; Staubus, M. (2005). *Equity, Why Employee Ownership is Good for Business,* Boston: Harvard Business School, Publisher

Strauss, George and Sayles, Leonard R. (1972) *Personnel-The Human Problems of Management,* Upper Saddle River, NJ: Prentice Hall, Publishers.

Segil, L. (2004). *Measuring the value of partnering: How to use metrics to plan, develop and implement successful alliances.* New York: AMACOM

Taulbert, C. L. (1999). *Eight habits of the heart: Embracing values that build strong families and communities.* New York: Penguin.

Vlasic, B. (2011*). Once upon a car: The fall and resurrection of America's big three auto makers - GM, Ford, and Chrysler.* New York: William Morrow.

SUPPLEMENTAL SOURCE:

U.S. Department of Labor Employment Law Guide –
This *Guide,* a companion to the suite of FirstStep Employment Law elaws Advisors, (available at www.usdol.gov) describes the major statutes and regulations administered by the U.S. Department of Labor (DOL) that affect businesses and workers. The *Guide* is designed mainly for those needing "hands-on" information to develop wage, benefit, safety and health, and nondiscrimination policies for businesses.

For businesses and other employers that do not know which of DOL's major laws apply to them, please start with the *First Step Overview Advisor* (www.dol.gov/elaws/firststep). The Advisor asks the user a short series of questions to determine which of the major DOL-administered laws apply to their organization. The Advisor takes into account relevant variables, (such as size of business and type of industry,) that determine coverage for these laws.

I. Wages and Hours Worked

- Minimum Wage and Overtime Pay - *Fair Labor Standards Act*

- Wage Garnishment - *Consumer Credit Protection Act*

- Worker Protections in Agriculture - *Migrant and Seasonal Agricultural Worker Protection Act*

- Child Labor Protections (Nonagricultural Work) - *Fair Labor Standards Act - Child Labor Provisions*

- Child Labor Protections (Agricultural Work) - *Fair Labor Standards Act - Child Labor Provisions*

- Workers with Disabilities for the Work Being Performed - *Fair Labor Standards Act - Section 14(c)*

II. Safety and Health Standards

- Occupational Safety and Health - *Occupational Safety and Health Act*

- Mine Safety and Health - *Mine Safety and Health Act*

- Worker Protections in Agriculture - *Migrant and Seasonal Agricultural Worker Protection Act*

- Child Labor Protections (Nonagricultural Work) - *Fair Labor Standards Act - Child Labor Provisions*

- Child Labor Protections (Agricultural Work) - *Fair Labor Standards Act - Child Labor Provisions*

III. HEALTH BENEFITS, RETIREMENT STANDARDS, AND WORKERS' COMPENSATION

- Employee Benefit Plans - *Employee Retirement Income Security Act*

- Black Lung Compensation - *Black Lung Benefits Act*

- Longshore and Harbor Workers' Compensation - *Longshore and Harbor Workers' Compensation Act*

- Defense Base Compensation - *Defense Base Act*

- Family and Medical Leave - *Family and Medical Leave Act*

IV. OTHER WORKPLACE STANDARDS

- Lie Detector Tests - *Employee Polygraph Protection Act*

- Whistleblower and Retaliation Protections - *Occupational Safety and Health Act, Surface Transportation Assistance Act and Other Statutes*

- Notices for Plant Closings and Mass Layoffs - *Worker Adjustment and Retraining Notification Act*

- Union Officer Elections and Financial Controls - *Labor-Management Reporting and Disclosure Act*

- Reemployment and Nondiscrimination Rights for Uniformed Services Members - *Uniformed Services Employment and Reemployment Rights Act*

V. WORK AUTHORIZATION FOR NON-U.S. CITIZENS

- General Information on Immigration, Including I-9 Forms - *Immigration and Nationality Act*

- Temporary Agricultural Workers (H-2A Visas) - *Immigration and Nationality Act - H-2A*

- Temporary Non-Agricultural Workers (H-2B Visas) - *Immigration and Nationality Act - H-2B*

- Workers in Professional and Specialty Occupations (H-1B, H-1B1, and E-3 Visas) - *Immigration and Nationality Act - H-1B, H-1B1, E-3*

- Workers Seeking Permanent Employment in the United States - *Immigration and Nationality Act*

- Crewmembers (D-1 Visas) - *Immigration and Nationality Act - D-1*

- Registered Nurses (H-1C Visas) - *Immigration and Nationality Act - H1-C*

VI. FEDERAL CONTRACTS: WORKING CONDITIONS

- Wages in Supply & Equipment Contracts - *Walsh-Healy Public Contracts Act*

- Prevailing Wages in Service Contracts - *McNamara-O'Hara Service Contract Act*

- Prevailing Wages in Construction Contracts - *Davis-Bacon and Related Acts*

- Hours and Safety Standards in Construction Contracts - *Contract Work Hours and Safety Standards Act*

- Prohibition Against "Kickbacks" in Federally Funded - *Copeland "Anti-Kickback" Act*

VII. FEDERAL CONTRACTS: EQUAL OPPORTUNITY IN EMPLOYMENT

- Employment Nondiscrimination and Equal Opportunity in Supply & Service Contracts - *Executive Order 11246 - Supply and Service*

- Employment Nondiscrimination and Equal Opportunity in

Construction Contracts - *Executive Order 11246 - Construction Contracts*

- Employment Nondiscrimination and Equal Opportunity for Qualified Individuals with Disabilities - *The Rehabilitation Act of 1973*

- Employment Nondiscrimination and Equal Opportunity for Covered Veterans - *The Vietnam Era Veterans' Readjustment Assistance Act*

INDEX OF LAWS OF PARTICULAR APPLICABILITY TO AN INDUSTRY

AGRICULTURE

- Worker Protections in Agriculture - *Migrant and Seasonal Agricultural Worker Protection Act*

- Child Labor Protections (Agricultural Work) - *Fair Labor Standards Act - Child Labor Provisions*

- Temporary Agricultural Workers (H-2A Visas) - *Immigration and Nationality Act - H-2A*

Note: Under the authority of the Occupational Safety and Health Act, OSHA has issued a number of safety standards that address such matters as field sanitation, overhead protection for operators of agricultural tractors, grain handling facilities, and guarding of farm field equipment and cotton gins. Contact the local *OSHA office for more detail (1-800-321-OSHA).*

MINING

- Mine Safety and Health - *Mine Safety and Health Act*

- Black Lung Compensation - *Black Lung Benefits Act*

CONSTRUCTION

- Prevailing Wages in Construction Contracts - *Davis-Bacon and Related Acts*

- Hours and Safety Standards in Construction Contracts - *Contract Work Hours and Safety Standards Act*

- Prohibition Against "Kickbacks" in Federally Funded Construction - *Copeland "Anti-Kickback" Act*

- Employment Non-Discrimination and Equal Opportunity in Construction Contracts - *Executive Order 11246 - Construction Contracts*

Note: Under the Occupational Safety and Health Act, OSHA sets and enforces construction safety and health standards. Contact the *local OSHA office for more information (1-800-321-OSHA)*

CHAPTER SEVEN
Entering the Market

"First say to yourself what you would be;
and then do what you have to do."

Epictetus

You have decided what you want to do, planned for success, and attracted sufficient funding to begin this new venture. It's time to think about what the new venture is going to be known for. If your innovation is big enough, its name may dominate the market. For example, the product labeled from the Greek words for "dry" + "copy" changed a company's name and reframed an entire market – Xerox.

There is a great deal of truth in the expression: *"you only get one chance to make a good first impression."* You are about to enter the arena of your targeted market segment; joining the ranks of others with whom you will be competing within an industry. The challenge that lies before you is to find a way to make an early presence recognizable, positive and different from the myriad of transactions that are currently taking place within your market sector. This is not a mere "branding exercise" or an "advertising plan;" this is "market strategy" discussion.

CREATING A PLACE IN THE MARKETPLACE-

Three critical elements must be considered when planning to enter a market. First, is the development of a market strategy, a deliberate assessment of what place in the market you are seeking and the position within your industry which your company will be known for. Second, is the development of a marketing communication plan; the marketing message sent to potential customers, suppliers and others - describing who you are and what you do. And, third is a product plan that clearly establishes the features and benefits of your company's products and services.

Think of this also as a three legged stool, each leg supporting its share of the weight. The legs of the stool are able to contribute to stability because they have been designed and arranged, (positioned) to do so. If a leg is too short or long, or located in the wrong position, the stool will not work. .

MARKET STRATEGY - FINDING YOUR SWEET SPOT

In a maturing circus industry, dominated for more than a century by old giant players like Ringling Brothers and Barnum & Bailey, unemployed Canadian former circus workers Guy Laliberté and Daniel Gauthier founded Cirque du Soleil (Circus of the Sun) in 1984. Cirque was a new entrant into an industry which was afflicted with falling revenues and declining profits for a long time. During this time, children, the traditional patrons of the circus, were becoming more attracted toward televisions, computers and video games - compared to circus animal acts, clowns and jugglers.

Rather than sticking to the age-old formula for running a circus, Laliberté and Gauthier built their new circus along unconventional lines. After identifying that the three core elements of any circus were the tent, the clowns and the acrobatic acts, they did away with the dangerous and expensive animal acts and launched acrobatic shows that included sophisticated live music, elaborate costumes and sets integrated with unique themes. Every show tells a story (Heward & Bacon, 2006); with most shows leaving patrons wondering whether they have witnessed ballet, musical concert, theater or circus. See www.cirquedusoleil.com for more information.

Cirque's unique shows resembling blended theatric and ballet performances are targeted to adults, rather than children. From a small Quebec-based club, Cirque Du Soleil has grown to become one of the world's most recognized entertainment operations and became a $500 million company by 2003; annually grossing almost $1 billion. Unlike traditional circuses, Cirque shows do not include ringmasters or animals. By combining the traditional elements of circus and the theater, Cirque was able to create a product that is totally differentiated from any other live show and circus; increasing its entertainment value proposition from low ticket price and low perceived value to high perceived value and a higher ticket price.

Marketing wisdom suggests that there are three strategic options available to a new enterprise or new product to consider as it gets ready to enter into an existing market:

1. Price - You can elect to compete on price, which will require you to find ways to be a low cost provider of the goods and services you are planning to offer. Wal-Mart is an example of a successful retailer who utilizes this strategy, *"always the low price, always."* Even as Wal-Mart tries to re-position itself to handling designer products, it is dogged by the branding it has effectively established.

2. Features and Functionality - You can compete with technology, (features and functionality) that differentiate your products and services from others. Apple's i-Pod, i-Phone, and i-Pad are examples of being first to market with new innovation. Apple does not compete on price; it competes on features and enhanced functionality. It has established itself as a market leader in this regard.

3. Change the Rules - You can "change the rules" and create new value or even new markets by re-introducing existing concepts in new ways. This is exactly what Cirque Du Soleil did when it re-defined the circus industry; from a child genre to an adult genre and from modest ticket prices to very expensive tickets that are almost always sold out.

Empirical observation shows that being the first to the market provides a significant and sustained market-share advantage over later entrants. Still, later entrants can succeed by adopting distinctive positioning and marketing strategies. For the pioneers in most industries, once they have reached the status of an incumbent, they have become powerful influences over competitor price and perceived value. But, industry giants can get complacent or are not positioned for adapting to shifting marketplace demands – paradigm paralysis. For example, Microsoft actually created the tablet computer idea (circa 2001); but the vice president in charge of Microsoft Office did not like the concept and the tablet group was eliminated (Gallo, 2010). Apple, on the other hand, obviously embraced the idea of a tablet.

New entrants can take advantage of the gaps in the product features, innovation functions, and perceived benefits to the customer. Often they can provide lower prices than these aging market sector pioneers who now have sizable infrastructure to pay for.; Successful new entrants usually find innovative ways to market their products and services.

While every innovation, by definition of being new, must have features that differentiate it from competitors, successful marketing is not done on "features." Instead, marketing should be based on "customer benefits." Examine any Sunday newspaper electronic product advertisements insert and analyze the marketing strategies of the advertisers; looking for listings of computer features or benefits. What you will find is Monitor size, Cache Memory, RAM Capacity, Hard Drive Size, Optical Drive Speed, Networking and Drive Capacity. Expert marketing agencies are making the tacit assumption that the average person walking into the retail store will know the relative benefits of choosing a computer with capabilities of such features. My experience in consumer retail electronic stores is that sales associates almost totally focus on computer features. Most of us everyday consumers greet this plethora of technical information with a resounding: "so what?"

In the 1970s, the fledgling personal computer industry was dominated by technical wizards capable of constructing their own hardware from available parts and programming their devices to accomplish a limited number of functions. International Business Machines (IBM) initially dismissed minicomputers as too small to do real computing tasks; their focus was mainframes for business and not on consumer level computing devices.

Steve Jobs did not invent the computer; he just realized that computer operation could be simplified for layman use. Even by 1985 it was still estimated that home computers would have limited utility. Jobs, "the man who could see past the horizon," pioneered mass marketing of personal computers by marketing its "benefits." He emphasized "how it could be used," and ignored expounding on "its features;" though features were necessary to deliver the benefits. Gallo (2010) cites the Steve Jobs 1977 list of benefits from using, what has come to be, the "Apple Computer" product family, as including items such as:

- Personal enjoyment

- Increased variety of entertainment

- Time, money saved

- Better financial decisions

- Increased leisure time

- Security of personal information

- Elimination of wasted paper, energy, and storage space.

- Improved standard of living

- Increased learning efficiency

- Reduced pollution

As compared to its origin in the mid-1970s gatherings of the "Homebrew Computer Club," (an informal group of people fascinated by the mechanics of building small computers,) the personal computer industry has become relatively commoditized – where low price for adequate performance is the sales metric. However, Apple has continued to market user benefits thereby increase their product's perceived value and successfully garner a higher purchase price.

To help find your place in your industry, use the fairly simple technique called "Perceptual Market Mapping" (Kotler, 2008). As part of your business planning process, you will have conducted a great deal of competing product research. Now you need to systematically analyze this information to enable the development of a market entry strategy. Though this approach is not 100% fool proof, it will help guide your thinking about product positioning in your targeted market sector.

For example, if you want to become a watch manufacturer, will you be making *Timex*-type watches or *Rolex*-type watches? Both are reasonably accurate chronometers, but the respective products are positioned at very different product prices and have very different perceived values; with the combination of price and perceived value being inextricably connected to subliminal messages about individuals who are wearing these respective watches. Marketing is about establishing a price and value identity that positions products and services relative to competitors in a market sector – or with competing market sectors.

Another example, Scott Cook and Tom Proulx founded Intuit in 1983 to provide mathematical information management software – software that moved across sector lines into the bookkeeping and accounting. Intuit recognized that the information services market sector they were entering was served by application specific providers that enabled only one or two of the necessary financial functions; billing, accounting, etc. By integrating multiple applications, Intuit created new market space for their integrated software. Intuit's Quicken (Quickbooks) software for individual and small business enables operators to track income, expenses, prepare and send invoices, manage inventory and prepare financial compliance reports

Consider your target market sector as the "playing field" for your company. Like any other competitive undertaking, it is very much like a game with boundaries, competitors, strategies and rules. Thus, it is important to understand the relative industry positions that your competitors occupy; so that you can take advantage of areas where there is limited competition. Entering the market in areas where there is less competitive pressure is a good strategy because it provides lower barriers for entry. After achieving financial success, you can then develop other in-house spin offs to participate in the higher and/or lower market sectors that are more competitive. .

A good example is the early Honda automobiles of the1960s that were barely operative; entered into the low value and low price market space, similar to the low price and low value Yugo. But then Honda began adopting the American business process guru's (W. Edwards Deming) vigorous quality control processes which enabled Honda to re-position itself as a moderately priced and moderate value vehicle. In order to enter the higher value and higher priced market space, Honda created its Acura premium luxury car brand in 1986, Nissan followed suit and added Infinity in 1989 and Toyota introduced Lexus in 1989; each with very little identifiable relation to their respective parent companies. Pick your spot, think through your strategy.

One way to represent the perceived value and price relationship you are trying to identify is to construct your own Perceptual Market Map; as shown in Figure 6.1. For practice, try to conduct the analysis on some easily accessed products such as laptop computers – comparing Apple, Acer, Dell, Gateway, HP, Samsung, Sony and Toshiba. However, unless you understand the value difference between having 320 GB Hard Drive Size combined with 2.2GHz Processor Speed versus 250BB Computer Hard Drive Size and 2.3Ghz Processor Speed, you and most other customers could have difficulty deciphering relative benefits. The electronics retailer Best Buy offers a free feature comparison at http//:wwwbestbuy.com, but there is no mention of the user benefits enjoyed by any of these features.

It is very difficult to differentiate consumer preferences for many of these devices from just the technical specifications alone.

Assume for your product offerings that price and value are the key considerations to making most purchasing decisions. Draw a rectangle and let vertical axis of the marketing model represent price points; from low to high, and let the horizontal axis represent perceived value, what your customers believe they are getting for their dollars. Use circles to represent the identified competitors you have; using large circles for competitors with a larger percent of market share and smaller circles for your smaller competitors. Some could over lap and some may participate at totally different ends of the spectrum. As a result of this exercise you are hoping to discover "blank space," an area in the market where competitors do not have a dominant presence.

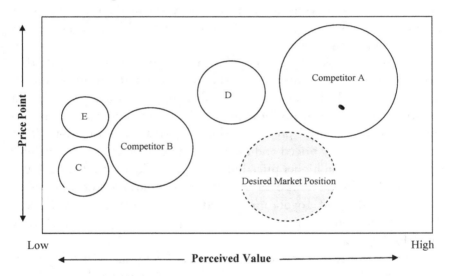

Figure 7.1. En Example of Perceptual Market Mapping for Market Entry in relation to competitive price and perceived value.

This illustration suggests that the largest competitor, "A," provides a set of products or services that are probably rich with features and functionality, but are priced in the higher end of the market. Smaller competitors, "B," "C," and "E" offer lower cost alternatives, but may only address specific niche needs; thereby limiting their ability to compete effectively within other parts of the industry. Competitor "D" has taken a middle of the road position, offering a relatively robust set of features, but charging a more moderate price. There appears to be an opportunity to for an entry in this industry sector for an enterprise positioned as a provider of quality products with a robust set of features and functionality that are priced below Competitor "A." Thus, the product development specifications must be written to create a product or service comparable to Competitor "A" that can be produced at a lower cost. A second strategic opportunity could be to simplify the product operation so it requires less employee or user training; marketing unique benefits over those of Competitor "A."

MARKETING COMMUNICATIONS FOR ESTABLISHING YOUR IDENTITY

Once you have decided the market position that you want to attain within your industry, you must begin to think about how you are going to communicate your arrival to the market. You have to decide "what" it is you want to be known as and for. Creating and communicating the right message is critically important, as it will become your "brand." When Toyota introduced Lexus they did so with a message that conveyed their desire for *"the relentless pursuit of perfection,"* implying that quality was the driving force behind their new automobile product. Rolex continually reminds us that their watch is the *"crown for every achievement,"* suggesting that highly successful people would chose and wear a Rolex. Whatever your product or service, it will become recognized and positioned by your customers perception of its perceived value. Therefore, set your expectations early in this process and do not allow the public or competitors to frame your marketing conversation. It's your choice.

Richard Branson, the charismatic leader of Virgin Airlines, recently granted Entrepreneur.com (2010) and interview on the topic of building a brand for your business. According to Branson, "The key to improving sales is to make sure your business or product stands out in the marketplace. We have always tried to ensure that Virgin products are innovative, that they offer good value and that there's a great attitude about service. When you have those basics right, you need to make sure people know about your business. Too many great businesses remain 'well-kept' secrets for too long and never get the attention they need to grow and thrive."

The marketing strategy team of Ries and Ries (1998) identified *"The 22 Immutable Laws of Branding;"* addressing a verity of influences from advertising and publicity to authenticity and market credentials for creating and defending a brand. It appears that establishing a reputation in the market for your new company and its products will not be as simple as designing a logo and putting it on your stationary. But, your "brand" is going to be noticed, so make sure it represents what you intend to stand for in many languages.

For example, sales of General Motors' "Nova" branded automobile, stalled in Mexico because the Spanish translation of "no" "va" means "does not work." Coors Brewing Company's marketing slogan "Turn it loose" translated into Spanish as "Suffer from diarrhea" and Coke Cola's popular slogan "Coke adds life" translated into Chinese as "Coke brings your ancestors back from the grave." Not so good!

To attract and retain the attention of the consumer is a perpetual undertaking, and whether or not it requires 22 branding touch points can be a worthy subject for debate. But, one take away from the branding experts deserving consideration is your logo. Your advertising, promotional displays and product packaging all need to reflect a consistent image and convey a consistent message. Human beings have "convenient" memories, and unless you keep your message in front of them they will forget.

Bob Lemons (2005), a 35 year veteran of business to business advertising, past chairman of the International Marketing Association and a member of the Business Marketing Hall of Fame, suggests that there are Seven Steps involved in successfully creating a brand or image in the business to business marketplace. He emphasizes that "positioning" is everything, meaning the necessity for identifying the space in the Perceptual Market Map that you are trying to penetrate. To ensure your market message and your market strategy are in synch, consider these:

- Step One – The first step in developing a business to business branding program is to get all of the key stakeholders involved and committed to a "theme." What do you want to be known for? For example: Intel – performance; Caterpillar – ruggedness; 3M – Innovation; UPS – reliability; etc.

- Step Two – Decide your brand "architecture." Will you create "freestanding" brands for your individual product categories like Proctor & Gamble does with 80 different brands; an "over brand" that identifies you with each of your product areas, like Ford does with each of their vehicles, Ford Taurus, Ford F150 trucks; or a "master brand" that is synonymous with your company, like General Electric, or IBM.

- Step Three – Recognize that the most important audience for your message is your employees. How can employees be more important than your customers? They are the face of the company to the customer and if they don't believe in the validity of your message, no one else will believe in it either.

- Step Four – Positioning is the foundation for branding, it is the "battle" for mind share. Just as you "positioned" your company and your products as the result of understanding what your competitors offer, you need to position your brand in relationship to what your competitors brand says about their firms.

- Step Five – Create a brand "personality" for your company. Mission statements are not personalities, stand for something. If your brand was a person, what kind of individual would it be" Caterpillar could be a hard working, non non-sense, rugged individual. Intel could be a race car driver, pushing the performance limits. What would your brand be?

- Step Six – Recognize the need to change your brands personality if it doesn't work for you. IBM for example, lived with the aura of "Big Blue" denial until a new CEO took office and changed their personality from "stogy" to "problem solving." "I'm an IBM'er and I am solving some of the world's most important problems."

- Step Seven – Be consistent with the execution of your brand strategy. We have seen the lonely May Tag repairman for decades, and Like a Good Neighbor, State Farm is still there. If the fundamental purpose of your company has not changed, then you brand personality does not need to either. Promote it differently, but be consistent with your theme.

Ultimately, branding comes down to common sense, introspective thinking, and hard work. Brand recognition doesn't happen overnight because brand development takes years to accomplish and it takes place in the minds of your customers, suppliers, and other audiences. It is difficult to accept the concept that you do not actually "own" your own brand. You should own your trademarks, but branding is strategic promotion that creates a perception in the marketplace. How valuable is a recognizable brand? Business Week estimated the 2004 "brand value" of General Electric to be $44.1 Billion, and IBM, Microsoft, and Coca-Cola's brands were considered even more valuable. It's important!

Publicity and press releases – As a new entity you will not have the millions that the larger organizations can spend to promote their brands or support the introduction of their new products. However, there are less expensive ways to announce your arrival and make the market aware of what you have to offer. One strategy worthy of pursuit is to mount your own publicity campaign. Media sources are always looking for stories about new companies, new products, or new entrepreneurs, and you can help them fill this void. Remember that the news media tell stories – stories about people and things that have affected or potentially will affect people. Stories are powerful and the ability to "put a face on a story" makes it even more powerful. Daniel Pink's (2006), *A Whole new Mind: Why Right-Brainers will Rule the Future*, is an excellent sourcebook for mastering the art of story.

Construct a "press kit" – A press kit is a collection of written materials designed to introduce an expert or a company to the media (Spector & McCarth, 1996). Often these materials are contained in attractive folders and are accompanied by a cover letter. The goal of a press kit is threefold:

- Highlight the issues that your company addresses - an innovative technology to save energy, store energy or enhance domestic energy production will be hot topics from now on.

- Establish your expertise or the organization's authority by demonstrating the depth of your company's knowledge and the experience. The background of your management team is often the key credibility factor for an early stage company.

- Make your organization's experts available for direct interviews by providing contact information. Include supporting information from industry article re-prints that connect the mission of your enterprise with broader societal issues. For example, Friedman's (2009), *Hot, Flat and Crowded*, and Toffler & Toffler (2006), *Revolutionary Wealth*, could be source books for relating your technology to broader societal problems.

The first page of the press kit is a cover letter introduction – you get one chance to make a good first impression. A cover letter introduces the person or the company and the kit, and includes the following information:

- Who the person or organization is - including name and title for a person, or a brief description of the organization. When writing for an individual, summarize the person's unique qualifications as an expert.

- What societal or business issues the organization or expert can address and why they are qualified to speak about the company strategies.

- How your experts or organization representatives can be contacted by phone or e-mail.

For press kits written for key individuals in your organization, summarize the person's background information, including relevant education and experience. For company press kits, include a description of your organization's purpose; explaining what your company does, why it exists, and what its goals are. For company press kits or kits written about specific issues, include brochures, pamphlets, fact sheets, and other collateral about relevant products, services or issues. Offer a list of suggested questions for your in-house experts. The value of this element is that it further establishes your expert's authority and places the interview in the editor's imagination; helping picture your expert's potential for a great story.

If your experts have published articles under or have been quoted in other articles, list the titles, publication names, and dates. Also, add dates, titles, and locations for speaking appearances at seminars, conferences, and events. Endorsements from customers (testimonials) or brief stories about how your organization or expert helped a client (case studies) reinforce credibility and provide the media with story ideas. Make it easy for deadline-pressed reporters by including a photograph of your experts, your organization in action, articles and project case study reprints. Brief video clips loaded on computer files are critical for get television exposure.

One-to-many marketing – Take advantage of the events within your industry that can increase your exposure for very little investment on your part. Look for speaking engagements, industry forums, and customer events, and then volunteer to be part of their agenda. You are seeking opportunities to communicate in a "one to many" fashion, so anytime you can promote your credentials, your products, or your company, you should take full advantage of it. You can have the most innovative products in the world, but if no one knows about them, they will not purchase them.

PRODUCT MARKETING-

An old marketing adage states: *"I know that 50 percent of my advertising budget is a waste of money, I just don't know which 50 percent."* Actually, it is not quite that bad, and in today's multi-media world, you are able to reach your target audience in an ever increasing variety of ways. This many options makes it important for you understand how your target audience will choose to seek and discover information about your products and your company.

Market segmentation – For companies offering consumer products, the challenge is quite formidable. There are over 300 million people in the United States and more than 6 billion people in the world. It is unlikely that you can contact each of them with a sales pitch, and more improbable that they will seek you out if they don't know that you exist. The challenge is to sort through this sea of humanity and identify the consumers with potential interest in your products – ignoring those who would not.

A variety of data base sources are available to identifying the potential customer base. The U.S. Census Bureau, (www.census.gov) provides listings of traditional demographic data for the national, state, county and local population. Local commerce organizations, like the Chambers of Commerce, can also be helpful in this regard as well. And, there are market research organizations that not only sort through this kind of information, but translate it into socioeconomic strata and lifestyle preferences to enable a more focused approach. Direct mail services have also developed sophisticated demographic desegregation tools; enabling direct mail contact sorted by name, age, income, children present, home value, lifestyle and hobbies for consumers and business type, employee size and sales volume for industrial customers. Search descriptors such as "direct mail" and "custom lists" for sources and services.

One popular data source, the Claritas (2004) organization, is affiliated with the Harris polling group; the people who track television viewing, etc.

The Claritas' database has identified 64 different socioeconomic groupings of consumer lifestyles and preferences. They also provide insight into media preferences, income, lifestyle and the kinds of purchases that these groups historically make. Utilizing a data source such as this enables you to target your consumer customers more specifically – wasting less time and money on low probability buyers.

Create your "ideal" or "generic" customer profile, describing people who would benefit from purchasing your product. Try to identify their lifestyle, their demographics, and their purchasing patterns. Next, find out where they are located, preferable by county, city, and zip code. For example, your consumer profile might be "Single women between the ages of 21 and 45 years, with annual incomes of over $50,000.00 who live in New England." Next, begin to explore your media choices within these locales. Consider internet presence, direct mail, print media, and radio advertising as options. Initially setting up a great website allows you to use social marketing and to drive consumer follow-up to the website with all other media sources. The objective is to reach as many as you can for the dollars you have to spend - you do not need to be on television in order to accomplish the goal.

Construct your message in an understandable way, specifically tailoring to your target audience's frame of reference. If your product is best suited for individuals who are striving singles under 34 who go to night clubs and live on pizza, then advertising to young families that live in the suburbs is not a good use of your funds. Fit the message to the audience, pick the audience that has a perceived need for your product and seek media outlets that provide a "one to many" communication opportunity. Your goal is to initiate a "pull" strategy, or a "demand" strategy that utilizes awareness to stimulate buyer interest and influence buying behavior.

The more you can learn about the desires, behaviors, and lifestyles of the customers you want to serve, the better you will be able to influence their buying decision process. In today's complex world, you are not only competing against similarly perceived products, but you are also competing for a share of the consumer's disposable income. Knowing who they are, where they are, how they buy, and what is important to them is critical for your success.

Product market sectors – The industrial, or business to business market, offers a different set of challenges. Your potential customer will probably be constrained by the checks and balances of a corporate purchasing protocol – where the buying process often includes more than one decision maker. In this environment you will need to offer a product or service that is integrated into the product or service that your customer offers to their customer; or that will facilitate their commercial processes. For example, Intuit recently introduced Quickbooks Point of Sale that replaces a company's cash register, tracks their inventory, records sales and customer buying information and also prepares reports.

Uses of the products or services you provide are often part of a larger consumption model that may affect multiple manufacturing or operational processes. Marketing to multiple sectors requires your offering to be "compatible" with these downstream environments and may require compliance with specific industry standards. In order for your potential customer to purchase from you, they must be satisfied that incorporating your wares will not upset their relationship with their up line suppliers or down stream customers.

Industrial or business customers are increasingly savvy about the economics of their purchases. They look at things from a broader point of view; considering the purchase price, the life cycle cost of an item and training requirements. Business purchasers consider the economic influence that comes from using your product or service to enhance their own products or services. What you often have to offer in a business to business environment, (B2B) is not just support for their business operations; it is also part of their value proposition to their customers. For example, Pepsi and Coke Cola have managed exclusive soft drink dispensary sales to restaurant chains; providing both their soft drink brand and self service support that help to enhance the restaurant's business.

Industrial or business customers can also be categorized into identifiable industry segments. There are industry specific products that do not have application outside of that particular environment. This would suggest that it is extremely important to identify those industry groupings and understand the manufacturing and distribution activities that transpire within them. . Do your homework to identify product needs and purchasing patterns within your specific environments.

Displaying at industry trade shows is another way to introduce your company to the commercial marketplace. Trade shows are an excellent one to many communication venue to potential customer groups who are there to learn about what is going on within their industry. Organizers of these events look for product and service innovations and they may actually promote a new entrant as part of their trade show communication programs. This is great publicity for a new company; once again a free announcement is going to go directly to your targeted audience. The "biz tradeshows" website displays worldwide trade shows (http://www. biztradeshows.com/) listed by industry, by country, by show date, by organizer, by venue and by product. Check it out.

Specific industries have also their own trade publications, and these journals are frequently read by the influencers and buyers of the products you are planning to offer. The cost of advertising in these publications is often quite reasonable and they provide a great medium to announce your new arrival. Most importantly, you know that the message you are sending has a high probability of being received by your targeted audience. Although advertising may not have the same influence on commercial buyers as it can on retail consumers, your initial objective is to create awareness - letting them know you are here.

Construct your message as a value proposition so that your potential customers understand the problem you are trying to solve or the need that you are trying to satisfy. Steve Jobs understood the market cliché - "features tell but benefits sell." Make sure your message specifically describes the benefits your customer will gain by including your product or service in their business activities. Anything other than that kind of message will be ignored or considered just marketing fluff.

PRODUCT PLANNING, POSITIONING YOUR PRODUCTS

The concept of product positioning is one that gets misinterpreted regularly in many organizations. Too often we have heard someone suggest that when a sales opportunity is lost, "we did not position the product against our competition" or we must have been "out sold" by somebody else. These are useless clichés' because positioning a product is all about "making it easy to buy," "not easy to sell" (Cobb, 2007). If you recognize the true meaning of product positioning then you must be willing to construct strategies to make your offering more attractive than the competition.

Determining price – For example, if you are planning to offer a new kind of coffee maker, customers should be able to find it among the retailers who provide these kinds of products; easily identifying your product in terms of use and capacity. The same Perceptual Marketing Map used to develop your marketing strategy can be used to help you plan your price points for your new coffee maker.. Construct another model for each of your products, a representation that visually shows how your product is going to be perceived in relationship to competitive alternatives.

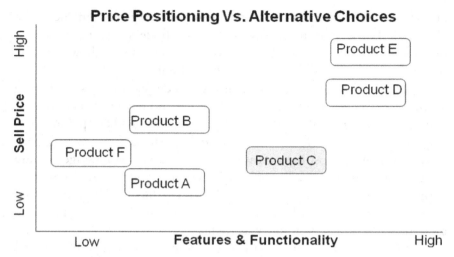

Figure 7.2 A Perceptual Marketing Map applied to pricing a product in a competitive environment

Make sure to note the similarity between the product positioning example in Figure 7.2 and the Perceptual Market Map for entry that we introduced in Figure 7.1. If you are seeking to capture a particular space within a targeted market segment, then everything you present to the market has to be representative of this distinction. Your market strategy, your market communications and your product positioning all must have been aligned in order to send a high impact message to the marketplace.

PRODUCT CHARACTERISTICS AFFECT CHANNEL STRATEGIES –

Individual product characteristics require different marketing channel consideration and deciding these choices will impact how your business operates. Products that sell for high unit values, automobiles for example, often require dedicated or specialized distribution channels. Products that have low unit values, pens and pencils for example, are usually standardized products that are offered through many distribution outlets. If the decision to purchase your products requires a technical evaluation, or a review by multiple influencers, then you will most likely need a direct sales effort to influence your customers purchasing decision. If your product's use is easily identified, then you could conceivably offer it through a catalogue.

Similar positioning dynamics exist around product complexity. The more complex the product, such as a custom engineered product for example, the more difficult it is to explain its value to its potential buyers. In this instance, the product may only be available from the original source, and it would be represented in the marketplace by a select group of sales engineers who understand the details of its application. Highly specialized products or services such as these would usually be offered at a price point specific to the customer benefits derived.

Commodities, on the other hand, can be mass marketed; custom engineered products cannot. Low cost or commodity items can be mass produced, specialized products cannot. Therefore, if your products are simple, look for many channels and consistent pricing. If your products are complex, you will be looking for specialized channels to represent your capabilities. Regardless of the kind of products you intend to offer, you need to find channels to get them introduced to potential buyers.

Use the matrix shown in Figure 7.3 to help you better understands your channel options for the kinds of products and services you plan to offer:

Product Characteristic	Product Line Strategies	Channel Choices
Unit Value High	Many Models	Selective or Direct
Unit Value Low	Standardize	Multiple
Purchase Event High	Many Models	Selective
Purchase Event Low	Standardized	Multiple
Purchase Effort High	Many Models	Selective or Direct
Purchase Effort Low	Standardize	Multiple
Tech. Change High	Many Models	Selective or Direct
Tech. Change Low	Standardize	Multiple
Tech. Complex High	Many Models	Selective or Direct
Tech Complex Low	Standardize	Multiple
Service Need High	Many Models	Selective
Service Need Low	Standardize	Multiple
Frequency High	Standardize	Multiple
Frequency Low	Many Models	Selective
Consumption High	Standardize	Multiple
Consumption Low	Many Models	Selective
Usage Broad	Standardize	Multiple
Usage Narrow	Many Models	Selective

Figure 7.3 The less complex and more standard the offering is, the less discriminating your channel selection needs to be. The more complex and less standard the offering is, the more deliberate you need to be in your channel selection. (Cobb,2007)

SELECTING YOUR CHANNELS FOR REACHING YOUR CUSTOMERS-

Skillfully announcing your arrival should generate some interest about the kind of company you have formed and the products you plan to offer. But, now you must provide a way for your customers to find your products and services so that they can actually purchase them. In marketing terms, this is all about selecting the appropriate channels, the "vehicles," that will deliver your products from the manufacturing source to the actual buyer. Characteristics of your products or services will have a significant influence on the kinds of distribution methods you can select for this purpose (Cobb, 2007).

CONSUMER PRODUCTS-

Examining options for consumer products reveals that there are three different alternatives to consider. The first option is to establish a direct channel, whereby your company is communicating directly with, and selling directly to, the end user or consumer – such as internet sales. Second is to utilize retailers to present your products, or as some refer to them, "the big box stores." The third option is to sell to wholesalers, or distributors, who will then in turn re-sell your products to other retail outlets. Each model has advantages, and disadvantages, depending on the characteristics and profitability of the products you have to offer. If you choose to use all three, be sure to protect your re-sellers by fixing the price point ranges. Manufactures using Big Box Stores for distribution can protect other preferred sellers by designing products with features specific to the retail giant; with a product feature set that would not be available elsewhere. Therefore, comparison shoppers will be unable to directly compare product features and price between large and small retailers.

Direct channel marketing – Economically establishing a direct channel to millions of potential consumers is relatively easy to do using the worldwide web. But, merely opening your virtual store doors or creating a website does not induce anyone to come visit it. You still need to advertise and promote your existence if you expect customers to come by. A virtual store may be intriguing, but some products may still require hands on viewing, and for them, an actual store front may be necessary.

The advantages to dealing with the consumer directly include keeping more of your profit margin, obtaining direct feedback on the quality of your products and services, and receiving "real time" information about your sales activity. The big disadvantage is that you are now engaged in a transaction by transaction process, and that will require a higher level of day to day staff involvement, processing capability, and customer service support

Big Box marketing – Selling to the "big box stores" (retailers), can sound attractive, but getting them to carry a new product is often difficult. Retailers want to know that your product will sell and will sell at the price point that you have planned. The advantage of selling through large retailer is that distribution costs are minimized; however, some large retailers systematically drive down suppliers profit margins – forcing a backwards flow of wage and cost cutting. Their business is all about making money from utilizing shelve space, so they are interested in high volume items that attract consumer interest. They also require a substantial profit margin of their own to off-set their operating costs, so don't be surprised when they ask to keep 50 percent of the retail price. The other wrinkle is that if your product doesn't sell, you may be asked to take it back, at your own expense and provide a refund.

Recently, these large retail outlets have been requiring new vendors to prove that there is a market for the products being offered before they will buy them and that the vendor provides some "proof" that consumers are willing to purchase them at recognizable price points. This model now requires all new vendors or suppliers to list their wares on the retail store's website where consumers can find it and consider purchasing them. If sufficient volumes can be generated within this environment, then the retail store will consider putting the products on their shelves. If sufficient volumes are not achieved, they will often allow new vendors to continue selling their products via the store's website.

There are advantages to working with the large retailers, as they have been strategically located in large customer's bases and they are able to attract higher levels of consumer traffic because of the variety of goods they offer. They will often allow promotional displays for items, and will include your products in their advertising campaigns. The disadvantages are that they will only carry what sells, so you will always be competing for shelving space, and they do require a substantial margin in order to represent your product.

Marketing through wholesalers – Selling to wholesalers is another alternative that is used successfully by some industries. Wine and beer, for example, are brought to market using this model. The producer concentrates on making the product, the wholesaler buys in larger quantities to take advantage of volume discounts, and then distributes and sells to the various retail outlets. The reason that this model works for this industry is that there is significant cost avoidance available to each of the participants throughout this consumption chain. The producer eliminates the need to market, store and ship the product, the wholesaler gets to purchase at a lower price point to off-set the distribution cost and the retailers gets the product delivered to them for a reasonable cost, enabling them to make a profit.

The advantages to selling to wholesalers is that you have a limited number of transactions to manage, a formal or contractual distribution arrangement is often arranged, and a mutually beneficial commercial relationship exists that can be leveraged for future growth. The disadvantage is that you will be foregoing incremental margin opportunity and limiting your marketing presence to the number of distributors you engage. Still, you would be amazed at how many industries thrive with this kind of arrangement, among who are the automotive, furniture, grocery and beer industries.

INDUSTRIAL PRODUCTS (B2B)-

For industrial products and services, marketing channel selection requires a different approach. If the product that is being offered is "standardized," meaning that it meets some predetermined specification that is known and accepted by the industry, then it can be marketed in more than one fashion. If the product or service is "specialized," then it normally requires a skilled distribution channel that can adequately present its attributes in a credible manner. This creates a different kind of role for the selected channel that often goes beyond just representing your product.

There are several choices available to you for the delivery of industrial or technical products, and here are four popular choices to consider:

- Direct sales requiring the establishment of your own sales force to take your message directly to your targeted customers.

- Value Added Re-sellers (VARs) who take your product and integrate it with their own and products from others to increase the packaged value to the customer.

- Wholesalers or distributors, who will purchase from you in volume and re-sell your products to other industrial outlets or users.

• Entering into what is known as an "O.E.M." (Original Equipment Manufacturer) relationship with companies that will re-sell your products under their own brand name.

Just as with your choices for consumer products, there are advantages and disadvantages to marketing with each of these channels as well.

Establishing a direct sales force will provide you with the advantage of influencing how your products and services are being represented. You can designate the target market, the products or packages of products and the transaction circumstance or conditions. Company sales representatives provide feed back about desired features and benefits directly to the customer. Pharmaceuticals typically use this model.

The advantages of employing a direct sales force are many for companies offering complex products or services – like a pharmaceutical line. Candidly, without subject matter experts to describe their offerings, these companies would have an extremely difficult time getting their prospective clients to understand the value they have to offer. The disadvantage is that this is one of the most expensive ways to reach the market, as direct sales usually require investments in personnel, training, and travel.

Value-added resellers have become popular with the providers of technology products. An individual electronic component is valuable, but only if it is incorporated into a circuit board and can work well with other electronic components on that board. Value-added resellers are technically savvy, and they understand both the industry and the application consumption cycle for many different components. VARs can be found in other market segments as well, and their common characteristic is that they enhance the value of the product you provide them by applying it in unique or creative ways.

The advantages to working with a VAR is obvious, they can expand your market opportunity. They can introduce your products into market niches that you may not be aware of and they can find new and creative uses for the products you offer. The disadvantage to working with VARs is that they may find substitutes for your products for comparable quality and lower price. They will also seek to purchase at reduced prices and are reluctant to enter into volume marketing agreements with the product sources they utilize. When you are working with a VAR, you are usually isolated from the ultimate end user customer and product feedback is limited.

Wholesalers and distributors have their place in the business to business environment as well, and they are a good choice for "standardized" parts and products. Standardization enables mass production, and mass production is a good feed source for mass distribution. If you are planning to offer a product that has universal appeal, such as nuts and bolts do, then you definitely want to consider working with wholesalers and distributors to deliver your products.

The wholesaler advantages are that you will be able to reach a larger number of outlets through these arrangements than you would be able to cultivate on your own. This greater visibility should translate to higher sales volumes, and larger individual transaction values. The disadvantage is that you are one layer removed from the actual consumer of your product, and will not necessarily receive timely or accurate market feedback. You will also need to make a portion of your margin available to the distributors to enable them to cover their operating costs.

Working with OEMs requires the producer of a product to produce sufficient quantities of a particular item or model in a fashion that meets the OEM's unique application requirements. This is often referred to as a "factory sales model" because a significant portion of your production will be dedicated to meeting the OEM's needs, and they in turn can be the ones who will dictate changes in design, and economics.

The advantages to working with an OEM partner are that you do not have to concern yourself with either marketing or fulfillment; the OEM Company handles that for you. You avoid these costs and can concentrate on producing predictable quantities of product in the most efficient fashion. These factors also permeate throughout the business in other ways, as administrative functions are not as tedious, and supply chain management is simplified.

The disadvantages to working with an OEM partner are that a large portion of your revenues are concentrated in just one customer. Because the OEM accepts the marketing risks and the logistics costs of the arrangement, they will expect very favorable pricing. This is a high volume, low cost, low margin environment to operate in.

MARKETING CHANNELS AFFECT PRODUCT PERCEPTION –

In addition to all of these economic and logistical considerations, it is important not to loose sight of the marketplace perceptions you will be creating because of the channel choices you are making. The process by which your channels represent your product or service will now become your company's reputation. Seek channel partners that compliment your business strategy, that are able to support your proposed marketing campaign plans, and can provide you with incremental market knowledge. It would also be helpful if they are willing to participate with you in your media campaigns, as well as contribute to the promotion of your products within the industry. Your goal in selecting your channels is to create a "win-win" scenario that benefits everyone who touches your products so that they will continue to support your present and future marketing efforts.

ORGANIZING THE EFFORT- EXECUTION

Once you have strategies defined, your advertising campaigns ready to launch and your products packaged and ready to go, you are officially in business. Being in business is a good thing; it represents the start of a journey that will hopefully provide the opportunities and rewards that you are seeking. But, like any exploration headed into the unknown, complete preparations are needed to ensure that you are able to manage the challenges confronting all new businesses. You need to define your business processes and business practices.

BUSINESS PROCESSES-

A business "reference model" is a means to describe the business operations of an organization; independent of the organizational structure assigned to perform them. These reference models can be constructed in layers, and offer a foundation for the analysis of service components, technology, data, and performance. They are often used to provide the framework for the development of business processes that are necessary to operate the business.

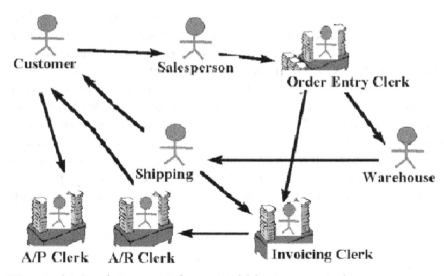

Figure 7.4 A Simple Business Reference Model for Customer Order Entry

Business processes, on the other hand, are a series of logically related activities or tasks (such as order entry, production, distribution, etc.) performed together to produce a defined set of results. A business process can be dissected into several sub-processes, all of which have their own attributes, but all contributing to achieving the goal of the overall process. The creation of a business processes typically includes mapping of processes and sub-processes down to individual employee activity levels.

In the 18th century, Adam Smith, in his famous (1776) description of a pin factory, Smith described the business process for the production of a pin in the following way: "One man draws out the wire, another straights it, a third cuts it, a fourth points it, a fifth grinds it at the top for receiving the head: to make the head requires two or three distinct operations: to put it on is a particular business, to whiten the pins is another ... and the important business of making a pin is, in this manner, divided into about eighteen distinct operations, which in some manufactories are all performed by distinct hands, though in others the same man will sometime perform two or three of them."

Rummler & Brache (1995) use a different kind of definition that clearly encompasses a focus on the organization's external customers, when stating: "a business process is a series of steps designed to produce a product or service. Most processes are cross-functional, spanning the 'white space' between the boxes on the organization chart. Some processes result in a product or service that is received by an organization's external customer. We call these primary processes. Other processes produce products that are invisible to the external customer but essential to the effective management of the business. We call these support processes." A business process model is usually represented with flow chart diagrams, and typically is one that has one or more individual business processes involved.

Launching your new enterprise will require you to have some understanding as to how the work you are about to perform is going to get done. We will touch on this topic again as part of your on going business operations in Chapter 9, Managing Financial Success, but it is important to make sure that you have considered this reality when you open your doors. How are you going to take an order? Does it require a contract? Who do you hand it to once you accept it? How are its requirements fulfilled? Who makes sure that it gets delivered on time? When do we bill the customer? How to we keep track of accounts receivable? Use business reference models to help you with this, and then formalize you business processes.

There are inexpensive tools that are now available in the market to help you get going with these business processes; some of which can be found within early stage company accounting packages. Intuit, Inc., for example, offers *Quick Books* as a small business/start up business accounting package. It provides a logical representation of how various business transactions are related, and includes the financial interactions that are necessary to keep track of your transactions. It also provides a basic business process diagram that can be extremely helpful to you if you have had no previous experience with business financial systems or process modeling.

Another effective approach to identify your needs in this area is to simulate the actual experience your customer will encounter. Pretend that you have just contacted your company and would like to know more about your products and services. Once you are comfortable with how that will be handled, go through the process of purchasing the product. Then examine how the order will be processed, fulfilled, and delivered. Ensure that the transaction will get recorded appropriately, and that the customer will be invoiced. It is critical that you establish a protocol for how transactions are to be conducted and recorded prior to the roll out.

Key Performance Indicators (KPIs) are key business statistics that measure a firm's performance in critical areas; such as the number of new orders or cash collection efficiency. KPIs show the progress (or lack of it) toward realizing the firm's objectives or strategic plans by monitoring metrics which (if not properly performed) would likely cause severe losses or outright failure. Since there is no standard metric for business performance, you will have to determine what is important to your organization and how you will keep track of it. Acquiring an understanding of what these are within you industry is a good place to start

An example of a key performance indicator could be the number of new customers being acquired and the quantity of new products being sold. In order to measure the success or failure of this effort, there needs to be visibility into the activities that are involved in generating new customers and new orders. For a consumer products company, it could be as simple as tracking the volume of sales on a daily basis to ensure that the actual number of transactions taking place is consistent with what you had expected. Collins (2001), in his classic *Good to Great: Why Some Companies Make the Leap and Others Don't*, found that performance metrics include strategies such as profit per transaction or profit per square foot of retail space; measures that are more descriptive of performance than just quarterly profit or loss.

For a business to business products company, it could be tracking the number and value of the sales proposals being presented to the market and the subsequent value of the new purchase orders received from that effort. If you are a manufacturing company, you may want to be watching the key performance indicators that measure your production activities. You will want to watch your supply chain, so that you have enough component parts; your production capacity, so you know how many items you can produce; and your finished product inventories, so that you don't produce more product than you need to meet expected customer demand. You would once again seek to establish a "norm" consistent with your planned expectations and track any variances to that norm so that you can make adjustments if needed.

There are numerous examples of key performance indicators that can be established for a variety of different business environments. The objective in taking this step is to ensure that, as the management of the organization, you have visibility into what's taking place within each critical functional area of the business. It is too late to make corrections or adjustments after the financial report tells you that things turned out differently than you hoped for. The greater the visibility you can access in the earliest stages of a process, the greater the likelihood is that you can influence the outcome of that activity.

BUSINESS PRACTICES –

Business practices are the methods, procedures, processes, and rules employed or followed by a firm in the pursuit of its objectives. This would imply that you may need to: think about whether or not you are going to provide a warranty, (guaranty) in support of the quality of your products; think about how you are going handle requests to return items; think about how you are going handle requests for additional services that are not recognizable in your initial contracted arrangements. In other words, start thinking about how your company is going to behave in the marketplace.

Ethics in action – For a new company, or any new organization, formalizing your business practices is more important than just the policies that may evolve over time. It is the recognition of a set of values and beliefs by which you are going to run your company, and the "creed" that you will be asking your employees and suppliers, distributors, and others to abide by. If you and your associates have a common understanding of what is important to the organization, than those beliefs will become the principals by which operating habits become engrained and decisions will be made.

An example of what a "credo" could contain is simply a definition of what the company is, what the company sees as its vision or mission, and what the firm believes in terms of how it intends to conduct its transactions. Here are some thoughts to consider:

> "Your Company is a growth company that is market driven and customer focused"

> "Your Company is a company that seeks mutual benefit from its relationships with partners, suppliers, customers and its employees"

> "Your Company intends to become the high quality, low cost provider of your products to your industry"

> "Your Company believes that its customers are the most important people in its business and that they are the purpose for its work"

> "Your Company believes in the dignity of the people it employs and the importance of their work and expects them to make the most effective use of their skill, effort, and time on the job"

The Better Business Bureau (2003) has addressed a number of business practice issues over the years, and as a result of this experience, it has defined a set of ethical business principles it recommends businesses to follow. Monitoring these ethical practices has become a more challenging task in recent years because of the proliferation of internet commerce. For example, they have now had to established and recommend a *"Code of Online Business Practices,"* that includes "the principles for ethical business to customer conduct." In summary, it provides the following guidelines:

Principle I: Truthful and Accurate Communications. Online advertisers should not engage in deceptive or misleading practices with regard to any aspect of electronic commerce, including advertising, marketing, or in their use of technology.

Principle II: Disclosure. Online merchants should disclose to their customers and prospective customers information about the business, the goods or services available for purchase online, and the transaction itself.

Principle III: Information Practices and Security. Online advertisers should adopt information practices that treat customers' personal information with care. They should post and adhere to a privacy policy based on fair information principles, take appropriate measures to provide adequate security, and respect customers' preferences regarding unsolicited email.

Principle IV: Customer Satisfaction. Online merchants should seek to ensure their customers are satisfied by honoring their representations, answering questions, and resolving customer complaints and disputes in a timely and responsive manner.

Principle V: Protecting Children. If online advertisers target children under the age of 13, they should take special care to protect them by recognizing children's developing cognitive abilities

Recognizable business practices establish long term relationships. The stories of customer service at Nordstrom's, the highly successful retailer, are legendary. As a matter of fact, there is even a book written about their obsession with customer satisfaction entitled: *The Nordstrom Way* (Specter & McCarth, 1996). Every associate who comes to work at Nordstrom knows that the one thing that is most highly valued by this organization is the customer relationship. There are multiple stories about Nordstrom taking back returned items that were either obviously worn, or in some cases, not even sold at their store, just to ensure that the customer returning the item held Nordstrom in the highest possible regard. No one has ever complained about doing business with Nordstrom, because if they are not 100 percent satisfied, Nordstrom will do everything it possibly can to make things right.

Nordstrom is a prime example of having a corporate culture that is understood and practiced throughout the organization. Your new enterprise is going to be challenged to develop its own set of values that will build your company's culture. When customers choose to do business with you, what can they expect? Will you return phone calls in a timely fashion? Will you follow up on deliveries to make sure that your products arrived in good condition and that your customer was satisfied with their purchase? These operating choices will determine how you are going to behave in the marketplace and influence your company's reputation.

CELEBRATE –

Launching your new business is an exciting event; something that should be celebrated and remembered. In the weeks and months ahead you will learn a great deal about your customers, your products, your processes, and your practices. Listen carefully to the feedback you will receive from each of your stakeholders and make your adjustments accordingly. You are experiencing a new adventure, so be sure to enjoy the challenges and opportunities that are part of the journey.

MARKETING CIRQUE DU SOLEIL

Business Description: Cirque du Soleil (Circus of the Sun) could easily be dismissed as an anomaly, not a real business, except for the odd fact that in 1984 two unemployed Canadian sidewalk circus street performers created an artistic experience that annually grosses approximately $1 billion; employs over 4000 people in 23 shows and will have played in more than 271 cities on every geographic continent by the end of 2011. Shows please the eyes and ears of audiences and bottom-line concerns of bankers. While maintaining original show genre, Cirque recently introduced Beatles, Elvis Presley and Michael Jackson tributes; with seven permanent shows in Las Vegas, a Disney Orlando Show and a permanent venue planned for the United Arab Emirates by 2012. See www.cirquedusoleil.com

Market Strategy: In 1984, circus had become passé in the entertainment field; circuses often having to give away children's tickets through schools to get paying adults to attend. Tents were expensive to transport and set up, animals were potentially dangerous and using them incited animal right activists. Adding a few more acrobatic features did little to raise ticket prices or ticket sales. Faced with dismal employment futures Guy Laliberte and Daniel Gauthier changed the rules; creating something that had never been done before. They broke the "circus paradigm;" cobbling together several performing arts into an audience experience that typically receives standing ovations. Instead of three simultaneous rings of activity, the famous "Three Ring Circus" format, Cirque builds every show around a story; dramatically telling it with live music, acrobatic and theater skills.

Market Communications: In changing the circus entrainment industry rules, Laliberte and Gauthier changed a major sector of the entertainment industry into its own version of the experience industry. A successful publicity stunt, walking 56 miles on circus stilts in 22 hours, worked to get a start up grant. An early decision was made to frame the brand architecture as an umbrella (Over brand) of different shows that served opportunity venues. From the beginning, marketing communications have been based on building a person to person rapport with the audience – creating experiences that no one has ever felt. To introduce Saltimbanco to Paris, local artisans were invited to conduct a workshop for the Cirque staff and a workshop was reciprocated. Relentless pursuit of performance perfection has positioned the Cirque brand to a High Value and High Price spot on the Perceptual Marketing Map. The company developed a world class website; including trailers for each show and it has a significant video clip presence on You Tube.

Product Marketing: Competition for discretionary spending money is fierce; including athletics at multiple levels and multiple types, theater, music and television. The traditional circus target markets to children; as each Ringling Brothers and Barum & Bailey show is begun by the ringmaster saying, "Ladies and gentlemen, children of all ages…." However, Cirque consciously positioned itself into the adult market segment – specifically attracting adults capable of purchasing premium entertainment tickets in the $90.00 to $160.00 range. Even at premium ticket prices, most of the shows are sold out every night.

Business Practices: Cirque du Soleil is an organization that thrives on getting ordinary people to do extraordinary things - creative things that translate into spectacular success. Corporate accountants, attorneys, make up artists, clowns, musicians, acrobats and performance support technicians work together to produce spectacular shows. The contributions of everyone are valued in building the corporate team. While many individual performances appear to be "death defying," that is a purposeful illusion – as performance support technicians ensure that the risk is quite minimal. Every part of every show is 100 percent safe or it will not be included in telling the story. The illusion of risk is derived from countless hours that artists spend with support personnel to minimize risk and maximize artistic value – "making the impossible possible." Now into its third decade, Cirque's relentless pursuit of excellence facilitates introduction of new shows – a "pull marketing strategy."

Check out: As an exercise in comparative business product and business practices, go to You Tube and search "Cirque du Soleil" and "Ringling Brothers, Barum & Bailey Circus. For more information on Circus du Soleil and its business model, see the following:

Babin, T. & Manchester, K. (2004). Cirque du Soleil: 20 years under the sun. New York: Harry N. Abrams Publisher.

Heward, L. & Bacon, J. U. (2006). The spark: Igniting the spark that lives within us all.

New York: Currency Books.

CHAPTER SUMMARY

KEY POINTS

- Entering the market requires that you have alignment between a) market strategy, b) marketing communications and c) product positioning.

- The Perceptual Market Map is a useful tool for identifying potential space in the marketplace.

- The Perceptual Market Map is a useful tool for price point decisions.

- The three generic market entry strategies are: a) Provide lower cost, b) Introduce new features and/or functions or c) Change the rules - deliver a different business practice.

- A marketing "message" must communicate your a) marketing strategy and the marketplace position you are seeking to establish

- All marketing communication mediums from advertising to packaging must convey the same message.

- Trademarks should be filed with the U.S. Office of Trademarks and Patents, but a "brand" is a perceived thing – in the eye of the beholder.

- Ultimately, brand identification is in the minds of the customer and other stakeholders.

- Product positioning should be consistent with your desired market positioning

- Different products may require different marketing channel considerations; a) direct customer sales, b) sales through major retailers or c) wholesale distribution.

- Launching into the market requires the establishment of business processes.

- Participating in the market requires the establishment of business practices.

- An ethical corporate culture fosters long term relationships.

TAKE ACTION NOW

- Create an industry "playing field" and assign the factors that are important to your success to the horizontal and vertical axis. (e.g. price and functionality)

- Populate this "arena" with your perceptual market map, using different size circles for different size competitors.

- Identify "market space" where your competitors have the least amount of influence, the "blank areas within your arena.

- Choose the market entry position that you intend to address and understand the nuances associated with assuming this market position

- Create your communications strategy, and identify the name, logo, and message that will best describe what you intend to be

- Create a press kit for your business – as it will open many doors to free publicity and can also be useful to support searching for start-up funding.

- Identify industry trade associations and take advantage of their gatherings and trade shows to introduce your new venture

- Design your product packaging, stationary, displays, and advertising in a similar format that communicates the same message in the same fashion; who you are

- Position and price the products you intend to offer in a manner that is absolutely representative of the market message you are creating

- Re-examine your "ideal target customer" profile and make sure you know who it is you are going to convey your market message and product introductions to.

- Identify and select distribution channels that can introduce you to these customers and adequately represent the features and benefits of your offerings

- Establish contractual relationships with these channels that adequately identify both qualifications and expectations

- Go through the process of buying your products from your organization and make sure that the process is seamless and that all elements of the transaction are recorded properly

- Insure that your have fulfillment processes in place to enable the delivery of customer orders in an accurate and timely manner

- Make sure that you team knows what is expected from them and that the company's desired practices are know and supported

- "Walk the talk" It is one thing to express a desire to do things right, it takes a commitment to make sure that things are actually done right.

- Make continuous learning and continuous improvement part of your culture, and always seek new ways to make things run more effectively.

REFERENCES:

BBB Online.Org (2003) *A Better Business Bureau Program*, Council of Better Business Bureau Inc., publisher

Branson, Richard (Oct 15, 2010) *Building a Brand for Your Business*, Entreprenueur.com, Publisher.

Cobb, William R. (2007) *Targeted Tactics: Transforming Strategy into Measurable Result.* Philadelphia, PA: Xliris Publishers

Claritas Inc. (2004) *Calritas Prizm,* , San Diego, CA: Claritas Inc. Publisher.

Chan, K. W. & Mauborgne, R. (2005) *Blue Ocean Strategy,* Harvard Cambridge, MA: Business School Publishing Corp.

Collins, J. (2001). *Good to great: Why some companies make the leap and others don't.* New York: HarperCollins Publishers.

Deming, W. E. (2000). *Out of crisis.* Cambridge, MA: MIT Press.

Friedman, T. L. (2008). *Hot, flat, and crowded: Why we need a green revolution – and how it can renew* America. New York: Farrar, Straus and Giroux.

Kranz, Jonathan (no date) *Constructing a Press Kit,* Dummies.com, Publisher.

Kotler, P., (2008)) *Principles of Marketing,* (13th Ed.), Upper Saddle River, NJ: Prentice Hall.

Lemons, B. (2005). *The Case for B2B Branding,* Stamford. CN: The Thomson Corporation Publisher

Moore, G. (2002). *Crossing the Chasm: Marketing and selling high-tech products to mainstream customers.* New York: HarperCollins Publisher.

Pink, D. H. (2006). *A whole new mind: Why right-brainers will rule the future.* New York: Riverhead Books.

Spector, R. & McCarth, P. (1996) *The Nordstrom Way,* Hoboken, NJ: John Wiley & Sons.

Toffler, A. & Toffler, H. (2006). *Revolutionary wealth: How it will be created and how it will change our lives.* New York: Currency Books.

Ries, Al, Ries, Laura (1998) *The 22 Immutable Laws of Branding,* Harper Business, Publishers

Rummler & Brache (1995). *Improving Performance: How to manage the white space on the organizational chart.* Jossey-Bass, San Francisco

SUPPLEMENTAL SOURCES:

Halligan, B., Dharmesh, S. & Meerman, D. (2009). *Inbound marketing: Get found using Google, social media and blogs.* Hoboken, NJ: John Wiley & Sons.

Jantsch, J. (2008). *Duct tape marketing: The world's most practical small business marketing guide.* Nashville, TN: Thomas Nelson Inc.

Kerin, R., Hartley, S. & Rudellus, W. (2010). *Marketing.* New York: McGraw-Hill.

Kotler, P. & Armstrong, G. (2009). *Principles of marketing* (13th Ed.). Upper Saddle River, NJ: Prentice Hall, Inc.

Scott, D. M. (2010). *The new rules of marketing and PR: How to use social media, blogs, news releases, online video and viral marketing to reach buyers directly* (2nd Ed.). Hoboken, NJ: John Wiley & Sons.

Sernovitz, A. (2009). *Word of mouth marketing: How smart companies get people talking* (2nd Ed.). New York: Kaplan Publishing.

Shenk, D. (2010). *The genius in all of us: Why everything you've been told about genetics, talent and IQ are wrong.* New York: Doubleday.

Trout, J. & Rivkin, S. The new positioning: The latest on the world's #1 business strategy. New York: McGraw-Hill.

CHAPTER EIGHT

Growing Your Enterprise

*"Only those who will risk going too far can
possibly find out how far one can go."*

T. S. Eliot

In Chapter Five we made reference to the infamous "S" curve, the model used to illustrate new enterprise financing needs, evolution and growth. The model, shown here again in Figure 8.1, has also been successfully applied to technology adoption, product life cycles, and business maturation. We are referring to it again to help us focus on the right priorities at the right time for the expansion of a new venture. Once a new company with a new product enters the market, the work has just begun. It must grow if it is going to enhance its value.

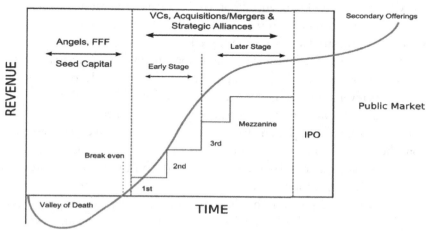

Figure 8.1 Growth requirements of the new venture project stage progression. Image representation from The TAPMI BLOG, T. A. Pai Management Institute

New business ventures, and the products that they offer, will go through a somewhat predictable life cycle. There will be the challenge and exhilaration that comes from a successful introduction into the marketplace. There will be a period of time when the new venture and its products start to gain market momentum and the company will experience a period of early growth. Eventually though, you will approach a period where the enthusiasm for the new innovation has slowed and things start to settle into a more stable pattern of maturity.

THE GROWTH PROCESSES

In order for an entrepreneur, or any other stakeholder, to benefit from the creation of a new venture, the business will have to grow in sales volume and profitability. Investors and acquirers are usually interested in businesses that have demonstrated revenue growth, achieved consistent profitability, and have a competent management team in place to run the company. To achieve this, you will have to grow to a level of critical mass that enables these factors to come to fruition. For most new ventures, this requires a series of thoughtful steps and recognition of the financial requirements for each step.

It is important to recognize that rapid growth can put a strain on any organization and there can be serious financial consequences to this undertaking if the growth is not planned for. We will be introducing several different financial approaches to accommodating growth in the next Chapter Nine, Managing Financial Success, but within the context of this Chapter, we will concentrate on the strategies and tactics available to grow revenues. Growing your business will be both fun, and challenging, but the rewards are usually worth the effort.

There are five generic strategies that management can pursue to accelerate the growth of the enterprise: a) explore new ways in which to increase the company's revenues from their current customer base so that additional sales can be realized from existing efforts; b) explore ways to enter new industries and new markets to acquire new customers so that one can expand revenues from the sale of their existing products and services; c) expand geographically by entering new geographies and introducing the business to new customers; d) franchise the operations to "clone" their business model into new markets; e) merge with or acquire another firm or firms that have similar products or complimentary capabilities to one's own that can be integrated and leveraged for growth. We may have over-simplified this a bit, but essentially these are the best options for achieving rapid, incremental growth.

INCREASING REVENUES FROM EXISTING CUSTOMERS

Increasing revenues from existing retail customers: Increasing sales in an existing market is one of the easiest ways to grow your business. You already have established customers, and, like all businesses, you've collected all kinds of information about them. The key to successfully increasing new sales to your existing customers is to learn from your customers' buying histories, both generally and individually. The goal, of course, is to get your existing customers to buy more.

Different kinds of business models will be required to do different things to accomplish this goal. For example, in retail operations, one that sells directly to the consumer, it can be as simple as adding a new line of products. If your customers are telling you that they like a particular grouping of products, such as sold through Bath & Body Works or The Body Shop, Inc., it is most likely because these are the things that support their lifestyle. Seek to understand what other products or services are valued within this group, and then search for ways to provide them. This process is often referred to as developing your "marketing mix" (Schewe & Hiam, 1998).

The major considerations for making these new product selections are the same decision factors that you encountered when you first launched your business. The goal remains the same; to bring value to your target market and be consistent in the way you represent your company. Figure 8.2 illustrates how the four "Ps" of marketing can be applied to help with your new product selection process: Product, Price, Place and Promotion (Cobb, 2007). The *"marketing mix"* you are creating is part of what defines the personality of your business. For example, if consumers wanted to buy sporting equipment to go camping with, they would not be going to Macy's or Nordstrom. They will probably head to stores like REI, Eddie Bauer or LL Bean because they know they can find what they are looking for at these retailers.

Product	**Price**	**Place**	**Promotion**
Functionality	List Price	Channel Partners	Advertising
Appearance	Discounts	Channel Motivation	Personal Selling
Quality	Allowances	Market Coverage	Public Relations
Packaging	Credit Terms	Locations	Message
Brand	Leasing Options	Logistics	Media
Warranty		Service Levels	Budget
Service / Support			

Figure 8.2 Summaries of Marketing Mix Decision Considerations (Cobb, 2007)

Bulk buys, purchase incentives, and frequent buyer reward programs are all examples of business growth strategies for increasing sales to existing customers. An individual customer's buying history gives you insight into his or her preferences and attitudes and allows you to customize your sales and marketing efforts. One to one marketing does require some degree of effort, but it has been proven to be a very effective model for building customer loyalty.

Increasing revenues from existing business customers – Businesses that are providing products or services to other businesses (B2B) have a more challenging set of issues to consider, particularly where the customer's business uses the producer's product to manufacture goods for the retail market. Products, such as an automated lathe, are expensive to design, produce and manufacture, which makes changing the make-up of these products both costly and difficult. Since very few organizations can exist for long with a single product or machine-type focus, it is incumbent that a *"product line"* strategy will be required to grow and sustain the new enterprise. If you only envision one product, you have an invention and not a sustainable business idea.

Product planning is the process that businesses engage in to determine the products or goods they wish to sell to accomplish their business objectives. Product planning may take weeks or months, or even years, depending on the type of product and/or production process. Companies that have these requirements need to make sure that they can earn sufficient gross margin from the sale of their products to support the research and development effort necessary to sustain this process.

The decision process to determine an overall product plan can include any number of practical considerations. It normally starts with a realization of what it is the company does well, or what is generally referred to as its "core competency." Core competencies are the collective learning within organizations, and they involve how these companies coordinate diverse production skills and integrate multiple streams of knowledge. This ability, or core competency, is the foundation from which they are able to develop and produce their products and services.

Theodore Levitt (1983) is known for his development of what is now referred to as the "donut model," the "total product concept." His representation of how a business can expand illustrates how the inherent expertise of an organization can be leveraged to diversify a company's product and service offerings. Often, by simply enhancing an existing product, a new model can be created that will appeal to a broader set of purchasers than already buy. The automobile industry, for example, does this quite successfully; they use the same core competency production techniques to produce many different models that appeal to a variety of consumer preferences.

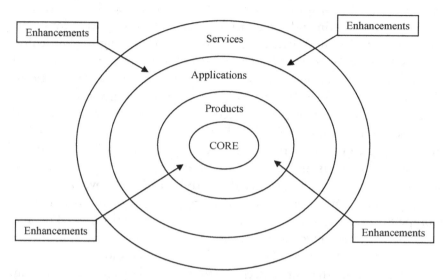

Figure 8.3 Representation of Theodore Levitt's Total Product Concept (1983)

One of the insights from Peters and Waterman's (1982) *In Search of Excellence,* research of successful company's business practices, was that these successful companies tend to "Stick to Their Knitting" - capitalizing on what they know how to do and thus fared better than those that diversified into unfamiliar areas. Collins (2002) extensive research data for his book *From Good to Great* validated the concept to staying with core competencies - terming the practice of staying in familiar sectors as "the Hedgehog Concept." Developing new products, or enhancing existing products, should evolve from what your company knows how to do best - core competencies and products that build the reputation your company is known for.

Building from core technology – Many of today's corporate giants started from very simple beginnings, and that is certainly the case for Armstrong World Industries (DaVita, 2010). Thomas M. Armstrong, the founder of Armstrong World Industries, began his career by working as a shipping clerk in a glass factory in, Pittsburgh, Pennsylvania. To supplement his income, he investing his savings in a machine that cut cork stoppers for bottles which he hand-finished and embossed with the Armstrong name. The production of the cork stoppers resulted in a significant amount of useless cork shavings and Armstrong, a frugal man, looked for ways to use the shavings.

Earlier, Frederick Walton (England) had observed that dried linseed oil formed a flexible skin and thought it to be a possible substitute for plant-based rubber. His 1860 patent application for accelerating the hardening process by heating it with lead acetate and zinc sulfate was intended as a product competition with water repellant fabrics such as oil cloth. His 1863 patent refinement specified that "For these purposes canvass or other suitable strong fabrics are coated over on their upper surfaces with a composition of oxidized oil, cork dust, and gum or resin.... The back or under surfaces of such fabrics are coated with a coating of such oxidized oils, or oxidized oils and gum or resin, and by preference without an admixture of cork." Walton named the cloth-backed floor covering product *linoleum,* from Latin terms *linum* meaning *flax* and *oleum* meaning *oil*. Competitors devised different methods for hardening the linseed oil and abandoned the patented cloth backing; with Walton losing rights to his *linoleum* brand name, since he had failed to trademark it.

Floors up until that time, except for the very wealthy and were generally bare. Rugs, mats, stone, and tile were used for flooring but were expensive, and in the case of rugs and mats, difficult to keep clean with 19th Century technology, and expensive beyond the means of the average individual. Linoleum was fairly inexpensive, hard wearing, easy-to clean, and could be mass produced. It was also coming into vogue in England and by 1869 Walton's factories were shipping to Europe and America. With geographical expansion, he founded the American Linoleum Manufacturing Company on Staten Island in 1872; it closing in 1928.

Meanwhile, though Thomas Armstrong had propelled his cork business to the largest worldwide supplier of cork bottle stoppers when he saw demand abating from other container closing technologies. Seeing the need to expand his product line and to use the cork shavings, Armstrong correctly versioned that "The (Company's) solid foundation of the future was covered with linoleum." Two years later Armstrong linoleum factory rolled out its first product to the market; a venture that has made the company synonymous with high quality consumer products.

Armstrong's success was based on two principles which he achieved: a) creating a superior product and b) earning and keeping the trust of his customers. Armstrong's products were superior to others in that he applied quality cork backing in the production and offering both color and patterns in the product. Though, several competitors saw only the utilitarian side of the product, the Armstrong Company saw its "linoleum carpeting" as a way to beautify the home.

From the humble beginnings of producing bottle corks, the business developed by Thomas Armstrong has expanded to producing high quality wood flooring, kitchen and bathroom cabinets, commercial carpeting, and linoleum that included high quality "inlaid" grades. The Armstrong Company employs over 10,000 people in 36 manufacturing plants worldwide and has sales in excess of $2.8 billion annually. It all started with an understanding of the utility of cork and total commitment to brand excellence.

Whatever your business model, expanding your marketing mix or making more of what you know how to make, selling more to existing customers are effective ways to grow a company. Here are a few pointers to help you implement a program to take full advantage of whatever customer relationships you may have already developed. Similarly, regional economic developers have found that the most productive strategy is to, first, get existing companies to stay and expand. Do not interpret this to say that new companies shouldn't aggressively go after new customers. The purpose here is to suggest that substantial growth lies in repeat sales to existing customers, via the following techniques:

- Stay in touch with existing customers to learn their ongoing needs. Inquire into their challenges so as to discover needs they have that you can fulfill. It may be that someone in another department has a problem that one of your company's products or services can solve. It is only by being in touch with customers that you learn about such opportunities.

- Try to find up-selling opportunities -- not only more of the same, but larger orders and new features. A satisfied customer is a great candidate for expanded sales. The customer has respect for your capabilities and ability to deliver and will therefore listen to your pitch, and likely tell you about possible obstacles, limited budgets, or opposition from another department or, even more valuable, the existence of a competitor. Then, you are in a position where you can help solve the problem--perhaps by offering a quantity discount or throwing in some additional service that will convince others in the company that you should provide more of your product or service.

- Let existing customers know when you come out with a new product or service. Regardless of whether they buy or not, they can provide feedback, and may become buyers or references for a new product in the future.

- Seek out new sales leads from existing customers. They can often provide referrals to others in their companies or to individuals associated with other firms they do business with. It always helps in soliciting a prospect to be referred by someone the prospect respects.

Existing customers represent a growth opportunity--not only for the present, but for helping to expand your company's future.

EXPANDING INTO NEW MARKET SEGMENTS –

After some period of time, many companies reach a point where they have "saturated" their existing market opportunities, or customer preferences have changed, and they begin to start looking for new customers. New customers can be found within a different market segment, a different geography, or even a different country. Seeking new terrain in which to sell your mix of products and services is another proven way to grow and expand your business.

Very often the products or services that have been designed to solve a problem or fulfill a need within one industry or market can be adapted to meet similar requirements for another. With obesity becoming a national problem and sweeten drinks being identified as a contributor, consumers began looking for alternatives. Who would have ever thought that water would become the packaged thirst quencher that it has, and that water would be available in so many different formats?

Take PepsiCo's Aquafina as an example. PepsiCo began distributing Aquafina in Wichita, Kansas in 1994, before it expanded distribution across the United States, Canada, Lebanon, Turkey, Saudi Arabia, Vietnam, Pakistan, India and Spain. As of 2003, it had become the United States' top-selling bottled water brand in measured retail channels. Aquafina is sold in 12-fluid ounce, 500-milliliter (16.9 fl oz), 20-ounce, 24-ounce,

1-liter, and 1.5-liter bottles. And, that is just the container size part of the story.

PepsiCo also produces other products under the Aquafina label: *Aquafina Sparkling*, carbonated flavored water, available in *Berry Blast* (Raspberry) and *Citrus Twist; Aquafina FlavorSplash*, flavored water (without carbonation), and artificially sweetened with Sucralose, available in *Grape, Citrus Blend, Wild Berry, Strawberry Kiwi, Raspberry* and *Lemon*; *Aquafina Alive*, a low calorie, vitamin-enhanced water beverage, available in *Berry Pomegranate, Peach Mango*, Lemon and *Orange Lime*; *Aquafina plus+*, a low calorie (120 calories per 591 ml bottle), vitamin supplement water beverage available in *Blackberry Grape, Pomegranate Cherry, Passionfruit Citrus* and *Orange Tangerine.*

Product diversification is an excellent example of how one business took a relatively simple product, water, and re-packaged it differently to penetrate deeper into the market by making moderate modifications to the original product. One could speculate that adding flavoring or sweeteners to water was not too difficult a task, nor was adding carbonation. But, Aquafina found a way to adapt their product to meet these unique taste requirements, and as a result, it has realized an increase in revenues and market share for their company.

EXPANDING INTO NEW GEOGRAPHIES –

Another approach to reaching new customers is to go directly to them, and you accomplish this via geographic expansion. If you are a retailer, it may require that you open new stores in different market locales. If you are selling to other businesses, it may require you to establish a new sales territory or a new channel of distribution. The objective to deploying this strategy is to enable your enterprise to reach a new set of target customers that you couldn't have reached unless you expanded your product distribution "foot print."

Once again, the same set of considerations needs to be applied to geographic expansion that was utilized in your original market entry decision process. Before incurring the expense of opening a new facility, or entering into a new distribution agreement, it is important to understand the characteristics of the new arena in which you are about to compete. Remember the phrase from Willson's "The Music Man" - "You've got to know the territory!" You will need to construct a new perceptual market map for this arena and recognize the competition you will be competing with. For retailers, this can be readily understood by simply surveying the area or searching the Yellow Pages of this new environment.

The best example of a successful geographical expansion program for a retail operation has to be Wal-Mart. Growth through new stores on both the home and overseas fronts continues to be a major part of the Wal-Mart story. Much of the U. S. growth is focused on urban and fill-in markets. Overseas, the strategy is more diverse. Internationally, Wal-Mart plans to add 155 to 165 stores. These will join 1,500 existing stores, clubs and restaurants. Since the retailer opened a single store in Mexico 10 years ago, international sales have reached $50 billion.

Mike Duke, Executive Vice President and President and CEO of the Wal-Mart Stores division, provided an update of Wal-Mart's expansion plans at the company's shareholders meeting in 2005. In the U.S., Wal-Mart operated more than 3,000 stores across multiple formats and employs 1.3 million associates. The previous year, (2004) it added 35 Wal-Mart discount stores, 242 Supercenters and 21 Neighborhood Markets. In 2005, the retailer was adding 40 to 45 discount stores, 240 to 250 Supercenters and 25 to 30 Neighborhood Markets. Today, 2010, Wal-Mart operates more than 4,500 stores.

For business to business efforts, geographic expansion can be a little more challenging to analyze within these new markets because many of the potential competitors will have sales efforts underway that are managed from other locations. Because of this, geographical expansion decisions are often linked to different kinds of considerations than you would find with retailers. Below is a list of things you may want to consider as you contemplate your expansion plans:

- Will you be seeking the benefit of being the initial mover into this new territory?

- Will you be reacting to an initial move of your competitors?

- Is the potential level(s) of new business to be acquired attractive enough?

- Can you provide cross location services to these new customers to control costs?

- Can you find and recruit the necessary skills to engage in these new market areas?

If your strategic plan is to ultimately position your organization as a regional or national company, than you do need to develop a migration plan to get there. Having business operations in multiple markets can offer the benefit of mitigating market risk: The larger the number and diversity of markets or locations, the greater the risk normalization. If speed to market is important to you, then consider engaging a third party distributor or re-seller who will enter into a mutually beneficial contract with you and give you instant access to X number of new customers and locations.

Moving your business to a new geography is a lot like moving your family into a new neighborhood. You need to consider the cost, the benefits that the new opportunity provides, and the impact on the members of your team. Needless to say, many an organization has grown successfully by systematically "marching" across the country and expanding its customer base. Establishing a new operation in new markets and geographies is a proven and effective way to grow revenues.

INTERNATIONAL EXPANSION –

There are often unforeseen perils involved in any international expansion program that can challenge every company's original planning assumptions. Latitude Partners Ltd. (Hacking, 2009) an English strategy consulting firm, recently conducted a survey of 74 international expansions and found that successful attempts at international expansion require a very high level of management commitment. Profitable expansions take up large amounts of senior management time, on average 28 percent. This sounds like a very large time investment to make something work, until you realize that unsuccessful expansions took up even more time, on average of 39 percent.

Despite the time commitment, many companies have found success in tapping into developing markets "overseas." In recent times, the focus seems to be on China, India, and Brazil because of their large population base. If your company is considering expanding into foreign markets, then you may want to consider Latitude's Partners' advice. For successful international expansions they have identified four stages, which are essentially a series of steps designed to improve the odds in your company's favor. There were exceptions of course, but these recommendations bear consideration:

1. *Prepare the company for geographic expansion* – Successful

companies develop a replicable business model that can be adopted easily by the new country team and can serve other cross-geography teams. Ensure that there is agreed to accountability and a defined decision making process between head office and any of the potential new country teams Develop a consistent review and evaluation process with no differences between the various global offices.

2. *Be sure to select the right country or region to enter-* "Follow the money" - set up your new organization to serve existing clients with sufficient budget to cover a long time frame where the market offers long term possibilities. Choose a new location within a new country where you have some knowledge, experience and contacts.

3. *Prepare the market for your entry-* Leverage your existing relationships where the head office can give introductions to potential buyers of your products or services. When selecting your team, recruit, or ideally transfer, local sales people and nationals who have local relationships and know the local language and culture. The ideal employee is a country national who has previously worked for you; the next best is recruiting the same kind of national several months in advance of starting your business in the new country.

4. *Be prepared to commit to the chosen geography-* Take one country at a time and make each successful before moving onto the next, and commit to the geography only if you want to be there for the long term. Take your time, and integrate new recruits properly into your company. They will be familiar with the culture and local business practices, but unfamiliar with your company's methods and models.

Latitude Partners offers some additional encouragement about the benefits of undertaking such a deliberate approach and the following of these four stages. They claim that the clients of theirs that have taken this approach have on average grown local sales by 25 percent annually, all have been profitable within 12 months, and their new offices have supported international growth by an average 10 percent annually. Apparently, it can be done successfully, but attaining some experienced help to support your efforts might be of value.

FRANCHISING-

Franchising is the practice of allowing someone else to use your successful business model to operate their own business; while retaining an income stream from downstream operations. Isaac Singer, in the 1850s, who made improvements to an existing model of a sewing machine, was among the first franchising efforts in the United States. He was followed by Coca-Cola, Western Union, etc. and the ensuing agreements that developed later on between automobile manufacturers and their dealers.

Modern franchising came into prominence with the rise of franchise-based food service establishments. In 1932, Howard Deering Johnson established the first modern restaurant franchise based on his successful Quincy, Massachusetts Howard Johnson's restaurant that he founded in the late 1920s. The idea was to let other independent operators use the same name, food, supplies, logo and even building design in exchange for a fee.

The franchisor owns the overall rights and trademarks of the company and allows its franchisees to use these rights and trademarks to do business. The franchisor usually charges the franchisee an upfront franchise fee for the rights to do business under the franchise name and standardizes the products or services - McDonalds Restaurant's products are the same nationwide. In addition, the franchisor will usually collect an ongoing franchise royalty fees from the franchisee.

According to the U.S. Small Business Administration, franchising is the fastest-growing kind of small business. Furthermore, each new franchise generates 8-14 new jobs and a new franchise opens at an average of every eight minutes per business day. Overall, franchises create over 300,000 new jobs per year.

There are four major types of franchises: business format franchises, product franchises, manufacturing franchises, and business opportunity ventures, according to the *Franchise Opportunities Handbook* (Ludden,1998) Business format franchises, the most common type, enables a company to expand by supplying independent business owners with an established business, including its name and trademark. The franchisor company generally assists the independent owners considerably in launching and running their businesses. In return, the business owners pay fees and royalties. The franchisee also often buys supplies from the franchisor. Fast food restaurants are good examples of this type of franchise.

Franchising offers a number of advantages not only to franchisors but also to the franchisees, which helps to explain why franchising has been so successful. Franchisors benefit from these agreements because they allow companies to expand much more quickly than they could otherwise. A lack of funds and workers can cause a company to grow slowly. However, through franchising a company invests very little capital or labor, because the franchisee supplies both.

A company also can ensure it has competent and highly motivated owner/managers at each outlet through franchising - Since the owners are largely responsible for the success of their outlets, they have an ensured self-interest for providing a strong, and constant effort to make sure their businesses run smoothly and prosper. In addition, companies are able to provide franchising rights to only qualified people. Moreover, franchisors can raise money from franchise sales without diluting company equity.

Camp Bow Wow has been referred to as *The Accidental $40 Million Franchise* (Dahl, 2010). After losing her first husband in a plane crash and divorcing her second, Heidi Ganahl decided to dust off an old business plan for a pet day care facility. Today, Camp Bow Wow boasts some 200 franchises and $40 million in revenue. Camp Bow Wow has become one of the fastest-growing pet services companies, but the company almost never came to be.

At one time, founder Heidi Ganahl found herself at rock bottom until her brother convinced her to reconsider a doggie day care and boarding facility in her hometown of Denver Colorado. Ganahl (2010), who has written a book about her life called *Tales from the Bark Side*, finds herself now running a company that recently posted more than $40 million in revenue.

It started in 1994, when her husband and she could never find enough friends and family to take care of their two furry pets whenever they wanted to travel. The idea of doggie day care was just getting started at that time and they thought it would be a great idea if they offered boarding as well. So, they wrote a business plan and scouted out an old VFW hall near downtown Denver as their first location. It was in rough shape, and they did a lot of work on it before opening the doors in December 2000. At the time, it was just the third doggie day care facility in the area, and things took off from there.

After they opened their second location in September 2002, they were approached by a client who worked for Mrs. Fields Cookies. He told them that he didn't think there were any pet services franchises out there and that they might want to look into franchising as a way to grow their business. After making the announcement that she was offering franchises, she sold the first franchise in a week. There were other contributing success factors to this story as well, like making the decision to incorporate a Webcam so that pet owners could actually see how their "family members" were doing while they were at facility. One of the key moments came when they were featured on the front page of AOL as "the next great franchise." They got thousands of phone calls from that event and have not looked back since.

Based on the success companies have enjoyed since the franchising boom began in the 1950s, the future of franchising is positive. The U.S. Department of Commerce predicts that slower population growth, population shifts to new metropolitan areas, and the introduction of new technology will create new opportunities for franchises. Schools and universities are now adding franchising studies to their business curricula. These factors, combined with the low rate of franchise failure, stability in the industry, and a considerable return on everybody's investment, have made franchising a major force in the American economy, and a very viable option for expanding your business.

MERGERS AND ACQUISITIONS (M&A)-

This is another possible growth strategy that incluses the buying, selling, dividing and combining of different companies and similar entities that can help an enterprise grow rapidly in its sector without creating a subsidiary or using a joint venture. The distinction between a "merger" and an "acquisition" has become increasingly blurred in various respects (particularly in terms of the ultimate economic outcome), although it has not completely disappeared in all situations.

A merger and acquisition strategy is not one that fits every business operation. There should be a specific purpose for an acquisition strategy, and a clear understanding as to how you are going to integrate these companies before you ever consider acquiring one. Although mergers and acquisitions can clearly "jump start" the growth of a new enterprise, the complexity of the process can often be a deterrent for an immature or early stage organization. Growing your business by acquiring other peoples businesses can be a risky strategy (Harding & Rovit, 2004). But, there are success stories for this strategy as well. Rupert Murdoch's Clear Channel Communications, Inc., which spent more than $40 billion since 1986 to build a leading market position in radio, out-door advertising displays, and live entertainment venues, provides a good example as to playing the merger and acquisition game. The company started making acquisitions in the 1970's, and had accumulated 43 radio stations and 16 television stations by the time the U.S. Congress deregulated the industry in 1996.

When restrictions on radio ownership were lifted, Clear Channel had gained enough experience at buying stations, one at a time, to lead the ensuing consolidation taking place within the industry. By 2003, Clear Channel had grown to 1200 radio stations and 40 television stations in the United States, five times more than its closest competitor, Viacom International, Inc. In addition, Clear Channel has accumulated equity in 240 international radio stations and had diversified into outdoor displays and live entertainment.

If you are considering merging with or acquiring other firms as a growth strategy, than you can gain by testing your reasoning against these top five reasons to merge with or acquire a company (Lyon, 2010):

- *Gain Market Leadership-* There is not a defined leader in the mobile ad market. Consequently, many of the largest tech companies are acquiring mobile ad networks in the race for market leadership. Google and Apple are two clear competitors vying for market share. Apple's recent acquisition of Quattro Wireless for over $250 million dialed-up the competition with Google, which acquired AdMob in Nov. 2009. "The (AdMob) deal is similar to mobile advertising acquisitions that AOL, Microsoft, Yahoo, and Apple have made in the past two years," writes Google, "and experts have called mobile advertising a 'very fragmented' space, in which 'no ad network is dominant' and 'no one really knows what ad network is biggest.'"

- *Acquire New Customers* - When MySpace acquired online music site, Imeem in Dec. 2009 the social network funneled all of the Imeem accounts to MySpace.com. It was a natural fit as MySpace and Imeem had a similar product offering — both sites built communities around avid music enthusiasts. In June 2009, Imeem Mobile reached the milestone of 1 million downloads on the iPhone and Android and had nearly 10 million site visits in July 2009, according to Compete.com. In an attempt to curb declining usership, MySpace bought Imeem to grow its user-base.

- *Expand Your Product Portfolio-* Since Google's rise to the top of the search engine market, it has greatly expanded its product portfolio. The search giant has acquired nearly 60 companies to expand its capabilities in the tech world. The largest acquisition was of DoubleClick in mid-2007. While AdSense served as Google's primary advertising platform, the search giant sought to expand its product portfolio by acquiring the banner advertising company for $3.1 billion.

- *Achieve Scale-* Macy's was able to achieve incredible scale in a short period of time. The historic NYC-based retailer grew from several stores to a national brand. Macy's parent company, Federated, acquired the May Departments Stores Company for $11 billion in stock. Soon thereafter, the Macy's company grew from a handful of stores to a total 850 locations in 2006.

- *Obtain New Talents and Skill-Sets-* While there were many underlying elements for Bank of America's acquisition of Merrill Lynch, one reason the main street bank purchased the famed Wall Street all-star was to obtain new skill sets. "The most forward thinking integration strategies also capture key pieces of elusive core competencies, such as an organization's best practices, skills, knowledge bases, and routines," (Graziadio Business Report, 2011). Bank of America's $50 billion merger tapped into Merrill Lynch's nearly 16,000 financial advisers. After the acquisition, the main street bank had Wall Street prowess.

Merging with a competitor or acquiring a distributor may indeed help to accelerate the growth for your organization. Make sure that you have a good reason for taking this step and that you understand the operational challenges of absorbing these new additions. If your management team is up to the challenge, mergers and acquisitions can not only help your organization to expand, it can offer economies of scale for operations and strengthen your company's competitiveness.

The M&A Process –

Remarkably, many companies embark on acquisitions without a proven written process for getting a deal consummated. Developed and refined through years of successful implementation, the Capstone Road Map (Braun, 2010) offers a logical process for executing acquisitions with maximum advantage and minimum risk. Their process recommendation includes these three major elements:

- *Build the Foundations:* a clearly defined acquisition strategy, consistent with business objectives is the foundation for successful growth from acquisitions.

- *Build the Relationship:* the art of acquisition is the art of relationships, from initial contact to full-scale purchase negotiations.

- *Build the Deal:* a successful close and harmonious integration are the benefits from all of the strategic work that went before.

The merger and acquisition process can be further summarized into some basic implementation steps that contribute to ensuring the profitability of the deal. Here is a list of suggested activities that are part of the M & A process (Graziadio, 2011).

- Preliminary Assessment or Business Valuation- This is the first step of the merger and acquisition process, determining the market value of the target company to be purchased. In this process the current financial performance of the company examined along with the estimated future market value. The company which intends to acquire the target firm engages itself in a thorough analysis of the target firm's business history. This includes the products of the firm, its' capital requirements, organizational structure, brand value, intellectual property and everything else are reviewed strictly.

- Phase of Proposal- After a complete analysis and review of the target firm is completed; the second step is to offer a proposal for merger or acquisition. Generally, this proposal is given through issuing a non-binding offer document.

- Exit Plan- When the company decides to buy the target firm and the target firm agrees to be purchased, then the acquired company becomes engaged in exit planning. The ownership, and often the management, of the acquired firm plans the right time for exit. It considers the entire spectrum of exit alternatives, like full sale, partial sale and others. The firm also does the necessary tax planning so that the owners can evaluate the options of reinvestment if appropriate.

- Marketing the Deal- After finalizing the exit plan, the acquired firm involves itself in the marketing process to try and achieve the highest selling price for its business. In this step of the acquisition process, the acquired firm concentrates on structuring the business deal.

- Offer of a Purchase or Merger Agreement- In this step, the acquiring company will create the purchase agreement, in the case of an acquisition deal. In the case of merger, the final agreement papers may be constructed by both parties and the terms of the merger agreed to by the owners of both entities.

- Integration- In this final stage, the two firms are integrated through a merger or acquisition operating agreement. Both companies work to ensure that the participating companies communicate the same messages, rules and policies throughout the new organization so that operations can continue effectively.

Earlier we made reference to the belief that companies considering a merger and acquisition strategy to grow their organizations could benefit from some of the "lessons learned" by others. Merrill Data Site provided a interesting white paper entitled *"The Seven Critical M & A Mistakes and How to Avoid Them"*(2012) that we thought should be included to emphasize this point. Acquiring companies is not without risk, and avoiding these pitfalls will help your organization to mitigate some of the perils. Here is the list they provided:

- *Overindulgent Optimism-* This is a common mistake that occurs when both parties perceived greater opportunity than is shown in the hard data surrounding the deal. The implications from this can be that the buyer pays too much for the acquired company. This risk, unfortunately is for the buyer, and is only realized after the deal is closed.

- *Poor Structural Engineering-* Both parties, (buyer and seller) can overlook critical building blocks that can contribute to organizational problems. Over leveraged financial statements, legal agreements, or contractual employment agreements are examples of these kinds of issues. The implications from this are that the buyer will have to assume these obligations or renegotiate them in order to operate the business as initially anticipated.

- *Ineffective Organizational Integration-* There are often harsh restructuring issues associated with mergers and acquisitions that can result in plant closings, lay offs, and other unpopular measurers. A clearly defined management and communication plan is needed to communicate the organizational benefits of the merger or acquisition. The implications of doing this poorly are that the buyer may not recognize existing employment agreements which can result in higher levels of post acquisition attrition.

- *Insufficient Time Allotment-* Completing an acquisition or merger takes longer than expected, and is often made more difficult because of impediments such as poison pills, golden parachutes, white knights, and others. Working through these issues takes time, and often results in "deal fatigue," diminishing the enthusiasm to complete the process. This usually is the result of the buyer not having access to all of the information they need to fully evaluate the opportunity, and the implications are that both parties could wind up dropping out of negotiations all together.

- *Inability to Execute the Plan-* Highly effective managers are the catalyst that brings successful mergers and acquisitions to fruition. Ineffective managers can bring mergers and acquisitions to their knees. Often in an attempt to cut costs as the result of a merger key functional managers are overlooked and laid off. The implications are that the acquiring company will need to "re-learn" these critical skills in order to execute the intended business plan.

- *Lack of Proper Data Preparation-* Successful business acquisitions are the result of a disciplined approach to the organizing and evaluation of business data. Some information can be shared by the seller with all suitors, but more sensitive information should be reserved for the serious buyer. The buyer needs to recognize that they will receive information at the appropriate stage of the acquisition process and to be comfortable in asking for it when it is appropriate to do so.

- *Absence of Secure Business Tools-* Information security is an important part of the discovery and negotiation period. Both buyers and sellers need to secure their information that holds sensitive documents that could provide competitive information if it fell into the wrong hands. The implications are that other suitors could learn of the pending details of the offer, or copyrighted or patented information could leak into the marketplace unintentionally.

ACQUISITION ROLL-UPS —

A roll up is the consolidation of several small businesses under one roof, usually through a publicly or privately held holding company. The concept works extremely well with mom and pop business owners. The roll-up strategy can be very successful if you have capable management steering the ship and an industry where the synergies for consolidation make sense.

Roll-ups can provide greater efficiencies to the smaller operations such as merging back office accounting, marketing efforts and purchasing arrangements. The roll-up also provides an exit strategy for many mom and pop owners who are seeking to retire in the not to distant future. Being associated with a larger company that is national or international in scope also adds credibility and transparency to current and future customers. Typically, the holding company pays for an acquisition with a combination of stock and cash, and usually puts limits on how quickly the seller can liquidate the shares.

The earliest roll-ups were funeral homes such as SCI, and Loewen Group Inc., in Vancouver, British Columbia; and trash companies like Waste

Management Inc. and Browning-Ferris Industries Inc., both now in Houston, Texas. They each acquired hundreds of mom-and-pop like companies beginning in the 1970s and then became famous growth stocks.

Both industries grew exponentially until fundamental problems caused a hic up in the 1990s. There were fewer than expected deaths along with greater use of cremation, and a glut of dump space for trash, respectively. However it is important to note that the roll-up concept worked for these industries and their stock flourished for almost 20 years before they experienced a downturn. Indeed, fortunes have been made in the roll-up game. US Filter Corp. had $17 million in sales in 1990. Nine years, and 260 acquisitions later, it had a big share-price run-up and the company sold for $6.2 billion.

Roll-ups can be a benefit to the small-businesses being acquired in some industries, as companies competing against each other for acquisitions have boosted the value of their businesses. United Rentals Inc., based in Greenwich, Conn., has paid cash to buy hundreds of small-equipment rental companies in the past few years, businesses that had few buyers lining up before the consolidator's appearance. Contractors of mechanical equipment, who could have expected to get no more than book value for their businesses a few years ago, can now sell them for several times that amount in roll-up shares and cash.

Companies that have a roll-up strategy have to be careful not to get caught up in the frenzy of deal making. It is easy to postpone the basics of instituting back office efficiencies, cutting costs and focusing marketing efforts when you on "on a roll" of consolidating an industry. Companies must remember the reasons they embarked on this type of a strategy in the first place. To create a large company that would be more profitable than a bunch of little ones. It isn't easy. Waste Management, 30 years into the roll-up game, is rumored to be still working to centralize its purchasing activities.

IMPLEMENTATION TACTICS –

Regardless of the strategy you choose to select, it will not yield the results you are looking for unless it is implemented and executed appropriately. While each of the aforementioned strategies has its own set of unique attributes, there is a generic model you can utilize to test you theories before you actually commit to spending your resources. Just as there are factors to consider in selecting a strategy, there are factors to consider in selecting the appropriate tactics to implement your strategy. When you are getting ready to enter your "new terrain," be sure to view each of your tactical choices from three perspectives: 1) is the opportunity real? 2) Are you ready to compete? 3) Can you focus your resources to win?

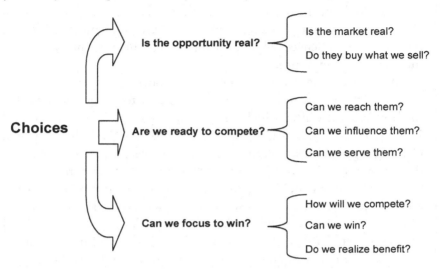

Figure 8.5 Targeted Tactics Implementation Model (Cobb, 2007).

From each of these key questions, comes another set of factors to recognize, and from that set of discoveries comes a next set of action steps that will help you to develop your path forward: Have you identified your targeted customers? Are your channels selected and contracted? Are expectations aligned and assigned? Establishing your implementation plans in a logical fashion will enable you to avoid making costly mistakes and significantly improve your chances for success.

There are other possibilities for growing an enterprise, but we wanted to provide you with some of the proven techniques that have been used successfully by entrepreneurs and established companies alike. This growth phase of your company's development is where you are creating the incremental value. The marketplace votes with its purchasing dollars, and their willingness to part with them to acquire your products and services is the strongest endorsement you could possibly have. Companies that can grow rapidly and profitably will become prime acquisition targets for the larger industry players, and often qualify as excellent candidates for an Initial Public Offering, (I.P.O.).

SAM WALTON

Sam Walton, the founder of Wal-Mart, grew up poor in a farm community in rural Missouri during the Great Depression. The poverty he experienced while growing up taught him the value of money and perseverance.

After attending the University of Missouri, he began work for J.C. Penny Co., where he got his first taste of retailing. He served in World War II, after which he became a successful franchiser of Ben Franklin Five-and-Dime stores. In 1962, he had the idea of opening bigger stores, sticking to rural areas, keeping costs low and discounting heavily. The Ben Franklin management disagreed with his vision. Undaunted, Walton pursued his vision, founded Wal-Mart and started a retailing success story. When Walton died in 1992, the family's net worth approached $25 billion. Today, Wal-Mart is the world's #1 retailer, with more than 4,150 stores, including discount stores, combination discount and grocery stores, and membership-only warehouse stores (Sam's Club). Here is Sam Walton's winning formula for business success:

Rule 1: Commit to your business. Believe in it more than anybody else. I think I overcame every single one of my personal shortcomings by the sheer passion I brought to my work. I don't know if you're born with this kind of passion, or if you can learn it. But, I do know you need it. If you love your work, you'll be out there every day trying to do it the best you possibly can, and pretty soon everybody around will catch the passion from you — like a fever.

Rule 2: Share your profits with all your associates, and treat them as partners. In turn, they will treat you as a partner, and together you will all perform beyond your wildest expectations. Remain a corporation and retain control if you like, but behave as a servant leader in your partnership. Encourage your associates to hold a stake in the company. Offer discounted stock, and grant them stock for their retirement. It's the single best thing we ever did.

Rule 3: Motivate your partners. Money and ownership alone aren't enough. Constantly, day by day, think of new and more interesting ways to motivate and challenge your partners. Set high goals, encourage competition, and then keep score. Make bets with outrageous payoffs. If things get stale, cross-pollinate; have managers switch jobs with one another to stay challenged. Keep everybody guessing as to what your next trick is going to be. Don't become too predictable.

Rule 4: Communicate everything you possibly can to your partners. The more they know, the more they'll understand. The more they understand, the more they'll care. Once they care, there's no stopping them. If you don't trust your associates to know what's going on, they'll know you really don't consider them partners. Information is power, and the gain you get from empowering your associates more than offsets the risk of informing your competitors.

Rule 5: Appreciate everything your associates do for the business. A paycheck and a stock option will buy one kind of loyalty. But, all of us like to be told how much somebody appreciates what we do for them. We like to hear it often, and especially when we have done something we're really proud of. Nothing else can quite substitute for a few well-chosen, well-timed, sincere words of praise. They're absolutely free — and worth a fortune.

Rule 6: Celebrate your success. Find some humor in your failures. Don't take yourself so seriously. Loosen up, and everybody around you will loosen up. Have fun. Show enthusiasm — always. When all else fails, put on a costume and sing a silly song. Then make everybody else sing with you. Don't do a hula on Wall Street. It's been done. Think up your own stunt. All of this is more important, and more fun, than you think, and it really fools competition. "Why should we take those cornballs at Wal-Mart seriously?"

Rule 7: Listen to everyone in your company and figure out ways to get them talking. The folks on the front lines — the ones who actually talk to the customer — are the only ones who really know what's going on out there. You'd better find out what they know. This really is what total quality is all about. To push responsibility down in your organization, and to force good ideas to bubble up within it, you must listen to what your associates are trying to tell you.

Rule 8: Exceed your customer's expectations. If you do, they'll come back over and over. Give them what they want — and a little more. Let them know you appreciate them. Make good on all your mistakes, and don't make excuses — apologize. Stand behind everything you do. The two most important words I ever wrote were on that first Wal-Mart sign: "Satisfaction Guaranteed." They're still up there, and they have made all the difference.

Rule 9: Control your expenses better than your competition. This is where you can always find the competitive advantage. For twenty-five years running — long before Wal-Mart was known as the nation's largest retailer — we've ranked No. 1 in our industry for the lowest ratio of expenses to sales. You can make a lot of different mistakes and still recover if you run an efficient operation. Or you can be brilliant and still go out of business if you're too inefficient.

Rule 10: Swim upstream. Go the other way. Ignore the conventional wisdom. If everybody else is doing it one way, there's a good chance you can find your niche by going in exactly the opposite direction. But, be prepared for a lot of folks to wave you down and tell you you're headed the wrong way. I guess in all my years, what I heard more often than anything was: a town of less than 50,000 populations cannot support a discount store for very long

CHAPTER SUMMARY

KEY POINTS

- Growing your enterprise requires management to constantly re-evaluate the original business plan assumptions and anticipate new requirements.

- Accelerating the growth cycle of your business will accelerate the creation of incremental value, as growth and profitability are key considerations in business valuation

- Different business models adapt differently to the five generic expansion models presented in this chapter. No single business model can use all of these suggestions

- Selling additional products to existing customers is referred to as developing your marketing mix. The mix of products offered should have relevance to the nature of your business

- Marketing mix considerations include pricing, product attributes, placement or access to purchasing the products, and advertising and promotion compatibility

- Product line expansion is a good strategy for a design and / or producing company to gain a larger portion of their customer's purchasing dollars.

- Products can often be modified relatively inexpensively to enable them to be attractive to new market segments or different industries.

- Products should continue to evolve from the core competency of the business so that their expertise in these areas continue to mature and their reputation for excellence in their chosen field continues to grow in the marketplace

- Geographical expansion is a proven way to grow market presence and mitigate market single market risks

- Expanding geographic focus for business to business sales also expands market presence and provides access to new customers

- Expanding Internationally requires careful planning and a recognition of the management time necessary to establish and mange a foreign operation

- Franchising is a growing and proven way to expand a business by allowing others to duplicate your business model for fees and other arrangements

- Mergers and acquisitions have been used successfully to enable organizations to gain market leadership, acquire new customers, expand product portfolios, achieve economies of scale, and obtain new talents and skills

- Acquisition roll-ups have been used successfully to acquire a number of smaller operations that can be consolidated into a larger identity to gain market leadership or economies of scale

- Establishing well thought through expansion implementation plans will help you to avoid costly mistakes and improve your opportunity for success

TAKE ACTION NOW

- Revisit your business plan and your business model and update what you have learned as a result of your first year of operations

- If you have not initiated a repository for customer information, (customer data base or customer relationship management system) do so to record customer preferences

- Select a growth target that you are comfortable with supporting, both financially and operationally, and establish this as a goal for your enterprise

- Select a growth strategy that compliments your business model, your management expertise, and your available resources

- Engage the professional services element of your business, (legal and finance) to address any of the contractual issues you my be facing, such as new leases for new facilities, or new distribution agreements, or due diligence reviews if you are considering acquisitions

- Develop an implementation plan to support your growth strategy selection that outlines the timelines to accomplish which steps and in what order

- Assign team members to the tasks identified in each of the implementation plan elements so that there is someone responsible for the accomplishment of these critical success factors

- Establish key performance indicators (KPIs) for each of the tasks assigned so that you can measure your progress and adjust to any unforeseen challenges that may occur

- Review your resource pool to make sure that you sufficient personnel with the appropriate skills to execute your plans

- Develop your implementation "tree" so that you recognize what it is you need to do in order to accomplish your expansion plans

REFERENCES:

Amato, R. (5/8/2007). *Reverse Shell Mergers Explained,* Howto.com /:Roll Ups

Braun, D. (2010). *Mergers and Acquisitions Daily,* Capstone Strategic, Inc. Publisher.

William R. Cobb and M. L. Johnson, Ed.D, Ph.D.

Cobb, W. (2007). *Targeted Tactics- Transforming Strategy into Measurable Results.* Philadelphia: Xlibris, Publisher.

Collins, J. (2001). *Good to great: Why some companies make the leap and others don't.* New York: Harper/Collins Publishers.

Dahl, D. (5/11/2010). *Camp Bow Wow: The Accidental $40 Million Franchise,* AOL.com /small business

De Vita, T. (7/23/2010). *Armstrong- From Cork Residue, to Linoleum, to Modern Flooring.* Suite101.com

Ganahl, H. (2010). *Tales From the Bark Side,* Denver: Heidi Inc., Publisher

Graziadio Business Review, (2011). Pepperdine University, Graziadio School of Business Management, Malibu, CA.

Hacking, S. (2009). *Geographic Expansion – How to Make It Work and Not Lose Your Shirt.* city: Manager Wise, a division of Klebanoff Associates, Inc., Publishers

Harding, D., & Rovit, S. (2004). *Mastering the Merger: Four Critical Decisions that Make or Break the Deal,* Boston: Harvard Business Press, Publishers

Levitt, T., (1983). *Marketing Imagination,* The Free Press, a Division of Simon & Schuster, Inc., Publisher.

Ludden, L. L. (1998) *Franchise Opportunities Handbook,* New York: Park Avenue Productions, Publisher.

Lyon, E. (2010) *Top Five Acquisition Strategies,* Sparxoo.com

Merrill Datasite, (2012), *Seven Critical M & A Transaction Mistakes,* Merrill Communications, LLC, St. Paul, MN

Peters, T. J. & Waterman, R. H. Jr. (1982). *In Search of Excellence,* New York: Harper & Row, Publishers.

Schewe, C. D. & Hiam, A. (1998), *The Portable MBA in Marketing,* San Francisco: Wiley and Sons, Publisher.

SUPPLEMENTAL SOURCES:

Dicke, T. S. (1992). *Franchising in America.* Chapel Hill, NC: University of North Carolina Press.

International Franchise Association. (1999). *International Franchise Association.* Washington: www.franchise.org

Ludden, L. L. (1999). *Franchise Opportunities Handbook.* Indianapolis, IN: JIST Works, Inc.

Shook, C. &. Shook. R. (1993). *Franchising: The Business Strategy That Changed the World.* Englewood Cliffs, NJ: Prentice Hall, Inc.

Webster, Bryce. (1986). *The Insider's Guide to Franchising.* New York: AMACOM.

CHAPTER NINE

Managing Financial Success

"It's not the employer who pays the wages. He only handles the money. It is the product that pays the wages."

Henry Ford

The language of love may be French, but the language of commerce is finance. By definition, "financial management" encompasses "the processes for planning, directing, monitoring, organizing, and controlling of the monetary resources of an organization (Web Finance, 2010). Whether you are planning to go big with your business or simply sustain the life style company you are creating, you can never neglect the importance of financial management. Business communicates its activities and operating results via a collection of financial references and reports. Neglect the financials at your own risk!

Just as with all business disciplines, there are many different perspectives about what constitutes financial management. Although there are literally thousands of different applications for financial principles, they can be broken down into three major categories: a) financial reporting; b) operating management accounting; and c) the treasury function or cash management.

FINANCIAL REPORTING-

To assure transparency and report comparability, a private sector organization was established in 1973 to develop financial accounting standards for nongovernmental entities. Thus, the Financial Accounting Standards Board (FASB, 2010) is officially recognized as authoritative by the Securities and Exchange Commission (SEC) (Financial Reporting Release

No. 1, Section 101) and was reaffirmed in its April 2003 Policy Statement and by the American Institute of Certified Public Accountants (Rule 203, Rules of Professional Conduct; as amended May 1973 and May 1979). These financial reporting standards provide a level of trustworthiness that is necessary for the efficient functioning of the U.S. economy. Decisions about the allocation of resources rely heavily on credible, concise, and understandable financial information.

The mission of the FASB is to establish and improve standards of financial accounting and reporting by nongovernmental entities; providing decision-useful information to investors and other users of financial reports. Standardization is accomplished through a comprehensive and independent process that encourages broad participation, objectively considers all stakeholder views, and is subject to oversight by the Financial Accounting Foundation's Board of Trustees.

FASB is independent of all other business and professional organizations and includes the Financial Accounting Foundation (Foundation), the FASB, the Financial Accounting Standards Advisory Council (FASAC), the Governmental Accounting Standards Board (GASB), and the Governmental Accounting Standards Advisory Council (GASAC).

In the U.S., "Generally Accepted Accounting Principles," commonly abbreviated as U.S. GAAP, or simply GAAP, are the accounting rules used to prepare, present, and report financial statements for a wide variety of entities, including publicly-traded and privately-held companies, non-profit organizations and governments. Generally, GAAP includes a local applicable accounting framework, related accounting law, rules, and an accounting standard. Although the financial information reported by different businesses in different industries can look very different, the framework in which the financial information is sorted and recorded is quite similar.

GAAP has a specific meaning for accountants and auditors. The AICPA Code of Professional Conduct prohibits members from expressing an opinion or stating affirmatively that financial statements or other financial data "present fairly ... in conformity with generally accepted accounting principles," if such information contains any departures from accounting principles promulgated by a body designated by the AICPA Council. GAAP rules are based upon a few basic principles that must be upheld by all GAAP subscribers. These principles include consistency, relevance, reliability, and comparability.

- *Consistency* means that all information should be gathered and presented the same across all periods.

- *Relevance* means that the information presented in financial statements (and other public statements) should be appropriate and assist a person evaluating the statements to make educated guesses regarding the future financial state of a company.

- *Reliability* means simply that the information presented in financial statements is reliable and verifiable by an independent party.

- *Comparability* is one of the most important GAAP categories and one of the main reasons having something similar to GAAP is necessary.

By ensuring comparability, a company's financial statements and other documentation can be compared to similar businesses within its industry. The importance of this principle cannot be overstated, as without comparability investors and other stakeholders would be unable to recognize the differences between companies within an industry sector in order to benchmark how one company is performing as compared to its peers.

Why is all of this important? The financial reports that you generate about your business will reflect the financial health of your enterprise, and you need to have this information available in a reliable and consistent format for financers and government auditors. The GAAP accounting principals provide the framework to do just that, and it is in your best interest to establish your financial reporting system under these rules right from the start.

For new entrepreneurs, particularly those who have not had any exposure to the financial world before, the requirements of accurate financial reporting can seem a bit cumbersome. It requires your business to identify and record each of your business transactions into predetermined accounting categories. These categories are created via the establishment of what is known as a "chart of accounts." A chart of accounts is nothing more than a listing of all of the different categories of business activities that you will need to keep track of. For small enterprises, this can be a relatively short list, for larger companies, it can be quite extensive. But, just recording transaction information is only the first step in understanding your financial health. The second step is to recognize how these various transactions relate to each other.

There are three principal financial reporting formats: a) operating statement; b) balance sheet, and c) cash flow statement. ALL of them are interrelated, and a change in an input to one will result in a change to a related field in the others. They are dynamic, which means that the information flowing in and out of these reports is constantly changing. Therefore, to assess the financial condition of your firm, you will need to establish a definitive reporting schedule; designated days that you will take the "snap shot" of your company's financial health. In most organizations, this is done at the end of each calendar month, but for some smaller firms, a minimum of quarterly reports can suffice.

Operating statement – This is sometimes called the *income statement* or the *profit and loss statement* (P&L), P&L of financial performance, earnings statement, operating statement or statement of operations. It is a company's financial statement that reports how the revenue, (money received from the sale of products and services before expenses are taken out) also known as the "top line" is transformed into net income, the result after all revenues and expenses have been accounted for, also known as the "bottom line." It displays the revenues recognized for a specific period, and the cost and expenses charged against these revenues. The purpose of the income statement is to show managers and stakeholders whether the company has made or lost money during the period being reported.

The income statement can be prepared in one of two methods (Warren, 2008). The Single Step income statement takes a simpler approach; totaling revenues and subtracting expenses to find the bottom line. The more complex Multi-Step income statement (as the name implies) takes several steps to find the bottom line, starting with the gross profit. Gross profit is calculated by subtracting the direct costs associated with making a product from the revenues generated from selling the product. Operating expenses when deducted from the gross profit, yields income from operations. Adding to income from operations is the difference of other revenues and other expenses. When combined with income from operations, this yields income before taxes. The final step is to deduct taxes, which finally produces the net income for the period being measured.

Category	Mo. 1	Mo. 2	Mo.3	Mo.4	Mo.5	Mo.6
Sales						
Product A	100	150	200	250	300	350
Product B	50	75	100	125	150	150
Product C			75	150	225	300
etc.						
Total Sales	150	225	375	525	675	800
Production Costs	75	115	175	250	325	400
Gross Margin	75	110	200	275	350	400
Expenses						
General & Admin	25	35	50	75	100	100
Sales & Marketing	25	40	80	90	100	125
Others	10	10	15	10	10	15
Total Operating Expense	60	85	145	175	210	240
Income from Operations	15	25	55	100	140	160

Figure 9.1 Representative Operating Statement Example

Business managers and entrepreneurs gain familiarity with this report quickly, as they recognize the importance of making a profit. But, as you will see as we progress through this chapter, you can easily become a highly profitable company that goes broke. There is a reason why there are three critical reporting formats needed to run the business. The single operating statement will not suffice.

Balance sheet – Balance sheets are condensed statements that show the financial position of an entity on a specified date - usually the last day of an accounting period. Among other items of information, it states (1) what assets the entity owns, (2) how it paid for them, (3) what it owes (its liabilities), and (4) what is the amount left after satisfying the liabilities. Balance sheet data is based on a fundamental accounting equation (assets = liabilities + owners' equity), and its content is classified under subheadings such as current assets, fixed assets, current liabilities, (Williams, et al, 2008). An audited balance sheet is often demanded by investors, lenders, suppliers, and taxation authorities; and it is required by law under corporate legislation (such as the Companies Act). To be considered valid, a balance sheet must give a 'true and fair view' of the entity's state of affairs, and must follow the provisions of GAAP in its preparation.

			XYZ Company		
			12/31/2010		
Assets			**Liabilities**		
Cash		1,000	Accounts Payable		750
Accounts Receivable		1,250	Lines of Credit		1000
Inventory		5,000	Curr. Portion of LT Debt		1,000
Other		500	Other		500
Current Assets		7750	Current Liabilities		3250
Fixed Assets		5,000	Long Term Debt.		12,500
Machinery & Equipment		10,000			
(Accumulated Depreciation)		-3,000	Total Liabilities		15,750
Net Value of Assets		12,000	Equity		4,000
Total Assets		19,750	Total Liabilities & Capital		19,750

Figure 9.3 Representative Balance Sheet Example

The balance sheet reflects the overall financial condition of the company at one moment in time. Obviously, these numbers are dynamic; as new obligations are incurred and existing ones retired, the balance sheet will reflect these events. The value of this report should be obvious; for it measures whether or not the company is keeping its obligations in check with the assets it has to satisfy these obligations. When total liabilities exceed total assets, the enterprise is usually in trouble.

Cash flow statement – Also known as a *statement of cash flows* or a *funds flow statement*, it is a financial statement that shows how changes in balance sheet accounts and income affect cash and cash equivalents; an analysis of operating, investing, and financing activities. Essentially, the cash flow statement is concerned with the flow of cash-in and cash-out of the business. The statement captures both the current operating results and the accompanying changes in the balance sheet (Helfert, (2001).

A cash flow statement is a financial report that describes the source of a company's cash and how it was spent over a specified time period. Because of the varied accrual accounting methods companies may employ, it is possible for a company to show profits while not having enough cash to sustain operations. A cash flow statement neutralizes the impact of the accrual entries on the other financial statements. It also categorizes the sources and uses of cash to provide the reader with an understanding of the amount of cash a company generates and spends in its operations; as opposed to the amount borrowed from stockholders or sources outside the company. A cash flow statement also tells the reader how much money was spent for items that do not appear on the income statement; such as loan repayments, long-term asset purchases, and payment of cash dividends. Cash flow statements classify cash receipts and payments according to whether they stem from operating, investing, or financing activities.

Operating activities include the production, sales and delivery of the company's product as well as payment collected from customers. This could include purchasing raw materials, building inventory, advertising, and shipping the product. Examples of *investing activities* would be the purchase or sale of an asset. *Financing activities* include the inflow of cash from investors such as banks and shareholders, as well as the outflow of cash to shareholders as dividends as the company generates income. Other activities which impact the long-term liabilities and equity of the company are also listed in the financing activities section of the cash flow statement.

Category	Mo. 1	Mo. 2	Mo.3
Cash In			
Income from operations	15	25	55
non cash expenses [increase (+)]	5	5	5
Operating Cash Flows	20	30	60
Changes in Assets [increase (-) decrease (+)]			
Increase/ decrease in Receivables	50	100	150
Increase / Decrease in Inventory	-50	-100	-150
Increase / Decrease other Assets	0	25	15
Changes in Liabilities [increase (+) decrease (-)]	0	25	15
Increase / Decrease in Payables	25	35	50
Increase / Decrease in current obligations	15	0	-15
Net Cash From Balance Sheet Changes	60	90	110
Purchase of Asssets [decrease (-)]	0	0	50
Sales of Assets [increase (+)]	0	0	0
Net Cash from Investing Activities	0	0	-50
Changes in Short Term Debt [increase (+)	10	15	20
Changes in Long Term Debt [decrease (-)]	-125	-125	-125
Additional Paid in Capital [increase (+)]	0	0	0
Dividends Paid [decrease (-)]	0	0	0
Net Cash from Financing Activities	-115	-110	-105
Period Changes in Company Cash Position	-35	10	15
Beginning Cash Balance	500	465	475
Changes in Company Cash Position	-35	10	15
Ending Cash Balance	465	475	490

Figure 9.3 Representative Cash Flow Statement Example

Understanding these three types of financial reports is crucial to the successful management of your enterprise. But, it is equally important to recognize that each of these reports represents a period in time that has already passed. They are providing you with a summary of what has already occurred, and although this is important to know, it only reveals where you have been - not where you are going. It is for this reason that you need to be introduced to the practice of management accounting.

OPERATIONS MANAGEMENT ACCOUNTING -

According to the Chartered Institute of Management Accountants (CIMA), management accounting is "the process of identification, measurement, accumulation, analysis, preparation, interpretation and communication of information used by management to plan, evaluate and control within an entity and to assure appropriate use of and accountability for its resources. It also includes financial report preparation for non-management groups such as shareholders, creditors, regulatory agencies and tax authorities" (CIMA, 2011). The American Institute of Certified Public Accountants (AICPA) extends management accounting to the following three areas:

- Risk Management - Contribute to frameworks and practices for identifying, measuring, managing and reporting risks to the achievement of the objectives of the organization.

- Performance Management - Develop the practice of business decision-making and managing the performance of the organization.

- Strategic Management – Advance the role of the management accountant as a strategic partner in the organization.

RISK MANAGEMENT–

Cost accounting has historically been used to help managers understand the costs of running a business and it is an important component of risk management. Modern cost accounting originated during the industrial revolution, when the complexities of running a large scale business led to the development of systems for recording and tracking costs to help business owners and managers make decisions. The main objectives of managerial/cost accounting are (Hilton, 1988) as follows:

- Providing managers with information for decision making and planning.

- Assisting managers in directing and controlling operations.

- Motivating managers towards the organization's goals.

- Measuring the performance of managers and sub-units within the organization.

In the early industrial age, most of the costs incurred by a business were what modern accountants call "variable costs" because they varied directly with the amount of production. Money was spent on labor, raw materials, power to run a factory, etc. in direct proportion to production. Managers could simply total the variable costs for a product and use this as a rough guide for decision-making processes.

Some costs tend to remain the same even during busy periods, unlike variable costs, which rise and fall with volume of work. Over time, the importance of these "fixed costs" has become more important to managers. Examples of fixed costs include the depreciation of plant and equipment, and the costs unique to various departments such as maintenance, tooling, production control, purchasing, quality control, storage and handling, plant supervision and engineering. However, in the 21st Century, these costs may have become more important than the variable cost of a product. Thus, allocating them to a broad range of products can be challenging. Managers must understand their fixed costs in order to make informed decisions about their products and pricing.

In modern cost accounting, the concept of recording historical costs has been taken further. Allocating the company's fixed costs over a given period of time to the items produced during that period, and recording the result as the total cost of production, allowed the full cost of products not sold during the production period to be recorded as finished goods inventory. A variety of complex accounting methods are employed to calculate these values consistent with the principles of Generally Accepted Accounting Principles (GAAP). Cost accounting principals essentially can enable managers to ignore fixed costs, and now look at the results of each time period in relation to the "standard cost" of production for any given product. Although there are any number of different scenarios that can be imaged for compiling the various costs associated with a specific business activity, they all seem to stem from one or more of the following general classifications:

Variable Costs	Variable costs change in total in proportion to the level of activity. For example if a carmakers production increases by 5%, its tire costs will increase by about 5%.
Fixed Costs	A fixed cost remains unchanged in total as the level of activity varies. For example, the property tax on a rental apartment is the same regardless of the number of building occupants.
Direct Costs	A direct cost is the cost of direct labor and material used in making the product or delivering the service.
Indirect Costs/ Overhead Costs	Indirect costs are costs of an activity which are not easily associated with the production of specific goods or services.
Opportunity Costs	The benefit that is sacrificed when the choice of one action precludes an alternative course of action.
Sunk Costs	Costs that have been incurred in the past and cannot be changed by current actions

Figure 9.4 General Cost Classifications

While the manager, and not the controller/accountant, has the ultimate responsibility for making operations decisions, such decisions will not be effective if the manager does not understand the cost data and analyses used to make decisions. . For example, the manager may be working with the costs of a product, and not realize which costs are fixed and which are variable. The controller understands the different types of data that are available, the rules used to accumulate the data, and the limitations that exist on the data. Therefore, the manager and the controller need to interact in the decision-making process. The controller provides the relevant data and an explanation of its suitable uses. Therewith, the manager then can make better decisions for operating the business.

William R. Cobb and M. L. Johnson, Ed.D, Ph.D.

Performance Management –

Moving financial analyses from historical reports to anticipation of the company's future is essential for sustaining profitability, market share and for growth. Obviously, in exercises such as projecting future sales, assumptions are being made and these assumptions must be validated in an open and honest manner. Each alternative considered will have an impact on the financial future of the firm, and its future financing requirements.

Business forecasting – Financial forecasting is an essential element of the budgeting and planning process and it enables the estimating of future financing needs (Barron's Educational Services, 2005). Financial projections (forecasts) begin with forecasting sales and their related expenses. The basic steps in financial forecasting are: (a) to project the firm's sales; (b) to project variables such as expenses and assets; (c) to estimate the level of investment in current and fixed assets that is required to support the projected sales; and (d) to calculate the firm's financing needs. The basic tools for financial forecasting include financial modeling, the percent-of-sales-method, and a regression analysis.

Financial modeling – Modeling is the task of building an abstract representation of a financial decision-making situation (Bennings, 1997). This mathematical model designed to represent (a simplified version of the performance of a business, a project, or any other investment. Financial modeling is a general term that means different things to different users; the reference usually relates either to accounting applications, or to quantitative finance applications.

In general usage, a financial model (also referred to as a financial plan) can refer to an annual projection of income and expenses for a company, division or department (Meigs & Meigs, 1970). A financial plan can also be an estimation of cash needs; providing the basis for a decision to secure financing through borrowing or issuing additional shares in the company. While a financial plan interlocks with estimating future income, expenses and assets, a financial plan is also used to manage company operations. If you want the company to produce the financial result you expect, then you need a way create the capital to facilitate the plan.

In Chapter Four we spent considerable time explaining the creation of various elements of the financial model needed to support the business plan.

As part of that process, it was necessary to make any number of financial assumptions about how your business was going to operate. These included everything from estimating the salaries and expenses you expected to pay, to the pricing of your products, the timing of your customer billing and the corresponding timing of payment receipts from customers. Now that you are operating, you want to determine whether or not your assumption were correct.

The original business plan's financial model should now become your first year's operating budget and it should be represented in the same format that you use to track and record your revenues and expenses. The operating financial reports should provide you with three sets of numbers for each of these major categories: a) the budgeted amount from your original plan - what you thought was going to occur; b) the actual amount incurred from operating the business, and c) the variance or the difference between the planned and the actual.

As you begin to create these reports, be sure to consider elements that are not always represented in the formal financial reporting. For example, your business plan assumed that you could produce and sell a certain number of product or services within a given period at a stated price. Your entire business model was predicated upon these assumptions; as you subsequently built your expense budget and cash requirements in relationship to revenues assumed to be generated from these sales.

Needless to say, you need to determine if you were actually a) able to sell the number of units you thought you could, b) at the prices you assumed you could, and c) produce them for the cost you estimated. So, in addition to the normal operating statement variances, you may want to consider a product variance report as well. This report should reconcile to the number of units that were sold, the revenues generated from sales, the margin derived from the sale, and identification of any variance.

Product Sales Variance Report						
	Units Budget	Units Actual	Units Variance	Revenues Budget	Revenues Actual	Period Variance
Product A	18	15	-3	450,000	375,000	(75,000)
Product B	9	10	1	225,000	250,000	25,000
Product C	1	-	-1	75,000	-	(75,000)
etc.						
Revenues from Sales	**28**	**25**	**-3**	**750,000**	**625,000**	**(125,000)**
	Budget Unit Cost	Actual Unit Cost	Unit Cost Variance	Budgeted Cost	Actual Cost	Cost Variance
Cost for product A	12.5	12.5	0	225000	187500	(37,500)
Cost for Product B	12.5	12.5	0	112500	125000	12,500
Cost for Product C	40	65	25	40	65	25
etc.						
Total Cost of Goods	**65**	**90**	**25**	**337,540**	**312,565**	**(24,975)**
Contribution Margin from Product A				225,000	187,500	(37,500)
Contribution Margin from Product B				112,500	125,000	12,500
Contribution Margin from Product C				74,960	(65)	(75,025)
etc.						
Total Gross Margin				**412,460**	**312,435**	**(100,025)**

Figure 9.5 Representative Product Sales Variance Report Example

Balance sheet items are the other elements of variance reporting that seem to be overlooked. The cash flow statement is always impacted by any changes in the composition of the company's assets or liabilities, and these changes often occur without management recognizing their impact. For example, there are two categories of assets that can dramatically effect the company's cash position: a) accounts receivables - money owed to the company for products or services sold - and b) inventory - the product or materials needed to provide a product that is needed to make the sale.

Days Sales Outstanding (DSO) is the metric used to express sales made, delivery done and payment owed - accounts receivable. Days Sales Outstanding represents the average amount of time between the creation and presentation of an invoice to a customer and the time it takes to get the cash in the bank. It is calculated by: *total outstanding receivables at the end of the period analyzed* divided by *total credit sales for the period analyzed* (typically 90 or 365 days), times *the number of days in the period analyzed* or DSO = Receivables/Sales. Calculating the average receivable amount produces a more conservative estimate.

If DSO is getting longer, customers are taking longer to pay their bills, which may be a) a warning that customers are dissatisfied with the company's product or service, b) an indication that sales are being made to customers that are less credit-worthy, or c) that salespeople have to offer longer payment terms in order to generate sales. Whatever the reasons, if the customer is taking longer to pay, the cash requirements for the business are going to increase because, in effect, you are "lending" the amount owed to your customer for a longer period of time than you had anticipated.

The second balance sheet item that can quickly impact your cash position is the build-up of inventory, whether it is raw materials to build a product, or finished product sitting on a shelf. In accounting, the inventory turnover (referred to as *inventory turns*) is a measure of the number of times inventory is sold or used in a time period such as a year. The equation for inventory turnover equals the cost of goods sold divided by the average investment in inventory. The formula for inventory turnover is calculated as follows: Inventory Turnover = Total Cost of Goods Sold / Average Inventory; (Average Inventory = Beginning Inventory + Ending Inventory / 2.)

An item whose inventory is sold (turns over) once a year has higher holding cost than one that turns over three times, or more in that time. Stock turnover also indicates the briskness of the business. The purpose of increasing the number of inventory turns is to control inventory levels for three reasons; because a) increasing inventory turns reduces holding cost, b) the organization spends less money on rent, utilities, insurance, theft and other costs of maintaining a stock of goods to be sold and/or c) reducing holding cost increases net income and profitability as long as the revenue from selling the item remains constant. There is reason why the larger, publicly held companies have an annual budgeting process and a set of *Key Performance Indicators* (K.P.I.'s) with which to operate. Financial modeling is the most predictable form of forecasting because it uses both historical information and planned operating adjustments that have been qualified and quantified.

Percent of sales – Sales percent forecast approach is commonly used as a "quick" way to forecast financial operations. Specifically, it is used for income statements, as balance sheets and cash flow statements are not directly related to percent of sales. This method is best used for an organization that has had the benefit of one or more full years of operations, as future assumptions will be based upon existing financial relationships.

Percent of sales will consider each line item in the income statement, from Revenue, to Operating Expenses, and others as a percent of sales. The fundamental assumption is that as revenues increase, so would each of the other items represented in the income statement in direct proportion to their "percent of sales." This provides a rough estimate of what the next several years' operating results might look like; based upon the forecast increase in sales or revenues for future years.

	Percent of Sales Forecast Model			
	Year End	% of	Forecast	Forecast
Current Year	Actual	Sales	Yr. 2	Yr. 3
Net Sales (less returns & allowances)	200,000	100%	300,000	400,000
Cost of Goods Sold (production costs)	80,000	40%	120,000	160,000
Gross Margin	**120,000**	60%	**180,000**	**240,000**
Insurance	250	0.1%	375	500
Licenses & Fees	80	0.0%	120	160
Office Expense (supplies, etc.)	200	0.1%	300	400
Outside Services	500	0.3%	750	1,000
Salaries & Wages	48,000	24.0%	72,000	96,000
Rent	8,000	4.0%	12,000	16,000
Repairs & Maintenance	125	0.1%	188	250
Shipping & Delivery	75	0.0%	113	150
Telephone	200	0.1%	300	400
Training & Development	150	0.1%	225	300
Travel & Entertainment	800	0.4%	1,200	1,600
Utilities	600	0.3%	900	1,200
Vehicle	1,200	0.6%	1,800	2,400
Miscellaneous	200	0.1%	300	400
Total G & A Expenses	**60,380**	30.2%	**90,570**	**120,760**
Advertising	600	0.3%	900	1,200
Conferences & Trade Shows	600	0.3%	900	1,200
Promotion Materials	250	0.1%	375	500
Public Relations	150	0.1%	225	300
Research	25	0.0%	38	50
Salaries & Wages	38,000	19.0%	57,000	76,000
Telephone	200	0.1%	300	400
Training & Development	150	0.1%	225	300
Travel & Entertainment	1,200	0.6%	1,800	2,400
Miscellaneous	300	0.2%	450	600
Total Sales & Marketing Expenses	**41,475**	20.7%	**62,213**	82,950
Total Operating Expenses	**101,855**	50.9%	**152,783**	203,710
Operating Income	**18,145**	9.1%	**27,218**	36,290

Figure 9.5 Percent of Sales Forecast Model Example

In creating a model of this nature it is important to recognize that not all expenses escalate at the same rate from year to year and that some others may be fixed and not subject to an increase at all. As you discover these items, you simply revise your forecast to reflect these adjustments, and work with the new information. Remember, a percent of sales forecast model will only estimate the operating statement of future years, and not produce the balance sheet or cash flow statements. A percent of sales forecast will provide you with information about the future profit or loss from operations for your company, but it can not provide any insight into what your cash requirements might be to support your proposed growth.

Establishing a management accounting practice within your enterprise will help you to operate more effectively and be able to forecast future results with more accuracy. Make it a point to select a competent financial reporting firm to help you with all aspects of your financial reporting, and consider having your own in-house financial professional to help you work with this aspect of your business. Knowing the financial condition of your company is critical, knowing how you got there is equally important, and knowing where you want to go is highly desirable.

STRATEGIC MANAGEMENT –

Strategic management is that set of decisions and actions that determines the long run performance of a company (Wheelen & Hunger, 1995). Models that are commonly used for this purpose include: a) review of the environment that the organization operates in; it's purpose or mission for existing; the strategies by which the organization will achieve its goals; b) objectives it sets for itself; the policies it will use to govern its actions; and the budgets, procedures and c) performance indicators it uses to manage the business, (K.P.I.'s).

Needless to say, financial analysis can contribute greatly to this process by providing both an evaluation of internal activities and their financial relationships as well as an external evaluation of factors that could impact the future performance of the business. An example of an internal analysis could be calculation of the financial impact of the different operating choices the business is considering. An example of an external analysis could be examining the relationships between things transpiring within the economy and their effect on the sale of the company's products.

Internal – A sensitivity analysis is the study of how the variation, or uncertainty, in the output of a mathematical model can be apportioned, qualitatively or quantitatively, to different sources of variation in the input of the model (Saltelli et al, 2008). Put another way, strategic financial management is a technique for systematically changing parameters in a model to determine the effects of such changes. A sensitivity analysis is used to support decision making or for formulating recommendations for decision makers and for testing the robustness of a result.

We suggested earlier that financial modeling was the most accurate method for understanding the financial impacts of business decisions on the total organization. Achieving the goals of company finance requires that any company investment be financed appropriately. The sources of financing will, generically, comprise some combination of debt and equity financing. Financing a project through debt results in a liability or obligation that must be serviced, thus entailing cash flow implications Equity financing is less risky with respect to cash flow commitments, but can result in a dilution of share ownership, control and earnings.

The *Pecking Order Theory* is one of the main financing decision theories for firms (Myers & Majluf, 1984); suggesting that firms avoid external financing while they have internal financing available and also avoid new equity financing while they can engage in new debt financing at reasonably low interest rates. The *Pecking Order Theory* states that "companies prioritize their sources of financing according to the *principle of least effort*, or of *least resistance*, preferring to raise equity as a financing means of last resort." Hence, internal funds are used first, and when that is depleted, debt is issued, and when it is not sensible to issue any more debt, equity is issued.

Strategic financial management is critically important to a company; because the implications of the choices made will impact the firm's operations, debt capacity, or ownership interests. Having the benefit of a financial professional to model these alternatives, evaluate the impacts, and convey the sensitivities of each alternative is extremely beneficial. This is a classic example of how "management accounting" can play a key role in shaping the organizations financial strategies.

External – Regression analysis is a statistical technique used to establish the relationship of a dependent variable, such as the sales of a company, and one or more independent variables, such as family formations, Gross Domestic Product (GDP), per capita income, and other economic indicators. By knowing exactly how large and significant each independent variable has historically been in its relation to the dependent variable, the future value of the dependent variable can be predicted. The term *regression*, like many statistical terms, is used in business quite differently than it is used in other contexts. The method was first used to examine the relationship between the heights of fathers and sons. The two were related, of course, but the slope is less than 1.0. A tall father tended to have sons shorter than him; a short father tended to have sons taller than him. The height of sons regressed to the mean. The term "regression" is now used for many sorts of curve fitting.

Regression deals with relationships between variables and also with prediction: the ability to more accurately predict behavior makes you more confident about decisions. Regression in all its shapes and forms remains the central workhorse of social science research, economics, sociology, psychology, and is used in many areas of business and technology.

For example, using regression analysis for forecasting could be made by plotting the index for personal income to help forecast auto sales (Decision 411, 2010). Personal income is chosen here as a predictor variable because it has been popular as a predictor variable for all kinds of other purchases made by consumers. The rationale behind using income as a predictor variable is obvious: the more discretionary income that consumers have, the more money they will spend on automobiles and other items.

In real life, however, there may be other factors to consider beyond these two variables, such as inflation and financing rates that could also impact the relationship between the two variables. The logic behind regression modeling is to try and understand the influence of one variable on the other, and from this relationship, be able to forecast the impact on one from the changes of the other.

Regression analysis allows a bank to set credit criteria for the general public, and build a statistical formula predicting how new accounts will perform in the future, that is, their ability to repay debt, by studying a sample of existing accounts. The banker wants to know the credit characteristics of consumers who are good payers, and those who are poor payers. Consumer credit ideally is suitable for statistical tools such as regression analysis because consumer behavior in handling credit is fairly predictable, based on a study of previous credit experience; even the credit losses are predictable.

People use regression on an intuitive level every day and probably do not realize it. In business, a well-dressed man is thought to be financially successful. A mother knows that more sugar in her children's diet results in higher energy levels. The ease of waking up in the morning often depends on how late you went to bed the night before. Quantitative regression just adds a degree of precision by developing a mathematical formula that can be used for predictive purposes.

Since regression analysis requires historical inputs to be meaningful, it may have little immediate value to a new enterprise. As your business begins to mature, and you establish a sustainable market position, you may begin to look for these kinds of external relationships within your business forecasting model. Suffice to say that regression analysis is a good tool for this purpose, and you can be well served by its effective use.

TREASURY FUNCTION AND CASH MANAGEMENT-

Cash management is a broad term that refers to the collection, concentration, and disbursement of cash. The goal is to manage the cash balances in such a way as to maximize the availability of cash not invested in fixed assets or inventories and to do so in such a way as to avoid the risk of insolvency. Factors monitored as a part of cash management include a) the level of liquidity, b) management of cash balances and c) short-term investment strategies.

Liquidity – Liquid assets are those things that can be immediately turned into cash by sale or leveraging. Stocks and bond are generally liquid; as they can be sold on a stock exchange. Antiques, art and collectibles are generally not liquid assets; since there is no intrinsic value on the open market. Since real estate cannot be readily sold, it is not considered liquid; though a line of credit can be issued for a large percentage of market value. Thus, to make payroll for a given time period real estate can be leveraged by establishing a secured line of credit well before it is needed.

Careful monitoring of cash management is particularly important for new and growing businesses. Cash flow can be a problem even when a small business has numerous clients, offers a product superior to that offered by its competitors and enjoys a sterling reputation in its industry. Companies suffering from cash flow problems have no margin of safety in case of unanticipated expenses or to meet payroll when accounts receivable are tardy. They also may experience trouble in finding the funds for innovation or expansion. It is ironic that it is easier to borrow money when you have money. This is the one segment of your financial management process where it is all about the money: Cash is King!

We suggest that you look at managing cash from three different perspectives: a) operating cash flows - the input and outflow of cash from managing the business; b) financing activities- short term and long term debt and c) managing the capital or equity account - dilution of ownership and dividend payments. All three of these activities may be needed to support a company that has plans for, and is experiencing, rapid growth. As discussed earlier in this chapter, it is very possible to be quite profitable and to go broke at the same time.

Operating cash flows – Management absolutely, positively, and unequivocally must know how cash moves through their business model, or the company will go broke. Although every business model has a different set of issues to manage, each is well served by taking an elementary approach to discovering their issues - A *day in the life of a dollar*. The "day trip" will be different for the dollar in every business, but the journey through the various charts of accounts may look familiar. To illustrate our point, we will track through these factors by modeling the cash flow of a service business and a retail business.

Service businesses – These enterprises have a tendency to run into cash flow difficulties very early because the cost to start these enterprises is not particularly steep. They generate revenues by billing out the time of their employees, either on an hourly basis or on a fee for service basis. Thus, the contracts they enter into with their clients require them to assign resources for a period of time before they can invoice the client for the completed work. The operating indicator that most service company managers pay close attention to is whether or not their employees produce "billable hours," or are assigned to projects that are billable. There is a mistaken belief is that if the associates are busy working for clients, the company is doing just fine and must be making money.

At least half of that assumption is probably true; "the company should be making money." As long as they are billing out at a higher rates than they are paying, the work being performed should generate profits for the business. The more hours they are able to bill, the higher the profits they should be able to generate. However, it does not necessarily mean that the company is not in trouble. Actually, the company could be running out of cash.

It is all about timing, the timing of when cash needs to go out of the company to meet payroll on a scheduled basis and when cash is expected to come back into the company after the work is completed and invoiced. Often, there is an additional float-time period between when the work is billed and when the payment is actually received. This is how services companies tend to get into difficulty; they accept a number of projects that require them to invest staff hours to complete without recognizing the cash flow implications of their choices. They are looking at the profit opportunity, and not the cash requirements.

Let's construct a simple cash flow model to illustrate what is occurring. For example, the company has taken a contract to provide services that will take six weeks to perform. All of their associates have been assigned to perform this work and the company expects to earn a good profit margin. However, the customer cannot be billed until the work is complete. The company's accounting system recognizes revenues, for reporting purposes, on what is known as a percentage of completion bases, accruing what they have earned each accounting period as the project moves along. This enables them to construct a profit and loss statement that reflects the effort they have expended for each of the reporting periods.

	wk. 1	wk. 2	wk. 3	wk. 4	wk. 5	wk. 6	wk. 7
Cash In	-	-	-	-	-	-	Paid
Billed Revenues	-	-	-	-	-	43,200	**43,200**
Work in Progress							
Accred Revenues	7,200	7,200	7,200	7,200	7,200	7,200	-
Cash Out							
Payroll costs	3,000	3,000	3,000	3,000	3,000	3,000	
Travel etc	250	250	250	250	250	250	
other expenses	50	50	50	50	50	50	
Overheads	500	500	500	500	500	500	
Total Operating Expenses	3,800	3,800	3,800	3,800	3,800	3,800	
Operating Profit	3,400	3,400	3,400	3,400	3,400	3,400	-
Cash Flow Impact	(3,800)	(7,600)	(11,400)	(15,200)	(19,000)	(22,800)	20,400

Figure 9.8 Project Cash Flow Statement Example

This is potentially a profitable project for this company; as it employs all of their associates and covers overhead to make a respectable margin. The project manager pays attention to performing the work and closely watches the projects profitability. But, in order to complete this work, under the terms it was accepted, the company will have to find a way to finance the cost of performing the work requiring some $22,800. It is not until the final billing is rendered and paid in week seven does the project turn cash flow positive. Multiply this scenario over several projects being worked on simultaneously and you can quickly see how a services firm can get into trouble.

Retail operation – Our second example is that of a retail operation that offers merchandise that it imports from overseas. In order to obtain the best price for the kinds of merchandise it offers, it purchases its inventory in bulk (containers). The typical negotiated terms are rather demanding. The manufacturer requires 25 percent in advance with the order and the balance upon delivery to US soil. Transportation time is required for moving the containers from the entry port city to the retail outlet. It takes approximately ninety days from order to receipt of merchandise. Our retailer has set up shop at an attractive location, and started its business with a "container of merchandise" on the shelves for their customers.

Just like our services company, our retailer has been challenged with good fortune, and several of the items they are offering are selling at an accelerated pace. They need to reorder inventory, and place their order now so that they can allow for the time it takes for shipping, etc. Since sales have been good, profits have been as well, and it looks like things are going to continue to improve as volumes increase.

Selling merchandise from stock, (off the shelves) creates an immediate cash flow benefit. The investment in inventory is reduced, and the retail sale converts almost immediately to cash. The store managers are feeling pretty successful about now, but they may be headed for trouble because of the timing issues associated with the replenishing of their inventory. They are going to need to advance 25 percent of the re-order cost when they place their replacement order and will need to pay the remaining balance when this new shipment arrives.

Let's once again construct a simple cash flow model to see what is actually going to occur. We will assume that a container of merchandise costs $10,000, and that it can be sold for $20,000 at retail. Obviously, it takes some period of time to sell all of this content, say 120 days. Their entire sales are for cash or cash equivalents, (credit card sales) so they don't have any accounts receivable to worry about. So, if sales are good why would any of this be a problem? Let's take a closer look.

	Mo. 1	Mo. 2	Mo. 3	Mo. 4	Mo. 5
Starting Inventory	10,000	8,000	5,750	3,500	11,500
Inventory Sold	2,000	2,250	2,250	2,000	
Ending Inventory	8,000	5,750	3,500	1,500	11,500
Retail Sales	4,000	4,500	4,500	4,000	-
Operating Expenses	2,000	2,000	2,000	2,000	
Operating Profit & Cash Flows	2,000	2,500	2,500	2,000	
Beginning Cash Balance	1,000	500	3,000	(2,000)	
25% Deposit w/ order	(2,500)				
Balance Due on Delivery			(7,500)		
Ending Cash Balance	500	3,000	(2,000)	-	-

Figure 9.9 Inventory Re-Order Example.

In this example, the faster the pace of sales increases, the more frequently inventory needed to be replenished. The more frequently inventory needs to be replaced, the sooner cash is required to order and pay for the merchandise. The profit and loss statement says that things are good, day to day operations are generating cash. In the example above though, this company runs out of cash, and equally dangerous, it is about to run out of merchandise to sell as well. Understanding this dynamic and being able to model it is a critical component for this company's success.

Every business plan will encounter some form of cash flow challenge as it grows and matures, so it is imperative that management understands how every dollar comes into their business and how it leaves. The bankruptcy courts are full of cases where the managers of the business were unaware of the cash flow implications of the decisions they were making. Even well established firms, like Eddie Bauer for instance, can over-extend themselves and run into difficulty. When you read their story at the end of this chapter, it will reinforce the principle to you once again that cash is indeed king!

FINANCING ALTERNATIVES

Very few businesses are able to operate on a consistent basis without the benefit of some external financing help. It would be a great advantage to the two companies in our cash flow examples to have access to short term credit facilities that would enable them to sustain operations until cash was received at a future date. We are going to look at financing alternatives in terms of short term debt and long term debt. Both have their place in financing the operations of an organization, but they should be used for distinctively different purposes.

Short term financing – This is defined as all debt obligations that come due within one year; as shown on a balance sheet for current liabilities. A current liability is defined as an obligation payable within one year or the normal operating cycle of the business. A current liability requires payment out of a current asset or the incurrence of another short-term obligation. Examples are accounts payable, short-term notes payable, accrued expenses payable, e.g., taxes payable, salaries payable (Barron's Educational Services, 2005).

Companies may need to consider three major categories of short term debt: a) accounts payable - payments you can defer to vendors and suppliers; b) working capital lines of credit - usually secured by current assets and c) revolving lines of bank credit - either as an independent instrument or company credit cards. Each of these financial tools has its place in smoothing out the ups and downs of cash flow needs within an organization.

Accounts payable – Accounts payable are the obligations you owe to your suppliers for the materials they supply to you in support of your business needs. Just as you may allow your customers 30 days or so to process your invoices, many of your supplier's will understand that your company needs this time as well. This will give you a short period of time to turn their product or service you purchased into cash from your product or service. The sooner you can collect for your goods or services, the less cash you will need to operate during this time period. Accounts payable time-float has the same value to your company as a short term loan. Most vendors and suppliers offer reasonable credit terms as part of doing business. Just remember that they are counting on your responsible payment of their invoices, just like you are counting on your customers' responsible payment of yours.

Working capital – Working capital financing is a flexible line of credit offered by banks to help smooth out the ebb and flow of business cycles. The most common is an asset based credit facility that is collateralized by inventory and/or receivables. Your bank will allow your company to borrow up to a fixed percentage of the investment the company has in these assets. Referring the service company we looked at earlier, if it needs cash to meet payroll, but the customer has not paid, cash can draw-down and repaid when the customer pays the account receivable.

It is a good business practice to have some sort of working capital financing arrangement in place for your company, as it enables you to smooth out cash flow disruptions and take advantage of unexpected opportunities. The best time to negotiate this kind of arrangement with your bank is when you do not need it; "Make friends before you need them!" As long as you recognize that the loan is not a fixed term instrument, but rather one that increases and decreases with need and repayment, it can serve your short term cash needs quite well.

Revolving credit and credit cards – These financial tools have their place in business just as they do in our personal lives. We use credit cards to acquire something we need now and choose to pay for it later. The same principal can be applied in business. You may have a need to travel and acquire some promotional materials in advance of attending a trade show. You purchase these items on your company credit card and pay for them as part of your normal accounts payable cycle. As long as you manage your purchases, just as you would in your personal life, it is another viable source of short term financing. It can also provide the added benefit of itemizing your purchases, making your bookkeeping easier.

Factoring – Factoring is a form of short-term, non-bank financing of accounts receivable. There are four main types of factoring arrangements: a) *Immaturity factoring* – (also called "service factoring), the factoring agent maintains the seller's sales ledger, controls credit, follows up on the payments, and pays the amount (after deducting a commission) of each seller invoice as it falls due - whether or not the payment was collected. b) *Finance factoring*, the factor agent (called the "financing factor") advances funds to a producer or a manufacturing firm, on the security of produce or goods that will be produced or manufactured utilizing those funds. c) *Discount factoring* (also called "service-plus finance factoring") the factor advances a percentage (usually between 70 to 85 percent of the value of accounts receivable) to the seller on a non-recourse basis and assumes the full responsibility of collecting the debts. d) *Undisclosed factoring*, a factor agent buys the goods from a primary party (producer, manufacturer, or seller) and then appoints the same party as its agent to resell those goods and to collect the payments. This arrangement prevents the disclosure that goods are being sold under a factoring agreement. The undisclosed factor, as in all other types of factoring, remains liable for uncollectible payments. Factoring is a type of off-balance sheet financing.

Although factoring is one of the more expensive forms of short term financing because the "factor," (the one advancing the funds,) is assuming a portion of the operating risks. The goods need to be produced; the "agent" (borrower) needs to perform some business process to enable the factor to collect the funds, or the account receivable owed to the borrower; they need to be paid from some third party. There are industries that utilize factoring as a normal part of their business practices, the garment industry being one of them. If you have a need for immediate cash, and sufficient profit margin available from the sale of your product, factoring can be a vehicle to consider as a short term financing option.

Managing the total short term debt obligations of the company is important, and here is a recommended guideline to work with. There is a financing term called the "current ratio," or the "liquidity ratio" that calculates the relationship between current assets and current liabilities. It is desirable to have twice as much value in current assets, (those assets that could be converted to cash within a year) as you have in current liabilities (those obligations that will come due within a year.) Bankers and financiers love to see current ratio's that are at 2:1 or better.

Leasing is a process by which a firm can obtain the use of a certain fixed asset for which it must pay a series of contractual, periodic, tax deductible payments. The lessee is the receiver of the services or the assets under the lease contract and the lessor is the owner of the assets. The relationship between the tenant, (lessee) and the landlord, (lessor) is called a tenancy, and can be for a fixed or an indefinite period of time (called the term of the lease). The consideration for the lease is called rent.

For businesses, leasing property may have significant financial benefits. Leasing is less capital-intensive than purchasing, so if a business has constraints on its capital, it can grow more rapidly by leasing property than it could by purchasing the property outright. Capital assets can also fluctuate in value. Leasing can provide more flexibility to a business which expects to grow or move in the relatively short term, because a lessee is not usually obliged to renew a lease at the end of its term. In some cases a lease may be the only practical option; such as for a small business that wishes to locate in a large office building within tight location parameters. Lease payments are considered expenses, which can be set off against revenue when calculating taxable profit at the end of the relevant tax accounting period.

Long term financing – Long term financing is any amount owed for a period exceeding 12 months from the date of the balance sheet entry. It could be in the form of a bank loan, mortgage bonds, debenture, or other obligations not due for one year. A firm must disclose its long-term debt in its balance sheet with its interest rate and date of maturity. Amount of long-term debt is a measure of a firm's leverage and is distinguished from long term liabilities; which may include supply of services already paid. Longer term debt is normally incurred for one of two purposes: a) the purchase of expensive assets necessary to run the business or b) as an alternative to having to invest additional capital to support business expansion and operations.

Leveraged financing – When debt is incurred for the purchase of an asset, such as equipment or machinery, a simple return on investment calculation may be all that is necessary to evaluate your decision. For example, if you have already purchased a machine that costs $5,000 that enables you to produce goods that earn $1,000 each year, you are earning a 20 percent annual return on that investment. If you wanted to purchase a second machine, and borrow the money to do so, say at an 8% interest rate, it would cost you an additional $400 in financing costs. But, you now have two machines, valued at $10,000 that produce $1600 in earnings ($1,000 from each machine less the $400 in financing costs) without having to invest any additional money of your own. So you original investment of $5,000 is now earning $1,600; or 32 percent.

This concept is often called "leveraged financing" because it enables the company to "lever" its original investment to earn more by using other people's money. As long as you are able to earn more on the amount of money you borrowed than you are paying for the use of the money, it can work well for everyone. The one factor to be conscious of with all longer term debt financing is that it requires repayment over a fixed time schedule, at a prescribed interest rate, in predetermined payment increments.

Although leveraged financing is an attractive source of funds, it too, like everything else in this chapter, has it pitfalls. All organizations have a ceiling as to how much debt it can handle. The financing term for this restraint is called "debt capacity," and it is important that you understand what the limitations would be for your company.

Another approach to acquiring fixed assets is called a *capital lease*. This is a lease of business equipment which represents ownership and is reflected on the company's balance sheet as an asset. A capital lease, in contrast to an operating lease, is treated as a purchase from the standpoint of the person who is doing the leasing and as a loan from the stand point of the person who is offering the lease.

For accounting purposes, a capital lease must meet at least one of these tests:

- Title to the equipment passes automatically to the lessee by the end of the lease term

- The lease contains an option to purchase the equipment at the end of the lease for substantially less than fair market value; sometimes this is a $1 purchase

- The term of the lease is greater than 75% of the useful life of the equipment

- The present value of the lease payments is greater than 90% of the fair market value of the equipment.

A capital lease obligation is normally recognized as a long term liability on the company's balance sheet and assets that are leased this way may be eligible for depreciation. Be sure to check with your tax adviser before you enter into a capital lease, to be sure it meets the criteria to be depreciable.

Borrowing limits - Debt capacity is an assessment of the amount of debt a firm can repay in a timely manner from available means or resources without jeopardizing its financial viability. It can also be influenced or restricted by the covenants of an existing loan agreement. Once again, we recognize the importance of cash management, because you will need cash from operations to repay these obligations as they come due. If the operating cash flows from the business produce $1,000 per month, then you can not service debt that requires repayment of $2,000 per month. Your debt capacity is limited by what you can repay on-time.

New businesses often start with loans from relatives or government supported Small Business loans from a local banks. When building you business plan's financial model, do not overlook this repayment requirement in the construction of your balance sheet and cash flow forecasts. The portion due within the first year is short term debt; the portion due in later years is long term debt. The interest expense is the same as any other operating cost, and the payments that are due each month will be paid from your cash account.

Virtually every business needs to establish some sort of a credit relationship with a financial institution in order to operate effectively. Use short term vehicles to accommodate the ebb and flow of daily operations. Use long term financing as you would investment capital, borrowing to purchase capital goods that make money for the company. Never obligate you company to more than it has the capacity to repay, as once you fall behind under that scenario, there is seldom a road to recovery. You will see an example of this when you read the Eddie Bauer story at the end of this chapter.

SHAREHOLDER EQUITY, INVESTMENTS AND DIVIDENDS -

Shareholder equity comes from two main sources. The original source is the money that was first invested in the company, along with any other additional investments made thereafter. The second comes from retained earnings which the company is able to accumulate over time through its operations. When a company is originally formed, ownership certificates, either "units" or "stock certificates," are exchanged for cash at some value. The future value of these ownership certificates changes with the changes in the value and makeup of the shareholder's equity account on the balance sheet.

New businesses that require investment for product development are often in need to raise additional capital in order to get products from concept, through development, and ultimately to market. Since these companies do not yet generate cash flows from operations, debt financing is not a viable option for them to consider. They have to convince their existing, or new stakeholders, to invest additional capital to fund their development phase. The process of selling additional interests in the company for needed cash will usually involve a management and investor discussion around *equity dilution.*

Dilution is the reduction of fractional ownership of each of a company's existing shareholders by the issuance of additional shares of ownership. These additional shares of ownership are sold to raise additional funds, which means there will be more shares outstanding and owned. The original stakeholders may still own the same number of shares when this sale is complete, but their percentage of ownership will have been decreased, or diluted, because there is now a larger total number of a share owned. Since equity dilution is an unavoidable part of raising company financing, it is advisable then to offer shares of the company at definable points in its evolution where milestones have been achieved and incremental value has been created.

For example, a company may need to raise $6,000,000 to develop its product from inception to market. Management has established a development timeframe that identifies four significant milestone accomplishments: the first is its engineering and design (Seed Round), the second is a working prototype (Series A), the third is a production model that can be readily produced and marketed (Series B) and the final round (Series C) will be for market launch. It may choose a financing strategy that calls for four different rounds of *equity financing* to accommodate their needs; as illustrated in Figure 9.10.

Round of Investment		Seed	Series A	Series B	Series C
Premoney Evaluation	$	500,000	$ 2,000,000	$ 6,000,000	$ 44,000,000
New Investment	$	250,000	$ 1,500,000	$ 5,000,000	$ 12,000,000
Post Money Evaluation	$	750,000	$ 3,500,000	$ 11,000,000	$ 56,000,000
% of Original Stakeholders Ownership		66.66%	33.33%	18.10%	14.20%
# of Original Stakeholder Shares		1,000	1,000	1,000	1,000
Individual Share Value	$	0.50	$ 1.00	$ 2.00	$ 8.00
Original Stakeholders $ Value	$	500,000	$ 1,000,000	$ 2,000,000	$ 8,000,000
Original # of Shares Outstanding		1,000	1,500	3,000	5,500
New Shares Issued and Sold		500	1,500	2,500	1,500
New Total of Shares Outstanding		1,500	3,000	5,500	7,000

Figure 9.10 Shareholder Dilution Example

In each round of financing, the original investor's interest has been diluted to reflect the issuance of new shares to new owners. But because management has timed the sale of the shares to the accomplishment of the milestones that added value, the dilution impact has been minimized because the value of the individual shares has increased. The result is that the original stakeholders may own a smaller percentage of the company than when they originally started, but the value of what they now own has increased substantially. This could not have occurred unless they were able to raise the necessary funding to enable the achievement of their required milestones.

Selling interests in the company will always result in the dilution of ownership; it is just the way the math works. However, if the opportunity is big enough, there should be enough reward to go around, and the early investors are taking just as much of a risk as the entrepreneur. For example, an early investor in Facebook might have had a 20 percent share, valued at $5 million; with equity dilution from later funding down to 10 percent. But, if the equity dilution for getting cash to grow the company results in only a 10 percent stake of a $20 billion company, dilution to grow the company is quite acceptable. These investors, whether they are venture capitalist or private citizens, are your partners and they have a vested interest in your success.

Examples of how dilution could occur include offering stock options to employees or utilizing company stock certificates for acquisitions. Although the purpose may be different, the math remains the same. Any time you make an adjustment to the value of the company or to the number of individual ownership shares, you will affect the value of the individual stock certificates. The book value of the individual shares is calculated by simply dividing the value of the shareholder's equity account on the balance sheet by the number of total shares outstanding.

Dividends – These are distributions of a portion of a company's earnings paid out to shareholders. The dividend most often is quoted in terms of the dollar amount each share receives - dividends per share. Dividend yield is a percentage of the current share market price. Companies that issue dividends generate surplus cash flows from operations, meaning that after they meet all of their financing and tax obligations, they have cash available for distribution to stakeholders.

Just as retained earnings reflect additions to the shareholder's equity account, dividends never make it there. Dividends are paid from operating profits, and therefore, they reduce the amount of "earnings" that will be available for reinvestment in the company. For a fledgling company trying to get started, the thought of having surplus cash is almost inconceivable. But, if you are creating a software company, for example, there is a real possibility that you could generate a very high percentage of cash flow from your operation once it matures. If that occurs, you could have the opportunity to decide if you want to reinvest the cash back into the business, or reward your investors with a dividend check.

Shareholder equity account – The shareholder equity account, sometimes referred to as the capital account, is all about the relationship with the owners of the business. If additional paid-in capital is needed to advance or expand the company, then the existing stakeholders are going to be impacted by the choices that are made. If surplus cash is available for distribution, then it is the stakeholders who will benefit. It is for these reasons that most companies establish Boards of Directors, or Advisory Boards, to represent the individual shareholder's interest. Management runs the company, but the shareholders own it.

SUMMARY-

Financial management is a very broad topic that includes a variety of business practices and processes and we obviously can not address them all within one book chapter. It is critically important that the entrepreneur, or business management, master cash flows in and out of the business. It is equally important to prepare timely and accurate financial reports.

We suggest that you take some time to establish and distribute financial policies in a manner that the members of your team can understand. Things such as who is authorized to make purchases? Who can sign for the delivery of merchandise? What are the limits of authority for entering into a contracting obligation? Who can write checks? Etc.

In today's business world, we are fortunate to have financial professionals to help set financial systems in place. Technology has also helped, as there are a number of good financial packages available "off the shelf" that can be readily applied to a new business venture. One that has gained popularity is Intuit's *"Quick Books;"* which is well suited for small business and start ups. The canned programs can also be expanded to add a number of the management accounting concepts we mentioned in this chapter as your company grows. The language of commerce is finance, and if you do not speak it, you will have to learn it, or will leave yourself vulnerable to its pitfalls.

A CLASSIC CASH FLOW PROBLEM
EDDIE BAUER DECLARES BANKRUPTCY

Summarized from an Article by: Lamm, G. (2009). Puget Sound Business Journal.

Overwhelmed by debt payments and a steep drop in customer spending, Eddie Bauer filed for bankruptcy protection, becoming another high-profile retail casualty of the recession. Eddie Bauer Holdings Inc. struggled with its high debt, a problem that worsened when revenues dropped as part of an overall trend affecting most retailers during the recent recession. The company lost nearly a half billion dollars in the past three years, and its inability to meet its debt payments apparently pushed the company into bankruptcy court. Eddie Bauer, along with Linens and Things, Circuit City, and Northwest retailer Joe's Sports & Outdoors, became another of the latest retailers to succumb to filing in bankruptcy court.

According to a filing with the Securities and Exchange Commission, Eddie Bauer had total assets of $525.22 million and listed total liabilities of $448.9 million. It reported losses of $165.5 million in fiscal year 2008, part of its total losses of $478.7 million during the past three fiscal years. For the first quarter of fiscal year 2009, which ended on April 4, Eddie Bauer reported an additional loss of $44.5 million. That was an even greater loss than the first quarter losses it suffered in 2008, when the company reported a $19.3 million loss. Net sales for the first quarter of 2009 were $179.8 million, a decline from net sales of $213.2 million in the first quarter of 2008.

Eddie Bauer has 370 stores, including 251 retail stores and 119 outlet stores in the United States and Canada. At the time of its bankruptcy filing, Eddie Bauer reported having $289.5 million in outstanding debt, including $187.8 million in term loans and $75 million in convertible notes, which company executives tried to persuade debt-holders to convert into equity shares of the company. But by filing for reorganization under Chapter 11 of the federal bankruptcy code, Eddie Bauer had hoped to avoid the fate of other retailers who have been forced to close their doors.

Eddie Bauer announced in early 2009 that it had amended its $225 million loan agreements with its lenders, but the company had a July 1 deadline to convert that debt or face big penalties, something that Eddie Bauer, which had depleted much of its cash and cash equivalences, could not afford to pay. In May, 2009 the *Wall Street Journal,* citing unnamed sources, said Eddie Bauer hired Peter J. Solomon Co. as its investment banker to negotiate any sale. The company was acquired at bankruptcy auction by Golden Gate Capital in July 2009.

Chapter Summary

KEY POINTS

- The universal language of commerce is finance, and businesses communicate their activities and operating results via a collection of financial references and reports.

- Three major categories of financial management include: formal financial reporting, management accounting, and cash management.

- The Financial Accounting Standards Board has been designated to establish the standards for financial reporting for non-government entities

- The accounting rules used to prepare, present and report financial statements is called GAAP, or "Generally Accepted Accounting Principles."

- By ensuring financial reporting comparability, financial statements and other documents can be compared to similar businesses within similar industries.

- Formal financial reports consist of an operating or income statement, a balance sheet, and a cash flow statement.

- It is possible for a company to show operating profits and not have enough cash to sustain its operations.

- Management accounting is used for the purpose of identifying, measuring, analyzing and preparing financial information to be used by management in the operation of the business.

- Examples of management accounting are cost accounting, performance management, forecasting, and strategic evaluations.

- The treasury, or cash management function, refers to the collection, concentration, and disbursement of cash.

- Operating cash flows are the ebb and flow cash generated from the process of performing one or more transactions within the business

- Financing alternatives can be recognized in two balance sheet categories: short term debt, (due within one year,) and long term debt (multi-year commitments)

- Examples of short term debt are: accounts payable to vendors & suppliers; working capital financing; revolving credit, (credit cards,) and factoring

- Long term debt examples are: mortgages, machinery and equipment financing; term loans used to establish or transition the business

- Equity financing is provided by selling additional interest in the company to existing or new stakeholders

- Equity financing can result in the dilution of the percentage of ownership of existing stakeholders if new shares need to be issued and sold to outsiders

- Dividends are paid to existing stockholders from operating cash flows that not need to be retained to support operations

- Including the services of a financial professional in the construction and maintenance of your financial systems is important and desirable

- Incorporating proven automated financial recording and reporting systems into your business practices is desirable as well as it keeps your accounting entries current.

- Establishing policies that clearly define the approval processes and individual authorities of those who manage your finances will mitigate financial risk

- Cash is KING !

TAKE ACTION NOW

- Revisit your original business plan financial model and use it to establish your initial operating budget.

- Make adjustments to your original assumptions to reflect what you have learned from operating the business and revise your operating budget to reflect this learning

- Engage a financial professional, (C.P.A.) to validate your assumptions, establish your chart of accounts, and arrange for the regularly scheduled production of your financial reports

- Incorporate an automated system if it is practical to do so, so that individual transactions get recognized in a timely manner.

- Establish a "cash" report that tells you how much cash came in, and how much of your cash is committed to go out within prescribed timeframes (weekly).

- Create a business practice that requires a more in-depth review of any transaction that is outside the norm so that it cash flow implications are known.

- Utilize financial modeling to establish your future years operating plans as this will enable you to understand you cash requirements to support your growth.

- Analyze the best sources and uses for capital to accommodate your plans, short term borrowing, long term borrowing, or equity investment.

- Make it a point to become familiar with basic financial terminology so that you can communicate effectively with potential stakeholders.

- Formalize your financial policies so that your associates understand what they can do and can not do. Your financial professional can help you with this.

REFERENCES:

Barron's Educational Series (2005). *Dictionary of accounting terms.* Haupauge, NY: Barron's Educational Series, Inc.

Bennins, S. (1997). *Financial Modeling,* MIT Press, Ambridge, MA Publisher.

CIMA (2011). *CIMA official terminology.* www.cimaglobal.com

Decision 411, (2010), *Forecasting,* www.duke.edu, Durham, NC: Duke University Publishing.

FASB (2010). *Financial Accounting Standards.* Norwalk, CT: Financial Accounting Standards Board director@fasb.org.

Helfert, Erich A. (2001). *Financial Analysis - Tools and Techniques - A Guide for Managers.* New York: McGraw-Hill Co.

Hilton, Ronald, (1988) *Managerial Accounting,* New York: McGraw Hill Co.

Meigs, W. B. & Meigs, R.F. (1970) *Financial Accounting.* New York: McGraw Hill Co.

Saltelli, A., Ratto, M., Andres, T., Campolongo, F., Cariboni, J., Gatelli, D. Saisana, M., & Tarantola, S. (2008,) *Global Sensitivity Analysis. The Primer,* San Francisco: John Wiley & Sons.

Frank, Murray & Goyal, Vidhan, (2003). *Testing the Pecking Order Theory of Capital Structure,* Journal of Financial Economics 67, 217-248

Warren, Carl (2008) *Survey of Accounting,* Cincinnati: Southwestern College Publisher.

Web Finance (2010). *Business dictionary.* www.businessdictionary.com

Wheelen, Thomas L. & Hunger, J. David (1995), *Strategic Management and Business Policy.* Boston: Addison-Wesley Publishing Company, Inc.

Williams, J. R., Haka, S. F., Bettner, M. S., & Carcello, J. V. (2008). *Financial & Managerial Accounting.* New York: McGraw-Hill Irwin.

William R. Cobb and M. L. Johnson, Ed.D, Ph.D.

SUPPLEMENTAL SOURCES:

Tracy, Tage C., Tracy John A., (2007) *Financial Management for Dummies,* Willey Publishing, Inc., Hoboken, New Jersey

Siciliano, Gene, (2003) *Finance for Non-Financial Managers,* McGraw Hill, New York

Ittelson, Thomas, (2009) *Financial Statements, A Step by Step Guide to Understanding and Creating Reports,* Career Press, Franklin, New Jersey

Rogers, Steven, (2003) *Entrepreneurs Guide to Finance and Business,* McGraw Hill, New York

Fields, Edward (2011) *The Essentials of Finance and Accounting for Nonfinancial Managers,* Amacom, New York, New York, publisher.

CHAPTER TEN

Operate or Sell?

"When someone makes a decision, he is really diving into a strong current that will carry him to places he had never dreamed of...."

The Alchemist/ Paulo Coelho

In the earlier chapters, we emphasized the necessity of deciding on the *fate* of your venture at the start of the initiative. By *fate* we mean "what happens when your business idea meets your definition of success." Do you reset higher goals or simply operate at the intended level? Some entrepreneurs are interested in establishing a "life style" business that provides their cost of living needs, and others are looking to build their enterprise for the sole purpose of selling it at a profit. Still others seek to build a privately held or publicly traded legacy company; one that will continue to provide useful goods and services long after their personal involvement.

Everyone can have their own definition for what "success" means. It is believed that success stems from the achievement of intention, within a specified period of time or within some specified parameter. Success can also be expanded to encompass an entire project or be restricted to a single component of a project or task. It can be achieved within the workplace, or in an individual's personal life. In the end, success is whatever we define it to be; so if you have achieved what you set out to do when you started the business, you are indeed successful. Here are several entrepreneurial success models for your consideration.

LIFESTYLE BUSINESS

Lifestyle businesses typically have limited scalability and potential for growth. Such greater growth would destroy the lifestyle for which their owner/

managers started them in the first place. However, lifestyle businesses can and do win awards and provide a great deal of satisfaction to their owners and customers. For example, Mary Jane Jossey opened her East Bay California wig store in 1959. It provided her a livelihood, artistic expression and community recognition. However, after 50 years she closed her House of Fashion when the last of the merchandise was cleared out – for more grandchildren time (Louie, 2011). Such firms depend heavily on the founder's skills, personality, energy, and contacts. Often the founders create them to exercise personal talent or skills, achieve a flexible schedule, work with other family members, remain in a desired geographic area, or simply to express themselves. But, without the founder's deep personal involvement, such businesses are likely to flounder if assumed or purchased by an outside party.

Apparently, the term *lifestyle entrepreneur* was coined in 1987 by William Wetzel, a director emeritus of the Center for Venture Research at the University of New Hampshire. Wetzel was using it then to describe the type and scale of ventures unlikely to generate economic returns robust enough to interest outside investors. In financial jargon, "There's no upside potential for creating great wealth." However, Wetzel views it a bit differently today. He recognizes lifestyle entrepreneurs as a specific breed of business owners who are neither financially independent hobbyists nor wealth-seeking empire builders. "Lifestyle ventures are usually ventures that are run by people who like being their own bosses. But they're in it for the income as well. Indeed, lifestyle entrepreneurs offer a different view of success than those who are mainly after wealth accumulation" (Henricks, 2011).

As it should be, everyone can have her/his own definition of what a successful "lifestyle business" could be. Suffice to say, if it meets the requirements of what the owner / entrepreneur had in mind, it is unquestionably a successful venture. Although each business operation is as unique as the founding entrepreneur, they do share a set of common characteristics. Here is what they tend to have in common:

- The owner/entrepreneur is "in charge" and there is no doubt about whom the "boss" is and who makes the decisions. Not to have a boss was one of the reasons why the entrepreneur formed the business in the first place.

- The owner/entrepreneur is very much engaged in the operation of the business, right down to the transaction level. The business practices of the enterprise reflect the personality of the owner.

- The legal structure of these businesses is usually a Proprietorship, a Limited Liability Corporation (LLC) or a sub-chapter "S" Corporation. Under all three of these structures the income generated by the firm is considered part of the owner's personal income.

- Start-up funding was, for the most part, provided from personal savings, friends and family, or a government backed S.B.A. loan. Seldom is third party equity investment required or involved. A loan does not dilute the owner's equity.

- The entrepreneur operates the business to sustain a minimal level of cash flow necessary to support a defined lifestyle; often passing up "growth opportunities" because they do not "need" the additional income.

- They take full advantage of the tax privileges that being a business owner can provide, right down to renting facilities from themselves, or charging vehicle operating costs to the business.

- They enjoy being part of their communities and are often highly visible in their local Chamber of Commerce, Rotary, or other civic organizations.

- They are not considering an "exit strategy" or any other form for leaving the business because the business has become an integral part of their identity and their life.

- If, and when, the time should come to "retire" from the business, they will often seek to transfer it to a family member, or simply close it down.

- If they do seek a buyer for their business, they are often subject to "earn-out" limitations because of the critical role they have played in the operation of the company. Earn-out refers to a requirement of the new owners to use future earnings of the business to pay a portion of or the entire purchase sale price.

- Professional investors, therefore, are rarely involved with lifestyle businesses (Soul Shelter, 2008).

A recent *New York Times* article was based on survey responses to the question, *"Is the Term Lifestyle Business an Insult?"* Barbara Taylor (2011) is co-owner of a business brokerage firm, *Synergy Business Services*, in Bentonville, Ark. She solicited her colleagues' opinions as to how a successful life style business should be described. Here are a few of the responses she reported:

> "I had what you could call a lifestyle business when my children were young. I don't think a lifestyle business is something someone does out of necessity. It is a deliberate choice. I would define a lifestyle business as an individual's creation that fulfills one's own ambitions, drives or values, while, at the same time, not sacrificing any of the other things in one's life that is important and worth doing. It's called a lifestyle business because it defines one's own life and style." - Rose Stabler, Certified Business Brokers

> "I'd say a lifestyle business is any company where the owner's motivations go beyond a strict definition of return on investment. If a business owner makes decisions that include more factors than just what will increase shareholder value, then he/she, at least to some extent, is running a lifestyle business. For example, maybe you want to live in San Diego, so you start a Search Engine Optimization agency in San Diego even though the best thing to do from a shareholder value perspective is to locate in foggy San Francisco or snowy New York." - John Warrillow, author of *Built to Sell*.

> "I would define a lifestyle business as a business under $500,000 in annual revenues where the owner's primary objective is the fulfillment of a non-financial personal passion. Typically, the freedom to pursue (and share) this passion supersedes the owner's desire to accumulate personal wealth. I most commonly associate a lifestyle business with a business-to-consumer model." — Scott Mashuda, River's Edge Alliance Group

A lifestyle business is usually one in which the founders live off the cash flow of the business; as opposed to trying to increase the equity value for themselves or other shareholders. Entrepreneurs who operate these businesses are seeking a "balance between their economic needs and their personal lifestyle desires," including being their own boss. There are so many great "lifestyle businesses" in our neighborhoods - ranging from successful franchise operations to the local cleaners or the hardware store on the corner.

THE ICE CREAM LADY

Originally reported by Richard Hewitt of the
Bangor Daily News staff (May, 2011)

BROOKLIN, Maine- Eating ice cream is a normal family activity, but for one local family, making ice cream is not only a family affair, but it has become a family business. Nancy Veilleux, her husband Chris Hurley, a full-time carpenter, and their daughter, a full-time 7-year-old, run The Ice Cream Lady, a business they purchased this spring. The business started in Stonington and now makes and markets homemade ice cream that is made in the family's Brooklin home.

The new venture has resulted in a slight change in the family's lifestyle. It was a desired change, Vellieux said, and one that involved switching places with the former owner. Veilleux and Hurley had operated an organic farm for a number of years, but had wanted a change in order to be able to spend more time at home where they home-school their daughter Isabelle. The former owner of The Ice Cream Lady owned some land and wanted to sell the business so she could focus on organic farming.

So they just did a switch. Veilleux reportedly said. "We home-school Isabelle, and working on the farm was just too much. I wanted to do something more home-based." Isabelle is now also involved in the ice cream operation and she was hand packing the Espresso Toffee Chip along with Hurley during the interview with Hewitt. She said the home business provides a multitude of learning opportunities for her.

Veilleux works about 20 hours a week making the ice cream, and also does much of the deliveries. That takes extra time because she and Isabelle often look for little adventures on the way back from their customer rounds. She also continues to work part time at a local dentist office. They use their own eggs and as much of the local produce as possible. Some of their ice creams are seasonal. Maple syrup from Carding Brook Farm just down the road provides the maple-flavored variety. Fresh strawberry and fresh blueberry ice cream will come later in their season as other local farmers and friends harvest their produce.

Their production process is straight-forward and takes place in a converted storage area-porch with a bank of windows that provide them with a view of the Benjamin River. They create a basic milk mixture, adding the various flavors as needed and pour the concoction into a 25-year-old Italian ice cream maker, which literally churns out a batch of ice cream in about 12 minutes. "It's 25 years old, but it just keeps chugging," Hurley reportedly said.

They bought the business in the middle of March, so they believe they are coming in just at the right time. Veilleux says she doesn't mind working every day, but she doesn't want to have to make ice cream on demand. Demand is the key word, she prefers to operate on her own terms. Initially, The Ice Cream Lady was stocked only in local markets in the Brooklin area, selling to a lot of mom and pop stores.

But, the couple has now tapped into contacts from their vegetable business and the demand is continuing to grow with larger super markets, such as Trade Winds in Blue Hill, along with area restaurants that are starting to carry The Ice Cream Lady ice creams. They are excited about expanding the business, but Veilleux and Hurley have slightly different ideas on how much or how fast the business should grow.

When they started farming, Veilleux said, they jumped in with both feet, and by the end of their first summer, they were exhausted. "I don't want to do that with this," she said. "We'll go slow and easy and keep it manageable." Hurley,on the other hand, says the sky's the limit, and he'd like to see the business grow large enough so that he too could work at home. His theory is that Ben and Jerry's started in a garage. Says Hurley: "We have no idea where this can go. But hope springs eternal."

BUILD IT TO SELL-

Start-ups designed for a merger or acquisition (M&A) exit strategy have a recognizable relationship to an industry sector or there would not be a holding of conglomerate interest. For example, a start-up possessing the intellectual property to make a lighter and more powerful lithium battery would quickly be on the M&A radar screens of every battery manufacturer – Eveready, Energizer and Duracell – as well as the automobile industry. Also, forward-looking companies would be interested in business ideas where demand is likely to increase – the energy sector. For example, Berkshire Hathaway, Inc. recently paid approximately $9 billion for

Lubrizol Corporation to bolster its energy sector portfolio. Lubrizol makes chemicals for pharmaceutical companies and fuel additives for both gasoline and diesel engines. Well managed start-ups, establishing a profitable presence in a growing market sector and with minimal annual revenues of $10 million, can certainly attract M&A interest. Current attractive demand sectors include pharmaceuticals, energy and internet services.

The volume and value of M&A transactions tend to follow demand and emerging technology cycles. Thompson and Walker (2010) of the Financial Executives Research Foundation (FERF) reported that M&A deal flow declined from 5,215 deals with a value of $1,510.5 billion in 2007 to 3,032 deals with a value of $763.6 billion in 2009. Approximately 56.6 percent of the total transaction value in 2009 occurred in three industries: life sciences and healthcare (24.9 percent), energy (19.7 percent) and financial services (12.0 percent). Transaction value is driven primarily by mergers involving a few relatively large corporations. In 2007 there were 484 acquisitions with transaction values greater than $500 million. In 2009 there were 163 large acquisitions (a decline of 66.3 percent). The total transaction value of these large acquisitions was $653.5 billion (or 85.6 percent of the total $763.6 billion).

Year	# of Deals	% Greater (Less) Prior Year	Total Value $ Billions	% Greater (Less) Prior Year	# Mid-sized *Acquisitions
2009	3,032	(24.7)	$763.6	(7.6)	1,027
2008	4,024	(22.8)	$826.4	(45.3)	1,477
2007	5,215	3.9	$1,510.5	(.01)	2,160
2006	5,021	12.7	$1,511.9	38.1	2,210
2005	4,456	8.6	$1,095.1	38.2	2,048
2004	4,105	52.1	$792.2	53.6	1,892
2003	2,698		$515.9		1,483

Figure 10.1 M&A deal flow in North America from 2003 thru 2009. Mid-sized acquisitions have transaction values between $15 million and $500 million (Thompson & Walker, 2010). The data also showed a similar decline in the number of mid-sized acquisitions. There were 2,160 mid-sized acquisitions in 2007, but only 1,027 mid-sized acquisitions in 2009.

Financial media frequently headlines the really big start-up exit sales like YouTube, Skype, and MySpace. Those are exciting company acquisitions and great startup success stories. But, for the other 99 percent of entrepreneurs and early investors, the really exciting news is that there are a large number of company acquisitions that are made for under $30 million. Many of these business acquisitions are so small they do not even warrant a press release, but for the entrepreneurs who sold them, it is very big news indeed!

Acquisition motivation – With too few exceptions, large corporations have difficulty generating new business ideas or have difficulty doing the commercialization translation. Large corporation operations management is focused on profitability and increasing short term stock value; leaving potentially profitable ideas on the shelf; as Blockbuster, Inc. did with its Total Access online video service concept in 2007. If the corporation is generating billions, adding a million dollars to the bottom line will not even move the profitability needle. However, that same idea outside the corporation that generates a million in profits is a BIG DEAL to a start-up. And, the entrepreneur that builds a five to ten million annual cash flow in an emerging market sector has an opportunity window to build and sell – for moving on to another innovation project.

Despite considerable research and development allocation, large companies often have difficulty in staying at the cutting edge. Microsoft functionally abandoned their computer tablet initiative, Blockbuster abandoned its internet video project some three years before filing for bankruptcy and Kodak stayed with its photography film technology too long and let others take the digital photography market. Also, the decision processes of large companies may not be attuned to market trends. For example, Cisco Systems spends millions annually on research and development, but in-house products are not sustaining competitiveness. Writing for *Forbes Magazine*, Hardy (2011) filed the following report:

Even for John Chambers, Cisco Systems' relentlessly positive chief executive, February 10 had to hurt. Cisco shed 15 percent of its market value after the news bomb of the day before; of its fourth quarter consecutive shrinking gross margins. Five years ago it netted 27 cents per dollar of revenue; now it gets just over a dime. Cisco looks like a company facing redoubled competition just as it diversified in the wrong directions and misread the greatest shift in business technology: computerization. In 2005 Chambers paid $6.9 billion for set-top-box maker Scientific Atlanta; figuring he could combine it with the old Linksys home-router business he'd bought earlier to offer pay-TV service providers a premium product for voice and video. He didn't figure in how fast the home-router market would get saturated or how quickly the set-top-box would begin to move inside the guts of connected TVs.

After reviewing some 5,000 technology company acquisitions over several years, Malik (2004) reported an average acquisition price of $12 million. Peters (2009) conducted a Google search for more recent tech company acquisitions and provided the following list. Most of these are good start-up successes stories in their own right, but they are also great companies that were acquired for under $30 million.

- Google bought Adscape for $23 million (now Adsense)

- Google bought Picasa for $5 million

- Ask Jeeves bought LiveJournal for $25 million

- Google bought Writely for $10 million

- Google bought MeasureMap for less than $5 million

It would appear that many on the Fortune 500 company list are not very good at initiating new ideas or launching startup ventures. They seem to struggle with building business from zero to $20 million in value. But, they are really good at growing values from $20 million to $200 million or more. At $20 million, a growing start-up is an attractive proposition for a major company to acquire as a new or different capability. But, if they see an acquisition priced at $100 million or more, they tend to view the prospect as already out of their sweet spot for adding any significant value.

Design acquisition strategies – The practical strategy for a start-up seeking to be acquired is to design the company, and its management practices, so that everyone associated with it is aligned to the idea of the company being acquired in the $20 to $30 million range. The good news is that these exits can often be completed in just a few years from start-up. Well managed medium range start-ups also have a much higher probability of success than swinging for the fences and hoping for a big NASDAQ IPO. The recent Groupon (Group+Coupon) rejection of the Google $6 billion bid is raising conjecture that the start-up's corporate strategy is to float an initial public offering (MacMillan & Galante, 2010).

Businesses are usually acquired by larger companies for one of two reasons: a) the acquisition provides a strategic capability that fits with the overall goals and objectives of the acquiring company; or b) there is an immediate operating benefit to the acquiring company resulting from the acquisition. Occasionally, the acquired company will provide both of these benefits to its new owners. However, be prepared for the acquiring company to bring in its own management team and to re-format your financial protocols to fit its corporate accounting systems.

When we discussed acquisition as a growth strategy in Chapter Eight, we identified several reasons why acquiring someone else's company could be attractive to yours for acquisition. These same criteria can apply in reverse - for making your company attractive to someone else. In building to sell, design a strategic corporate plan to answer these questions. Can you provide access to customers they don't have? Are you delivering a new technology or a product family a larger corporation needs to offer? Does your company employ a set of talents and skills that would enhance their operations? Chances are, if your company is providing one or more of these capabilities, then you would be considered an acquisition candidate. When Steve Jobs acquired, what became *Pixar*, from Lucas films in 1986 for only $5 million, he eventually provided customers what they did not have (digitally animated feature film entertainment) and secured the technical talents needed to produce a litany of highly profitable award winning films.

Every company that is acquired offers something that is unique or different to the firm that acquires them – though some acquisitions are made to minimize competition. And, although their methods of formation and operation may be different, they all seem to have a set of common characteristics that make them attractive to their suitors. Remember, it is the company that is being acquired, not just the products the company offers, so it is your company "profile" that needs to meet the acquiring company's criteria. Acquired companies tend to share the following characteristics:

- The owner / entrepreneur is the founder and visionary for the company, but not necessarily the day to day operator of the business

- The business is well positioned in a growth market sector.

- The legal structure of these businesses is either a Limited

Liability Corporation or a "C" Corporation that has divided its ownership into shares that can be acquired by others.

- Initial funding to start these enterprises was typically a combination of the founder, angel investors (Regulation D) or venture capitalists.

- Entrepreneurs operate the business to build value and have a financial goal in mind that represents their success achievement criteria.

- They enjoy being part of their industry and seek recognition for their innovation, market leadership, or business model to separate themselves from other participants who could also be acquisition candidates.

- They are conscious of their "market window" and realize that they need to accomplish their objectives within certain timeframes to be attractive to others.

- Their company's have demonstrated revenue growth and profitability so that they are attractive to potential suitors.

- They have established a management team that can operate the business without their personal involvement, so that they can exit when the time comes.

- When the business is sold, they are open to considering various purchasing options that work to the benefit of both the acquiring company and their own personal interests, (e.g. stock vs. cash).

Before the value of a business can be measured, the basis for the valuation must specify the reason for and circumstances surrounding the business valuation. These are formally known as the *business value standard* and *premise of value* (Malik, 2004). Business valuation results can vary considerably depending upon the choice of either the a) standard or b) premise of value. In an actual business sale, it would be expected that the buyer and seller, each with an incentive to achieve a respective optimal outcome, would determine the fair market value of a business asset that would compete in the market for such an acquisition. If the offer becomes known, a bidding competition may ensue that will realistically determine the "fair market value."

Determining company worth – Three different approaches are commonly used in business valuation: a) the income approach, b) the asset-based approach, and c) the market approach (Pratt, Reilly & Schweihs, 2000). Within each of these approaches, there are various techniques for determining the value of a business using the definition of value appropriate for the appraisal assignment. Generally, the income approach determines value by calculating the net present value of the benefit stream generated by the business (discounted cash flow). The asset-based approach determines value by adding the sum of the parts of the business (net asset value). And the market approach determines value by comparing the subject company to other companies in the same industry, of the same size, and/or within the same region.

Income Approach – The income approach takes a look at the earnings potential from running the business. Here is where the economic principle of *expectation* applies: If a bidder invests time, money and effort into business ownership, what are the economic benefits and when is it provided? Notice the future expectation of economic benefit in the above sentence. Since the money is not in the bank yet, there is some measure of risk – risk of not receiving all or part of it when you expect it. Therefore, in addition to figuring out what kind of money the business is likely to make, the income valuation approach also factors in potential risk. Since the business value must be established in the present tense, the expected future income and risk must be translated to today. The income approach uses two ways to do this translation: Capitalization and Discounting.

Capitalization method – The *capitalization method* basically divides the business's expected earnings by the so-called capitalization rate. The capitalization rate is the ratio between the net operating income produced by an asset and its capital cost (the original price paid to buy the asset) or alternatively its current market value (Pratt, Reilly & Schweihs, 2000). The formula to calculate this rate is to divide the net operating income by the cost or value of the asset. For example, if the assets are worth $1.00 and the projected earnings are expected to be 33 cents, then the capitalization rate is 33 percent (1.00 / .33). The value of the business would then be calculated by multiplying the projected earnings (.33) times the inverse of the capitalization rate, (33 percent or 1/3 inverse is 3). The business would be then be worth three times projected earnings, (3 X .33 = $1.00).

Discounted method – The discounting method works differently. First, you project the business income stream over some future period of time, usually measured in years. Next, you determine the discount rate which reflects the risk of getting this income on time. Lastly, calculate what the business will be worth at the end of the projection period. This is called the residual or terminal business value. Finally, the discounting calculation gives you the so-called present value of the business, or what it is worth today.

Since both income valuation methods do the same thing, you would expect similar results. If fact, the capitalization and discount rates are related; as shown in the formula CR = DR – K -where *CR* is the capitalization rate, *DR* is the discount rate, and *K* is the expected average growth rate in the income stream. If the discount rate is 25 percent and your projections show that the business profits are growing at a steady 5 percent per year, then, the capitalization rate is 25 - 5 = 20 percent.

Perhaps the biggest difference between capitalization and discounting is what income stream you choose to use. Capitalization uses a single income measure such as the average of the earnings over several years. The discounting model is done on a set of income values, one for each year in the projected valuation period. If your business shows smooth, steady profits year to year, the capitalization method is a good choice. For a growing business with rapidly changing and less predictable profits, discounting gives the most accurate results

Asset Approach – The asset approach views the business as a set of assets and liabilities that are used as building blocks to construct the picture of business value. The asset approach is based on the so-called economic principle of substitution that addresses the question: "What will it cost to create another business like this one that will produce the same economic benefits for its owners?" Since every operating business has assets and liabilities, a natural way to address this question is to determine the value of these assets and liabilities. The difference is the business value, or "book" value of the company.

The challenge is in the details of a) determining which assets and liabilities to include in the valuation, b) choosing a standard of measuring their value, and then c) determining what each asset and liability is actually worth. For example, many business balance sheets may not include the most important business assets; such as internally developed products or a proprietary way of doing business. If the business owner did not pay for them, they don't get recorded on the "cost-basis" balance sheet. Thus, the real value of such assets may be far greater than all the "recorded" assets combined. Imagine a business that does not own the intellectual property it uses to create the products that it sells. Valuing these kinds of contingent assets is always a challenge.

Market Approach – The market approach, as the name suggests relies on indicators from the real market place to determine what a business is worth. Here, the *economic principle of competition* actually applies: "What are other businesses worth that are similar to my business?" If what you do is really great, then chances are there are others doing the same or similar things. If you are looking to buy a business, you decide what type of business you are interested in and then look around to see what the "going rate" is for businesses of this type. If you are planning to sell your business, you check the market to see what similar businesses are sold for.

Fair market value *is* that which a willing buyer will pay and a willing seller will accept for the business. Both parties are assumed to act in full knowledge of all the relevant facts, and neither being under any obligation to conclude the sale. The comparable market approach to valuing a business is a great way to determine its fair market value. Comprehensive market data is great for supporting your offer or your asking price.

Deal Structure – The way in which a proposed acquisition is structured will have a lot to do with the success or failure of the transaction. A buyer and seller agree on a price and draft a basic term sheet. The acquisition is essentially complete, right? Unfortunately, many inexperienced sellers have this view. But, agreeing on a deal structure isn't always easy. And, the due diligence process for examining the seller's financial records can only be started after a purchase proposal is signed. Obviously, there will be numerous contingencies built into the purchase proposal; including verification of the financial records, assets and liabilities and ownership of any intellectual property.

The range of available forms, including asset sales and stock sales and consideration of relevant factors such as securities and tax laws, often create conflicting goals between buyers and sellers. Add a lender to the mix, and a third set of objectives further complicates the deal structure. Buyers and sellers need to understand these complexities. They also need to determine the amount and timing of cash proceeds during the deal process and anticipate their relative tax impact.

As a general rule, sellers prefer to sell stock rather than assets. A stock sale for a C corporation is taxable to the seller only if there are capital gains. Even when capital gains are realized, these taxes are lower than ordinary income tax rates. On the other hand, asset sales get taxed twice: First there are capital gains taxes at the corporate level, then shareholders are taxed at ordinary income tax rates for the receipt of any dividends.

Buyers, on the other hand, generally prefer to acquire assets. Because an asset purchase gives the acquirer the opportunity to step up the cost basis of an asset to its fair market value, the result is increased depreciation deductions, lower taxes and increased future cash flow. By acquiring assets instead of stock, buyers also avoid any contingent liabilities that might transfer in a stock purchase.

In an asset transaction, all assets of the target business may be transferred, including real estate, equipment and inventory, and intangible property such as patents and trademarks. But, in some cases, buyers negotiate to buy only specific assets, such as inventory, equipment and intangible assets, but not cash, receivables or real estate. Buyers also generally agree to assume certain liabilities of the selling company.

Although buyers enjoy tax advantages, asset-based deals can be more costly than other types of transactions. Asset-based sales require the legal transfer of each asset, which in some cases triggers additional transfer and real estate taxes. Also, legal fees and other advisory fees are higher with asset purchases. Finally, many intangible assets, such as customer contracts and leases, may not be assignable in an asset sale without the consent of third parties such as lessors (property or equipment leases) or customers (supply contracts).

In a stock sale, the seller transfers shares of its company to the buyer for an agreed-upon price. In addition to the negative tax impact for buyers, disadvantages to stock sales may include more difficulty in securing transaction approval if there are minority shareholders. If the buyer wants to acquire all of the company's outstanding shares, any one shareholder could hold up the deal. Transaction costs however, particularly legal fees, are generally lower with stock sales.

Acquisition Payments – Although every individual transaction is subject to its own puts and takes, generally most companies are acquired one of three ways: they are purchased for a) cash, b) stock of the acquiring company or c) for some combination of both. Secure advice of your tax accountant to help you understand the impacts for each of the choices you are considering. Usually, an "all cash" stock purchase results in an immediate recognition of any value created and a capital gains tax liability. For example, the 2011 Berkshire Hathaway cash purchase of Lubrizol stock, at a 28 percent premium over the previous closing price, presented stockholders with a $135.00 per share cash-out and a capital gains tax problem. However, when the stock of a company is acquired for shares of a publicly traded company, then the capital gains implications do not occur until the publicly traded shares are converted to cash at a future date.

Occasionally, companies are acquired under the terms of what is known as a "Leveraged Buy Out," (LBO), which requires some entity or individuals to provide a loan for a portion of the purchase price. These loans are made upon an evaluation of the earnings forecast and cash flow projections of the company being sold. Although it is most desirable to have a third party, such as a bank or private equity firm, provide this lending facility, sometimes the company being sold is forced to consider this as an option. A LBO often occurs when a company is being acquired by its existing employees, and the current owners are willing to accommodate this arrangement and defer their selling price cash payment accordingly. This arrangement can often provide favorable tax, and future income, benefits to the seller, so it should not be casually overlooked.

Build to sell companies are started and acquired every day within our economy and they provide a welcome source of new innovation and business practices that enrich our lives. The entrepreneurs who start and develop these firms may do so with the intent to sell them for a profit, but it is that very motivation that sparks their imaginations and drives their commitment to make these new ventures successful. Often, entrepreneurs, successful with this model, will go on to create multiple companies, becoming "serial entrepreneurs" who continue to develop our economy. If you are starting a company for the sole purpose of being acquired, remember you need to make the company successful first, so that you have something of value to sell.

SERIAL ENTREPRENEUR MICHAEL GORTON - FROM A REPORT BY (JEAN, 2010) *THE DALLAS MORNING NEWS*

At 11, Michael Gorton wanted to become the first person to walk on Mars after watching astronauts Neil Armstrong and Buzz Aldrin land on the moon. Gorton, who was reported to be 52, pursued his Mars goal all the way through the late 1980s before recognizing that he would be too old to Mars. Instead, he went on to launch six differenet companies. Perhaps the best known was TelaDoc, Inc., a Dallas-based telephone medical service firm that's attracted about $18 million in venture capital, and Internet Global Services, a Lewisville Internet service provider that developed the first DSL and an early phone-over-Internet network. Michael grew up as an Air Force brat who lived in six states and three foreign countries, and was the first in his family to earn a college degree. He began his career as an engineer with TXU Energy.

Gorton credited his engineering background as the cornerstone for all of his business ventures. He's somewhat of a true Renaissance man, with experiences in physics, law, astronomy, fiction writing. He stumbled upon his first venture when he shipped two computers to Mexico for an international trade class in law school (he actually did graduate from Law School but never did take the bar exam). That experience led to the creation of G Squared International in 1993. He later sold the assets in 1995.

Around the same time, Gorton founded Internet Global Services, and once again, sold the company in 2000. Global Services was generating annual revenues of about $10 million at the time, and he was able to sell it for $122 million in stock. In 2002, he once again stumbled upon an idea that led to the creation of TelaDoc, which provides telephone medical consultations. Gorton had to fight off skepticism from 17 state medical boards to prove his concept, but by getting industry experts, such as former U.S. Health and Human Services Secretary Tommy Thompson, he was able to overcome the skeptics. When Gorton left the company last year, TelaDoc's patient base had doubled to nearly 2 million in just two years.

Gorton's energy transfers to his hobbies, which include running (18 marathons so far) and hiking (climbed the highest peaks in 38 states toward a goal of all 50). He has published two political thrillers and has co-written a book on global warming with his teenage daughter. Gorton also teaches math, astronomy and physics at local colleges, right up until 2007.

At the time of this article, he was busy with Principal Solar, a company that he started in 2010 to become a major owner-operator of solar power plants by acquiring existing companies. Gorton plans are to amass 1 (one) gigawatt of solar power, enough to support just under 1 million homes, within the next three years. He was quoted as saying: "I sat at my desk 18 months ago and thought, 'What am I going to do next?' he further said."I like audacious things that will change the world."

LEGACY COMPANIES AND THE INITIAL PUBLIC OFFERING (IPO)

Occasionally some entrepreneur, somewhere, comes up with the big idea that is so different, and so unique, that it can impact the way things get done within the economy. These are the ideas that traditionally have broad impacts, and as they begin to take shape, they start to take on lives of their own. Think for a moment about the impact that this early group of entrepreneurs have had on the world:

- Alexander Graham Bell (1847-1922) - Innovator in communications, his patents led to the formation of The American Bell Company in 1877. American Bell went on to become American Telephone and Telegraph (AT&T).

- Thomas Edison (1847-1931) - Innovator and founder of the Edison General Electric Company which went on to become the present General Electric Company.

- Henry Ford, (1863-1947) - Henry Ford improved the "assembly line" for automobile manufacturing, received a patent for a transmission mechanism, and popularized the gas-powered car with the Model-T. He founded Ford Motor Company and helped pioneer commercial aviation..

- Herman Hollerith (1860-1929) - Herman Hollerith invented a punch-card tabulation machine system for statistical computation. His machines were used for the 1890 census and accomplished in one year what would have taken nearly ten years of hand tabulating. Herman Hollerith formed the Computing Tabulating Recording Company, which went on to become International Business Machines (IBM).

- Robert Wood Johnson (1887-1920) - Inspired by a speech by antiseptic advocate Joseph Lister, the brothers James Wood Johnson and Edward Meade Johnson, formed Johnson & Johnson in 1885. Johnson & Johnson is today a global provider of pharmaceuticals, medical devices, and consumer packaged goods.

- Frederick Weyerhaeuser (1834-1914) founded the Weyerhaeuser Timber Company in 1900 after purchasing 900,000 acres of timberland in the Pacific Northwest. Weyerhaeuser is now one of the largest producers of lumber, pulp and paper in the world; operating in 13 countries around the globe.

Obviously, the list could go on, and on, but we wanted to make our point. Some concepts, ideas, and institutions actually do live on well beyond the entrepreneurs who discovered them. In recent years, we have been introduced to an equally innovative group of entrepreneurs who are leaving their own impacts on our society as well. Consider the following list of current business leaders who were able to see new opportunities resulting from the changes within our economy:

- Jeff Bezos (1964 -) - Founder, president, chief executive officer and chairman of Amazon.com; the Internet on-line retailer.

- Sergey Brin (1973 -) and Larry Page, (1973 -) - Co-founders of the Google search engine. Google began in March 1996 as a research project at Stanford University; as the result of working on the Stanford Digital Library Project.

- Bernie Marcus (1929 -) - One of the founders (along with Arthur Blank, Ron Brill, and Pat Farrah,) of Home Depot Stores. First opened in 1979, Home Depot today operates some 2,242 big box format stores across the United States and is the largest home improvement retailer in the country.

- Lawrence J. Ellison (1944 -) - Co-founder (with Bob Minor and Ed Oates) of Oracle Corporation that was launched in 1977. Although, it began under the name Software Development Laboratories (SDL.) in 1982, it was renamed, Oracle Systems, to align more closely with its flagship product, Oracle Database.

- Bill Gates (1955 -) with co-founder Paul Allen, the Microsoft Corporation was officially established in 1975. However, it was the introduction of DOS, (Disk Operating System) in 1980 that established the company's software industry dominance.

- Steve Jobs, (1955 -) Co-founder of Apple Computer Co. (along with Steve Wozniak) in 1976. Apple saw the use of Graphical User Interface as a means to attract consumers to desk top computers.

- Martha Stewart (1941-) - In September 1997 Martha Stewart, along with the assistance of her business partner Sharon Patrick, founded Martha Stewart Omnimedia Corp.; which she successfully took public in October, 1999. It has become one of the most valuable brands for home decorating products.

This list could go on, and on as well, as we have many gifted entrepreneurs in America. They all seem to have envisioned a new concept that becomes a substitute for what is presently being used, or they introduce a new business model that changes the way individuals and businesses interact with one another. More importantly, they all seem to understand that success is never permanent and that failure is never final. They do not stop their efforts until their "Victory" makes "History."

In Chapter Three we introduced several different methods for evaluating a new business concept or idea. Among the methods was a "check list" provided from the investment banking community that suggested the different types of new businesses that were of most interest to them, the ones that could potentially be considered for an Initial Public Offering. They would have to meet the following criteria:

- The new concept or idea would have to address a high level of underserved need or unconstrained opportunity within its market.

- It would be able to capitalize on interaction that exists between major customer segments, the customers that it will serve

- The forecasted likely rate of continued market growth is credible, the greater the growth the better the opportunity

- The overall potential size of the market and the volume of available transactions is significant to be captured

- Desirable levels of profitability can be achieved by satisfying this need

The obvious observation from this list is that it is all about the business opportunity, the chance to meet an underserved need, in a desirable market segment that is growing at an attractive rate. So, if what you are planning to offer and provide fits into this profile, than you may be looking at something that has the potential to go public – find a place in the world's stock exchanges.

An Initial Public Offering (IPO) is the initial sale of a corporation's securities (almost always as stock) under the auspices of the Security and Exchange Commission. According to a recent report (Ritter 2011), between 1990 and 2010, a total of 5,486 companies went public and collectively raised a total of $617 Billion in new funding. Price, Waterhouse Coopers (2010), in their *2009 US IPO Watch Analysis and Trends Publication,* reported an increase in the number of IPO's in the $500 million to $999 million range, as well as the $50 million to $149 million range. IPO's raising more than $500 million doubled in 2009 to 11, from 5 in 2008. IPO's of less than $50 million declined from 11 in 2008 to 7 in 2009.

Offering $ Value	2005 # of deals	2006 # of deals	2007 # of deals	2008 # of deals	2009 # of deals
1.0 Billion+	2	8	7	2	3
500m-999 m	10	15	15	3	8
150m-499m	68	61	109	22	23
50m-149m	88	105	129	19	28
Less than $50	47	47	36	11	7

Industry Sector	2009 # of deals	2008 # of deals	2007 # of deals
Financial Services	13	22	97
Business Services	11	8	27
Technology	11	3	55
Healthcare	10	4	43
Consumer	8	1	13
Energy / Utilities	5	9	34
Other	2	1	2
Industrials	7	6	12
Transport	2	3	13
Totals	69	57	296

Figure 10.2 Volume of IPO's by Range and Industry Sector

Price Waterhouse Coopers further stated that they expected IPO's from the technology sector, including biotech, as well as financial services, healthcare and retail to increase in 2010. They based this forecast upon the recognition that fifty-four companies registered for an IPO in the fourth quarter of 2009 across the United States.

Although an IPO can potentially raise large sums of capital, it is probably the most expensive way to raise money in terms of the amounts you have to invest upfront. The cost for accountants, lawyers, printing and miscellaneous fees for even a modest IPO will easily reach a minimum of six figures. However, given the potential of the amount of funding that could be raised, an IPO remains an attractive way to finance the future growth and expansion of a business. For example, the Riverbed Technology (2006) initial public offering process, recognized as the most successful IPO in the year, is summarized as follows:

San Francisco – September 21, 2006 – Riverbed Technology (Nasdaq:RVBD) today announced an initial public offering of 8.7 million shares of its common stock at a price of 9.75 per share. Riverbed has also granted its underwriters a 30-day option to purchase up to approximately 1.3 million additional shares. Riverbed's common stock will be listed on the Nasdaq Global Market under the symbol "RVBD" and will begin trading Thursday, September 21, 2006.

Goldman, Sachs & Co. acted as sole book-running manager, Citigroup and Deutsche Bank Securities acted as joint lead managers, and Thomas Weisel Partners LLC acted as co-manager for the offering. When available, a copy of the final prospectus relating to the offering may be obtained from Goldman, Sachs & Co. A registration statement relating to the offering was filed with and declared effective by the Securities Exchange Commission.

When a company is privately owned, the founders, certain members of the management team (or all the employees, depending on the company) and private investors who helped fund the company all hold shares in the company. Those shares have little liquidity since they aren't publicly traded. For example, Facebook, Inc., see the film "Social Network," is still privately held and its investor's millions will be difficult to cash out until there is an IPO. And, the multi-billion dollar Mars, Inc. has been held privately by the Mars family for four generations. However, after a successful IPO those shares can be traded on one of the stock exchanges and can potentially increase in value as the company continues to grow. In short, investors, founding principals and equity share employees owning a lot of those shares could become very rich by selling them to the general public. Initial public offerings have made instant billionaires of entrepreneurs such as Yahoo's Jerry Yang and Broadcast.com's Mark Cuban.

Creative individuals who are responsible for these innovative companies are usually smart enough to know that they can not bring these large scale ideas to life without the help of others. They are willing to include the experience of others in the management of their firms and they typically need to invite in institutional investors. However, early stage investors typically seek a return on their investment that yields 10 to 100 times their initial investment. Prime candidates for successful IPOs tend to possess the following characteristics:

- The owner / entrepreneur is the founder and visionary for the company, but not necessarily the day to day operator of the business.

- The owner / entrepreneur is engaged in the strategy and direction of the business, but the responsibility is now shared with other financial stakeholders.

- The legal structure of these businesses is either a Limited Liability Corporation or a "C" Corporation that has divided its ownership into shares that can be acquired by others. Often, in the case of a "C" Corporation, their can be more than one class of shares (common and preferred); with different voting rights associated with each class.

- Initial funding to start these enterprises may have included angel investors, but the majority of the capital needed is provided from venture capital firms with industry knowledge. Since the amount of capital needed to launch a venture with this kind of potential will be significant, the entrepreneur understands and accepts the process of ownership dilution.

- These entrepreneurs contribute their expertise to the operations of the business, but are often relegated to a functional role, allowing professional management to grow the enterprise to the critical mass needed to be considered for an IPO.

- They remain a visible part of their industry and receive recognition for their innovation, contributions to the enterprise, and act as a spokesperson for the company.

- They are conscious of their company's "market window" and realize that they need to accomplish their objectives within certain timeframes to be attractive to the public financing markets.

- Their companies have to demonstrate significant revenue growth and profitability so that they can meet the criteria for an IPO.

- Their company needs to have established a professional management team that can operate the business under the same guidelines and requirements of a publicly traded enterprise.

- When their companies eventually do go public, the entrepreneur's interest may be subject to the same restrictions and timeline factors as other investors with respect to the selling of their stock.

Taking a company public is no small undertaking. As a matter of fact, there are a number of challenges that need to be addressed before the process can even begin. Ernst & Young (2008), one of the premiere public accounting firms, produced an excellent guide entitled: *"Top 10 IPO Readiness Challenges,"* which defines readiness benchmarks and timelines for taking a firm public. Their report was written from the perspective of C-level executives, worldwide, who have successfully completed this journey. A summary of the Ernst & Young suggestions include the following:

Step One- Transaction readiness and planning (24 to 36 months prior to IPO)

1. *Develop a compelling strategic plan-.* The first step in an IPO journey is a careful exercise in defining success. The business plan needs to be long term, including 24 months before and after the IPO. The plan needs to provide a clear road map for the company and its future direction which then may be communicated to the stakeholders. While private companies may be able to function with an informal planning process, institutional investors expect a public company to have a compelling strategic plan.

2. *Keep your options open-* Successful executives explore potentially attractive alternatives to a public listing, before settling on the traditional IPO. The goal is to achieve optimal value for a company's current situation and future objectives. Compared to the public markets, private capital sources may be more realistic, feasible, lucrative, and less costly. Increasingly, businesses are keeping their options open by grooming for more than one source of funding. During IPO preparation, a company's transaction options may include an investment by a private equity firm, strategic sale through the Merger and Acquisition market, joint ventures or alliances.

3. *Timing the market-* While it is best to go public at the most opportune moment, it is just as important to be able to operate as a public company. E&Y has found that the most common mistake made by newly public companies is that they tend to hurry into their IPO before their company is ready. Typically, the rush to go public is driven by a pre-listed company's need for capital, pressure from their board, or the desire to capitalize on the limited window of opportunity in the midst of changing market conditions.

STEP TWO – IPO EXECUTION (24 MONTHS PRIOR TO IPO)

4. *Building the right team-* The process of transforming from a private company to a public company depends to a large degree on the coordinated effort of the internal management team and the external advisors. In the successful cases that E&Y identified, the internal management team is already in place and performing well in advance of the IPO. The top managers already have the experience and expertise to undertake the IPO and operate a public company during the road show and long after it is over.

5. *Building your business processes and infrastructure-* The infrastructure and systems of a publicly traded company are very different from a typical private company structure. Before listing, an organizations financial, accounting, tax, operational and IT processes, systems and controls all must be able to withstand the rigors and scrutiny of public company status. Before going public, management needs to have in place the infrastructure (of people, systems, policies and procedures); which will enable the production of quarterly and annual reports in compliance with regulations.

6. *Establishing corporate governance-* Management of the top performing companies adopts the best practices and corporate governance principals that protect shareholder interests. They take the time to build a company board of directors with a disparate mix of compensation, compliance, and governance specialists, corporate strategists, and experienced business and financial executives. With heightened corporate governance standards for public companies, the process for attracting qualified independent board members is more complicated and more critical for IPO candidates than in the past.

7. *Managing investor relations and communications-* The investor relations function involves educating the public about the company's position in the industry, providing a regular update on forecasts and identifying key business issues that could impact the company. Specifically, when a company acquires a group of shareholders it needs to keep them informed of corporate developments in a variety of disclosure vehicles, including

annual and quarterly reports, proxy statements, press releases, direct mailings and shareholder meetings. Shareholders, analyst, and the financial press will critically evaluate management's performance and focus on the share price.

8. *Conducting a successful IPO road show-* Completion of a road show is one of the more challenging steps in the period between the publishing of the company's IPO prospectus and the final closing. It is a vital step, since it is the only time a company's senior management team meets the investor. Institutional investors rarely visit the companies they invest in, preferring instead to rely upon information presented at road show meetings and other sources. During the road show, underwriters take senior management on a whirlwind tour and introduce the company to investment audiences, including the underwriting sales forces and institutional investors.

STEP THREE-IPO REALIZATION (12 TO 24 MONTHS AFTER THE IPO)

9. *Attracting the right investors and analyst-* Once the IPO is over, the process for retelling and fine-tuning the company's investment story begins. Early on, many firms are fortunate to enjoy a high share price fueled, in part, by investor's interest in IPOs and by the press coverage for such companies. However, unless the market interest is carefully maintained after the IPO, the euphoria quickly fades. The senior executives of the company must continue to communicate the intangible business drivers of the company. The successful executives are able to determine what information to convey to the investment community and effectively monitor and react to news about the company.

10. *Delivering on your promises-* Once a company goes public, the work has just begun. A publicly traded company must meet, or exceed, the expectations it has set for itself. After the IPO, the executive challenge is to deliver the shareholder value, (and, ultimately share price appreciation) promised to stakeholders by the business plan, offering prospectus, and

other communications. Promises will have to be made as part of the company's road show to many different stakeholders, including investors, analyst, employees, customers, and the board, as well as regulatory authorities, the financial community and the press. Being a public company means having to keep the promises made – under promise and over-deliver.

Given the challenges of taking a company public, why would anyone want to subject themselves to the vigor of creating something that requires all of this? If you were to ask the successful entrepreneurs who have completed this journey, you would get very a similar response. They all envisioned the potential of what their ideas could become, the contributions that their innovations could make to their industry, and the impact it would have on the people who helped them to create the success. It is estimated that Google's August 2004 IPO created at least 900 instant millionaires of the company's 2,300 employees. What's not to like?

Entering this new decade, 2011 – 2020, we will witness the impact of the social networking companies on the world of commerce and communication. With the likes of Twitter, Linkedin, and Facebook gaining large scale popularity, and a new internet marketing concept called Groupon (Group + Coupon) taking hold, there are new and exciting IPO's in the works. Groupon recently turned down a $6.0 billion acquisition offer in hopes of driving up the price of its IPO stock even higher.

Are you the next innovator creating a billion dollar Legacy Company? If you are, you now have a road map!

Summarized from the Biography posted by the
Academy of Achievement (2010)

ORACLE CORPORATION, LARRY ELLISON'S COMPANY

Lawrence J. Ellison was born in the Bronx, New York. At nine months of age, he contracted pneumonia, and his unmarried 19 year-old mother gave him to her great aunt and uncle to raise. Lawrence was raised in a two-bedroom apartment on the South Side of Chicago. Even as a boy, he showed a strong aptitude for math and science, and he was named science student of the year when he attended the University of Illinois. During the final exams of his second year, Ellison's adoptive mother died, and he dropped out of school. He later enrolled at the University of Chicago the in fall, but once again dropped out after the first semester. But Ellison had learned the rudiments of computer programming in Chicago, and he took this skill with him to Berkeley, California.

For the next eight years he bounced from job to job, working as a technician for Fireman's Fund, and Wells Fargo bank, until he began working as a programmer with large databases at Ampex. While working at Ampex, he built a large database for the CIA, code name: Oracle. In 1977, Ellison and his former supervisor from Ampex, Robert Miner, founded their own company called Software Development Labs. They supported themselves by doing consulting work for an assortment of corporate clients.

Then Ellison read a paper called "A Relational Model of Data for Large Shared Data Banks" by E. F Codd, describing a concept Codd had developed at IBM. IBM didn't see any commercial potential in the concept of a Structured Query Language (SQL), but Ellison and his partner did. They created a database program that was compatible with both mainframe and desktop computer systems, and renamed their company Oracle. They found their first customers for the database program shortly thereafter- Wright Patterson Air Force Base and the CIA. Back in 1980, Oracle had only eight employees, and their revenues were less than $1 million. But the following year, IBM adopted Oracle's SQL for its mainframe systems, and for the next seven years, Oracle's sales doubled every year. The million dollar company was now on its way, and Ellison renamed the company to Oracle Corporation for its best selling product..

Oracle went public in 1986, raising $31.5 million with its initial public offering. But like many other early stage companies, Oracle experienced its first set of challenges in 1990 and posted its first ever operating loss. Oracle's market capitalization fell by 80 percent and the company appeared to be on the verge of collapse. Ellison was faced with the need to replace much of the original senior staff with more experienced managers in order to correct his course. For the first time since forming the company, he was willing to delegate the management side of the business to professionals, and re-channeled his own energies into improving product development. The newest version of the company's database program became a solid success and in only two years the company's stock had regained much of its previous value.

Starting in 2004, Ellison set out to increase Oracle's market share through a series of strategic acquisitions. Oracle spent more than $25 billion in only three years to buy a flock of companies, makers of software for managing data, identity, retail inventory and logistics. The first major acquisition was PeopleSoft, purchased at the end of 2004 for $10.3 billion. Next Ellison trumped rival SAP to acquire retail software developer Retek, followed by the acquisition of competitor Siebel Systems. Ellison completed this buying spree with the acquisition of business intelligence software provider Hyperion Solutions in 2007. Two years later Ellison once again acted boldly by acquiring computer hardware and software manufacturer Sun Microsystems for $7.4 billion. Oracle has now become the world's largest business software company, supplying all 100 of the Fortune Global 100.

Oracle's fortunes continued to rise throughout the 1990s as America's banks, airlines, automobile companies and retail giants all began depending on Oracle's database programs to operate their businesses. Oracle has also benefited from the growth of electronic commerce and its net profits increased by 76 percent in a single quarter during the year 2000. While the stocks of most high tech companies fluctuated wildly, Oracle has held its value, and its largest shareholder, founder and CEO Larry Ellison, is coming very close to a long-cherished personal goal; that of surpassing Microsoft's Bill Gates to become the richest man in the world.

The Academy of Achievement is a non-profit foundation that has sparked the imagination of students across America and around the globe for 50 years by bringing them into direct personal contact with the preeminent leaders of our times. (www.achievement.com)

CHAPTER SUMMARY

KEY POINTS

- Entrepreneurial success is measured in the eye of the entrepreneur, and success is determined by the satisfaction that he or she enjoys from their creation

- Lifestyle companies are usually formed to provide operating autonomy, and individual income needs for the founding and operating entrepreneur

- Lifestyle companies are very seldom managed for value creation, and as a result, are not attractive to financial investors.

- Build to sell companies are created by entrepreneurs who are seeking to create businesses that increase in value for the sole purpose of selling them.

- Serial entrepreneurs are individuals who have successfully built and sold a company and elect to repeat the process again and again

- Build to sell companies often require larger amounts of startup and operating capital and seek additional investors to meet this requirement.

- Acquisitions that are valued under $30 million are more attractive to the Fortune 500 companies than those that our more mature and more expensive.

- Companies are valued by either an income approach, asset based approach, or a market approach

- Income approach evaluates the anticipated earnings from

operation the business and assigns a "present value" to determine its value at the time of sale.

- The asset based approach views the business as a set of assets and liabilities and enables the purchaser to value both to determine the businesses "book value."

- The market approach is used to determine the "fair market value" of a business by comparing it to other companies of similar circumstance that have been recently purchased.

- Legacy companies are often started by entrepreneurs who introduce ideas and concepts that live on long after their personal involvement

- Big ideas often require large amounts of capital to bring to fruition and the entrepreneurs who introduce these concepts are open to institutional investment.

- An IPO, Initial Public Offering is the introduction of a company's stock for sale under the Security and Exchange Commission's regulations governing a public company.

- Trading of a company's stock on one of the exchanges enables the stock to easily transfer ownership, providing liquidity to both the company and its stakeholders.

- Taking a company public requires a great deal of preparation, a professional management team, and a significant investment of dollars and time to accomplish.

- Introducing the company to the investment community will require a "road show" where the underwriters will introduce the company's senior management and their plans to potential investors.

- Post IPO the company's management will have to communicate openly with investors, the financial press, and industry analyst about their plans and performance.

- There is an expectation that the management of a publicly traded company delivers on forecasts and projects that continue to increase shareholder value.

TAKE ACTION NOW

- Go back to the beginning of this publication, and determine if you are ready to begin the journey of owning you own business.

- Examine what your personal goals and ambitions are for the new enterprise you are about to create and compare them to the different models we described in this chapter.

- If you have already started this journey, review the different attributes of the business models we described and determine if you want to run your company, sell it, or develop it to its full potential.

- Be open to the help and support of others, whether they are investors, advisors, or highly valued employees. You will most likely need their help, regardless of the type of business you operate.

- If you are preparing to sell your company, seek the advice and counsel of professionals who can help you with valuation and tax issues.

- If you are considering a large scale expansion, then begin a relationship with an accounting firm, and investment banking firm, who can help you consider the advantages and disadvantages of going public.

- Enjoy the journey, and the pay day, as there are very few things in life that you could do that would have as positive an impact as starting and operating a successful business.

REFERENCES:

Ernst & Young, (2008) *Top 10 IPO Readiness Challenges, London, EN:* EYGM Ltd.

Hardy, Q. (2010). Chambers challenged: Cisco tried to report its business success just as the world became consumer dominant. *Forbes,* 187(4), 30-32.

Henricks, M. (2011). Startup journal reports, *The Wall Street Journal*, 02/2011.

Jean, S. (2010). Serial entrepreneur Michael Gorton let dreams of space flight rocket him to success. *The Dallas Morning News*, 11/13/2010.

Louie, E. (2011). Alamo style maven decides to call it a career, *San Ramon Valley Times*, 03/15/2011, A2.

MacMillan, D. & Galante, D. (2010). Google's Groupon bid said rejected. *Bloomberg Business Week*, 12/04/2010.

Malik, O. (2004) *The new road to riches*, www.CNNMoney.com New York: Cable News Network/Time Warner.

Market Capitalization Rate, *Finance Glossary* http://abinomics.com

Oracle Corporation: Larry Ellison's Company. (2011). Washington, DC, Academy of Achievement. http://www.achievement.org

Peters, B. (2009). *Early exits, exit strategies for entrepreneurs and angel investors,* Vancouver, Canada: Meteor Bytes Data Management Corp.

Pratt, S.; Reilly R. F. &. Schweihs R. P. (2000). *Valuing a business,* New York: McGraw Hill Professional.

Price, Waterhouse, Coopers, (2010). *2009US IPO watch, analysis & trends,* London, EN: Price Waterhouse Coopers.

Ritter, J. R. (2011*). Initial public offerings: Tables updated through 2010,* Gainesville, FL: University of Florida Press, http://bear.cba.ufl.edu/ritter

Riverbed Technology (2006). News Release: Riverbed Technology Announces Initial Public Offering, San Francisco: Riverbed Technology.

Soul Shelter (2008). *Balancing meaning and money,* www.soulshelter.com

Taylor, B. (2011). *Is the term "Lifestyle Business" an insult? The New York Times,* 01/2011.

Thompson, T. Jr.,. & Walker, M. M., (2010). *M&A deal flow in the post recessionary period,* Morristown, NJ: Financial Executive Research Foundation, Inc.

Warrilow, J. (2010) *Built to sell.* New York: Portfolio Hardcover.

SUPPLEMENTAL SOURCES:

Anderson, S., Beard, T. R. & Born, J. A. (1995). *Initial public offerings: Findings and theories.* Norwell, MA: Kluwer Academic Publishers.

Beaton, N. J. (2010). *Valuing early stage and venture backed companies.* Hoboken, NJ: Wiley Publishers.

Ghosh, A. (2008). *Pricing and performance of initial public offerings in the United States.* Piscataway, NJ: Transaction Publishers.

Gregoriou, G. N. (2005). *Initial public offerings (IPO): An international perspective of IPOs.* Burlington, MA: Elsevier.

Kleeburg, R. P. (2005). *Initial public offerings.* Mason, OH: South-Western Educational Publishers.

Kollar, T, Goedhart, M. & Wessels, D. (2010). *Valuation: measuring and managing the value of companies,* (5th Ed.) Hoboken, NJ: Wiley Publishers.

Rosenbaum, J. Pearl, J. & Perella, J. R. (2009). *Investment banking: Valuation, leveraged buyouts, and mergers and acquisitions.* Hoboken, NJ: Wiley Publishers.

Thomas, R. & Gup, B. E. (2009). *The valuation handbook: Valuation techniques from today's top practitioners.* Hoboken, NJ: Wiley Publishers.

Epilogue

As we were getting ready to publish *Business Alchemy: Turning Ideas into Gold*, the *Wall Street Journal Report*, (March 19, 2012) raised the question of whether entrepreneurism can be taught. The obvious alternatives are to either learn from the mistakes and successes of others or to be doggedly determined to learn only from your own mistakes - and good luck on getting startup capital for that kind of a new venture. Since only ten percent of business ideas and inventions ever reach profitability, it is obvious that help is needed to increase that success rate.

The Ewing Marion Kauffman Foundation, Kansas City, Missouri, has done extensive research into the entrepreneurial challenge and presently offers a number of educational programs, (e.g. Fast Trac® Tech Venture™; Fast Trac® New Venture™; Fast Trac® Growth Venture™) designed to transfer knowledge and experience to new entrepreneurs. We have been both instructors and coaches for several of these sessions and concluded that the quality of the information provided was directly proportional to the knowledge and experiences of the session facilitators and subject matter presenters. Content varied dramatically from session to session.

In conducting our own research for *Business Alchemy: Turning Ideas into Gold*, we further discovered that many Junior Colleges and Colleges were considering, or have already begun offering, entrepreneurial programs. Once again, the content of these efforts was inconsistent from institution to institution, as there is no "standard" set of principles that has been agreed upon for instructional purposes. There is a plethora of itinerant consultants and related book titles in categories such as "Entrepreneurism," "business start-up," "innovation," and "marketing," but we didn't find a single publication that pulled all of these elements together into an understandable format for Entrepreneurs to actually use.

Given the troubling start-up success rate of new ventures, certainly offering improved education about the topic can only be beneficial.

Though we reference the ancient mystical alchemy concept, *Business Alchemy: Turning Ideas into Gold,* it is as contemporary as the business opportunities in the New Global Economy. To be successful, innovations must be relevant to the larger cultural context, as Guttenberg's printing press success closely followed learning's renaissance and an emergent wave of literacy in Europe. Thus, we address the emerging global environmental, cultural and economic realities; as context for creating and commercializing both business ideas and intellectual property. *Business Alchemy* is your personal guidebook - from creating ideas to successfully commercializing them - that integrates best-practices and case examples to make you a successful entrepreneur. This is the very reason why we wanted to publish this book.

GLOSSARY OF FINANCIAL TERMS

Accounts Payable: Amounts owed by the business for purchases of products or services made on credit. These amounts are usually paid by the business after a time period that is measured by Days Payable Outstanding (DPO).

Accounts Receivable: Amounts owed to the business from customers for merchandise or services purchased on credit. The business receives payment for these amounts after a "term of sale" delay measured by Days Sales Outstanding (DSO).

Accrued Expenses: Expenses that the business has incurred for which it has not yet received an invoice, and that have not yet been paid.

Accumulated Depreciation: The total amount of depreciation expense recorded to date for the company's fixed assets that qualify for depreciation.. On the balance sheet, this value is subtracted from the total value of Property, Plant and Equipment assets to derive a net figure.

Acid Test Ratio: Current Assets divided by Current Liabilities

Acquisition Cost: The amount actually paid to purchase an asset. This includes all of the costs associated with the purchase, such as freight, sales tax, and installation labor.

Actuals: Financial statements that describe the actual financial results of the business. Actuals often pertain to a predetermined "historical" period before the start of a new forecast period.

Additional Paid-in Capital: The additional amount of capital paid by investors for stock over and above its par value. See also contributed capital.

Adjusted Book Value: The reported equity of a company which is arrived at after the values of assets and liabilities are adjusted. It represents the estimated market value.

Adjusted Net Asset Method: The methodology by which net asset value is calculated after deducting the net deferred taxes.

After Tax Income: Another term for net income.

Amortization: The recognition of part of an intangible asset's cost as an expense during each year of its useful life. Examples of items that are often amortized include goodwill, start-up expenses and purchased patents.

Appraisal: This is a way of judging the performance of a business as compared to others that are similar. Financial comparisons are made whereby comparative benchmarking is done for this purpose.

Arbitrage Pricing Theory: This is an asset pricing model .This model specifies that the returns earned by a business are a function of multiple factors.

Asset: An asset is anything that has economic value. In addition to tangible items such as cash and equipment, assets can also include intangibles such as intellectual property or goodwill.

Asset Accumulation: A calculation that states that when you liquidate the property, plant and equipment (PP&E) assets of a company, and pay off the company's liabilities, the net proceeds would accrue to the equity of the company.

Asset Based Approach: It s a business valuation method where the primary source of income for the business is the assets it owns. The assets and liabilities are valued at current market and intangible assets are added.

Average Annual Return: The expected financial return on an investment, including interest and dividends that is expressed as a percentage.

Average Cost: A method of valuing inventory whereby the total cost of all units bought or produced is divided by the number of units.

Bad Debt Expense: The actual losses incurred from uncollectible accounts receivable.

Balance Sheet: A financial statement that lists the assets, liabilities, and capital of a company at a certain point in time.

Benefits: The amount of indirect compensation that the business will provide to employees during each operating period. Benefits can be statutory, such as payroll taxes and worker's compensation; or discretionary, such as health insurance, life insurance, and 401(K) plans.

Book Value: The recorded value of an asset for accounting purposes. For assets where depreciation is applied or reserves booked, this is often expressed as the net book value. The book value of a company is the difference between assets and liabilities, which is equivalent to total owner's equity.

Breakeven Analysis: An analysis tool that calculates the effect of changes in expenses, and profit vary with changes in sales volume. Breakeven analysis estimates the sales volume necessary to cover fixed and variable expenses.

Breakeven Point: The sales volume level at which revenues equal expenses (fixed and variable).

Budgeting: The process of determining and recording the expected financial results of a future accounting period, generally the next fiscal year. Budgets usually include Income Statement, Balance Sheet, and Cash Flow Statement.

Business Risk: It is the uncertainty attached with the operations of an business entity wherein the realization of future returns is unpredictable.

Business Valuation: It is a process by which the market value of a firm or an entity is determined. It differs from an appraisal in the sense that appraisals only take into consideration tangible assets, but a valuation considers intangible assets as well.

Business Valuation Services: These are professional valuators of businesses and intangible assets who provide expert analysis for litigation, tax planning, and business transactions.

Capitalization: It is the value of the economic benefits earned by an entity during a financial reporting period.

Capitalization Factor: It is the expected rate of return that an investor anticipates to receive. It also takes into consideration the risk that the expected earnings could not be achieved.

Capitalization of Earnings Method: It considers the past earnings performance as the primary consideration for deciding the value of a business. This method does not value the inventory or work in progress.

Capitalization Rate: It is a ratio of a company's net operating income divided by the sales price It is used to define the estimated value of income producing properties.

Capital Structure: It is the combination of an entity's debts and paid in capital which constitutes the firm is termed as capital structure.

Capital Lease: A long-term lease of property, plant, or equipment in which the lessee acquires the risks and benefits associated with the ownership of the leased item. Because resembles the financing of an asset purchase, a capital lease is treated as a long-term debt for accounting purposes.

Cash & Equivalents: Cash plus highly liquid and safe investments, such as money market funds and treasury bills.

Cash Flow: Cash Flow represents the difference between the inflow and outflow of the entity's money.

Cash Flow Statement: A financial report that expresses a company's sources and uses of cash.

Chart of Accounts: The establishment of an accounting system that lists the accounts to which transactions are posted.

Common Stock Equivalents: Financial instruments such as convertible preferred stock plus convertible bonds, stock options, and warrants.

Contra Accounts: Off-set accounts, such as Accumulated Depreciation, that decreases the value of a related account, usually an asset. The contra account is subtracted from the related account to arrive at the net book value of an asset.

Contributed Capital: The total amount paid into the business for its common and preferred stock.

Contribution Margin: The difference between revenue generated from sales and the associated variable costs.

Control: Control is the authority to manage the workings and operations of an entity.

Control Premium: A Control Premium is the additional price paid by a controller to exert the powers to manage the firm.

Cost: A term for expenditure. See expenses.

Cost Approach: It is a method of re-assessing the value of an asset by recognizing the cost of replacement or reinstatement of its appreciated or depreciated value.

Cost of Capital: It is the opportunity cost (measured by rate of return) that a firm would have been able to earn had it invested in some other business activity at the same risk level.

Cost of Goods Sold: Another term for cost of sales, (see below).

Cost of Sales/Services (COS): All the direct costs associated with the goods or services that were sold during a specified accounting period, including materials, labor, and overhead.

Covenants: Conditions agreed to in a formal debt agreement designed to protect the lender's interests. Covenants may include restrictions on debt/equity ratio, working capital, owner's draws or dividend payments.

Current Assets: Assets that can be converted to cash within one year in the normal course of business. This group usually includes cash, accounts receivable, inventory, and prepaid expenses.

Current Liabilities: Obligations that will come due within a year from the current reporting date. This group usually includes accounts payable, accrued expenses, and the portion of long-term obligations that are due within one year.

Current Ratio: Current assets divided by current liabilities. This ratio is used to determine a company's ability to meet its financial obligations in a timely manner.

Days Payable Outstanding (DPO): The number of days a business takes to pay its accounts payable, on average.

Days Sales Outstanding (DSO): The number of days it takes a business to collect its accounts receivable, on average.

Debt: A form of liability that represents money borrowed from banks or other lending institutions.

Debt to Equity Ratio: The ratio of total debt owed to owners' equity, used as a measure of leverage and ability to repay debt obligations.

Debt Free: Debt Free defines a situation created in the absence of any liabilities.

Deferred Revenue: A liability that arises when a customer pays for goods or services before delivery is complete; for example, a one-year service contract billed in advance.

Depreciation: The recognition that part of an asset's cost is an expense during each year of its useful life. There are several acceptable methods for calculating this expense, including straight-line depreciation and various accelerated methods.

Direct Costs: Expenses, such as labor, overhead, and materials, that vary in direct proportion to the number of units produced or services rendered.

Direct Labor: Wages paid for activities directly related to production of units sold or services delivered, and are considered part of cost of sales. Sometimes referred to simply as labor.

Discounted Cash Flow Method: A business valuation method that determines the present value of future cash flows based on a discount rate. This valuation method uses the future free cash flow of the company (meeting all the liabilities) discounted by the firm's weighted average cost of capital.

Discounted Future Earnings Method: It is another business valuation method that determines the present value of future financial benefits based on a discount rate.

Discount for Lack of Voting Rights: It is a discount applicable on the share value of minority interest voting shares due to the lack of voting rights.

Discount Rate: It is the interest rate at which the expected future cash flows of a business can be discounted.

Double Declining Balance (DDB): A method of recording accelerated depreciation. Also called the 200 percent declining balance method, this system applies twice the annual straight-line depreciation rate to the undepreciated balance of the asset.

Earnings Before Interest and Taxes (EBIT): Operating income before income tax expense and interest expense. This is a popular measure for comparing the earning power of companies, because it eliminates the impact of capital structure and effective tax rates, two non-operating factors.

Earnings Per Share (EPS): Net income divided by the number of outstanding shares of common stock and equivalents.

Earnings Before Interest, Taxes, Depreciation and Amortization (EBIT/DA): Operating income before income tax expense, interest expense, depreciation expense and amortization expense. This is a popular measure for comparing the free cash flows generated from operations because it eliminates the impact of capital structure, effective tax rates, and non-cash expenses.

Economic Life: This is the expected time span in which a firm's assets continue to produce economic benefits.

Equity: Also known as the net worth or owners' equity of a company. Equity is the net value of a company's total assets, less its total liabilities.

Equity Net Cash Flows: These are the cash dividends paid to the shareholders after making the other necessary funding adjustments.

Expenditures: All purchases made by a business, whether in cash or on credit; not equivalent to expenses. Also referred to as costs.

Expenses: The resources used to support the ongoing operations of a business for a specified time period; not equivalent to expenditures or costs.

Fair Market Value: This is the expected price at which a seller will be willing to sell an asset and the buyer would be willing to purchase the asset.

Fairness Opinion: This is a report or opinion which is developed to assess whether a transaction occurring is fair and correct from the financial aspect.

Financial Risk: This risk is the same as 'business risk' and differs only in the sense that it is concerned with only the financial uncertainties.

Finished Goods: Inventory that is ready for sale.

First In, First Out (FIFO): A method of inventory valuation whereby the goods first purchased or manufactured are considered the first ones sold.

Fiscal Year: The 12-month period, not necessarily coinciding with the calendar year, chosen to constitute a single year for external financial reporting and taxes.

Fiscal Year End: The last month of a company's fiscal year.

Fixed Assets: Another term for Property, Plant and Equipment.

Fixed Costs: Expenses that are assumed not to vary with sales volume or within the expected range of sales volumes. Fixed costs are things such as rent or administrative costs, and are important to recognize when calculating a breakeven analysis.

Forecast Start Date: The month and year on which the forecast period begins.

Forecast Year: The forecast year can coincide with either the January-December calendar year, but this is not a requirement. Depending on the forecast start month, the first year of the forecast period may cover less than 12 months.

Forecasting: Financial forecasting is the process of estimating future financial performance. The projected financial performance of a business is measured by using pro-forma financial statements as well as other indicators such as trend analysis, ratio analysis, and return on equity.

Free Cash Flow: This is the cash left with a firm after it has met its expenses. It is the excess amount left over after the funding activities are completed.

·GAAP: An acronym for Generally Accepted Accounting Principles. Accountants follow GAAP standards, conventions, and rules in recording and summarizing financial transactions, and in preparing financial statements. GAAP standards are issued by the American Institute of Certified Public Accountants.

Going Concern: This defines a concept which assumes that a firm will continue to be in existence indefinitely and continue its business operations into the future.

Going Concern Value: This defines the value of a firm that will remain in existence in the future. It takes into account the value of the intangible assets like goodwill.

Goodwill: The accounting term for amounts paid for assets over and above their fair market value. Goodwill theoretically represents the value of the business's name, reputation, and customer relations, which increase the true value of the business beyond the value of its assets alone.

Gross Margin: Net Sales less cost of sales; often expressed as a percentage of sales. Also referred to as gross profit.

Gross Sales: The total of amounts received (sales for cash) and amounts expected (sales on credit) in return for products sold or services rendered during the given time period. Gross sales reflect sales at invoice values, before sales discounts, returns, or credit card fees.

Income: Another term for net income.

Income Statement: A financial report that shows a company's performance over a specified period of time by subtracting expenses from revenues to obtain net income. Also known as a profit and loss statement (P&L) or an earnings report.

Income Tax Expense: Levies on the income of a business imposed by federal and state governments. This expense appears on the income statement simply as Taxes.

Intangible Asset: A long-term asset that represents a financial, legal, or accounting concept rather than a physical item. Intangible assets include: Goodwill , the value of a patent, copyright, or trademark, the value of a franchise or operating rights. Under accounting rules, an intangible asset must have a useful life greater than one year, and a portion of its value must be amortized over time as an expense.

Interest Basis: The interest rate, such as prime, that is used as a reference point for quoting borrowing rates. For example, using the prime rate as the interest basis, a loan might be offered at prime plus one percent.

Interest Expense: Money paid by a business in exchange for the use of capital for a specified time period. On the income statement, "Interest Expense (Income)" is a single account that is the net amount of interest income and interest expense.

Interest Income: Money earned by a business in exchange for the use of capital for a specified time period. On the income statement, "Interest Expense (Income)" is often a single account that is the net amount of interest income and interest expense.

Interest Rate: The cost of borrowing money, expressed as a percentage per period of time, usually one year.

Internal Rate of Return: This is the rate of return on an asset, which is also the discount rate, that makes the present value of future cash inflows equal the current market price of the investment or the outflow.

Inventory: Goods purchased or manufactured by a business and held for production or sale. Inventory is often subdivided into raw materials, work in progress, and finished goods.

Inventory Targets: The numbers of months of inventory that the user requires to be in stock at a given point in time. For Raw Materials, this amount represents the number of months of future production. For Finished Goods, the amount represents the number of months of future sales.

Inventory Turns: The ratio of annual cost of sales to inventory commonly used as a rough measure of inventory management efficiency. Also known as inventory turnover ratio or simply turns.

Investment: The expenditure of cash to create additional capital. Investment can be in income-producing vehicles such as stocks and bonds, or more risk-oriented ventures such as the purchase of another company.

Intrinsic Value: This is the difference of the value perceived of an asset from the actual market value. It is the inherent value.

Invested Capital: Invested Capital is the collective of a firm's equity and debt.

Invested Capital Net Cash Flows: These are the dividends (paid to shareholders) and interest (paid to investors and creditors) comprise the invested capital net cash flows.

Investment Risk: These risks are the uncertainties attached while making an investment that the investment may not yield the expected returns.

Investment Value: This is the value an investor estimates of a security. It is the amount according to the investor at which the security should be trading for.

Key Person Discount: This is the reduction in value resulting from the actual or potential loss of a key person in a business enterprise. This is reflected by deducting an amount or percentage from the value of an ownership interest.

Labor: Another term for direct labor.

Last In, First Out (LIFO): A method of inventory valuation whereby the goods most recently purchased or manufactured are considered the first ones sold.

Lease: A long-term contract granting use of real estate, equipment or other fixed assets in exchange for a rental payment. All leases entered into for Property, Plant and Equipment are considered capital leases; operating leases should be entered as expenses.

Leverage: The relationship between debt and equity. A company is considered highly leveraged if its levels of debt are high compared to its equity.

Leveraged Buy Out (L.B.O.): The acquisition of another company using a significant amount of borrowed money (bonds or loans) to meet the cost of acquisition.

Liabilities: Obligations used to fund the operations of a business, including bank loans, accounts payable and accrued expenses.

Limited Appraisal: This appraisal is an appraisal done with limitations in analyses, procedures, or scope. It is the process of determining the value of a business, business ownership interest, security, or intangible asset with the limitations.

Line of Credit: The amount of short-term credit available to a business from banks.

Liquidity: A company's ability to generate cash in a timely manner in order to meet its obligations, often measured by the quick ratio or the current ratio.

Liquidation Value: This is the net amount that will be realized if the business is terminated and the assets are sold and the liabilities are satisfied.

London Interbank Offered Rate (LIBOR): The interest rate used among the most creditworthy international banks for large loans in eurodollars. LIBOR is an important reference number, because loans to businesses can be tied to it on a percentage basis.

Long-Term Asset: Any asset that has an economic life greater than one year. Under accounting rules, intangible assets must always be classified as long-term assets, even if their remaining life is less than one year.

Long-Term Borrowing: Liabilities that represent money borrowed from banks or other lenders to fund the ongoing operations of a business and that will not come due within one year.

Majority Control: Majority control is the degree of control which one stockholder has due to a majority ownership position.

Majority Interest: Majority interest exists if the ownership interest is greater than fifty percent (50%) of the voting interest in a business enterprise.

Market Capitalization of Equity: Market Capitalization is the share price of a publicly traded stock being multiplied by the number of shares outstanding. This amount is known as the market capitalization of Equity.

Market Capitalization of Invested Capital: This is the market capitalization of equity and the market value of the debt component of invested capital added together.

Market Approach: Market Approach is a method of determining the value of a business, security, or an intangible asset by either comparing it to similar businesses, securities or intangible assets that have been sold.

Market Value: The price at which an asset would pass from an informed and willing seller to an informed and willing buyer, assuming that goodwill played no role in the transaction.

Marketability: Marketability is the ease or difficulty with which an interest can be resold in the secondary market. Good marketability means a security can be resold easily in the secondary market.

Marketability Discount: This discount is an amount or percentage that is deducted from the value of an ownership interest to compensate for the relative absence of marketability.

Marketable Securities: Securities that can readily be converted into cash, including government securities, bankers' acceptances, and commercial paper.

Market Value: Market value is determined by multiplying the quoted share price of the company by the number of issued shares. This valuation reflects the price that the market at a point in time is prepared to pay for the shares outstanding.

Materials: The physical inputs to manufacturing treated as part of cost of sales. Also known as raw materials.

Merger and Acquisition Method: This is a valuation method derived from comparing pricing multiples from transactions of significant interests in companies engaged in the same or similar lines of business.

Minority Interest: Minority interest is an ownership interest which is less than fifty percent of the voting interest in a business enterprise. This means that the control of the minority interest holder is very limited.

Miscellaneous Expenses: An account for operating expenses that do not fall into any of the predefined categories such as salaries, utilities, advertising, and depreciation.

Miscellaneous Non-Current Assets: An account for assets not including current assets, property, plant and equipment, intangibles, deposits, and loans made.

Miscellaneous Non-Current Liabilities: An account for non-current liabilities not including long-term debt (mortgage debt, lease debt, long-term borrowing, and shareholder loans) and deferred taxes.

Mortgage: A long-term debt instrument for the purchase of property by which the borrower uses the property itself for collateral.

NAICS Code: North American Industry Classification System industry category

Net Book Value: The acquisition cost of an asset less any accumulated depreciation. See also book value and contra accounts.

Net Cash Provided By Operations: On a cash flow statement, net income plus non-cash transactions and the net amount of changes in operating assets and liabilities.

Net Income: Total revenues minus total expenses, including taxes and depreciation, for a specified time. Also known as profit, net profit, or net earnings.

Net Income Before Taxes: Total revenues minus total expenses except the income tax expense, for a specified time. Also known as pretax income.

Net Operating Loss (NOL): The excess of business expenses over income in a given tax year.

Net Operating Loss (NOL) Carry-forward: The amount of Net Operating Losses accumulated over past tax years that are available for offsetting taxable income in the current and future tax years.

Net Present Value (NPV): A measure of a project's future value in current dollars. Future income is summed and then discounted using a required rate of return to adjust for the time value of money. Net present value is, theoretically, the best method for evaluating projects.

Net Property, Plant and Equipment: Gross property, plant and equipment minus accumulated depreciation. This number represents that portion of PP&E acquisition cost that has not yet been recognized as an expense.

Net Sales: Sales revenue less sales discounts, returns and allowances.

Net Tangible Assets: Assets of the organization minus the liabilities. In the calculation of Net Tangible assets one does not include excess assets and non operating assets.

Non-Current Assets: Assets that are not convertible to cash within one year in the normal course of business. Property and Goodwill are examples of non-current assets.

Non-Current Liabilities: Obligations that will not come due within one year of the current date.

Non operating assets: Assets that are not used and hence are not necessary in the present ongoing operations of the organization.

Non-Operating Expense: Expenses not related to the ongoing operations of a company; for example, interest expense, one-time events, and taxes.

Non-Operating Income: Income not related to the ongoing operations of a company; for example, interest income and sale of fixed assets.

Normalized Earnings: Earnings which have been adjusted to eliminate unusual items or anomalies in order to facilitate comparisons.

Normalized Financial Statements: Financial statements which have been adjusted to eliminate unusual items or anomalies and facilitate comparisons.

Operating Expenses: All expenses related to the ongoing operations of a company, including research and development, sales and marketing, and administrative expenses. Any costs directly attributable to producing goods or services are not included as they are recognized in cost of goods sold.

Operating Income: Sales revenue minus cost of sales and operating expenses. Similar to earnings before interest and taxes. Also referred to as operating profit, operating earnings, and income from operations.

Operating Lease: A type of lease, normally involving equipment, classified as a rental not as a purchase over time. An operating lease must be shown as an expense, unlike a capital lease, which is treated as a long-term debt.

Operating Profit: Another term for operating income.

Other Assets: Assets exclusive of current assets and property, plant and equipment. Other assets can include intangibles, deposits, loans made, and miscellaneous non-current assets.

Other Expenses: Expenses due to activities outside the normal operations of the business, for example, loss from foreign exchange and loss from investments.

Other Income: Income due to activities outside the normal operations of the business, for example, dividends from investments and gain from foreign exchange.

Other Liabilities: Liabilities other than debt, line of credit, and accounts payable, for example, deferred taxes, accrued expenses, and customer deposits.

Overhead: Expenses incurred in operating a business, such as rent, executive salaries, and insurance, that is not directly related to the manufacture of a product or delivery of a service. A portion of overhead can be attributed to cost of sales, the remainder is considered an operating expense.

Owners' Equity: Another term for equity.

Par Value: The stated value of a share of stock. Par is usually a minimal value (such as $.01) and bears no relation to the market value of the shares.

Payables: Another term for accounts payable.

Payroll: The total wages, not including benefits, paid by a business during each forecast year.

Period Expenses: A term for expenses recorded in the period in which they occur regardless of whether or not they pertain to a prior or later period. R&D and advertising expenditures are examples of costs that benefit future periods, but must be treated as period expenses according to Generally Accepted Accounting Principles (GAAP).

Periodicity: The level of detail in terms of time, at which data is forecast or reported, specified as months, quarters, or years.

Periods: Discrete intervals of time. The word period generally refers either to the interval of the entire forecast (as in forecast period) or the granularity of data in financial statements.

Plan Period: Another term for Forecast Period.

PP&E: See Property, Plant & Equipment.

Portfolio Discount: Portfolio discount applies when a business enterprise owns dissimilar operations or assets that do not fit well together. When this occurs an amount or percentage is deducted from its value as portfolio discount.

Precision: The scale at which forecast numbers are displayed. Choices include dollars, hundreds, thousands, and millions.

Prepaid Expenses: Services, goods, and intangibles paid for prior to the period in which they provide benefit. Prepaid expenses are accounted for as assets until their benefit is realized.

Present Value: Present value is the current value of a future economic benefit calculated using an appropriate discounting method.

Price Earnings Multiple: A price earnings multiple can be arrived at by dividing the price of a share of stock by its earnings per share.

Price Earnings Multiple Valuation: A price earnings multiple valuation or Price-earnings ratio (P/E) is simply the price of a company's share of common stock in the public market divided by its earnings per share. By multiplying this P/E multiple by the net income, the value for the business could be determined.

Price/Earnings Ratio (P-E): The market value of a company's stock divided by net income.

Prime Rate: The interest rate that banks charge to their most creditworthy customers. The prime rate is an important reference number, because loans to companies are often tied to it on a percentage basis.

Pro-Forma Financial Statements: A set of financial statements and other schedules that show projected results for a future period. The three major financial statements are the Income Statement, Balance Sheet, and Cash Flow Statement.

Profit: Another term for net income.

Profit & Loss Statement (P&L): Another term for the income statement.

Prompt Payment Discounts: Discounts that a business gives to credit customers who pay within a specified period of time; also called sales discounts. On an income statement, this amount is subtracted from Gross Sales to yield Net Sales.

Property, Plant and Equipment (PP&E): Assets used in the operations of a business that have a useful life greater than one year, including land, buildings, machinery, equipment, and furniture.

Purchases of PP&E: The acquisition cost of new property, plant and equipment assets in a given year, minus the proceeds from the sale of existing PP&E.

Rate of Return: Rate of Return is the return one gets over one's investment expressed as a percentage of the investment.

Quick Ratio: Current assets, excluding inventory and prepaid expenses, divided by current liabilities. Also known as the acid test ratio.

Ratio: A comparison of financial statement elements in the form of a quotient. Ratios such as the price/earnings ratio, return on assets, and quick ratio are often used for analyzing financial statements.

Raw Materials: Another term for materials.

Receivables: Another term for accounts receivable.

Redundant Assets: These are assets are assets that are not used and hence are not necessary in the present ongoing operations of the organization.

Replacement Cost New: This is the cost of replacing an existing property with one which is similar to it and is of equal utility.

Report Date: This is the date on which the valuation conclusions are transmitted to the client.

Reproduction Cost New: Reproduction cost is the current cost of producing a new property which is identical.

Required Rate of Return: This is the rate of return demanded by an investor from an investment to compensate for the amount of risk involved. The required rate of return increases with the risk involved.

Residual Value: Residual value is the expected value of an asset or a capital item at the end of a specified period.

Retained Earnings: Net profits kept within a business in the Owners' Equity account after stock dividends are paid.

Retired Liabilities: Debt paid off within a given period of the forecast.

Retirement of Long-Term Debt: The repayment of a non-current liability.

Return on Assets (ROA): Net income for a time period divided by total assets. This ratio is often used to measure profitability or the efficiency with which assets are being employed.

Return on Invested Capital: This shows the company's ability to create value and is calculated as the relationship between earnings and invested capital (net interest-bearing debt + capital and reserves.)

Return on Tangible Equity: Net income for a time period divided by tangible equity. The value of intangible assets such as goodwill is excluded from this ratio in order to better reflect actual operating profitability.

Return on Equity (ROE): Net income divided by equity. This ratio is often used as a measure of the return on funds invested in a business.

Return on Investment: Return on investment is the standard measure of project profitability. It is the discounted profits over the life of the project expressed as a percentage of initial investment.

Revenue: The total income received in exchange for goods or services during a specific accounting period. Revenue can be recorded using either the cash basis (as received), or the accrual basis (as earned). Also referred to as sales or sales revenue.

Risk Free Rate: Risk Free Rate is the rate of return available in the market which one can get with certainty on an investment without any risk being involved.

Risk Premium: Risk Premium is an additional return over the risk-free rate earned by investors for taking risk.

Rule of Thumb: Rule of Thumb is a mathematical relationship between or among variables which is derived through experience, observation, hearsay, or a combination of all of these.

Salaries: Compensation provided by a business to employees, excluding benefits. On an income statement, Salaries refers only to that portion of compensation that does not vary in direct proportion to sales.

Sales: Another term for revenue.

Salvage Value: The scrap value of an asset. Acquisition cost minus salvage value yields the total amount that an asset is depreciated over its useful life.

Shareholder Equity: Another term for equity.

Short-Term Borrowing: Liabilities that represent money borrowed from banks or other institutions to fund the ongoing operations of a business that will come due within one year.

SIC code: the four-digit code prescribed by the Standard Industrial Classification System to categorize businesses according to the types of activities they perform.

Solvency: A company's ability to satisfy its obligations to creditors when they are due. A company is "technically insolvent" if it has sufficient assets to pay creditors, but cannot generate enough cash to meet payment deadlines.

Special Interests Purchasers: Special interest purchasers are those purchasers who believe they can enjoy economies of scale, synergies, or strategic advantages after the purchase of a company by combining the acquired business interest with their own.

Standard Costs: A target or average cost that can be used either to value inventory or as a basis of comparison with actual costs. Standard costs can often be used to calculate cost of sales.

Statement of Cash Flows: Another term for cash flow statement.

Stockholders' Equity: Another term for equity.

Straight-Line Method: The simplest form of depreciation, in which an equal expense is recorded in each year of an asset's useful life. For example, if the asset has a purchase price of $1,000,000, a useful life of four years and a salvage value of $200,000, straight-line depreciation would record $200,000 of depreciation each of the four years.

Sum of the Years' Digits (SYD): A method of recording accelerated depreciation. It allows the depreciation of an asset based on an inverted scale of the total digits of the asset's useful life. For example, if the useful life is four years, the years' digits (1, 2, 3, and 4) are summed to produce ten, and 4/10ths of the asset's depreciable cost is recognized as an expense the first year, 3/10ths the second year, and so on.

Sustaining Capital Reinvestment: This is the periodic addition of capital which is required to maintain operations at existing levels.

Systemic Risk: Systematic Risk is market risk which occurs to the entire market. This risk cannot be diversified because if the market gets affected it will equally affect all. Thus systematic risk is a risk affecting the whole economy.

Tangible Asset: An asset that represents a physical object such as land, furniture, and buildings. Under accounting rules, a tangible asset must have a useful life greater than one year, and must be used in business operations rather than being held for resale.

Tangible Equity: Equity less intangible assets. See the ratios of debt to tangible equity, fixed assets to tangible equity, and return on tangible equity.

Terminal Value: Terminal value is the expected value of an asset or a capital item at the end of a specified period.

Treasury Stock: Stock that has been reacquired by the company that issued it and is available for retirement or resale. Also called reacquired stock and treasury shares.

Useful Life: An estimate of the period of time over which an asset will be of use to a company. Along with acquisition cost and salvage value, this measure is used to calculate the amount that the asset is depreciated each year.

Valuation: The act or process that determines the worth of a business or a security or an asset.

Valuation Approach: This is the general way which is followed to determine a value of a business, business ownership interest, security, or intangible asset using one or more valuation methods to do the same.

Valuation Date: The valuation date, also known as effective date, appraisal date or date of evaluation, is the day when the evaluation has been made or the date when the evaluation applies.

Valuation Method: Valuation method is a specific method used to determine the value of a business or an asset.

Valuation Procedure: Valuation procedure is the act, manner and technique of following the steps of a valuation method.

Value to Owner: This is the value an investor estimates of a security. It is the amount according to the investor at which the security should be trading for.

Variable Costs: Expenditures that change in proportion to increases or decreases in sales or production volumes.

Variance: The difference between actual and targeted numbers for revenues, expenditures, or productivity. Variances are usually described as either favorable or unfavorable.

Working Capital: The net amount of current assets and current liabilities. This is equivalent to a company's liquid assets.